THE RISE AND DECLINE OF THE REDNECK RIVIERA

THE RISE AND DECLINE OF THE

Redneck Riviera

An Insider's History of the Florida-Alabama Coast

HARVEY H. JACKSON III

The University of Georgia Press

Athens & London

a
Friends Fund
publication

Publication of this work was made possible, in part, by a generous gift from the University of Georgia Press Friends Fund.

Maps by David Wasserboehr
Designed by Erin Kirk New
Set in 10.3/14 Chapparal Pro with Mullen Hand display

Printed digitally in the United States of America

Library of Congress Cataloging-in-Publication Data

Jackson, Harvey H.
    The rise and decline of the Redneck Riviera : an insider's history of the
Florida-Alabama coast / Harvey H. Jackson III.
        p. cm.
    Includes bibliographical references and index.
    ISBN-13: 978-0-8203-3400-4 (hardcover : alk. paper)
    ISBN-10: 0-8203-3400-6 (hardcover : alk. paper)
    1. Gulf Coast (Fla.)—History. 2. Gulf Coast (Ala.)—History.
3. Gulf Coast (Fla.)—Social life and customs.
4. Gulf Coast (Ala.)—Social life and customs.
5. Tourism—Florida—Gulf Coast—History.
6. Tourism—Alabama, Gulf Coast—History.
7. Tourism—Social aspects—Florida—Gulf Coast.
8. Tourism—Social aspects—Alabama—Gulf Coast.
I. Title.
    F317.W5J34   2011
    975.9'9—dc23   2011040110

British Library Cataloging-in-Publication Data available

To Suzanne, who brought me back to the beach

Contents

THE RISE AND DECLINE OF THE REDNECK RIVIERA

Alabama Dreaming

I N SEPTEMBER 1944, on the island of Oahu, half a world away from his south Alabama home, a lonely Corporal Jewel Rivers, "Jack" to his friends, wrote his wife and infant son of the wonders he had seen—the coast, an active volcano, and Honolulu, which he described as "quite a town." His journey had been a long one; it would be longer still. "This is only a stepping stone to where I am going," he told them. The war with Japan had brought him this far, and it would take him the rest of the way.

While his mind was on what came next, it was also on what would be waiting in the States when the fighting was over. He had seen Waikiki Beach, with its curving stretch of sand domi-nated by the famous Royal Hawaiian Hotel and Diamond Head. Waikiki was "very pretty," but there was somewhere else he would rather be. "I'll take the good old Gulf Shores any old day," he wrote. "Give me Ala., in the U.S.A., and I'll be satisfied."

Not long after he mailed that letter Corporal Rivers shipped out to New Guinea. Promoted to sergeant, he served as the waist gunner on a B-24 Liberator, flying with the Ninetieth Bomber Group. On November 19, his plane took off to attack a Japanese base on Mindanao Island in the Philippines.

It did not return.

Jack Rivers never saw Gulf Shores again.

But many who served in that war did come back; and in the years that followed, veterans of the front lines and of the home front sought out sand and surf to relax and recover. Along the Alabama and Florida Gulf Coast, from the mouth of Mobile Bay east to St. Andrews Bay at Panama City, residents of the lower South made the beach their own. Children of the Depression and of conflict, more hopeful, indeed optimistic, than they had been in a decade, they drove down on New Deal–paved, military-improved roads in automobiles they bought on easy credit or with cashed-in war bonds. They came on vacations from jobs that they were trained and educated for under the GI Bill. They left behind homes financed through that same program. Few if any cared that their ticket to the middle class had been punched by the federal government.

Along this coast folks from the lower South found a way of life, a culture and context, much like the one they left back home—segregated (where blacks existed at all), small town, provincial, self-centered, and unassuming. Only the landscape was different. Few of the postwar visitors, even the ones who had served in the Mediterranean, would likely have made the connection that was made by a prewar WPA writer who saw in Gulf Shores and Orange Beach reflections of "little fishing villages that reminded the visitor of the southern coast of France." Nor is it likely that they would have made the alliterative association that years later Howell Raines, writing for the *New York Times*, made when he referred to this stretch of the Alabama shoreline as the "Redneck Riviera." From there east to Panama City Beach was, as historian Patrick Moore of the University of West Florida described it, "a provincial environment committed to tradition, conservative values, and a close tie to regional identity."

Or that is what it has been for as long as I have known it, which is pretty much the length of time covered in this book.

Let me explain.

I grew up in south Alabama, in a little town about a three-hour drive from Gulf Shores. That beach became our beach—our Disney World, a friend from childhood called it. Though I was just a tot, I still recall going down with the family in those years after my father returned from defeating Hitler. Later I went back again and again, to deep-sea fish from Orange Beach, to dance at the Hangout, and to sleep in my car or on the sand.

Meanwhile, even as all this was occurring, my attention was being drawn east, over to a spot in Florida, between Destin and Panama City Beach, where ancient dunes had formed a high bluff and where a developer was selling lots. In 1954 my grandmother bought one. In 1956 she built a cottage

"Bubba's Dream"—what the Redneck Riviera was and is to so many. Cartoon by Jeff Darby; courtesy of the *Mobile Press-Register*.

there, and from then until now Seagrove Beach, "Where Nature Did Its Best," has been my other home.

It was there that I decided to write this book.

So here it is: my account of how people from the lower South created a coastal playground, a place where they and their families could get away from constraints and restraints of home and job and school and responsibility but without going too far—physically or culturally—from where they were. It is the story of how those who were already there, and those who came later, turned "fishing villages" and "bathing beaches" into tourist destinations for millions, places where parties were pitched, dreams were dreamed, and fortunes were made and lost. And it is the story of how people keep coming, searching for something new, something old, something upscale, and something sleazy.

What follows is how the Redneck Riviera began, what it became, and what is happening to it now. In the narrative are a number of themes that also deserve exploration and analysis on their own, and hopefully, what I have written will inspire others to have at it. In the evolution of the region one can see how efforts to build a tourist economy led to new and innovative ways to promote the Gulf Coast. However, the new and innovative ultimately altered, threatened, and even destroyed the simple, laid-back, guilt-free enjoyment of tropical indolence that attracted lower South southerners at the start. Toward the end of the story, the region is increasingly dominated not by those who want to get away but by those who want to create a coast with all the amenities and attitudes they left back home, only with sand and surf instead of suburbs and cul-de-sacs.

This is also the story of how a desire to make money off tourists forced Gulf Coast folks to reconsider their attitude toward local government and the authority, bureaucracy, and taxes that came with it. Ultimately they would give up their freedom from civic oversight in exchange for better roads, better tasting water, a dependable sewage system, fire protection, and law enforcement. Many would not like what they got in return, but the deal was made nonetheless. Woven into this are accounts of the pioneers who found ways to cater to the desires and urges of visitors and investors and in the process reshaped the land and the landscape. They turned tourist courts into condominiums and bulldozed palmetto and scrub to make way for houses and communities that some would herald as the future of urban design and others would criticize for their clawing conformity.

Then there are those who have been left behind, descendants of the first arrivals who came to the coast for the simplicity, watched as it changed, and didn't like the result. The "no growth" attitudes of residents who "have theirs and don't want to share it" would run headlong into the policies of those who consider the coast a commodity to package for consumers, developers who want to tame it, homogenize it, and make it palatable to people who are not rednecks or at least do not consider themselves so. All of this has been played out in rituals that, like the coast, have become increasingly commercialized—Spring Break, Fourth of July parades, and a host of "festivals" that celebrate everything from the bounty of the Gulf to Beaujolais.

At times along the way, this rush to capitalize on the opportunities the beach offers has been influenced, redirected, and sometimes stopped dead in its tracks by economic factors taking shape far from the coast. Burps and bubbles in national and international finance have been felt along the Riviera as developers and speculators have gotten rich and gone broke as a result of policies crafted in Washington and on Wall Street. And as if it were not enough that the fate of the coastal economy rests on decisions made by financiers in suits instead of locals in shorts and T-shirts, increasing concern for the fate of coastal creatures and their habitats has come in conflict with the belief, deeply held by many at the beach, that the coast is there for humans to exploit and enjoy and that what happens to a mouse or a turtle is small stuff in the bigger scheme of things.

But at the end of this story, mice and men, turtles and tourists, rednecks and real estate tycoons have found themselves facing the same situation. When the BP/Deepwater Horizon well blew and oil spewed into the Gulf, everything that walked, crawled, swam, or soared became threatened. Optimism, already dampened by recession, disappeared. As the extent of the disaster became known, a few people along the Redneck Riviera began to wonder if the compromises made to find the petroleum that fueled the cars and planes that brought people to the motels and condos were worth the danger offshore drilling posed to their way of life. However, most, in true coastal fashion, avoided alternatives that might involve sacrifice and restraint. Instead they began to press the governments they so often held in contempt—local, state, and federal—to make a company once praised as a fine example of free-market capitalism clean up the mess and reimburse coastal interests for what they lost. Though it was a time for serious soul-searching, the fact that so little of that was done may be one of the clearest indications of how attitudes that shaped the coast at the beginning of this story shape it still.

Poutin' House South
Seagrove Beach, Florida, Summer 2011

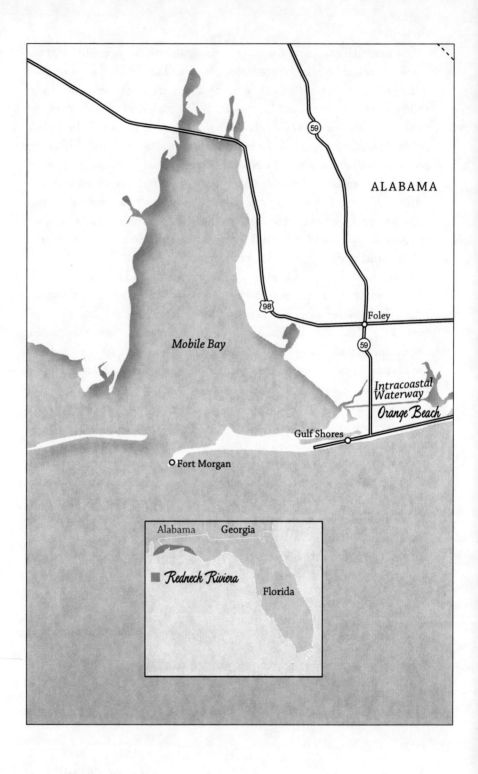

ALABAMA

59

98

Foley

59

Mobile Bay

Intracoastal
Waterway

Orange Beach

Gulf Shores

O Fort Morgan

Alabama   Georgia

Redneck Riviera

Florida

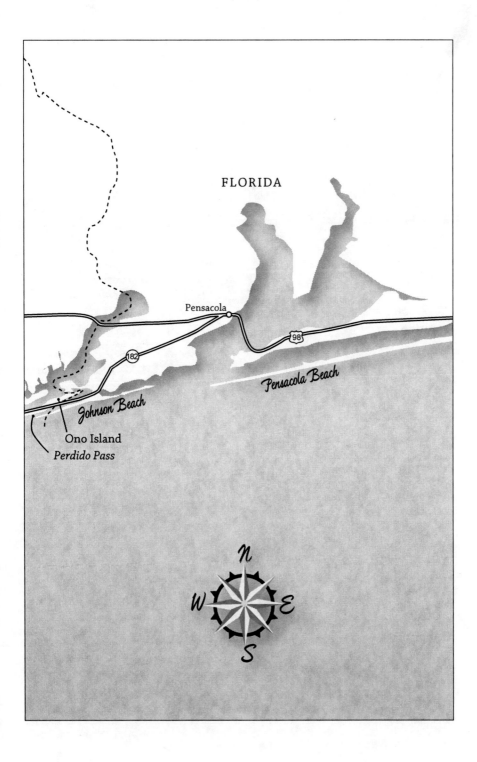

FLORIDA

Pensacola

98

182

Pensacola Beach

Johnson Beach

Ono Island
Perdido Pass

N
W   E
S

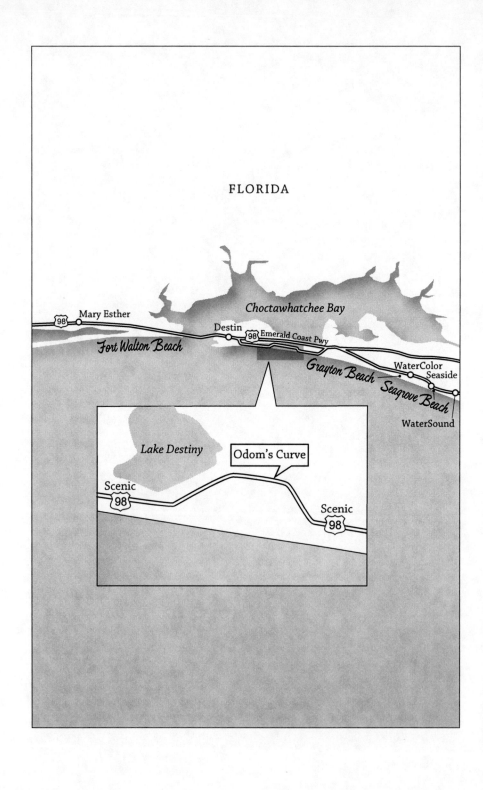

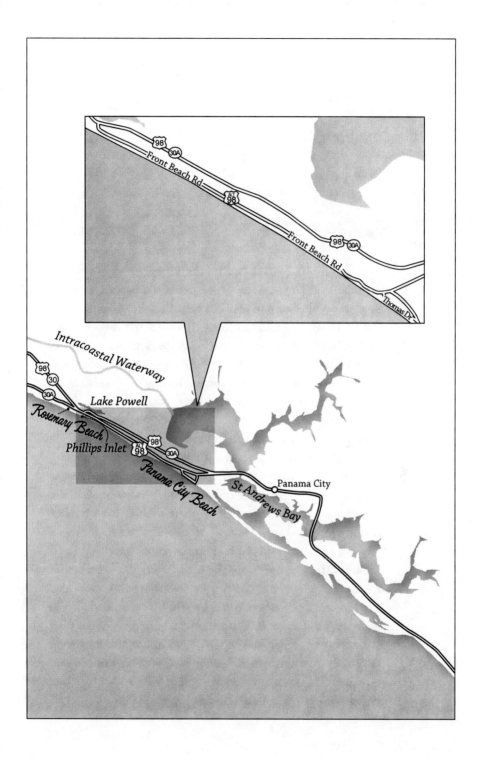

ONE

The Coast Jack Rivers Knew

*T*HE BEACH THAT Jack Rivers wanted to see again was not much by Waikiki standards. The same could be said for most of what would become the Redneck Riviera. Down on the Alabama coast there was no Royal Hawaiian, but there was the Orange Beach Hotel, which opened in 1923 and offered guests comfortable rooms with Delco System electrical lights and running water but no indoor toilets. The building took a beating in 1926, when the unnamed hurricane that did so much damage in the Miami area entered the Gulf, turned north, and made landfall again near the mouth of Mobile Bay. But the Orange Beach Hotel survived and was modernized (plumbing and all) in the 1930s, with cottages added to accommodate the growing number of families coming down. The year after the hurricane, the Gulf Shores Hotel opened. Built from lumber salvaged from a storm-damaged Mobile Bay hostelry, it was a two-story structure with a bathhouse on the lower level and private cottages—one owned by Mrs. Dixie Bibb Graves, wife of Alabama's governor, Bibb Graves. Vacation homes were also springing up, the first built in the 1920s by a couple of Mobile businessmen. Laid out on the mill-town, shotgun-house plan with screened sitting/sleeping porches all around, they were harbingers of things to come. By the 1930s these retreats were joined by other cottages of similar design—"a green box roofed by a green pyramid and propped on creosote poles" recalled a member of the family that built theirs "from cheap pine mill-ends and cheaper Depression labor" and named it Sand Castle.

Getting to the coast was no easy matter. Travel was routine as far as Foley, some fifteen miles inland, but from there the trip continued on a teeth-rattling, wooden, corduroy road and over a one-lane pontoon swing bridge that could be opened to let boats pass up into freshwater creeks to ride out storms or clean sea worms off their hulls. Anchored and docked in the coves and bayous behind the beach, these boats were among the many reasons visitors came down. As early as 1913, and maybe earlier, there were locals who would take tourists out through the pass to fish deep water—for seventy-five cents a day. Once beyond the breakers it was only a brief run to the "100-fathom curve," a dramatic six-hundred-foot drop in the floor of the Gulf where red snapper, grouper, and other popular fish clustered to feed. There upcountry folks, who had only fished for catfish and crappie, could catch the big ones, and as word of this bounty spread, "fishing for hire" became the Orange Beach industry. By 1938 a booklet titled "Tour Guide to South Baldwin County" told of fishing camps "opposite the Gulf of Mexico inlet [that led] to Perdido Bay," and of "a fleet of charter boats . . . available at most reasonable rates, with experienced fishing guides and navigators in charge." That same year captains and crew organized as the Orange Beach Fishing Association, and off into the promotional future they sailed.

About this same time there began to appear among coastal folks an atti-tude that might have passed unnoticed had it not later become a defining characteristic of the people and the place. You could see it in Carl Taylor "Zeke" Martin who, after the 1926 hurricane, homesteaded acres of beach-front that the government told him he could keep only if he tilled the soil. But the soil was sand, and raising crops was not what Zeke had in mind. So he planted fig trees, which he proudly pointed out to the homestead inspec-tor as evidence of his intention to do what the government told him he must do, only of course it wasn't. When the federal official left, Martin let the birds eat the figs, such as they were, and settled back to enjoy life on the beach. Charter boat captain Herman Callaway was cut from the same cloth. In the 1930s, the federal government levied a tax on charter boats and yachts. Callaway refused to pay it. Revenue agents arrived and Callaway ran them off. Then down from Mobile came the president of Waterman Steam Ship Corporation, who had heard of Callaway's defiance and wanted to tell him that his company was going to fight the tax as well. It did, it won, and the tax was repealed. Corporate giant and charter boat captain, united in a common wariness of what the federal government, or any government for that matter, might do that they didn't want done.

However, during the same period, and not for the last time, that same federal government pumped money into the Alabama coast and made the region more than it might have been. In 1931, the U.S. Corps of Engineers began building the Alabama section of the Intracoastal Waterway, and when it was finished two years later it had turned south Baldwin County into an island— Pleasure Island, Governor James E. "Big Jim" Folsom would later christen it. The construction brought jobs and people, improved the roads, and finally gave residents of Orange Beach and Gulf Shores a dependable bridge to what had become the mainland. A few years later another government, Alabama's this time, struck a deal with a local landowner who gave and sold the state around 4,500 acres, including some prime beachfront, in return for helping develop roads in the villages. Then, with the heavy lifting done by federally paid Civilian Conservation Corps boys, the state cleared the scrub and palmetto and built Gulf State Park, complete with a casino for dancing and dining, a bath house, and cabins that families could rent for ten dollars a week. By the end of the decade Gulf State was well on its way to being the most popular park in Alabama. If government was going to do anything, coastal citizens concluded, this was the sort of thing it should do.

Slowly but surely the region attracted more visitors, and as they came local folks and outside investors scrambled to accommodate them. When "two prospectors from Iowa" appeared "looking for a hotel site," the *Foley Outlooker* reported that they were "very profuse in praise for our bathing beach," and local landowners eager to sell began speculating which site the visitors would select. They didn't select any, but that disappointment hardly dampened the almost infectious optimism of coastal dwellers. With little or no state, county, or municipal authority down there to tell residents what they could or could not do, could or could not be, they could dream great dreams unfettered by regulations or reality. So when the "prospectors" left, locals returned to their normal routine and waited for the next opportunity to arise.

In Orange Beach the normal routine was fishing. Camps, complete with "lodge-sleeping accommodations" for anglers, were built along the bayous and coves. One even had "a small Texaco gas station and store offering day snacks and ice" and most had "skiffs for rent." Soon the newspaper in Foley was reporting month-long visits by families and friends from as near as Montgomery and as far away as Illinois, there to enjoy the "good bathing and fishing"—"bathing" being what they called "swimming" until the 1940s, when "bathing" came to be associated with personal hygiene and "swimming" with recreation and physical fitness. To attract fishers and bathers the Fishing Association began advertising what its members had to offer and encouraging those interested to telegraph Foley for reservations. From there the messages would be hand carried to captains in Orange Beach. Not the most efficient and certainly not the swiftest way to secure accommodations and make arrangements, but it had to do until the 1950s, when telephone service finally arrived.

Thus the seeds of a future were sown. Prosperity would come to the coast if locals could attract more visitors with promises that they could leave their cares (and maybe their inhibitions) behind, while they fished, surf-bathed, and relaxed. It was paradise, Alabama style, and in the late 1930s, as the Great Depression seemed to lose steam and before war took so many away, it was what increasing numbers of Alabamians enjoyed—if they could afford it.

Across the Florida line, things were a little different, but not much.

The Florida Panhandle and Alabama were so closely connected, physically and culturally, that back in 1900, as the new century opened, the Young Men's Business League of Pensacola began lobbying for Alabama to annex Florida all the way to the Apalachicola River. Arguing not only the economic advantages of such a union, proannexation forces pointed out that there were "more natives of Alabama in West Florida than of any other state, not counting native Floridians, who are in many cases children of natives of Alabama." Obviously the effort failed, but the connection on which it was predicated continued to influence the growth of west Florida, whose beaches many Alabamians found easier (and often more fun) to visit than their own.

Despite the sentiments of its Young Men's Business League, by the end of the First World War, Pensacola had settled comfortably into being Florida. With tourism, timber, and the military, the city had the largest and most diverse economy on the Panhandle. The beach, however, was not the city's main attraction. Although in years past there had been talk of how Pensacola's part of Santa Rosa Island would become "the Coney Island of the South" it did not happen. The beach, across the bay and on the other side of the island, was difficult to reach. In 1924, after reading about the wonders of Pensacola and the Gulf, a couple of Alabama boys rode their bikes all the way down to the coast. Pensacola was pretty much as advertised, but across the bay on the island biking was difficult. The closer they got to the water the deeper the ruts in the sandy road became, "so deep we had to push on level ground," one of them wrote later. That part of Florida, the young adventurer recalled, "was nothing like the stuff I had been reading about." But interest in the island was growing. A few years later the Pensacola Bridge Corporation was formed. It leased a couple of miles of island and shoreline and began constructing a bridge from the mainland that would draw people to the resort the company planned to build. In 1931 the bridge opened, just in time for the onset of the Great Depression. Despite the odds against it, the Pensacola Beach resort was built, a little smaller than initially planned, and it survived, though barely. It would be the core of what would later be known simply as Pensacola Beach.

Pensacola residents were quick to take advantage of the new span. Those who could afford it built cottages on the island, which was close enough to allow them to leave town after work on Friday and be sitting and sipping on their porch at sunset. Soon a weekend migration to the beach became part of affluent Pensacolians' summer routine. Local entrepreneurs came as well and built motels, though they weren't called that yet. By the end of the decade the beach was illuminated for "night bathing," a casino for dining and dancing had opened, and a fishing pier had been built out into the Gulf. It was a start, albeit a slow one. Though city fathers touted the sand and surf, there was more to do in Pensacola than visit what was still a largely undeveloped island. So most of the Depression-era tourists who visited the town, what few there were, spent most of their time on the mainland and took day trips over to the coast. In 1937, not long after U.S. 98 was completed to connect Pensacola to the rest of the Panhandle, the Florida State Road Department put out a tourist booklet, *Highways of Florida*. There was no mention of Pensacola Beach.

To the east of Pensacola were little communities like Navarre, best known in the 1930s for the story of how its founder, a Colonel Guy Wayman, chased off his ex-wife (who was also his adopted daughter—things can get a little strange down there) and warned her that if she came back he would shoot her. She came back. He shot her. But having warned her, local law enforcement figured she should have known better, so Wayman went free. A little further east was the town of Mary Esther, which had been settled before the Civil War and named, locals think, for a member (or members) of the founder's family—along the coast, precision is often optional. Neither Navarre nor Mary Esther was on the beach. They were on the north side of Santa Rosa Sound, the narrow body of water that separated "tree-crowned Santa Rosa Island" from the mainland and protected settlements from storms. The 1939 WPA publication *Florida: A Guide to the Southernmost State* told how both communities attracted visitors and investors who built "tourist and summer camps, beach cottages, and substantial houses that overlook the placid waters" of the sound. Those who wanted to enjoy bathing and fishing could jump or drop a hook off their dock into the water, or row over to the island, walk across and play in the surf. The eldest son of an Alabama family that lived on one of the lakes north of Montgomery told of how in the 1920s his family would go down for a week or so. Lake-raised and experienced in water, he and his siblings refused the boats offered them and swam across to the island instead. Once there they had the beach all to themselves.

Then there was Fort Walton, also on the north side of the sound, which also had no beach, and no fort, for that matter. It had been Camp Walton once, but was renamed, and by the early twentieth century there were a couple of small hotels for tourists and salesmen traveling through. Then in 1927, a local visionary, Thomas E. Brooks, leased land on Okaloosa Island— not a separate island really but the east end of Santa Rosa, across the sound from Fort Walton. There Brooks set to building cottages for the visitors he knew would come. Only they didn't. Okaloosa was isolated from the mainland without much to do but play in the water and sit in the sun, and the first season he could not get anyone to stay overnight. That, however, would change.

Across the pass that led from the Gulf to Choctawhatchee Bay and separated Fort Walton from the eastern Panhandle was Destin. Settled before the Civil War by a New England fisherman whose descendants still live there, "The Luckiest Little Fishing Village in the World," as it came to be known, was lucky because it was as close to the "100-fathom curve" as Orange Beach, if not closer. And as they did from Orange Beach, charter boats took out visitors from Destin to catch everything from mackerel to snapper to grouper to an occasional billfish. Destin was also "lucky," it was told, because during Prohibition boat captains were well positioned to sail out, connect with rumrunners, and bring the liquor in to thirsty folks on shore. Orange Beach and other coastal communities had their share of that trade and there would not be better bootlegging until the 1960s and 1970s when marijuana became the contraband of choice. While Destin was blessed with a beautiful and easily accessible beach, fishing was what brought people there, and accommodations like those in Orange Beach were the rule. Though the opening of U.S. 98 in the mid-1930s made it easier for beach-loving tourists to get to Destin (and the rest of the Panhandle), at the end of that decade it was still being described as a "fishing resort." With only twenty-five year-round residents in Destin, anyone visiting on the eve of World War II would have believed its future would forever be linked to its charter fleet and to the men who operated the boats.

They would have been wrong.

Between Destin and Panama City was some sixty miles of largely deserted coastline, distinguished by tall dunes and coastal dune lakes. In ancient times, much of this was an island, cut off from the rest of the coast and countryside by Destin Pass to the west, Phillips Inlet to the east, and Choctawhatchee Bay to the north. Old folks still called it "the island" though they had never known it when it was. With a few exceptions, the completion of U.S. 98 did little to immediately relieve the isolation of most of the people who lived there—the shrimpers and oystermen back on the bay, the few timber crews cutting what was left of the longleaf pine cover, and the handful of beachside residents, some who lived almost as hermits and liked it that way. The highway ran down the middle of the island, not along the beach, but there would not have been much to see, other than beach, if it had taken a more coastal route. So in the 1930s (and for the next three decades) travelers through south Walton County turned off the highway only if by some prior arrangement or out of curiosity they wanted to visit Grayton Beach or Seagrove.

Grayton, one of the oldest vacation beaches on the Panhandle, had been homesteaded in the 1880s. Around the turn of the century its namesake, Major Charles T. Gray, built a house that evolved into the hotel that became known as the Washaway after what the 1926 hurricane almost did to it. (According to another account the Washaway was built by the McCaskill Land and Timber Company to house its workers, and the name came from its location near a pond that eroded the foundation—another case of people

Washaway Hotel, Grayton Beach, Florida, circa 1985. Built in the 1890s—though over the years raised, repaired, and updated—it still looks much the same as it did back then. Photograph by the author.

along the coast not getting hung up on precision.) In time the village's few permanent residents built cottages for renting and Grayton became a popular summer resort for folks from inland Florida and south Alabama. Better roads and bridges built in the 1930s brought more people, some of whom constructed cottages of their own that would become family seasonal retreats, but accommodations remained spartan for years to come—no electricity until the 1940s. Even the leading member of the town's leading family, Van Ness Butler, did not live there year-round. Principal of Point Washington School back on the bay, where his wife taught, Butler packed up the family and moved to a home near the school for the winter rather than drive the thirty-mile round-trip every day.

When the tourists returned, so did the Butlers, who rented out cottages and ran the town's only store, Butler General, which sold staples to residents and visitors, and doubled as a dance hall. Of all the "island" settlements, Grayton may have benefitted most, or at least first, from the completion of U.S. 98. On weekends during the late 1930s Butler General was a partying place, a honky-tonk for folks who liked their honky-tonking a little less redneck than some other places were known, or at least rumored, to be. "We'd have a hundred people here on Saturday night," Butler recalled. "People would come from as far as Destin to dance." Business boomed. A soft-drink salesman told Butler that "the year before the war [Butler General] sold more Coca-Cola than any store in Fort Walton Beach." Of course the "stores" in Fort Walton offered a wider variety of drinks, not all of them "soft," though imperfect memories recall that what Butler sold was often mixed with, or used to chase, something stronger. The good times rolled.

About three miles east of Grayton, Seagrove Beach sat atop an oak-covered bluff that some claimed was the highest point between Key West and Brownsville, Texas. It was said that when a hurricane approached, locals flocked there (and even climbed up into the trees) to escape the storm surges. Sea captains called it "green hill" and used it as a navigation point, for they could see it from far out in the Gulf. In 1923, the location got its permanent name from the Seagrove Company, which came in, bought up land, laid out streets, and "dedicated for public use . . . for bathing and fishing" the beachfront that the developers felt would be the community's main attraction. A few lots were sold. Later a hotel was built, which served for a while as a retreat for members of the Dixie Art Colony, a group of painters under the direction and inspiration of Alabama artist Kelly Fitzpatrick. But the Depression closed the hotel, the artists returned to Alabama, and by the time World War II began, there was not much to see at Seagrove except a couple of cottages, the beach, and the trees.

Although they were not far apart, getting from Grayton to Seagrove, or between any of the other small beach settlements of south Walton, was a long and often unpleasant trip. Travelers had to drive back out to U.S. 98 on the rough and sandy road that brought them in, then drive a few miles east or west to a similar road that would take them back to the coast. As a result, there was little interaction between the villages and people. Each Walton County beach community was a world unto itself, having much in common with its neighbors but little shared. Not that there was much reason to cooperate. Political power in Walton County was inland, at the courthouse in DeFuniak Springs, where entrenched agricultural interests called the shots. The same was true for most other Panhandle counties as well as coastal counties in Alabama—Santa Rosa County was run by the courthouse gang in Milton, in Okaloosa the power brokers were at Crestview, and in Alabama there were the good old Baldwin County boys in Bay Minette. The folks who controlled these centers of authority cared little for the concerns of small beach communities such as Destin, Fort Walton, Gulf Shores,

Orange Beach, Seagrove, and Grayton. With few year-round residents to vote, the coast was not much of a constituency. Even county seats close to the Gulf—Panama City in Bay County and Pensacola in Escambia—paid scant attention to nearby beach villages. So it followed that with few rules and regulations, and only a distant sheriff's department to keep order, beach folks were pretty much on their own—and most liked it that way.

Crossing Phillips Inlet and Lake Powell, where the Fleming family from Geneva, just inside Alabama, built a cabin and spent summers fishing, swimming, and sweating, U.S. 98 left the "island" and drew closer to the beach. Constructed in part along the dune line and violating most modern environmental regulations, this stretch of highway and the roads leading off it would in time be home to much of the tasteless, trashy, unsophisticated amusements and activities that other folks in other places will think of when they hear people talk of the "Redneck Riviera." But it did not start out that way, nor would it end that way.

In between start and end, this is what happened.

At the turn of the century, and even later, when people spoke of Panama City (if they spoke of it at all) they were talking about a city that, like Pensacola, was separated from the coast by a bay. Early on, however, city fathers could see that most tourists were not content to just stay in town. "It is already very evident," the local newspaper wrote in 1909, "that about everyone who visits this bay desires to go to the gulf beach and take a dip in the surf." Evenings on the shore with bonfires and picnics were especially popular, and the press reported "scarcely a night but there are from one to five boat loads of people going there." Looking to the future, the writer predicted that "when the trains begin to bring in those who come here almost solely to enjoy the water and bathing, this number will greatly increase."

Automobiles, not trains, turned out to be what brought folks to the Gulf Coast. Though Panama City could boast the downtown ten-story Dixie-Sherman Hotel where guests could see the Gulf from the rooftop garden, in the 1920s local developers began to turn their attention away from the town and out to the beach. One of the first was W. T. Sharpless who envisioned a resort at Long Beach, west of the city and across the bay. He built some cottages and a large casino for dancing, but when he began charging a fifty-cent fee for anyone who wanted to cross his strip of sand to get to the water, people who were used to using the beach as if it were their own were outraged. In 1931, Sharpless attempted to collect the fee from one of the interlopers, who said he wouldn't pay it. Sharpless told him to pay or get off his beach. So the interloper shot him. It would not be the last time tempers would flare over access to sand and surf, though in the future the lawsuit will be the weapon of choice.

Developers were not deterred. J. E. Churchwell purchased the Sharpless property, built some more cottages, refurbished the casino, and turned Long Beach Resort into what has been described as "a miniature fiefdom of the Churchwell family." About the same time, Gideon "Gil" Thomas bought a little over one hundred acres adjacent to Churchwell's resort and named it Panama City Beach. Selling the project to investors was not easy. Located where U.S. 98 curved back away from the coast, the property could only be reached by a sandy road with ruts so deep that at times visitors had to get out and push their cars through. But Thomas's enthusiasm was contagious. He raised the money, laid out the streets, and made them passable with oyster shells brought in from Apalachicola. Then he built a two-story, twelve-room hotel, along with a few tourist cottages for visitors who wanted more privacy and less luxury. Gated with an arch and so brightly lit at night that it could be seen from the downtown Dixie-Sherman Hotel, Panama City Beach became the destination for so many that in time visitors, paying little attention to names, came to think of the town and beach as one.

Entrance to Panama City Beach, circa 1940. The lighted arch could be seen from the roof of a downtown hotel. Courtesy of Bay County Public Library, Panama City, Fla.

Despite the Depression, the beaches of Bay County west of Panama City continued to draw developers. In the fall of 1936, two Dixie-Sherman Hotel investors—including the "energetic, high-strung Broderick Lahan of Birmingham's Lahan & Co."—drove the "Gulf Coast Scenic Highway" and noticed "the natural beauty of the spot, with its ideal advantages as a locale for vacation cottages." They bought up four thousand feet along the Gulf and U.S. 98, laid out cottage sites, and within the first week sold thirty-seven lots, all "to Alabamians who longed for just such a spot to call their own." Meanwhile plans were being made to increase accommodations and facilities at Panama City Beach and at new resorts named Laguna, Sunnyside, Bahama Beach, Mara Vista, El Centro, and Gulf Beach Resort. Located just west of the landmark Y where the highway that brought so many down from the north dead-ended at U.S. 98, the developments were easily reached by automobile. With this market on which to draw, the press reported that planners were already envisioning "two hundred new cottages by spring along this beautiful highway and beach." Beyond any doubt, the writer observed, "Panama City is coming into its own as a vacation land." It was becoming something else as well. Because so many of the visitors and so many of the investors came from Florida's neighbor to the north, some folks were calling it "Lower Alabama." The name would stick, for a while.

Though Alabamians were discovering the wonders of the Panama City coast, Floridians were not so quick to pick up on the news. *Highways of Florida*, the 1937 promotional pamphlet that ignored Pensacola Beach, paid little attention to Panama City's resorts. While noting that the town, "only a fishing village a short time ago," was now home to over twelve thousand inhabitants, the guide reported that the source of this growth was "due largely to the paper mill there." Though it observed that Panama City "attracts tourists in all seasons," there was no comment on its beaches.

That may have been the last time for such an omission. The year after that account was published, Harry Edwards Lark and his son Jimmy built a semicircle of multicolored cabins on the north side of U.S. 98 and christened them Larkway Villas. Advertised as "The Most Exclusive on the Gulf," Larkway boasted of facilities "fully furnished" and a "private beach" just across the road. These "gay-colored summer cottages [that] line[d] the dunes" along U.S. 98 were built on the "dry side" of the highway, not from any particular concern for the dune environment, but because it was rightly believed that that side was safer from storms and because visitors were less likely to track sand into the cottages if they had to cross the highway. Besides, there wasn't much traffic, so it was easy to scurry safely across—for a while at least. As for the "private beach," where once making a beach exclusive led to a shooting, with U.S. 98 open those who were excluded couldn't have cared less. So much beach was available that anyone could pull off the highway onto the "hard surfaced parking places" and (according to the 1939 *WPA Guide*) "stop at intervals for a swim or picnic" on a beach they could and often did consider their own.

Larkway Villas, Panama City Beach, circa 1940. Individual cottages were popular with early tourists. Courtesy of Bay County Public Library, Panama City, Fla.

The Larks, who later developed the Miracle Strip Amusement Park, would become major players in defining the coast and promoting tourism. More interested in attracting visitors than in selling lots, they represented one side of the two-sided approach to beach development. On one hand were promoters such as Lahan who were essentially land speculators. While their interests were broad enough to include rental properties and businesses to attract and entertain visitors, their first priority was selling real estate. On the other side were people like the Larks and Bill Holloway, who created Holloway Beach sixteen miles west of Panama City and built the two-story Sea Breeze Hotel on the Gulf side of the highway. Boasting that every room had a "private tile bath" (where guests could wash off that pesky sand), the Sea Breeze also included a restaurant that served "The World's Best Fried Chicken" (a nod to his lower South clientele). The restaurant was an important addition, for being far down the beach, it was a long ride to find a place to eat. This is why many of the fully furnished cottages included kitchenettes so folks could come in loaded with groceries. For most families—and families were the core of their business—a meal "out" was an occasional treat, not a regular thing. Bologna sandwiches, peanut butter and jelly, and chips would keep the kids happy.

The families who came found families like themselves. Whether at Gulf Shores, Pensacola, Fort Walton, Destin, Grayton, Seagrove, or Panama City, visitors who came to frolic instead of fish were mostly the traditional wife,

husband, and kids. Most were white, southern, middle class, and protes-
tant (with a lowercase "p"; even the scattering of Catholics who came to
the coast brought with them sentiments and habits that were far down the
scale from high church). To call them redneck might be stretching the definition a bit. Although some couples left children behind with a sitter and
went out dancing at the Panama City Beach casino or one of the few clubs
that had opened, and some came in a bit tipsy from a little more liquor than
they might have consumed back home where neighbors would shake their
heads and click their tongues if they found out, most just enjoyed the beach
and each other in an atmosphere a little more laid back than what they left
behind. They did not come down to party, they came to relax. And that is
what the Panhandle beaches offered.

As for the locals, the residents who were there to make tourist trips
worthwhile, most were much like the visitors themselves. Along the coast
there was hardly a black face to be seen. In 1940, barely one-third of Bay
County's residents were African Americans and most worked inland in the
lumber and turpentine camps. That was the largest percentage in all the
coastal counties, including Baldwin in Alabama, where blacks were only a
quarter of the population. And as with Bay County, few African Americans
were found along the beach. If one of the characteristics of a redneck was
having a white neck that could burn in the sun, the coastal residents from
Mobile Bay to St. Andrews Bay met that critical requirement.

In time they would meet others as well.

TWO

The War and after It

AS THE 1940S OPENED, if Gulf Coast folks were troubled by the possibility that the United States might be pulled into the war in Europe, not to mention the one going on in Asia, it did not show in what they were doing, which was what they had always been doing. Over at Long Beach Resort, J. E. Churchwell recalled, people continued to dance at his casino, fish in the surf or out in the Gulf, and "generally play." More and more of his customers were from nearby Tyndall Field, but the great military influx was yet to come. The beaches of Panama City were still tourist beaches. Things were much the same off to the west. At Grayton, families played on the sand and in the surf in the daytime and on weekends folks came in to dance at Butler General. From Destin the charter boats (there were more of them now) still carried visitors out to pull 'em in till their arms were sore, a frenzy of catching (no release) that Howell Raines called the "redneck way of fishing." But across the pass, over in Fort Walton, another form of entertainment was popular. Although state law prohibited slot machines and certain casino-type gambling, the law was "openly violated" in Okaloosa County. Fort Walton, with good roads, summer visitors, and places that served alcohol, had become a little Las Vegas on the Gulf Coast. County officials inland at Crestview turned a blind eye to what was going on. As long as the money rolled in (and some of it was passed under the table) everyone was happy—except the losers. When the War Department

Casino and Bar, Panama City Beach, 1938. This casino was fairly typical of others along the coast. Courtesy of Bay County Public Library, Panama City, Fla.

began expanding nearby Eglin Air Force Base, Fort Walton was ready to offer airmen something more than swimming and fishing.

So was Pensacola. With the U.S. Naval Air Station and Fort Barrancas nearby, the city knew how to entertain off-duty servicemen. Add to that mix the commercial fishermen who went out into the Gulf, stayed for months, and came back to turn Pensacola's waterfront into "a scene of merrymaking." Beer and whiskey flowed until their money was gone and then they went back to sea, for according to local lore it was "considered unlucky for a professional fisherman to set out on another trip with funds in his pockets." Servicemen on a weekend pass fit right in. Meanwhile, Pensacola expanded west toward Alabama. The Paradise Beach Hotel opened on "Beautiful Perdido Bay" and offered a variety of "summertime amusements" along with "splendid meals," rooms with private baths and a "comfortable, home-like atmosphere" at $2.50 a night for a single, $4.00 for a double. If guests wanted to fish, the charter boats of Orange Beach were just across the pass.

A little further west was the Gulf Shores Hotel, which opened the decade with an advertising campaign in Mobile newspapers, inviting folks to "come to the Gulf" for "an afternoon, a week-end or an extended vacation at our delightful surf-pounded beach." There visitors could find complete hotel services, a restaurant with home cooking, a cocktail bar, and dancing. "Rest, relax and play at Gulf Shores Hotel," one ad beckoned, "Guaranteed against Boredom!" Yet despite increased emphasis on dancing, drinking, and other "amusements," Gulf Shores remained a family-focused resort. In the summer of 1941, the *Mobile Press-Register* ran a picture-filled page showing how "Surf and Sand Turn[ed] Gulf Shores into One of Dixie's Beauty Spots."

Girls at Gulf Shores, 1948. Taken in the heart of the resort, the photo shows typical beach cottages in the background. The girls were from Grove Hill, Alabama, about 150 miles inland. Note the swimsuits—a 1940s model two-piece and the coming fashion, a 1950s one-piece. From *A Pictorial History: Clarke County, Alabama*, published by the *Clarke County Democrat*, Grove Hill, Ala., 2006.

Though most of the pictures were of young women in bathing suits, on shore, in the water, and walking along the newly constructed pier that went three hundred feet out into the Gulf, at the top of the page was toddler Paul Porter Mathews Jr. of Jackson, Mississippi, who was "having the time of his life visiting the beach with his parents." The Alabama coast offered a little something for everyone, close to home and at a price visitors could afford.

In these late Depression years, price was no small matter, which is why, in the summer of 1940, people began to complain about the fees being charged at the Gulf State Park. The issue would appear time and again along the coast as more and more tourists came down to use facilities and resources they thought should be free. Since the park belonged to the state, or more specifically the people of the state, was it right for the public, most of them Alabamians, to have to pay to drive onto the property and picnic? It might be reasonable for it to cost citizens to stay overnight in a cabin, but should there be a fee to use the state-operated bathhouse? "With the various charges asked by the state from visitors to the park," the *Mobile Register* wrote in a scathing editorial, "the development might as well be a privately-operated casino and beach." Because of the fees, the writer continued, "numerous pleasure seekers are reportedly expressing their resentment to the charge by going elsewhere for similar amusements." Then the newspaper hit politicians in Montgomery where it hurt. "If the state had built the casino, bathhouses, cabins and other structures within the reservation, it would have further justification for charging admission; but all of the buildings were constructed, furniture included, by the federal government through the CCC camp located near the park." The fees, the *Register* concluded, should be removed.

Of course, they weren't—at least not all of them—and despite the cost, tourists kept coming. Even as the debate raged, the state conservation director reported that some three hundred families were turned away "because of a lack of cottages." Once again the CCC came to the rescue. In the winter of 1940–41, five new units were built and existing facilities were refurbished to get the park ready for the next tourist season—not enough accommodations to meet the demand, but a step in the right direction. And as far as one can tell, visitors didn't care who built the cabins, they just wanted a place at the beach, even if only for a week.

The mostly deserted coast to the west of Gulf Shores was also catching the attention of visitors and investors. Twelve miles out on the Dixie Graves Parkway, which took visitors to Fort Morgan, developers carved out "600 feet of sand beach playground" and announced in the *Register* that those who did not want to compete for reservations at the park or in the hotel could buy a "large cabin lot" of their own for as low as fifty dollars to one dollar down and the rest in monthly installments. Buy a lot, build a cottage, hop in your automobile and drive there whenever you wanted. And if you didn't have a car, H. J. Kittrell of Kittrell-Milling Motor Company would be happy to sell you one. Since "folks here on the Gulf Coast are given to aquatic sports," Kittrell pointed out in his company's bathing beauty–adorned advertisement, beach lovers would be happy with "the ease with which one may reach the swimming places in a 1941 Dodge." Yes, the Depression was fading and good times seemed just around the corner.

What came instead was Pearl Harbor.

On December 7, 1941, everything changed. The "complacency" that the *Mobile Register* found among Gulf Coast folks disappeared beneath "waves of excitement and apprehension" when reports reached the city that "enemy submarines" had been sighted off Texas. This, the *Register* warned, "offers necessary evidence that the southern coast of the United States is not as secure as it has thought." If that were not warning enough, soon other evidence began to drift in: oil, tar, and bits and pieces of ships washed onto the beach. The first German submarine commander who got into the Gulf wrote in his log how surprised he was at the lack of preparation he found. That soon changed. When "dimouts" were ordered for cities with populations of five thousand or more within thirty miles of the Gulf, Pensacola and Panama City lost their glow. Smaller towns voluntarily did the same. Floodlights and bright signs that advertised hotels and resorts were turned off; baseball and football games were rescheduled for daytime. Vehicles, even those with the top halves of their headlights darkened, were banned from the beach at night. And beach bonfires were prohibited, to the relief, surely, of parents of teenagers, though the youngsters who were determined to gather there were likely undeterred, perhaps even encouraged, by the dark. Windows facing the water were curtained, shuttered, or covered with black paper, and visitors to the coast recall sitting on porches at night, watching the Gulf, and wondering if the lights they saw were our ships or the enemy's.

They had reason to wonder. For years after the conflict ended the children of the family that owned the Sand Castle cottage at Gulf Shores would urge elders to "tell about the war [and] the German Submarine." Then out would come the tale of the night car lights were seen flashing on the beach and lights in the Gulf flashing back. The next day, the story went, the FBI arrived, and later locals learned of the arrest of "the old manager" of a local establishment. He was the same man who at hotel dances glided across the floor with girls of the family, but it turned out he had a "crystal set in his room" and was "spotting ships for the U-boats." U.S. vessels would run as close to shore as they could to escape the enemy. From shore he could see them and let the enemy know where they were. Some ships got through to Mobile Bay. Some were torpedoed. Some sank and today divers go down to them. Some were hit but limped to safety, with holes so big, it was told, "you could put Sand Castle through."

Stories like this might be written off as local lore were it not for confirming reports of U-boat sightings and ships lost. So all beaches, including those along the Gulf, "were closed to night bathing" as the military "intensified precaution against further landings of enemy saboteurs." At about this same time, out of patriotic duty or self-preservation or a yearning for excitement or maybe just the desire to get a little more rationed gasoline, charter boat captains, yachtsmen, and even folks with outboard driven skiffs volunteered to patrol close to shore. The U.S. Navy, fearing (with good reason) that this ragtag bunch might prove more trouble than they were worth, resisted until political pressure forced the real military to accept "help" from what became known as the Hooligan Navy. The captains of these vessels were given temporary rank in the Coast Guard Reserves, and their boats were equipped with radios so they could keep in touch with shore. Some boats were also armed, and though there was concern that Gulf Coast boatmen with weapons would be as much a danger to themselves as to the enemy, it turned out that they weren't. They took their job seriously and did the best they could.

Which, in the end, didn't amount to much. Despite interference from local congressmen who wanted the government to build a fleet of small, fast submarine hunters—"aqua bombers," as Alabama representative Frank Boykin called them—the Navy squashed the idea, and Coast Guard cutters, destroyers, and spotter aircraft with trained crews did most of the work. As far as the Germans were concerned, the Hooligan Navy made little differ-ence. As far as coastal folk were concerned, they were heroes.

Along the Florida Panhandle the military geared up. Pensacola was full of sailors and airmen, and the miles of empty beach became firing ranges for pilots in training. Relic hunters with metal detectors still find the bullets with which the planes pounded the dunes, and later, when environmental-ists would campaign to save the beach mouse, some people would observe that if the little rodents could survive that assault, surely they could sur-vive condo development. While the war put a crimp in the tourist trade, the Army and the Navy kept local economies in Pensacola, Fort Walton, and Panama City doing just fine. Even little Grayton benefitted from the war effort. When a forty-man Coast Guard station was established there the military rented vacation homes and the Washaway to billet the troops who patrolled the beach on horseback. With this new clientele Butler's store did a booming business. Over close to Panama City, cottages at Churchwell's Long Beach Resort were turned over to servicemen and the casino became their mess hall.

But soldiers weren't the only ones filling cottages, hotels, and newly opened boarding houses. Even before the United States got into the war, the government had ordered thirty-three freighters to be built in the Panama City shipyard. Pensacola experienced the same sort of industrial boom and to fill the jobs these contracts created, workers came down from inland Florida, south Alabama, and south Georgia. These were not the middle-class southerners who vacationed at the beach. Like the vacationers, they were white, and in some cases they had a patina of education that moved them up to supervisory positions, but most were rough-handed men (and soon women) who had worked on hardscrabble farms or in small cotton mills or perhaps nowhere at all. So, for the promise of steady employment, good pay, and the hope of a better life for themselves and their families, these folks came to the coast. They gave the shipyards a good week's work and on Friday and Saturday took families to the beach that was once the province of people just a little more affluent, and a little more, dare we say, sophisticated than the newcomers. They mingled well with charter captains and their mates, hung out around the docks and oyster bars, danced and drank at the local honky-tonks that were springing up, got in fights, went to jail, came home repentant, and went to church—few did all of those things at once, though some tried. And when the war was over many went back "home" and returned on vacations. But for others the coast had become home, so they stayed.

The same honky-tonks and dives that catered to this wave of civilian workers were also popular with servicemen, so commanding officers moved quickly to head off the trouble that experience told them would soon follow. (The fact that officers, even the noncommissioned ones, had "clubs" of their own was not lost on men in the ranks.) A couple of months after Pearl Harbor the commander at Ft. Barrancas told Pensacola city leaders that they had better clean up local saloons or the establishments would be put "out of bounds" to his men. The city responded with regulations that required all places selling alcoholic beverages to be closed at midnight and all day Sunday. Licensed businesses apparently accepted the new rules without complaint, but establishments described as "jook joints" that operated near the Army and Navy posts tried to get around the law and do business as they always had. Some were able to. Most weren't.

Bars weren't all the war closed. Though a trickle of tourists continued to arrive, with gasoline rationed few came from far away. People who owned homes on the Gulf and could stay for much of the summer came as they had before, but by 1943 some of the small stores that catered to fishermen and visitors were shut and shuttered. A few cabin owners put their property on the market at bargain prices—you could get a camp house at Gulf Shores, back on Little Lagoon, with an electric refrigerator, hot and cold water in the bath, and a garage on a 110-by-310-foot shaded lot for only two thousand dollars—but apparently there were few takers. If you wanted solitude, the Gulf Coast was the place to go—if you could get there, which was increasingly hard to do. As the summer of 1944 approached the Office of Defense Transportation asked the public to "refrain from burdening the country's transportation facilities with heavy vacation travel." Troops were on the move, mostly by train, so anyone planning to go by rail to Pensacola, Panama City, or the Alabama beaches by way of Mobile needed to change plans. Some vacationed elsewhere, but most stayed at home.

However, that summer marked a turning point in the war *and* for the coast. It may only be coincidental, but shortly after D-day the *Mobile Register* editorialized on the "Postwar Need for Resort Facilities." The editorial pointed out that despite "limited transportation and lessened opportunity for pleasure, the inadequacy of the facilities for full enjoyment of the Gulf Coast in the Mobile district is immediately obvious." Although not much could be done "in the way of development and improvement in beach facilities" until there was peace again, it was not too early for thinking and planning. Even before the fighting began, the *Register* noted, "facilities were not equivalent to the need," and with the coastal population surge brought on by the conflict, postwar demands for beach accommodations would be even greater. "Mobile," the writer concluded, "has never taken advantage of anything like the potentials which the coast country offers in seashore and bay shore attractions. After the war it should begin to treat itself to more of these benefits." The same editorial could have been written about Pensacola or Panama City, and the same thoughts could have been, and were, expressed by city promoters in all of these places. As the war slogged on toward its bloody end, without citing the biblical reference, probably without even knowing there was one, promoters echoed throughout the lower South what "the angel of the Lord spake unto Philip," recorded in Acts 8:26, when he told him "Arise and go toward the south."

As if in response to the *Register's* editorial, coastal developers moved in. Orange Beach got its first subdivision in 1944, carved out on Alabama Point, around Cotton Bayou, in the Catman Road area, a thoroughfare that got its name from the teenagers who slipped in and screeched like cats to scare lovers parked on the lane. That same year the Mobile Chamber of Commerce listed among the projects it wanted the state to undertake a "scenic drive" from Mobile to Pensacola, down the eastern shore of Mobile Bay and across south Baldwin County, a road that would make the coast more accessible. Then in the summer of 1945, with VE Day in the history books, social activities on the Gulf picked up. Mobile's Cavalier Club renewed a prewar tradition among the city's social elite and drove member-filled trucks down to Gulf State Park for an all-day picnic that included box lunches, swimming, sunbathing, and dancing at the casino. Sensing the change that was coming coastal newspapers advertised beachwear and announced, "Bare beauty is the keynote of 1945 Summer fashion." Picking up on that theme health advice columnists warned that "sleeveless dresses, midriff swimsuits, bare back play suits and drawstring necklines that leave little of the shoulders and neck to the imagination call for more complete skin care." That was as far as they went. Down in Miami Beach the City Council, shocked by the "growing scantiness of bathing attire and the popularity of shorts and play suits," had banned "Abbreviated Togs in Public Places," but the women on Alabama's shores faced no such restrictions.

Nor did the women of the Panhandle where beaches and beach towns quickly returned to prewar activities. Their civilian populations swelled by the war, Pensacola, Panama City, and many points in between had more people than ever taking day trips to the beach and spending evenings in the refurbished casinos, the bars, and the surviving jook joints. The military, at least some of it, was soon gone, but these others took their place. And then there were the traditional beach lovers from the lower South, coming back, the *Mobile Press-Register* reported, to carve out for themselves the months between Memorial Day and Labor Day "to play, swim, fish the salt water, sail boats, and do the night clubs." Though coastal promoters promised this summer crowd cool Gulf breezes, everyone knew that summer was just as hot on the coast as it was in Montgomery, Jackson, Macon, and even farther north—and no one seemed to mind. Cash registers rang as "free spending tourists . . . jam-pack[ed] the beaches and hotels from Gulfport to Panama City." Down there they could do things that they could not do at home, so they went down to do them. It had been their beach before the war and they were out to reclaim it.

After summer was over, southerners left. The winter beach held no charms for them. But there were people further north who felt otherwise. And because of them, after the war a second tourist season was born. From roughly January 20 to Easter Sunday a different crowd arrived. These "winter visitors," these "snowbirds" (though they weren't called that then) "hailed mostly from the Midwest." Though few at first, they were welcomed, for according to local businesses, northerners spent more, stayed longer, and were "on the average more settled people than Summer vacationists." Many of them had been stationed along the coast during the war, liked it, and came back. Only instead of the debauchery they sought out as service-men on weekend leave, those returning (and those coming down for the first time) were looking for "warm weather, sunshine, rest, and a spell of effortless living." The winter coast could give them that. Supplemented by this small but important second season, income from the Gulf coast's "tour-ist trade" jumped from a prewar $25 million annually to $40 million in 1946. Happy days were here again.

So naturally, politicians took an interest in what was going on. In the summer after the war ended, governor-elect James E. Folsom arrived in Mobile, "sun-tanned from a recent Florida vacation," to announce that his administration would "give serious consideration" to developing the thirty miles of beach from Gulf State Park to Fort Morgan. Pointing out the obvi-ous, that this Gulf front was "naturally one of the most beautiful in this part of the country," the ever-populist "Big Jim" promised its development would " be for recreational benefits of all the state's people, who ordinarily would go to Florida for recreation"—as he himself had done. When he'd fin-ished speaking, the Florida-tanned governor-elect left the coast to spend the rest of his vacation relaxing on Mobile Bay in the yacht that belonged to the State Docks. The beaches of south Baldwin would wait a while before he visited them again.

Although Florida had little reason to feel threatened by the future gov-ernor's promise to offer Alabamians amusements that would keep them home, the Sunshine State launched a "Choose Florida this Summer" cam-paign to entice neighbors over. Touting its parks, springs, gardens, nation-ally known attractions, and rustling palms, the state went out of its way to tell Alabamians what Florida had that Alabama didn't. It is hard to say how successful the campaign was. In the summer of 1946, a "bumper crop of tourists" filled hotels, cottages, and parks all along the coast. Gulf State Park had to turn people away, but apart from the cabins there, Alabama's coastal facilities were limited. In what would later be the heart of Gulf Shores there were only a few rental cottages and a couple of cafe–general stores, clustered where the road from Foley dead-ended just short of the water. There were also a few private homes, some of which were remod-eled, screened so folks could enjoy "bug free breezes," and enlarged so that "extended families and visitors" could be put up for a night, a weekend, or a

Gulf Shores in the summer of 1949. The June 30, 1949, *Foley (Ala.) Onlooker* article in which this image appeared declared Gulf Shores the "Nation's No. 1 Play Area." Courtesy of the Doy Leale McCall Rare Book and Manuscript Library, University of South Alabama.

week—"with the boys sleeping in hammocks and chairs on one side and the girls and families on the other." All comfortable and chaste. Anyone seeking more upscale accommodations could go to the Gulf Shores Hotel, a short distance off to the west.

To the east Orange Beach was still a fishing community with camps and cabins for anglers. There was a beautiful stretch of sand along the Gulf and a quiet bay and bayou for those who wanted to spend time in the water as well as on it, but at that point not many did. As for other "amusements," they were in the future, but to those folks coming down that did not seem to matter. "It looks like everybody," the *Press-Register* observed, "is taking the vacation [they] promised [themselves] through the strenuous war years."

Across the line in Florida, all along the Panhandle portion of U.S. 98, the boom was under way. In Pensacola, officials warned tourists to make reservations early, for "despite excellent facilities for boating, swimming, and fishing . . . housing accommodations [were] extremely limited." Even though the city still had jook joints and such, Pensacola boosters made it clear that they were promoting family fun. If visitors asked for something else, they would probably be told to go a little farther east, where Fort Walton offered more excitement for those seeking it and willing to pay the price. The influx of servicemen during the war had breathed life and money into the "down-home, low-key" gambling operations that were there. After the war these grew into what would be later described as the "coolest gambling dens outside Miami." The Shalimar Club and the Magnolia Club offered "Latin music and expensive entertainment" for the high rollers taking a break from the tables. It was said that "fortunes changed hands nightly," while local law enforcement took its cut and looked the other way. Meanwhile residents of Fort Walton and the rest of the county didn't seem to care. According to one, the "gambling scene was . . . laid back," and though airmen from Eglin would "lose their money one night, [they'd] come back the next and win it back." Just good fun.

Gambling beyond the "down-home, low-key" variety did not spread across the pass to Destin, where, as in Orange Beach, fishing paid the bills. Even though its beaches were beginning to attract attention the charter fleet kept the town afloat. On further east, if you ventured off U.S. 98 you'd find Grayton still humming with seasonal visitors and Butler General doing well. Shedding its prewar, weekend honky-tonk image, the store became a community center. Remembered as "sleepy during the day," Butler General "came to life on warm nights when people of all ages, children and adults, gathered to dance, watch others dance, or catch up on gossip." On those nights was born the tradition of adding your name to the "brightly colored graffiti [that] covered the walls . . . inside and out," documenting yearly visits and summer romances. A little more restrained, more sedate, more relaxed than the prewar crowd, Grayton's visitors—cottage owners and tourists— were successfully transforming the village into a family focused resort, and it would remain so for years to come.

If you turned off on the Seagrove Beach road, you'd have found that with the exception of a few cottages the bluff was deserted. But if you skipped that detour and drove on east, which most folks did, a few miles after U.S. 98 veered south to run along the coast, you would reach the outskirts of that string of prewar resorts, which by the summer of 1946 had grown to offer visitors over one thousand units from which to choose. Hotel rooms, single cottages, apartments, and duplexes—you name it, the beaches west of Panama City had it. As of June 1, most of the accommodations were booked for the summer. Those resorts attracted over 150,000 visitors that summer—a record that would stand for years to come. It was there, along the beaches of the eastern Panhandle, that the Redneck Riviera defined itself, and from there it spread. In addition to sand and surf, Panama City Beach and Long Beach were becoming "amusement centers" with rides, shooting galleries, roller skating, and bowling in addition to bars and dance halls. Tacky from the start with more tackiness to come, the resorts were soon joined by independent promoters who knew just what folks from the lower South would pay to see, and in 1946 the Snake-A-Torium opened, just in time for Christmas. Of course, not every visitor came for the dancing and the snakes. J. E. Churchwell, who ran Long Beach, quickly and correctly noted that many who came to his resort were "suffering from war fatigue." Needing a rest, they were content to "enjoy their cottages, a couple of swims a day—and let the minority go out for jive and the midway." That minority, in time, would become the majority, and for that majority "jive and the midway" would be almost as important as the beach.

But not everyone had to save up their money and block out time for a vacation. In at least one spot on the Gulf, the vacation was paid for and the vacationer was told when to take it, which they were happy to do. Just west of Panama City's beaches, away from the "jive and the midway," was Camp Helen, a beachfront retreat that Alabama textile magnet B. B. Comer created in 1945, as a place where his family and workers from his Avondale Mills in Sylacauga could come to swim and fish and relax. Comer brought employees down during the summer and as one of the workers at the camp recalled, "the lintheads loved it." Camp Helen was also the place where, for one or two weeks in August, one of the largest concentrations of African Americans on the coast could be found. Though the textile industry was not known for hiring blacks, Avondale Mills employed some, and after all the white workers had been down, black workers and their families got their turn. To entertain those who wanted to go out deep-sea fishing, Comer hired a local captain, and years later, well into his nineties, he told of how folks from upland Alabama were amazed at the size of the Gulf and afraid when he took his boat out of sight of land.

During these postwar years a new clientele began to make their presence known along the coast—kids. Local businesses quickly adapted. Adults who were children at Gulf Shores then remember that "each summer brought a new attraction, a goofy golf or a water-bike ride or a trampoline place or a baseball batting range." They also remember how kids who lived down there made their own fun. Older boys bought old cars cheap, stripped them down, and roared across the dunes with no regard for ecological consequences. One young man who did this in Pensacola out on the island in the 1950s later expressed regret at the damage done, but of the coastal sins committed against man and nature, dune riding would rank pretty low. It was not as if the young folks ran the place—not yet anyway. But they were making their presence known. High school fraternities and sororities from Mobile loaded up in trucks and came down for a day at the beach and an evening dancing at the casino, which was initially conceived as a place for teenagers to congregate, dance, and play games. In time, however, the state realized that the park would be more profitable if the casino served liquor and catered to an older crowd. So teenagers were excluded, and soon afterward a rash of fake IDs appeared on the beach.

Things were still pretty primitive down there. Gulf Shores had electricity now, and in 1947 got its first neon sign, but most roads were sand trails where visitors got stuck if they weren't careful. Where there was pavement the greatest hazard was roaming cattle that would sleep on the warm asphalt in winter, but there weren't many visitors in winter and locals knew how to avoid the beasts. The cattle problem was solved when Alabama finally passed a stock law, and rather than fence their herds as required, ranchers rounded them up and sold them off. Still, good roads, or the lack of them, remained a problem. Which is at least one of the reasons that some fifteen thousand citizens, many from the newly formed Baldwin County Recreation and Tourist Association, turned out in a DDT-sprayed, debugged field at the state park on July 4, 1947, in hopes that honored guest Governor "Big Jim" Folsom would promise them more asphalt. They were not disappointed. Among the beauty contest (at which "Kissin' Jim" did his duty), the air show, speedboat races, swimming contests, a hog-calling contest, and a fireworks display, the governor dedicated the short stretch of pavement already built, pointed proudly to the remaining beach route under construction, and told of plans to work with the governor of Florida to build a bridge across Perdido Pass. He also christened the park Alabama Beach (a nice name, but it wouldn't stick). Through the rest of the day other politicians spoke, other promises were made, fifteen thousand pounds of fish were fried and consumed, and most everyone went home happy.

No small part of their joy came from the fact that as in the previous summer, hotels, cabins, and cottages all along the coast were full and again tourists were being turned away. So crowded were the Gulf Park beaches that for the first time lifeguards were hired. Although Pensacola was still facing a housing shortage, it was reported that many tourists "seem[ed] to have anticipated this situation and [had] traveled by automobile trailer." Attracted by beaches and parks with "tennis courts, golf courses, and athletic fields" that (unlike Alabama's) were free to the public, visitors flocked to Pensacola. Although the *Mobile Register* praised the Florida city's efforts to attract tourists and suggested that the spillover from next-door benefitted Alabama, it was obvious that the newspaper felt that the state was not doing enough on its own to draw tourists in. There was, of course, talk about expanding Gulf State Park and adding convention facilities, but the key to that would be getting the legislature to appropriate the money, which was no easy task. Even when the Alabama Press Association, meeting in Biloxi because there was no place on the Alabama coast to host them, endorsed expansion and the need for a convention facility at the park, the legislature was unmoved. As far as folks in Montgomery were concerned, the beach was a novelty on which the state might make money, but it was no place for the state to spend it.

Off to the east, Panama City's beaches were showing Alabama how to profit by treating tourists well. In the summer of 1947, existing attractions were "daily . . . augmented by institutions of new amusement centers," and the local Chamber of Commerce reported summer visitors arriving at a record rate. Still coming mostly from Alabama, Georgia, Tennessee, and inland Florida, in daytime they flocked to the resort parks for the "customary concession entertainment," while at night the "dance casinos [were] filled." For day-trippers and tourists staying in cheaper accommodations off the beach, newly opened "Wayside Park," the first of a series scheduled to be built, offered well-lighted parking, showers and dressing rooms, walkways to the water, and a "steel barge" anchored off shore for diving—all free of charge. Panama City's in-town establishment warned that these visitors would destroy the charm of the city and depress property values, but at the end of the summer, as if to thumb their collective noses at the old guard,

Wayside Park, Panama City Beach, circa 1950. Parks like this appealed to day-trippers and to tourists who stayed at cheaper, inland cottages. Courtesy of Bay County Public Library, Panama City, Fla.

tourist promoters noted that property assessment in the area increased 17.13 percent that year, the greatest rise in Bay County.

Encouraged by the summer success, in the fall of 1947, the Panama City Chamber of Commerce placed ads in nine of the leading midwestern newspapers touting the off-season "tourist advantages" to be found along "scenic gulf coast highway U.S. 98." Aware that "winter vacationists" usually stayed two to three weeks, and in some cases up to a month, while summer tourists from the lower South stayed a week or two and went home, promoters wanted to attract as many Yankees as they could to fill cottages and hotels that would otherwise stand empty. Midwesterners and easterners were considered "experienced and determined vacationists" who had more money than the summer crowds, although even the warm-weather visitors appeared "more prosperous" and less concerned about cost than they had been before the war. While resort operators did not expect a repeat of the "heavy spending" of the summer after the boys came home, the future looked bright.

Then, as the ad campaign got started, nature reminded coastal residents just how vulnerable they were. On September 17, 1947, a powerful hurricane known in those prenaming days as Number 6, came out of the Atlantic and hit Fort Lauderdale. It crossed Florida into the Gulf of Mexico, turned north, strengthened, and on September 21 came ashore near the Mississippi-Louisiana line with winds approaching 130 MPH. The Alabama beaches, on the northeast side of the eye, took a pounding. To prevent looting, National Guard troops were called out to help local law enforcement. Residents who evacuated (not many did), and those who had vacation homes there, had to show proof that they were property owners before they could go back across the Intracoastal Waterway and assess the damage. The Gulf Shores Hotel took a hit. The storm surge pushed sand into the first floor, piling it to within six inches of the ceiling. So, in a manner if not characteristic of coastal folks at least in keeping with how people inland pictured them, the hotel owners ordered more sand bulldozed in, covered the first floor, and turned the second floor into the first, high enough, they hoped, to be safe from another storm.

After the damage was cleared away the tourists returned. Fall visitors, folks whose baby-boomer children were not yet in school, came down to enjoy October and November, which can be the most pleasant months of the year on this stretch of the Gulf Coast. People from not too far away piled into cars and trucks and went to the beach to picnic, dance, and even swim, for in October and early November the water can still be warm and inviting. Then, after Christmas, as snow fell in the north, the "experienced" and "determined" visitors arrived and the cycle began again. Summer was still "the season" as far as folks on the coast were concerned. That was when the most tourists came and the most money was spent. But the fall and winter business would grow and carry some resort owners over until summer came again.

With the three things that had become symbols of the good life after the war—a job, a car, and a vacation—Americans hit the road in record numbers, and a lot of them came to the Gulf Coast. Still, Alabama was not taking advantage of this growing tourist trade to the extent Florida was. In the summer of 1948, newspapers chided Alabama for being the only state that did not supply the American Automobile Association with information on road construction, so the association was detouring members elsewhere. Florida, on the other hand, advertised that if you wanted a "breezy, easy-on-your-budget vacation" you should choose the Sunshine State. Alabama may have failed to advise the AAA of construction projects because under the Folsom administration there were so many that it was hard to keep up with them, and while this negligence may have cost the Alabama coast some tourists from further north, accommodations down there were full. So many people were on the coast in late 1948 and 1949 that when September gales flooded highways and isolated visitors in resorts, officials began talking about the need for evacuation routes in case of a major storm.

At the same time officials were also concerned about the damage storms inflicted on the coast's major attraction—the beach. Early in 1948 the Southern States Erosion Control Association was formed for the purpose of "saving shorelines that are being washed away by the Gulf and Atlantic Oceans." At the organizational conference in Sarasota they discussed what was happening, what was causing it, how the shore could be protected, and how to get money from Congress and coastal states to do the job. The answer to one of these problems was revealed when those September gales hit the Alabama coast. Though houses, hotels, cottages, and cabins were battered, the Gulf State Park came through just fine. Why? Because, a damage assessment concluded, "high sand dunes protected the area." The message seemed clear enough: Save the dunes and the dunes will save what lies behind them. Unfortunately, that was not the solution coastal developers wanted to hear.

Meanwhile, despite the ever-increasing emphasis on family entertainment, a coastal subculture was forming that would in time give the beach the "outlaw" reputation on which the image of redneckery rests. Gambling thrived in Fort Walton, folks jived all along the coast, and in Alabama the Beverage Control Board approved jukeboxes for seventy-seven Gulf area establishments that were already licensed to serve beer. Now folks from inland, folks who would never think of drinking and dancing in hometown establishments (if there were any) for fear that neighbors and fellow church members might find them out, could come to the coast for all those things preachers and parents warned them about and taste some of those delights themselves. Also appearing were reports of an increase in the number of people arrested in the Mobile area for the possession of marijuana. The federal district attorney for south Alabama reported the seizure of a thirty-six-pound shipment, small potatoes in later years, but it sent a message to good, upstanding citizens that the scourge of "reefer" was among them. To make sure the public was aware of the danger the community faced, the local press warned the public that a person who smokes "the weed," will believe that "there is nothing he isn't capable of doing or saying" and "in some instances it makes the user run amok." Rather than risk a heavy fine, jail time, or both if they sold, used, or possessed marijuana, most folks on the coast stuck with alcohol and ran "amok" drinking rather than smoking—for a while at least.

The year 1949 opened with a cold January, which was followed by a bitter February and then a March that was no better. Even winter visitors complained. So when April and warm weather finally came, people along the coast were ready. The ring of hammers, the rasp of saws, and the roar of "mighty bulldozers" were heard as dunes were knocked down, sand was moved, and houses "ranging from simple cabins to magnificent residents" were built along the beach. The long-promised paved road from Gulf Shores east to Alabama Point was almost finished, and local authorities had been assured once again that Alabama and Florida would cooperate on the construction of a bridge across Perdido Pass. Meanwhile the *Mobile Press-Register* reported that "the paint brush [was] being applied copiously" to the already "booked to the hilt" cabins at the state park and that there were ambitious plans for building more. The Gulf Shores Lions Club, "a virtual Chamber of Commerce," took the lead promoting the community, although its members seemed to pay as much attention to real estate opportunities as to the tourist attractions springing up. For developers there were opportunities aplenty. Until the mid-1920s there were no private cottages in Gulf Shores. In the spring of 1949, there were at least two hundred on the "sand-duned beach section" and more were anticipated. Land values "skyrocketed." A tract that was once homesteaded for $100 reportedly sold for $100,000. Folks who had been around awhile shook their heads at the prices being asked and remembered some Chicago investors who tried to give their land away rather than pay taxes on it. There were no takers: no one else wanted to pay the taxes either.

Not everyone was happy with this rapid growth, and even this early many folks had the "not in my neighborhood" attitude that would characterize antidevelopment activities in the years to come. Out on the Dixie Graves Parkway, the state owned a 330-foot right-of-way. Word spread that to pay for coastal roads and bridges the Highway Department planned to lease some of this property to businesses. Residents and vacation-home owners protested, declaring that the people who donated the right-of-way land did not intend for it to be "cluttered up with all kinds of business places," some of them "operating almost within [our] back yards." For a while these and similar objections detoured developers' plans, but they hardly stopped the march of "progress."

West Florida was also expecting to close the 1940s with the biggest summer vacation crowd in its history. The "vast beach resort centers" from the Alabama line to Panama City were the "scene of feverish activity" as operators of hotels, cottages, and other facilities got ready. All chambers of commerce reported mail inquiries piling up, sent by folks who had learned to get their reservations in early for "despite the fact accommodations have been increased by leaps and bounds in recent years, they still [were] not adequate to care for the entire demand." Prominent among those wishing to visit the beach were "young Americans" who had trained at local bases, had served their country in war, and now wanted to return with their families. Escambia County officials, "deeply concerned" that those veterans would have no place to stay, set up the Santa Rosa Island Authority to develop beaches that would be accessible when the then under construction road running the length of the island was completed. To get people to build cottages to occupy or to rent, the Island Authority began signing over ninety-nine-year leases on lots just down from Pensacola Beach's $350,000 casino. The Authority also announced plans to construct three thousand rental units on the island in the next few years. This was Florida, and in Florida you never think small.

Fort Walton was still enjoying its gambling boom, and its location and facilities for vacationers made it an attractive destination. But not everyone came solely to visit the "dens." Prominent among the visitors were veterans who had spent time at Eglin and returned with their families to do what tourists were doing all along the coast—fish, swim, maybe take in a show at one of the clubs, and just relax. Some of these veterans had stayed in the military, made it their career, and were on active duty at bases scattered around the lower South. With Eglin's amenities available to them, including the Officers and Non-Com clubs down the road and on the Gulf, Fort Walton had everything they could want. So it comes as no surprise that later, when the career servicemen retired, many settled there and turned the community into a quiet suburb, the hometown they had always wanted when they were moving from assignment to assignment. Later still, when growth of the type that eventually consumed Destin approached their neighborhoods, they fought it.

But in the 1940s and 1950s and even into the 1960s, Destin had no development to fight. Fishing made Destin famous. Fishing put food on the table for most residents of the village. If they did not fish, they ran the stores where captains and crews and their families shopped, the cafes where they ate, and the bars where they went when the day was done. It was a tight-knit, one-industry town with a fragile economy, a community where folks fished six to nine months of the year and got by as best they could the rest of the time. Little wonder that when later someone offered them something that sounded better, they took it.

On the coast between Destin and the resorts west of Panama City, situated off the main highway, Grayton Beach remained like a village trapped and preserved in amber. One of the early residents recalled how as a child when a rare car came down the road they would "run to the windows and look to see who it was." All the streets were dirt, all the "quaint beach cottages" were wooden and "in various stages of repair." The ten or so families that lived there year-round kept their homes well, but "others suffered neglect from owners who lived in other states and seldom saw their property." But whether painted and protected or dilapidated and needing repairs, "most had one thing in common: screened porches that beckoned people to come and spend a lazy afternoon reading or sleeping." The single store in town still served as a community amusement center and grocery, but not much was going on. Families who had lived there or had visited for years knew each other, watched each other's children, and enjoyed each other's company. If you wanted peace and quiet, Grayton Beach was the place to go.

For visitors who wanted a variety of amusements and a little more excitement, there were the beaches west of Panama City. These resorts would, in time, stand as the best, most representative, and most successful examples of the early development and promotion of the northern rim of the Gulf. But Panama City's beaches were not alone in touting their wonders to any and all who might come and spend time and money. Year after year, all along the coast, there were more cottages, more motels, more amusements, more developments, and year after year more people took advantage of them. Although visitors came from many states, during spring, summer, and fall this was the playground of the lower South. Alabama governor Big Jim

Folsom, down in 1949 to take part in another Gulf State Park Fourth of July and to dedicate the newest section of the beach road, looked out at it all and, in what some people still believe was a moment of inspiration, unplanned, he announced, "In the name of all the people of Alabama and all its sixty-seven counties, I hereby proclaim this island, lying south of the Canal, to be known hereafter and in the future as Pleasure Island."

Pleasure Island.

He was talking about south Alabama. But he could have meant Santa Rosa across from Pensacola. Or the beaches from Destin to Panama City that were once on an island and which in many ways were on an island still.

In Alabama, the name stuck.

Panhandle Florida had not figured out what to call itself yet.

THREE

Bring 'em Down, Keep 'em Happy, and Keep 'em Spending

THINGS WERE LOOKING BRIGHT all along the northern
Gulf Coast as the 1940s came to an end, and at no place did
prospects seem brighter than at Fort Walton, where the local
chamber of commerce predicted that the last summer of the
decade would be the "biggest summer season in history."
Driving this optimism was the popularity of the towns gambling dens, for no small number of the visitors who came to
Fort Walton spent their time and money at the Shalimar Club
and the "swank" Magnolia, or simply played the slot machines
that seemed to be in almost every store and shop. Although
gambling was illegal, those involved seemed to have little to
fear from local law enforcement. It was not clear if Okaloosa
County sheriff Isle Enzor was on the take, was simply incompetent, or had more important crimes on his "to stop" list, but
even though there were also slot machines inland, even within
sight of the county courthouse, apparently the sheriff did not
intend to do anything about them.

Not that it mattered much to most residents. One man
recalled his wife getting upset when he came home with seventeen dollars he had won—she called it "dirty money"—but
little was said publicly until 1949 when the *Tampa Tribune* ran
a story that not only "exposed" the gambling industry in Fort
Walton, but also told of how "authorities let high-rollers and
penny-ante players have their fun despite the law." County
seat businessmen who had ignored the slot machines in their

own town expressed surprise and outrage at what was going on down along the decadent coast and joined the Florida Better Government League in its campaign to end gambling statewide. In retaliation, businessmen in Fort Walton proposed forming their own county, free from meddling uplanders—not the last time coastal interests would talk of such a separation. Then Florida governor Fuller Warren got involved. In 1950, in a move some claimed was calculated to divert attention from gambling in Miami and Tampa, Warren suspended Sheriff Enzor and two constables for failing to enforce the law. With that the clean up began. Two years later the popular Enzor was re-elected, but by then gambling was on its way out. The *Tribune* article had put the community in a bad light and city fathers worried that tourists would take their business elsewhere. Back on the job and converted to the cause, Sheriff Enzor began cracking down, and soon even the Shalimar Club was turning to more "legitimate" forms of entertainment. But without gambling, it was just another nightspot. The Shalimar closed for good in 1956.

However, by then Fort Walton had something it had not had before, something that in the future would be an even bigger attraction than gambling. Fort Walton had a beach. In 1953, the Florida legislature authorized Okaloosa County to lease for recreation and development a three-mile stretch of Okaloosa Island, across the sound from Fort Walton and linked to it by U.S. 98. With that Fort Walton became Fort Walton Beach. By the middle of the decade Okaloosa Island was home of the Tower Beach Casino, which advertised "All Around Family Entertainment on the World's Most Beautiful Beaches." Visitors could swim in the Gulf, drink in the lounge, eat at the snack bar, and buy things at the shops. They could also play in the amusement arcade and dance on the patio. With Pensacola on the west, Panama City on the east, and Okaloosa Island in the middle, U.S. 98 was becoming known as the Miracle Strip.

Now we must keep all this in perspective. Despite the publicity generated by chambers of commerce, civic clubs, and resort operators, in the 1940s and 1950s the coast from Mobile Bay to Panama City was just emerging as a tourist attraction. Although visitor records were set and broken year after year, the increases were marginal. Though new amusements appeared with seasonal regularity, like the people who enjoyed them, they were concentrated in resort areas—developments west of Panama City, on Okaloosa Island, across the bay from Pensacola, and in Alabama at Gulf Shores. Aside from a sprinkling of little communities—Orange Beach, Destin, Grayton—the rest of the coast was almost inaccessible and pretty much deserted. To tell the truth, outside of the resorts (and in some cases in them), the coast could be an unpleasant place. In those pre-air-conditioned summers, if there wasn't a breeze or a fan to move the heavy air, residents and visitors sat still and sweated. And then there were the bugs—mosquitoes and biting flies, "flying teeth" some folks called them—which was why Alabama authorities sprayed the field with DDT before Big Jim's address on July 4, 1947, and why porches were screened and ceiling fans were popular—though they rusted out quickly and had to be replaced. Fall brought better weather but also September gales and hurricanes. Winter was damp, chilly, and sometimes downright cold; spring came quickly and was over quickly. Then it was summer again.

Summer was "the season." Despite all the talk about attracting winter visitors, winter was, as native son and songwriter Jimmy Buffett put it, when "the coast was clear." Tim Hollis, who chronicled the rise of Gulf region amusement parks in *Miracle Strip*, told of how his parents honeymooned at Panama City Beach in 1954. Married on Christmas Day, they arrived at their destination to find "a deserted wasteland with very little sign of human habitation." They finally located some tourist cabins that were open, but there were no restaurants on the beach serving meals. Had the lady who managed the cottages not taken pity on them and brought them food, it would have been a short honeymoon. But the off-season could also be a good time for potential investors to get a sense of the region and its possibilities. That was how Birmingham businessman Elton B. Stephens discovered Seagrove Beach.

In the early 1950s, Stephens was driving along U.S. 98, headed to a football game in Jacksonville, Florida. He saw a sign telling travelers that down the side road was a place "Where Nature Did Its Best" and he decided to go see. There he found C. H. McGee.

Like so many people who came to Florida, McGee had dreams, and like those others he believed the Sunshine State was the place where dreams came true—you just had to make it happen. After the war, McGee settled in the Panama City area and got into the construction business. He did well in the postwar building boom and after helping develop Bahama Beach west of town, he purchased the 170 acres, 2650 feet on the Gulf, where the Seagrove Land Company had once operated. All that was there when McGee arrived

C. H. McGee at his sales office, Seagrove Beach, Florida, circa 1950. Courtesy of
Mrs. C. H. McGee Jr.

were a scattering of cottages in a small subdivision, SeaHighland, which a
few years earlier had been laid out by Alabamians who named its streets for
the towns from which they came—Andalusia, Dothan, Montgomery. To dis-
tinguish his from theirs McGee decided to keep the name Seagrove. He sub-
divided his land, laid out more streets, and, his son, Cube, later recalled, set
to building "three spec homes and a little store." Then McGee put a sign out
at the highway "inviting the public to come see his vision for a new beach
community." Stephens saw the sign, accepted the invitation, and, impressed
by the "beautiful country location," bought a cottage. Eventually he bought
another, and in the deal, he later recounted, "got all the hogs, snakes, coons,
possums and everything else that lived there." Seagrove Beach was primitive, but it was loaded with possibilities.

Decades later, when successful and often controversial developers such
as Robert Davis of Seaside would be considered pioneers in creating coastal
communities, C. H. McGee would be largely forgotten. He shouldn't have
been. Just as Davis's Seaside would tap into the utopian dreams of affluent Americans in the 1990s, what McGee created on that remote bluff was
designed to appeal to upper-middle-class white southerners who wanted
something other than a week at a beach motel in a resort full of tacky

amusements and the sort of people who enjoyed them. The only amusement Seagrove would provide would be the beach, which McGee deeded over to the community. Investors might own beachfront property, but not the sand and shore. In addition, he set aside some two hundred feet of bluff overlooking the Gulf, called it a park, and promised that it would remain undeveloped. To assure buyers that their investment would be a wise one, McGee drew up a covenant that promised "no trailer, tent, shack, outhouse or other temporary structure would be allowed." Lots were laid out for single-family dwellings, and the building code mandated that all houses would be within a certain size—none too big, none too small, all compact, simple, and functional. Building materials had to be "approved and accepted" and the white-trash tin roofing that Seaside would later make popular was prohibited. McGee's covenant also promised that there would be "no noxious activities, offensive noises or odors, nor any nuisance" to shatter the quiet and seclusion. No running amok at Seagrove.

Knowing his clientele McGee also assured potential buyers that none of his lots would "be sold, leased, or rented to or occupied by any person or persons other than the Caucasian race"—though, the covenant added, those homeowners with "domestic servants [of] either race actually employed by those residing on said property, may reside thereon while thus employed." So some of the first houses, including one built for Stephens, had a small, separate apartment, the maid's quarters, set back by the road, away from the beach so as not to waste a Gulf view on the "help."

Seagrove's covenant spelled out what would later become a common theme of developers along the coast, though few would be so open about it. At Seagrove, black folks and white trash were not welcome. Seagrove's covenant was written to keep out riffraff rednecks while preserving the racial arrangement that middle-class racists and the excluded riffraff valued in common. White folks who considered themselves among the "better sort" might have to deal with the lower orders back home, but on vacation they wanted to be as far from them as possible, unless, of course, those lower orders were in their employ. Seagrove Beach was to be a gated community without a gate. Isolated at the end of the road, if residents wanted to take part in "noxious activities," create a few "offensive noises or odors," and make a "nuisance" of themselves, they could drive an hour or more to the fishermen's bars at Destin and the "jive" joints along the Panama City beach strip, but there was little chance that the people they met in those places would follow them back. This is not to suggest that Seagrove homeowners were not capable of having a good time, and maybe even engaging in activities that violated the community code, but such violations were only occasional and involved their own kind. Seagrove Beach was not for everyone, and that, plus the natural beauty of the setting, was its attraction.

As for those southerners who found Seagrove too isolated and its restrictions too, well, restrictive, there were other communities along the coast that welcomed similar folks from similar places, but in a location more convenient to popular amusements. For example, if you were from Alabama, Laguna Beach, near the far west end of the Panama City Beach strip, was a place where you could find your own. So many from that state's largest city owned cottages or vacationed there that one enterprising barkeep named his establishment the Little B'ham and advertised it as the "home of 1000 satisfied customers and a few old grouches." Scores of Alabamians, me included, remember the Little B'ham fondly. It was there that my father bought me my first legal beer when I turned twenty-one. There were similar establishments all along the Panama City beaches. In clusters that more-upscale developers would later call "town centers," you could find bars, souvenir shops, cafes, motels, and amusements aplenty, most adjacent to residential areas with private homes and vacation cottages ranging from simple cabins to substantial homes. In these early days these neighborhoods of individually owned houses did what Seagrove Beach was designed to do—put a middle-class patina on the community and keep redneckery at bay. As in Laguna Beach, if you wanted beer, you just had to walk a little way to the local version of the Little B'ham. If you wanted a beer at Seagrove, you had to bring your own or drive ten miles to a little store on U.S. 98—at least for a while.

McGee was innovative in another way. Before the war most houses on the Florida Panhandle and the Alabama coast were built of wood. McGee preferred concrete block—cooler, more durable, and easier to maintain. Moreover, though he could and did build houses to a client's particular specifications, most of the houses he built in Seagrove Beach were of one of two basic designs that could be altered slightly to meet the buyer's needs or cater to aesthetic whims.

As if to ensure that redneck riffraff would not infiltrate his community, McGee priced lower-income whites out of the market. Gulf front lots were listed between one thousand and two thousand dollars, so high that Cube

Little B'ham, Panama City Beach, 1950s. The bar was named to attract Alabama customers visiting the coast. Courtesy of Bay County Public Library, Panama City, Fla.

"really wondered if we would ever sell the first lot or home." Apparently the price did not bother Stephens, whose houses were on prime wooded lots overlooking the beach. However Stephens later confessed that he was taken aback when someone, learning the price he paid, told him that if "I had set out from Seagrove towards Panama City, I could have had all the land I wanted for a dollar an acre." Exaggerated, perhaps, but McGee was demanding top price for the best locations, and getting it.

For lots away from the beach the price dropped dramatically, and that is where my grandmother bought hers in 1954. The daughter of a self-taught concrete engineer, as a girl she had lived on an island off Tampa while her father built fortifications for the U.S. Corps of Engineers. She loved the beach and had always wanted to own a cottage there. Living just north of Montgomery, the Florida Panhandle was the closest coast, so when she heard of Seagrove she and her daughter, my aunt, drove down to investigate. The location was right, the restrictions were right, and when they found that lots within easy walking to the beach could be had for half what gulf-front lots were bringing, she bought two. C. H. McGee died that year, but his son took over the development. Cube agreed to build my grandmother one of his father's standard design cottages—two bedrooms and one bath, with a living room, dining area, kitchen, and screened porch. Paradise for around five thousand dollars. It was finished in 1956.

That was the year Grandma Minnie learned that paradise was in danger.

The Jackson cottage was one lot in from the beach and separated from the more expensive property by a sandy trail that could only be traveled by jeep. It was wide enough for a two-lane road but no one really thought that one would be built. They were wrong. About the time her cottage was finished Grandma Minnie learned that the state intended to build a beach highway that would run from just east of Destin to just west of the Panama City beach strip and connect beach communities like Grayton and Seagrove. The idea of a road running through what she considered her front yard did not sit well with her, nor with other Seagrove homeowners. Late in the year Grandma Minnie received a letter from the vice president of the First National Bank of Birmingham, who owned a house near Stephens. He told her of a letter-writing campaign designed to get the Florida State Road Department to re-route the project. "It was because of the quiet seclusion," he wrote my grandmother, "that I was so happy to find Seagrove and I am sure you feel the same way"—which of course she did. He added, without direct reference to the riffraff that would travel in, "I am convinced that our property values would be badly hurt if a through highway were jammed along the present road site." Grandma agreed.

So Grandma Minnie wrote a letter telling the head of the highway department that the value of her property would be decreased by the "added traffic and noise" and the seclusion for which she "selected Seagrove, bought property there, and built a home" would be lost. She also noted that Cube and his mother had "offered to give a right of way for the new road behind the present developed section of Seagrove." If the offer was seriously made, the state didn't take it. Having reportedly already given in to protests by the Butlers of Grayton and routed the road around instead of through that community, another change would mean that there would not be much beach along the "beach route." Seagrove owners who were living in Alabama had less clout than full-time voting residents like the Butlers, so the state threw its lot with development interests that wanted the road where it was. Soon construction began on what would become Scenic Highway 30-A.

If anyone was curious about what the folks in Seagrove did not want to come down the road and into their village they needed only to drive east toward Panama City, and shortly after crossing Phillips Inlet they would begin to see it. It wasn't so bad at first—Hollywood Beach, Sunnyside, and Laguna Beach with the Little B'ham were mostly cottages and a store or two. But the closer you got to the bridge and the city itself the more developed the beach became. Seeing this area today, a string of beaches and resorts divided and defined only by an occasional sign or store bearing a community name, it is hard to imagine that in the 1950s all along the strip there were large blocks of empty land, which could be, and would be, bought and sold at prices significantly less than what C. H. McGee asked. Then, about eight miles west of the city you found what Seagrove did not want. Long Beach Resort—hard against Edgewater Gulf Beach and Panama City Beach—had already become, or so it advertised, "a gala playground for young and old." Right there on the "snow-white sand" was (the owners claimed) "a place for wholesome, out-of-doors fun," as well as "clean indoor recreation and amusement." And, they added, "there is no better exercise for any age than a refreshing swim in the clear waters of the Gulf of Mexico." It was not the sort of physical fitness hype that turn-of-the- century promoters used to lure people down when they advertised that "many a consumptive, rheumatic, nervous, worn out, and over-worked person whose case was thought hopeless have found health and a new lease on life" down on the coast, but they did say "swim" instead of "bathe," and that was something.

Long Beach and its neighbors had it all. If a visitor wanted to go deep-sea fishing, play golf, "visit famous restaurants, nightclubs and cocktail lounges," those things were just a short drive away. For families down for a week or so, there were "completely modern cottages right on the water's edge" into which father could fit mother, the kids, and maybe a grandmother or two. "Luxurious Beautyrest mattresses on the beds, tile baths and showers" offered tourists "all the comforts of home" and a few they likely did not have back where they came from. By 1954 the cottages were air-conditioned, and a couple of years later televisions were added. There was a supermarket close by if visitors wanted to prepare their own meals and "modern restaurants" available if they did not. Before the end of the decade Long Beach Resort also boasted "Florida's largest and newest skating rink" and an amusement park. The amenities and attractions appealed to the sorts of people that the folks at Seagrove hoped would go to Long Beach and stay there. For a while that was what they did.

If visitors couldn't get a cottage in Long Beach, they could find a room in one of the new motels, which had begun popping up all along the coast in the early 1950s. The first may have been the Beacon Motel, which started renting its eight rooms in 1951. The Beacon was soon joined by the nine-room Sandpiper, then the two-story, twelve-room Driftwood Lodge, the fifteen room Bell-Mar Court, and in 1955 "the classiest of motels," the Georgia Terrace. In 1956 the Plaza Motel invited the public to rent one of its twenty-seven rooms, "as modern as tomorrow," each with air conditioning, steam heat, a radio, a television, and in some rooms "intercom telephones." Knowing why their clientele came to the coast, these establishments were often connected with or close to amusement parks, miniature golf courses, cafes, and souvenir shops. But because of their family focus, few had bars or lounges. In south Florida after the war (according to the *Mobile Register*), "pale people with gaudy diamonds did not mind laying solid cash on the line to shed their mink and ermine and bask in the sun," but by the 1950s word reached the Gulf Coast that high prices down there had driven away "John Q. Citizen." So tourism promoters were beginning to "subscribe to the theory that the plain, everyday guy and his wife and kids may be the salvation of a glittering enterprise known as the 'tourist trade.'" On the Florida Panhandle and on the Alabama beaches of Baldwin County, businessmen knew that already, and they were doing all they could to attract the plain and the everyday.

As reasonably priced motel rooms gained popularity, so did a variety of independent operations that reminded visitors from the lower South of the traveling carnivals that arrived only seasonally in small towns back home. Featuring trains, Ferris wheels, roller coasters, and all the other shake-and-swing-me-till-I-puke rides country folks enjoyed at county fairs, plus midway attractions such as the ever-popular fortune-telling chicken, these were just the sort of amusement parks that the South's rising (but not yet risen) middle class would drive to the coast to see. Among the delights were rides that pushed young couples together in an intimacy parents would have frowned on otherwise, including a dark Tunnel of Love where summer romances were born and consummated with a kiss.

Which brings us to the teenagers.

When the first baby boomers reached that magical stage of life, the 1950s were about over, so they really weren't the ones who shaped beach culture in that era. During the 1950s the coast belonged to the war babies, born (as I was) before Daddy went overseas to defeat Hitler, or conceived during a passionate weekend leave. We weren't as big a bunch as the boomers who

The Hangout, beachside, with amusement park in background, 1950s. For teenagers in the 1950s and 1960s, this was the place to go. Courtesy of Bay County Public Library, Panama City, Fla.

followed, but my generation did things differently than our parents did, and at the Long Beach Resort and in Gulf Shores, we did it at the Hangouts.

Although there were similar gathering spots at other beaches, because Panama City and Gulf Shores became a favorite destination for so many southern families, the Hangouts at those two beaches are remembered most frequently and fondly by people today who were teenagers then. Coming down to the coast with their families, teens in the 1950s wanted to do what teens on vacation always want to do: get away from adults and siblings and be with people their own age. The Hangouts, the Casinos at Gulf State Park, Pensacola, and Okaloosa Island, and a sprinkling of "teen towns" and similar gathering spots gave them that opportunity. The Long Beach Hangout was really more of a small amusement park with an open-sided pavilion that was a dance floor some nights and a roller-skating rink others. There were snack bars and games where a guy could win a stuffed animal for his date or for the girl he'd just met and wanted to impress. There was jukebox music—popular tunes that will always remind those who were there of that summer—though most who attended watched the dancers rather than getting out on the floor themselves. Over the years, dances that had steps and partners you actually touched, such as the shag and the dirty-bop, gave way to the more improvised ones, such as the twist, and as the rules became looser, people who didn't know the steps but knew how to move in rhythm took their turn. However, for most, dancing at the Hangouts was a spectator sport.

What went on at the Long Beach Hangout in the 1950s reminded one observer of "something innocuous enough to be straight out of an Annette Funicello movie," and maybe it was. But it was a different Hangout that the writer Wayne Greenhaw remembered. As a teen, down from Tuscaloosa with his friends, Greenhaw recalled the thrill of sauntering around drinking from quart beer bottles, "symbols of manhood that summer," which they carried "right out there in broad daylight" and no one seemed to mind. Before his Hangout evening was done he had watched "two fat seniors from Murphy High in Mobile [have] a chug-a-lug contest before they fell like a pair of Hippos into the sand," had been punched in the face by a "tough guy from Ensley," and was taught the "be-bop" by Betty Sue from Atlanta. But maybe he was just there on a good night. In the 1950s the Hangout was never as wild as parents feared, or teenagers hoped it would be. It was just a lot of fun.

The atmosphere at the Gulf Shores Hangout was much the same—a "big elevated rectangle where everybody went to see and be seen" one regular recalls. There were fewer adjacent amusements and, it seemed to me at least, less tension between teens from competing towns or schools. My opinion, supported by some, but not much, anecdotal evidence, suggests that teens from Panama City proper who came over the bridge to party were not as receptive to out-of-town visitors, especially boys trying to meet local girls, as resident teens were in Gulf Shores. This may be, in part at least, because there were so few teens living on the Alabama coast. It may also be because there were out-of-town girls enough to make up for the local girls who danced with out-of-town boys—and who gave them fake names and bogus phone numbers so that whatever happened at Gulf Shores stayed at Gulf Shores. But the real reason may have been that in the 1950s and 1960s a goodly number of the kids at the Gulf Shores Hangout were farm boys from up the road at Foley where the Gulf Shores kids went to school, classmates who came down so often that they were almost like locals themselves. Both Hangouts are gone today, and though Gulf Shores has a modern version built close to where the old one was, veterans will tell you it is not the same.

Dancing at the Hangout, 1950s. Note the short-shorts, crew cut, pegged pants, and white socks. Courtesy of Bay County Public Library, Panama City, Fla.

Those who recall the earlier Hangout still hold yearly reunions every May where they dance a little and reminisce a lot.

Meanwhile along the coast, communities had begun to take on individual characteristics reflecting, for the most part, how businesses there made their money. Increasingly Gulf Shores and the resorts along the Panama City strip catered to the family tourist trade. Though real estate was a lucrative profession, the best money was being made in building and operating motels, restaurants, and amusement parks. Indeed it had become something of a running joke among some uplanders that what they really wanted to do was sell out the family farm, move to the coast, and buy a motel. What could be better? A great place to live; a job where the money was good and the work easy (just hire yourself a clean-up crew and a handyman to fix things that tourist break); and a three-month vacation every winter, unless you want to open up to Yankees and Canadians. Then there were communities like Destin and Orange Beach, which were (as a visitor described one but it could be either) "mostly charter boat wharfs, a handful of motels, the usual tacky souvenir shops, and a few seafood restaurants." Then there were the "island" getaways—Okaloosa and Pensacola Beach. And last, the residential resorts—Seagrove, Grayton, and such—where amusements were few and where the primary means of turning a profit were selling lots, building cottages, and renting long-term to summer visitors. Yet all the differences in class and circumstances notwithstanding, the people who visited the coast, bought there, rented there, and worked there were much the same. Some had more money, some had more education, some had both, but almost to the man (and to the woman) they were white, they were southerners, and they were part of Dixie's new middle class—though some just barely. They weren't what folks think of as your typical redneck, but this was their Riviera.

Local promoters wanted it also to be the Riviera for winter-vacationing and interested-in-relocating northerners, and if you believe the tales real estate agents told, efforts to attract this group were paying off. Stories like the one published in *Alabama* magazine, told of Yankees like the Illinois coal broker and his wife who on the advice of friends had vacationed in Gulf Shores rather than going to more expensive and distant south Florida. They liked it, and when he retired in 1954, with children grown and little reason for maintaining a large home, they sold out and "moved to Alabama's Gulf coast as permanent residents." There they spent their days "in their seaside cottage, enjoying the sun and surf, fishing and genuine relaxation." But even though a "well-planned advertising campaign" by the newly formed Gulf Shores Tourist Association reportedly brought in "hundreds of newcomers" from the north, most came to vacation; few came to live. In 1956 Gulf Shores had only 120 permanent residents, most of them southerners. Orange Beach had fewer still. Despite tourist association efforts, there were not many winter visitors, so most rental places closed after Labor Day and real estate offices cut back their hours. Come January, Gulf Shores was a lonely place.

But there were other things going on. Though tourism was and for some time would be the region's bread and butter, word was spreading that the coast was more than just a place for a vacation in the sun and the opportunity to do things that you could not do back home. More and more people were coming to Gulf Shores and other coastal communities because they believed what promoters told them, that the beach was a place where prosperity was possible, and they were all for prosperity. In a 1954 feature article, surrounded by advertisements for realty offices, *Alabama* magazine praised Gulf Shores as the "State Resort Paradise," and told of how investors from Alabama, Tennessee, Mississippi, and Arkansas had realized opportunities there and driven up the price of beachfront property "to more than $65 a front foot"—more, it should be noted, than C. H. McGee charged for the "overpriced" lots at Seagrove Beach when he opened in 1949. Some commercial real estate was "tagged at $100" a foot. There was money to be made on the coast. Buy low, sell high, buy again, sell again—the age of the speculator was at hand.

Still, the purpose of the tourist association was to promote tourism, not real estate, so it continued to advertise Gulf Shores as "strictly a family vacation resort with little or none of the hubbub or riotous activity so familiar at many beaches." Targeting traditional visitors, the association suggested that "Alabamians planning a sea-side vacation . . . [would] do well to investigate their own doorstep." They did, and locals set out to give visitors what they wanted and were willing to pay for. But times had changed. The beach lovers coming to the coast in the 1950s were not war-fatigued visitors who just wanted to rest and recharge. The families coming to the coast in the 1950s wanted accommodations near amusements other than sand and surf, amusements to which their increasingly influential children wanted to be taken. Seagrove, Grayton, and similar beaches might be ideal for adults, but kids who came with them found those communities dull and could not wait for the promised trips to the parks and arcades along Panama City's beaches or to the newly opened Gulfarium on Okaloosa Island, which offered something close to an educational experience with a "living sea" exhibit and porpoise shows—really bottle-nose dolphins, but visitors weren't particular. Besides, in comparison with Destin's Museum of the Sea and Indian (an interesting juxtaposition) where you could see the Drunken Fish and visit the Indian Fun House, the Gulfarium was nothing short of scholarly.

Of course some promoters did attempt to benefit from historical events that had taken place in their area. Gulf Shores tourist offices told visitors that a short drive west was Fort Morgan, one of the two antebellum forts built to guard the entrance to Mobile Bay. A magnificent brick fortress, it was well worth an afternoon, but that sort of thing appealed to a particular clientele and never became more than a side trip for most folks. Pensacola Beach also gave history a nod with a recreated Spanish village, circa 1723, but it never became Williamsburg South or anything close to it. It lasted just over a decade and then closed. So chamber of commerce types in Pensacola and Fort Walton decided to use history in a more traditional way: as an excuse for a party. Pensacola invented the Fiesta of Five Flags, a pseudo-historical celebration of the 1559 "discovery" of that piece of the Panhandle by Don Tristan de Luna. But at least the fiesta could claim a real man and a reasonably accurate date. To the east, Fort Walton Beach invented a pirate named Billy Bowlegs and created a Mardi Gras–like event that featured Bowlegs and his crew sailing into the harbor, capturing the city and mayor, and setting off a week of pirate rule, which included costumed buccaneers and their buxom wenches, a parade with bands and floats, and lots of parties. Visitors attracted by the goings-on joined in the merriment, which like any beach party included more than a few of what the folks at Seagrove considered "noxious activities [and] offensive noises." But for the Panhandle's good old boys and girls, and their counterparts in from out of town, these festivals were another excuse to eat, drink, and have fun, not that they needed one.

Alabama beaches developed more slowly than Florida beaches. Carnival-like amusements were few, individually owned cottages were scattered about with little sense of community planning, and though a couple of rental places used the name, Orange Beach did not get its first real motel until 1959, the White Caps, which also had the first motel swimming pool in the area. It may have been wishful thinking when Alabama boosters bragged that their beaches had "bitten deep into the vacation dollar formerly spent at . . . Pensacola, Fort Walton and Panama City" and that the Alabama coast would soon "outgrow older, longer established beach resorts" in Florida, but there was competition. By the middle of the 1950s "vacationers and fishermen" were spending $2 million annually in south Baldwin County, a tidy sum back then.

About this time Gulf Shores began offering amenities for people a little more affluent than the earliest visitors. In a significant shift, fewer and fewer cafes and hotel restaurants advertised home-cooked meals and more announced seafood as a specialty. Of course fish and shrimp had always been on the menu, and slurping oysters was something of a rite of passage for vacationers with a yearning for adventure, but in the summer of 1953 *Alabama* magazine highlighted the Gulf Shores Friendship House, where "longtime food specialists" from Birmingham offered a "varied" and "well-prepared" menu which "naturally featured seafood." However, prices higher than "what you would expect at home" sent the less than affluent, and the more traditional, back to the cafes where locals ate things fried or raw and drank what happened to have come in on the distributor's truck that day. What was happening there was happening all along the coast: Two different sets of tourists, classes if you will, were taking shape, and in time they would create different coasts, each in its own image.

Visibly at least, the tourists who were coming out ahead in the contest to a create a coastal "image" were the ones attracted to the growing number of amusements advertised by the reinforced concrete and stucco statues and buildings dotting the landscape. Created initially by welder and "concrete-artist" Lee Koplin and copied for years by other craftsmen with similar if not equal skills, they consisted of marvels such as Castle Dracula, out of place but enticing to a particular clientele (you know who); the Jungle Land volcano, which at least had a tropical theme; and Tombstone Territory, with its giant concrete Indian and replica of Mesa Verde. But of all the Koplin-inspired, redneck-embraced symbols of the country-come-to-town coast, none was more popular and representative than Koplin's own Goofy Golf.

The story goes that Koplin got his start in California where miniature golf was popular. He used his skills to make some statuary for a friend's course, receipts increased, and the artist was on his way. His way took him, eventually, to the Gulf Coast where in the late 1950s he built his first statu-ary-filled Goofy Golf course at Biloxi. From there it was only a short jump east to the beaches of Panama City, and in the summer of 1959 he opened the Goofy Golf that was to become the Panhandle's most famous miniature golf course. Giant figures of apes, dinosaurs of all sorts, skulls and sphinx and octopi, fish and fowl never seen in nature in sizes as fantastic as their shapes, all sprinkled throughout a twisting miniature golf course where Daddy, Mama, and the kids could putt about in friendly family competi-tion. And maybe the parents would wonder what it would be like to play golf on a real course, with rolling fairways and manicured greens, the kind where rich folks drove and putted. Those country club courses reflected the class and circumstances of the folks who played there; Goofy Golf courses did the same.

So it came to pass that each of these coastal resorts became a fantasy world for families from Alabama, Mississippi, Georgia, Tennessee, and points around and about, a place where, for a week or two, they could enjoy the beach and the sun and in that "wholesome atmosphere" entertain the children, whose numbers seemed to increase every year and who, in the future, would set out to shape the beach their way, just as their parents were trying to do. War babies had given the coast its first taste of teenage hormonal energy, but they were only a hint of the future. In the 1960s, the baby boomers came of age, and from their teens into their college years they and those who came after them took noxious activities and offensive noises to a new level—at least they did in the spring.

Children were not the only harbingers of change. Even though the motels close to the amusements had maintained their reputation as safe places for families to stay, the beach was beginning to attract people who wanted to do more than swim, play Goofy Golf, fish a little, eat seafood fried or raw, and go home with a carved coconut head. Among the southerners coming to the coast were good old boys and girls who figured lying in the sun was something to do for a hangover the day after. They wanted their own fantasy world, an exciting place where nights on the town could be spent. Of course folks of this sort had been coming there all

Goofy Golf, Panama City Beach, fiftieth anniversary, 2009. Photograph by the author.

along, just as the children had, but as their numbers swelled there would be enough of them to constitute a class of their own. Joined at times by respectable folks looking for a walk on the wild side, their noxious activities and offensive noises would be responsible for no small part of the Riviera's redneckery.

A few would even run amok.

As for those carved coconuts, Gary Walsingham, whose father, Alvin, created the chain of Alvin's Island souvenir and beachwear shops that have become as ubiquitous as Goofy Golf and water parks, once observed, "We've sold thousands . . . but you never walk into someone's house and see them." Well, not unless you drop in at one of the vacation cottages at resort communities such as Grayton, Seagrove, Gulf Shores, or Laguna Beach. Furnished in those pre–designer décor days with a combination of old furniture brought from home and thrift store treasures found locally, there among the paint-by-numbers masterpieces created by children on a rainy day and hung for a season, among the seashells and sand dollars found on the beach and mounted in shadowboxes, among the pieces of driftwood that had washed up after a storm, you might find a carved coconut head proudly displayed as if it were a trophy, won (or perhaps captured) on one of those infrequent forays into places where redneck families congregated and played.

FOUR

Times They Were A-Changing

A S THE 1950S came to a close the Alabama coast and the Florida Panhandle seemed settled comfortably into a skin of tacky resorts for southerners whose income and aspirations kept creeping up on middle class. In and around these amusements was a sprinkling of small, reasonably exclusive vacation-cottage communities for those who were a little (and in some cases a lot) better off. Most of the Panhandle's year-round residents lived away from the beach, back in towns like Pensacola, Fort Walton, Destin, and Panama City, and in villages north of the Intracoastal Waterway. If they did not work at the beach, and most didn't, uplanders seldom ventured across the bridge. Town folks—inland folks—looked down on beach folks and beach folks knew and resented it. But the attitude inland was in some ways justified. Things seemed to change when you got close to salt water. There was "something in Florida's humid, languorous air," a writer for *Fortune* observed, that over the years had "attracted pirates, derelicts, remittance men, thieves, madams, gamblers, blue-sky promoters, moneybags, exhausted noblemen, black-market operators, profiteers, [and] all the infections of Western life." The Panhandle and Alabama beaches had, at one time or another, been infected by most of these. (I haven't found an "exhausted noblemen" yet, but one might still turn up.) And they kept coming. Though Fort Walton's upstanding citizens had run out gamblers of one sort, all along the coast another breed of gambler was setting up shop, not in swanky clubs but in real estate offices. High and low rollers, they bet money on land—what could be built on it and what it could be sold for—and in the years to come, with the support of local governments, chambers of commerce, and civic groups, they made and remade the Redneck Riviera.

Meanwhile, the secession of seasons was set. During the summer the amusement parks at and around Long Beach, Okaloosa Island, Pensacola Beach, and Gulf Shores did a brisk business, while back in the cottages, as one summer-season resident wrote, "the breeze is blowing, the bourbon is flowing and life is easy." And it was. Whether for a long weekend, a week (maybe two), or the summer, people came to the coast to get away from the day-to-day grind, to forget that there was a boss or a business or even a work ethic to remind them that leisure was akin to laziness, which could slip into sloth, and too much of that and you'd end up, as the saying went, "sorry as gully dirt." So it followed that those who had only a short time to spend (or waste, depending on how you looked at it) played the hardest, and the locals who owned and ran the resorts worked equally hard to make the visitors want to come back again. "Be sure and greet everyone happy and with a smile," one operator told her daughter who was being brought up in the business. "These families might have saved for years for this one vacation and our bad day should not affect their family fun." But at the same time, the resorts were also there to make money, so behind the smile and the greeting was the determination that visitors would not go home with change in their pockets.

As the summer season grew, a labor problem developed. Between Memorial Day and Labor Day the motels, parks, and amusements needed lots of workers, but who would sign up for jobs where hours were long, the work was tedious and hot, the pay was low, and when fall came you got laid off. Family operations, of which there were many, solved the problem with family labor, when they could, as Lamar Triplett did. In 1959, Triplett left a successful Birmingham public school band directorship to take a similar job at Panama City High, for ten thousand dollars a year less. But he wasn't worried. He was sure he'd earn that and more during the summer, running the beach motel he had bought and named Trip's. Like so many who came to Florida, Triplett was chasing a dream, and like so many of the others, he took the family with him. In the years that followed, until the children were grown and gone, he, his wife, and his two daughters ran Trip's. During the school

Trip's Motel and Cottages, circa 1959. This beach establishment was operated by
Lamar Triplett, who came down from Alabama to live out his dream. Courtesy of
Paula Triplett Bailey and Karen Triplett Grant.

year they lived away from the coast in one of those nice, new, wrong-side-of-
the-bridge residential areas that were making a beach address a little more
"respectable." When summer came the family moved to the motel, where
they took up residence in one of the cottages, and ran the place until fall.
Then, when the tourists left, they closed up Trip's and moved back "home."

Not every owner had Triplett's labor force and even those who did often
found that family was not enough. To add staff, many owners hired out-of-
school teenagers from nearby towns who drove in to work and drove home
in the evening, but they were still shorthanded. Word drifted inland that
folks could spend the summer at the beach and get paid for it—another
dream Florida could make come true. Inland they heard and from inland
they came. Although the vice president of the Florida State Chamber of
Commerce had cautioned civic leaders "to be a bit choosy about newcomers
[you] invite to live within [your] borders" neither the Panhandle promoters
nor those over in Alabama were particularly mindful of the warning when it
came to hiring folks to run the rides, collect the tickets, make change, and
police the grounds. True, it would have been nice to do as the chamber VP
suggested and work to attract people "who can contribute to the economy
and social welfare," but the resorts needed cheap labor that would do what
had to be done and leave in the fall with the crowds. So they welcomed seasonal workers, home-from-college students who came down to the beach to
pick up extra money and have more fun than could be had clerking at a store

back home. Many of these pooled their resources to rent small, old houses away from the beach or rooms in cheap motels that had sprung up around the amusement parks. They were welcomed because they worked for little, spent most of what they made right where they made it, and at the end of the summer went back to school. But their presence left a distinct impression on visitors. While south Florida was becoming the province of affluent retirees who gave its activities and institutions an older, more settled, more sophisticated appearance, the Panhandle and its Alabama neighbor seemed more youthful, more active, and anything but sophisticated.

The Panhandle was also white, or at least that was how it seemed to white folks. However, there were a few spots along the coast where African Americans could and did go when they got a chance. Gulf Beach, on Perdido Key between Gulf Shores and Pensacola, was one. Remote, and segregated as much by geography and custom as by law, for years Gulf Beach had been a popular gathering spot for area blacks. In 1950, the Sunset Riding Club, which was owned by prominent black dentist Dr. Simon W. Boyd, leased the property from Escambia County and began operating it "for the sole use of bathing, beach, and recreational facilities for the 'colored citizens.'" Renamed Johnson Beach for Private Rosamond Johnson Jr., the African American who was the first Escambia County soldier to die in the Korean War, word of the playground spread and soon bus loads of black beachgoers were coming in from Mobile and other points inland. Ora Wills, who has written about African American life in the Pensacola area, tells of holidays when "men would rise early, heft out the fishing lines and nets and crab baskets and steal away in the darkness," off to the coast. The women and children would come later in the day, and soon a "black wash pot filled with hot, sizzling grease, squatted on short, spiked legs in the white sand." The adults cooked mullet, crabs, and "hush puppies, mixed with Spearman's beer," while the girls "strutted the beach, shaking up the boys."

There was also Wingate Beach, near Pensacola, which had a restaurant well known for its fresh fish sandwiches and a lounge where black beachgoers, some from as far away as Tennessee, congregated to enjoy the music and each other. "We used to dance the jitterbug, listen to the blues," recalled Rosie Wingate Reynolds, a member of the family that owned the resort. "Everything was booming."

Johnson Beach and Wingate Beach may have taken some pressure off Pensacola Beach, which was "white only." Gulf Shores, about twenty-five miles to the west, apparently did not prohibit blacks from using the public beach, but the shoreline there was long and largely deserted, so it would have been easy for both races to use it and never come in contact with each other. More interesting is the memory of Monroe McLeod, who was superintendent of Gulf State Park during the 1950s and 1960s. In 1990, McLeod told the *Mobile Press-Register* that when he was in charge blacks used park facilities "whenever they wanted to." Maybe so. But considering Alabama's record on race relations, it is also possible that the superintendent's recollections had become rose-tinted with time.

Still, if McLeod was right that blacks were not excluded from the Alabama coast, patrons of Johnson Beach soon lost what beach they had. In 1956, Escambia County officials cancelled the Sunset Riding Club's lease. No one can (or perhaps will) say for sure why the county did this. Some believe that there had been fights and other disturbances out there. Others recall concern that the area might become a staging ground for civil rights protests. But it's also possible that officials cancelled the lease simply because they could—one more way to show restive blacks who was in charge. It would not have been the first time something like that was done, nor the last. Wingate Beach, which was privately owned and not dependent on a county lease, continued on until the storms of the 1970s wrecked the restaurant and lounge, and the family decided to develop the land for homes, apartments, and condominiums.

The Johnson Beach matter notwithstanding, during the 1950s and 1960s there seems to have been little racial tension along the coast, a situation due in no small part to the fact that there were not many African Americans living there or visiting the beach. By 1950, only two of the coastal counties had an African American population of more than 20 percent. In Alabama's Baldwin County and in adjacent Escambia County, 22 percent of the population was black. The majority of Baldwin's black residents lived in farming and timber areas well inland. Most Escambia African Americans lived in Pensacola, which contained 63 percent of the county's black population and likely provided much of Johnson Beach's clientele. Bay County's African American community comprised 17 percent of the population, and 74 percent of that group lived in Panama City proper. There was a segregated beach near St. Andrews State Park, but apparently it was never as formally organized as Johnson Beach was. Thirteen percent of Walton County's population was black, while in Okaloosa and Santa Rosa counties less than 10 percent of the population was African American. And in each of these counties few if any of this minority lived on or near the coast. Ten years later the 1960 census showed that the number of blacks increased in every county with the exception of Walton, where it remained roughly the same. However, the percentage of the population that was black declined. This made it even less likely that blacks would come in contact with whites, especially whites vacationing at the beach. The few black faces seen at the resorts were maids, janitors, or musicians who played at local clubs. When the work day was done and the last set finished, they disappeared. It was not necessary for coastal communities to draw up covenants as C. H. McGee did. Motels simply did not rent to blacks. Restaurants did not serve blacks. Stores did not cater to blacks. Black people either went to the few beaches set aside for them or did not go to the beach at all.

Just because there were not many blacks does not mean there wasn't racism. A racial liberal, someone at least sympathetic to the goals of the civil rights movement, was as hard to find among white coastal residents as in the upland communities from which the tourists came. Certainly there were some, but in those troubled times such opinions were considered better kept to one's self. More revealing of the people and place were the racist remarks and jokes that bonded whites—residents and visitors, affluent and not-so—together in the shared understanding that the coast "belonged" to them and they planned to keep it that way. African Americans, with neither the resources nor (one suspects) the desire to challenge this coastal status quo, spent time and energy on other things.

Which was at least one of the reasons why, despite changes that went on in the 1950s, there was a continuity to the coast, which author Tim Hollis noted was "comfortably reassuring" to visitors and residents alike. A new ride or even a new resort might appear but it would be much like the old, except bigger and, if possible, more garish. New restaurants opened but they fit right in or, if they didn't, they quickly closed. There were new clubs where tourist couples without kids could drink and dance much like couples had at beach casinos before their baby boomers were born. At some of these nightspots, performers with regional reputations entertained folks who had heard of them somewhere. Meanwhile, in the vacation communities away from the action new cottages popped up now and then, but they looked a lot like those already there, and because they did not stand out, they and their owners reassured neighbors that life would go on as everyone wanted it to. On the rides, in the restaurants, at the clubs, and back at the motels, everyone was comfortably, reassuringly southern and overwhelmingly white. This was Florida, only it wasn't like the rest of the state. This was Alabama, but it wasn't Alabama either. Visitors were not sure what to call it other than "the beach," but they liked it.

So they continued to come, visit, buy, retire, live. Meanwhile the folks who wanted to "develop" Alabama and Florida did all they could to get them there. With the help of the increasingly benevolent federal government Alabama finished paving its beach route to the Florida line. Across Perdido Pass, Florida had done the same. All they needed was a connecting bridge. As early as 1949, state officials were talking about constructing the bridge together, a joint project to share the costs and the benefits. Then complications arose. Although it was generally assumed that the line between Florida and Alabama was Perdido Pass, engineers surveying the site noted that over the years the channel of the pass had shifted west, and because of this drift either Florida had gained about three miles of territory or the actual line was farther east. And if the line was to the east, then both sides of the pass belonged to Alabama and any bridge built would be an Alabama bridge. So they talked, and argued, and went to court, but Florida did not push the point as it might today. The debatable land was almost-empty beachfront and the Sunshine State had plenty of that. A bridge would cost millions, and the strip of sand wasn't worth much. So Alabama got three miles of beach and the bill for a bridge. Work started in 1958 and in 1962, it was finished.

The next year, just across the line, on the Florida side, the Tampary family from Pensacola built a lounge and package store that would become the Flora-Bama. Although other bars and dives would come along and give it stiff competition, none would make such a long and enduring contribution as the "Bama" to the reputation of the coast as a place where people step outside accepted boundaries of behavior. As anyone will tell you, if you are looking for the Redneck Riviera, you will find it there.

The Flora-Bama almost went out of business before it got started. According to current co-owner Joe Gilchrist, near where the Bama was being built was the River Queen, a "Mississippi workboat that was pulled up" and turned into a honky-tonk. "They had strippers and unlicensed booze and other illegal activities going on," all protected because one of the owners was a state senator—Gilchrist did not say which state, not that it mattered. Could have been either. That owner and his partners didn't want the

Perdido Bridge, 1970s. At this time, there was still little development on either side of the bridge, just as when it was built a decade earlier. Courtesy of the Mobile Press-Register Collection, Doy Leale McCall Rare Book and Manuscript Library, University of South Alabama.

competition, so the day before the Tampary's bar was scheduled to open, Gilchrist said, "a crew of low-life characters came over and burned the Flora-Bama." Everyone knew who was behind it, but proof was hard to come by so no one was charged. But the Bama was rebuilt and as traffic along the beach route increased so did its business—which is hardly surprising since it was almost the only place to party on that lonely strip. Though advertised as "on the line" the bar was all "Flora" and no "Bama," which worked well because of Florida's more liberal liquor laws. However, Alabama supplied many, if not most of its customers, and as Orange Beach and Gulf Shores grew, the Flora-Bama became popular more for being across the line than for being on it. Popularity led to physical growth, with additions tacked on, according to one observer, as if cobbled together "by a kid with tree-house-building skills." As the Bama was located on the south side of the highway where customers could walk out the back door and onto the sand, it was easy for couples wishing to accept the challenge—"Let's do it on the line." Though the Flora-Bama has expanded, changed owners, and added activities to its reason for being, it remains the quintessential beach bar.

And for many along the northern Gulf Coast, the quintessential beach event will be Spring Break. According to both fact and myth, Spring Break began when the swimming team from a northern university sought to get a jump on its competition by escaping the snow and spending the Christmas break practicing in sunny Fort Lauderdale. The idea of getting out of the wintry grayness and into the sunshine caught on, and with the Easter break coming near winter's end it was only natural for students to want to celebrate the Resurrection or Passover in a place that was warm and pleasant. By the late 1950s an Easter expedition to south Florida was the dream of most northern students and, increasingly, the reality of many. If, as historian Gary Mormino has suggested, amusement parks for the working classes constituted something of a "social safety valve," Spring Break served the same function for winter-bound students with cabin fever. Then, in 1960, Hollywood turned out *Where the Boys Are*, a movie about Fort Lauderdale's Spring Break, and the cult of Spring Break was born—or so the story goes.

But Spring Break did not offer much for students from the lower South. Most of them did not have an Easter break. They got time off when the Alabama Education Association (AEA), the Georgia Association of Educators (GAE), the Mississippi Association of Educators (MAE), and similar organizations in other states—including Florida—held their annual meetings. But these breaks were short—two to three days plus a weekend, so a trip to Fort Lauderdale was all but out of the question. The Gulf Coast was nearer, but it was also cold, windy, and rainy there in March, the traditional month for Spring Break in the South. So southern students, of which I was one, stayed away until *Where the Boys Are* made it "cool" to go break at the beach, even if it was cold.

Or so I thought.

Although my friends and I believed then, and for years after, that we and others like us had more or less invented Spring Break on the Gulf, apparently we were wrong. On February 17, 1960, the *Mobile Press-Register* noted, with obvious satisfaction, that because "several hundred Alabama teen-agers" were expected to "pay an early visit to local beaches" during AEA holidays, Panama City area civic groups and city officials were cooperating to provide a "series of entertainments" to keep the young folks occupied. These diversions included "a beauty pageant, talent show, fishing contest, and treasure hunt"—just what teenagers wanted to do at the beach. However, another article, down the page a bit, revealed a more realistic assessment of the visitor expectations. According to that report the mayors of Panama City Beach, Long Beach, and Edgewater Beach "have joined in the move to ban the sale . . . of all beer and alcoholic beverages" from March 15 to March 20. Moreover, according to the article, this ban had been in place every year since 1954! So it would seem that even before *Where the Boys Are* inspired my generation to go to the coast, enough students were celebrating Spring Break on the beaches west of Panama City to draw the attention of local authorities, and they were drinking enough alcohol to cause concern.

But did they really ban beer? Checking with older residents of the Panama City area, some of whom were in local government in the late 1950s, I found none who could remember such an ordinance ever being passed. So I went digging into the minutes of the Panama City Beach Commissioners' meetings and sure enough, a few days before the *Press-Register* article, a representative from the Panama City Junior Chamber of Commerce appeared before the commission to explain his organization's plan for "supervised activities for the teen agers who will visit the beach during the AEA convention." The commissioners, feeling the cause was worthy, voted $150 to underwrite the cost of a dance for their guests. But no beer ban. Before adjourning city leaders did pass an ordinance making it unlawful to sell alcoholic beverages to anyone under twenty-one years of age, which was both odd and redundant since that was illegal already. It was also meaningless for, as a former police chief told me, those kids "could find beer in Saudi Arabia." As for the mayors calling for businesses to stop selling, if it happened it was a personal appeal, not an official act. But even if there was no ban, records and recollections reveal that regardless of the weather, before *Where the Boys Are* hit the screen, kids from Alabama and likely from other nearby states were taking their short Spring Breaks down on the Gulf.

The movie, however, ratcheted things up a bit, for by the early 1960s, Hangouts at Long Beach and Gulf Shores were full of Spring Breakers, and if "beverages" had been banned, that prohibition, like the one on underage drinking, was routinely ignored, for one of the memories of the Long Beach Hangout was how the smell of beer permeated the place. Aware, and no doubt fearful, of what unsupervised students might do, local forces of order and decency set out to sponsor "wholesome" activities for visitors who came down to sun (if there was sun), swim (if they could stand the cold),

Dancing at the Hangout, Panama City Beach, 1960s. Fashions and dances changed; kids did not. Courtesy of Bay County Public Library, Panama City, Fla.

and enjoy each other. In an effort to channel their energies into something other than drinking and dancing and drinking some more, local promoters welcomed students with contests they were certain would keep the kids out of trouble. In 1964, the beaches of Panama City offered Spring Breakers trials of skill such as sack races, "find the needle in the flour," balloon blowing, egg throwing, potato rolling, and such, which only confirmed what the students already believed—that adults didn't have a clue.

Guys and girls went to the beach over Spring Break to either be with someone in a place where you could do things you couldn't do back home or meet other guys and girls who were down to do what you were down to do—or so you hoped. There was drinking, certainly, and partying late into the night, and even casual sex (an oxymoron if one ever existed), but what took place when Spring Break was new and like the coast itself, relatively undeveloped, pales in comparison with what would come later. What started as a student rite of spring would in time become an event, popularized and promoted, to make a lot of people a lot of money. Spring Break would be different then. Students would be different. And the beach would be different as well.

If Spring Breakers had taken the time to look around, they would have seen the beach changing, even from year to year. So would everyone else. Back in the 1930s, someone asked Gid Thomas, for whom the now famous Thomas Drive was named, just what he expected to grow on the sand he had purchased. The founder of Panama City Beach replied, "I'm not growing vegetables out here. I'm growing people." Thomas's successors realized that you don't grow people on the coast, you bring them in, and in the 1960s such an explosion of promotional activity occurred that what had come before appeared tepid and amateurish in comparison. Panama City Beach led the way with a news bureau under "promoter extraordinaire Jim Sumter," who showed everyone who had a beach how to sell their product. Mixing sex (nothing like a girl in a swimsuit to get the public's attention) and gimmicks (such as appearing on a Canadian TV talk show and successfully slipping white Gulf Coast sand into the host's sugar bowl), Sumter made his point. Though stories are told that money under the table was a sure way to get your resort highlighted when Sumter hit the road, the fact remained that the Gulf Coast was getting more attention than ever before, and what benefitted Panama City Beach did not hurt its neighbors. Unless, of course, neighbors did not want Panama City Beach–type development in their backyards.

Symbols of promotional success could be found all along the coast. In 1964, Holiday Inn, the American icon that promised guests quality, consistency, and a homogenized tourist experience, opened on Panama City Beach. Four stories tall with one hundred rooms, it was said (with the usual Florida exaggeration) to be the tallest building on the Gulf—and north of Tampa it likely was. For a while. Three years later Holiday Inn built Destin's first high-rise, a nine-story hostelry with a revolving restaurant on the top. It was one of the first indications that people with money, big money, were beginning to consider Destin more than a little fishing village. Three more years and Holiday Inn opened in Gulf Shores. More modest than its Panama City Beach and Destin counterparts, it was nevertheless greeted by locals as evidence that the Alabama coast had as much to offer as those more widely known resorts to the east. It didn't of course. The beaches west of Panama City continued to set the standard. But Alabama was trying.

It might be well to pause here and consider the lay of the land.

As pointed out earlier, there was the city of Panama City and to its west, across the Hathaway Bridge, there was a string of beach communities and resorts, one of which was named Panama City Beach. However, by the 1960s the distinctions among four of them—Panama City Beach, Long Beach, Edgewater Beach, and West Panama City Beach—meant little to tourists who felt they were all one. And since Panama City was the city, tourists reasoned that the beach must be Panama City's beach. So when families loaded the car and pointed it south, they told the neighbor who agreed to feed the dog or watch the cat that they were headed to Panama City, and the neighbor knew they meant the beach. That was all that mattered. Finally, in 1969, those four beaches combined into one—Panama City Beach. For most visitors, however, they were that already.

But until the four became one, West Panama City Beach was where the action was. Long Beach had its day in the 1950s, when the Hangout was going strong, but by the 1960s the arcade and midway-type amusements around the pavilion were becoming shabby and clientele was becoming sleazy—and a little dangerous. There were rumors of gangs and of fights between locals and tourists, and occasionally the law had to be called. Although visitors looking for excitement a little rougher than surf and sun and Goofy Golf continued to show up at the Hangout, the folks who operated "family" motels were suggesting that their guests might want to venture out to the east end of the commercial development, where the Miracle Strip Amusement Park was rising out of the sand and scrub.

Of all the places between Panama City and Gulf Shores where tourists from the lower South came to be entertained, none will ever match the Miracle Strip Amusement Park in its appeal to the glorious lack of sophistication of regional visitors. Thanks to Congressman Robert Sikes, Florida's original "He-Coon," there was nothing in federal law to restrict development along the coast, so developers went at it. Jimmy Lark, a member of one of the beach's pioneering developer families, got one up on the rest when he brought in a Philadelphia company to build the longest and fastest roller coaster in the country. Then in a move loaded with irony, the story goes that Lark got in touch with city officials in Birmingham and made arrangements to buy and lease the rides from Kiddieland, a small municipal amusement park that the city had decided to close rather than integrate. So the Ferris wheel, the umbrella rides, the tilt-a-whirl, and the rest were brought to the beach so white folks could continue to enjoy the same amusements white folks had enjoyed back in the Magic City. According to another story, Lark simply bought up rides from a Birmingham carnival

Miracle Strip Amusement Park, 1960s. Note how relatively undeveloped the coast around it is. Courtesy of Bay County Public Library, Panama City, Fla.

operator, but either way, the rides arrived and in the summer of 1963 the Miracle Strip Amusement Park opened.

After that, every resort owner along the beach seemed determined to do the Miracle Strip one better, which led to a frenzy of offseason building and upgrading that yearly changed the face of the Panama City coast. Though competitors never succeeded in replacing Lark's park as the top amusement on the strip, they made good effort at it. There was Petticoat Junction just down the road, and after enjoying the "country" entertainment, visitors could dine at the Kona-Kia, "a bit of the South Seas transplanted right in the middle of Long Beach." In and around the resorts were attractions sprinkled with Koplin and Koplin-like concrete, fiberglass, and chicken wire creations—Tombstone Territory, the Magic Forest, and miniature golf galore. Attractions came and went, appeared and disappeared, only to appear again in a different form. Along Panama City Beach, change was the only constant. Miracle Strip Park grew to keep up and stay ahead, adding the Hurricane House that supposedly gave you a sense of what it was like being in a storm and, my favorite, the dark, dank, and scary Haunted Castle ride. Then you could wander over and take the Skyride for a great view of it all. It seemed that whatever a visitor's heart desired and budget could afford could be found at Panama City Beach. The beach itself often seemed an afterthought to tourists once they arrived and saw the other delights that awaited them.

Of course Panama City Beach was not alone in giving upcountry visitors the entertainment they preferred. Build it faster, longer, and bigger, paint it in colors that never appeared in nature, and you'd get their attention—and their money. But of all the resorts between Panama City and Pensacola, in the 1960s only Okaloosa Island Park, across from Fort Walton, came anywhere close to matching what the Miracle Strip Amusement Park had to offer. Or at least as best we can tell. Today the Okaloosa Park is something of a mystery. Apparently it consisted of a collection of older rides, a miniature golf course, a shooting gallery, a snack bar, and a place for teenagers to dance. But not even Tim Hollis's diligent research for his book on Florida Panhandle amusement parks could uncover much more than that. I am certainly not much help. Though I spent some time in the area when the park was in operation, I have no memory of it. If my friends and I, or our families, went to Fort Walton Beach we went to the Gulfarium. Otherwise, we headed for Panama City. Not that it mattered much to Fort Walton. Though the island was slowly developing, tourism was not what drove the local economy. Without gambling to attract visitors, before tourists and retirees discovered what Okaloosa had to offer, Fort Walton Beach was little more than a ward of the federal government. With Eglin Air Force Base nearby, airmen were Fort Walton Beach's tourists and their money kept the economy afloat. In 1969, according to a study of the region, military income comprised an "incredible" 92.1 percent of the total labor force income of the Fort Walton Beach metropolitan statistical area.

Pensacola Beach never had an amusement park, though it did have a giant slide. Always a little more tasteful, a little more upscale than their neighbors east and west, Pensacola folks seemed to believe that if surf, sand, pier, and casino were not enough to keep some tourists amused, then those folks should go somewhere else. As for Destin, though its beaches were beginning to attract attention and new motels were springing up, fishing remained the amusement that drew visitors. Out from the town you could drive along Highway 98 for miles, with an unobstructed view of the Gulf, and if you wanted to picnic or swim, all you had to do was pull over and walk down to the shore. The only thing to stop you might be the sandy shoulder where it was easy to get stuck and hard to get out. Though there were a few establishments along the way that announced that their beach was private, they were rare and no one paid them much attention. The beach belonged to everyone, or so everyone seemed to believe.

Destin did make one significant contribution to coastal statuary which became a landmark in the memories of locals and visitors alike. In 1967, a giant emerald knight was erected outside the Green Knight restaurant. Taller than most of the single story buildings around it, the Green Knight became a point of reference for visitors driving in from the east. When you reached the Green Knight you were in Destin. Less than a mile further and you would be at the harbor, ready to climb aboard and go fishing. The Green Knight soon evolved into a lounge and liquor store, which became the rendezvous point for travelers just arriving and locals already there—"we'll meet at the Green Knight, have a few drinks, and figure out what to do next" was how a lot of things got started that probably shouldn't have. Over the years the statue became the target of local high school students and college kids on Spring Break who heaped on it the indignity of diapers, painted-on private parts, and alternative colors. One local lady recalled that it was considered "rite of passage for teenagers and young men in the area to urinate on him." Once they even stole his spear. Nevertheless, for many residents the Knight was Destin's neighborhood bar. For others it was a warm, inviting place where anyone could fit right in. So they returned again and again.

Though change was coming, during the 1960s Destin remained focused on the deep sea, and the annual Fishing Rodeo was the town's biggest event. With fewer than one thousand year-round residents, the village remained a tight-knit community where the rodeo was kicked off by captains and crews gathering for "sho'nuff rib eating throwdowns" rather than a celebration carefully choreographed by the chamber of commerce. If you did not want to go out into the Gulf there was the Crystal Beach Pier where you could fish for fifty cents a day or go to the Blue Room and let them fry up what someone else caught. And there was the beach, as yet underappreciated and undeveloped. Without even a hamburger joint at which to hang out, local high school kids took their dates, a few blankets, and maybe a six pack or two out to Holiday Isle across the sound from the docks (everybody had a boat it seemed). There they built a fire and had a party. I have talked to a lot of adults who grew up on the coast and none would have wanted to be young anywhere else.

Though the beaches grew and prospered, rural-based county leaders in Walton, Okaloosa, and Baldwin hardly seemed to care. Firmly focused on their inland agricultural constituencies, county commissioners paid attention to the coast only when they were called on to keep the peace. The rest of the time they could and did ignore what went on down there. For many beach folks, that was just fine. Unincorporated, lightly regulated, and underserved, they were pretty much on their own. In 1958, after a bitter court fight, Gulf Shores got a corporate identity but the municipal staff consisted only of a policeman, a clerk, and a part-time street worker. The first few council meetings ended in shouting matches, city functions depended heavily on volunteers and donations, and though a zoning plan was passed in 1962, people routinely found ways to get around its restrictions. The town did purchase a water system and with the help of the American Civil Defense Association and surplus military equipment began a mosquito control program. For most residents, this was all the local government they wanted. As long as the state and county maintained the roads and the Sheriff's Department was there to quell any disturbance or investigate serious crimes, why pay taxes for anything more?

There were times, of course, when beach folks were less willing, and less able, to go it alone. When the weather turned and the storms came in, people learned quickly how vulnerable they were. Fortunately for the Panhandle and the beaches of Baldwin, the 1950s were relatively quiet, which meant that what development there was suffered little damage. But as more businesses and homes were built along the coast, the more concerned people became. In the 1940s and early 1950s washed out roads presented few problems for there were not many roads to wash out. There were not many reports of hotels filled with storm surge sand for there were few hotels. However, time passed and things changed. By 1960, there was more to wash away, more to be damaged. In 1965, when Hurricane Betsy came ashore near New Orleans, the Alabama beaches took a pounding. With little advance warning, locals either rode it out or battened down and headed north. The owner of the Flora-Bama and some friends, fearing looters might beat them back home after the storm, loaded up the liquor and prepared to leave. Then the weather worsened, so they decided to hunker down until it passed. According to the sister of one of the group, a highway patrolman came by and told them "they had better leave quick" and when they said they weren't going "he took names of next of kin." As she tells it, "they stayed [and] got quite drunk, but no whiskey was stolen," so the venture was judged a success.

Then it was calm until August 1969, when Hurricane Camille hit the Mississippi coast. No one knows the strength of Camille's winds because the gauges were blown away, but it is estimated that gusts were as high as 200 MPH. The storm surge washed inland, destroying everything in its way. When it was over, 143 people were dead. Property losses were calculated at $9 billion. Though Alabama and the Panhandle escaped relatively unscathed, many realized that what had happened to Mississippi could also happen to them. Others, however, figured it never would.

One of the two groups would be wrong.

FIVE

The Redneck Riviera Rises

I T CAN BE SAID, with some justification, that by the 1970s the Redneck Riviera had already risen and was pretty firmly in place. All along the coast, a less than sophisticated southerner could find just about everything he or she might want: carnivals, amusements, clubs, roadhouses, juke joints and honkytonks, fish to catch and fish to eat, drinking and dancing and (in some cases) fighting, and of course the beach. H. L. Mencken, who back in the 1920s wrote of a South that was "almost as sterile, artistically, intellectually, culturally, as the Sahara Desert," could have stood in the middle of any one of these coastal attractions and concluded that nothing had really changed. The "southerners inoculated with all the worst traits of the Yankee sharper" that Mencken detested were still in charge. And as they had done to Dixie in Mencken's day, modern "Philistines" turned the region between Panama City and Mobile Bay into a "gargantuan paradise of the fourth-rate." Instead of art galleries they built haunted castles, instead of symphonies there was the juke box, instead of white tablecloth restaurants there were oyster bars and smoked mullet. The only time people who had taken a college course outnumbered high school dropouts was Spring Break. It would have been to Mencken what so much of his South was—"an obscenity of the very first caliber"—but good old boys and girls loved it.

The one thing of which Mencken might have approved was the general absence of religion—at least of the populist,

Noah's Ark. The ark has remained a fixture on Panama City Beach and a gathering place for the faithful well into the twenty-first century. Photograph by the author.

Pentecostal, proselytizing variety that gave men like Mencken the heebie-jeebies. There were churches, certainly, but they were for the locals. Tourists down for an extended stay might drop in, but for short-termers Sunday morning was set aside for nursing a hangover, packing up, or getting in one last swim before hitting the road for home and work on Monday. Some denominations did have a coastal presence. The Methodist Church, in keeping with the architectural trends prevalent along Panama City Beach, built Noah's Ark, a house of the Lord designed to look like the vessel that rode out the flood. Although the purpose was to provide a place for vacationers to worship, the ark's appearance was so similar to amusements around it that it fit in too well. According to its first pastor, people would see the ship, "think it [was] a restaurant or an arcade," and stop. How many of the disappointed came back for Sunday services is hard to say, but by following the general rule of beach resorts—get the tourists' attention and bring them in—Noah's Ark and the Methodists may have picked up a few stray souls.

Meanwhile, more and more souls seemed to be straying. During the 1960s and into the 1970s the social revolution that buffeted the rest of the nation was also felt along the Alabama coast and the Florida Panhandle. Though there had always been "sex, drugs (of the alcoholic sort) & rock 'n roll" on the beach, what was once isolated and reasonably discrete, suddenly seemed to be open and everywhere. Numbers made the difference. In the

1950s and early 1960s baby boomers, down with their families, were still playing in the sand and surf during the day and going to the amusement parks at night. War babies like myself were few enough to be relegated to Hangouts and "teen towns," where we were with our own and, for the most part, out of sight and out of mind. What commotion we caused surely distressed our parents, and fears of juvenile delinquency were often justified, but compared to what would come next we were a pretty tame bunch—at least most of us. However, by the mid-sixties the first wave of boomers was out of high school, into college, and into trouble—or at least wanting to be. And the beach, which their parents, aunts, uncles, and older siblings had already established as a getaway where inhibitions could be shed, was embraced by this next generation as the place to do what they wanted to do with whoever would do it with them. So they shucked off the old, embraced the new, and headed for the coast.

And of the many things this generation shed, the most obvious to those around them, and most troubling to adults, were their clothes.

During the 1950s the two-piece swimsuits once so popular with "bathing beauties" were replaced by one-piece outfits that left everything to the imagination. On the beach and by the pool, women settled into the roles of well-covered stereotypical "Father-knows-best" wives and daughters. Bikinis might be found in magazines like *Playboy*, which had just come on the scene, and in French movies. But you would not find them being worn by respectable southern girls on southern beaches.

Then it began to change, and when it did, change came quickly. By the mid-1960s the modest one-pieces of the previous decade were replaced by "itsy bitsy" bikinis that seemed to get itsyer and bitsyer every summer. Some parents believed the inspiration for this fashion decision was the hippie movement with its "no bra, hip-hugging ideals," and maybe so. But along the Gulf Coast, among the conservative southern children of conservative southern parents, the influence of the counterculture was for the most part superficial. Coastal kids listened to the same music everyone else did, though you were more likely to hear "(I Can't Get No) Satisfaction" than "The Age of Aquarius." Bell-bottom jeans and tie-dyed shirts replaced madras shorts and button-downs, but when the weather turned hot the bell-bottoms became cutoffs—some with a little cheek showing. Guys let their hair grow longer, some girls went braless when they weren't wearing bikini tops, and flip-flops became the footwear of choice. But that was about it. About the only things the Redneck Riviera's beach-going baby boomers picked up from the hippie movement, other than attire and music, was a more open attitude toward sex and the acceptance and use of marijuana.

Along the Redneck Riviera, if you wanted pot you could get it. Miles of deserted beach made the region a smuggler's paradise. Police departments in the few coastal communities that were incorporated were too small to do much more than break up bar fights, settle domestic disturbances, and investigate burglaries. So patrolling the beach became the responsibility of county sheriffs with occasional help from the Coast Guard. Enforcement was spotty at best. One Alabama beach bar owner recalls seeing pot boats with bales piled on their decks, anchored just beyond the second sand bar, waiting for local distributors to come out and pick up the merchandise. If the authorities did appear, smugglers simply threw the stuff overboard and headed out to sea. From the few times this happened stories grew and were circulated about people who wandered the shoreline "fishing for square grouper," terminology borrowed from the scavengers in the Florida Keys, where the practice of searching for jettisoned marijuana was more prevalent and more profitable. Also appearing about this time was a T-shirt picturing the mythical fish and the slogan "Save the Bales." We'll never know how much pot got through, but in the late 1970s a local officer proudly showed a reporter some pictures of a captured vessel and bragged how "we got seventeen tons of grass off that cabin cruiser yesterday. Buncha damn hippies runnin' it up from Mesko."

Fearing the influence that hippies might have on their youngsters, communities in south Florida cracked down on "hippie hangouts," head shops, and such, but on the Redneck Riviera those establishments were few and far between. Pot may have been smoked, but beer was still the drug of choice and the roadhouse was the beer-drinking baby boomer's home away from home. All along the coast there were bars and clubs and honky-tonks where people could spend their nights and their money after spending a day on the sand and in the water. Tucked in among the "family" amusements, yet far enough away to shield the innocent from what they had to offer, these establishments may have attracted as many to the coast as did the rides and arcades—or at least they seem to hold more memories than the twists and turns on the "longest and fastest" roller coaster in the world, the tilts and jerks of the Tilt-a-Whirl, and the spins of the umbrella rides. The problem with describing and discussing these watering holes is that there were so many of them, and so many tourists visited them, that any attempt to include them all surely would fall short. Instead I will cover two representative establishments, both mentioned earlier, that just about every coastal barhopper claims to have visited: the Flora-Bama Lounge and Package Store, on Perdido Key, and the Green Knight, on the eastern edge of Destin. Both have remained fixtures on the coast for many decades, but it was in the decade after the sixties supposedly ran their course that these two institutions came to symbolize what the Redneck Riviera was all about.

Most people have forgotten that the Green Knight began as an effort to bring fine dining to the land of oyster bars and seafood platters. Norma Calhoun, who started working as a cocktail waitress in the lounge in 1973, tells of how at the start waiters in tuxes "served appetizers on Grecian urns," while diners surveyed a menu that included lobsters flown in from Maine. The Knight quickly became popular with Destin's upper crust and soon "all the middle-aged crowd would go there, have dinner" in a relaxed, refined setting, and head home early. The Green Knight was tasteful, proper, and, before long, losing money. Fine dining had a limited appeal among Destin's one thousand year-round residents. Visitors who came to the town to fish were mostly beer and gumbo folks. So it was not long before the restaurant had exhausted its market. Something had to be done to broaden its appeal or the Green Knight would have to close its doors.

The answer was in the lounge.

The Green Knight's lounge, where Norma worked, seemed to have been added almost as an afterthought. It was "a small place," she recalls, "for maybe seventy-five people to have a drink and a smoke before dinner." But as the restaurant began to fail, the owners asked Norma to build up the lounge's business to balance the books. She did, thanks in part to the arrival of Phil Calhoun, the man she eventually married. Phil came to Destin to work construction. In the late 1960s and early 1970s the village began to grow. It got its first high-rise, the Hawaiki, in 1971, so Calhoun's skills as a trim carpenter were in demand. But in 1974 the boom burst and the carpenter turned to a new line of work—lead singer for a group called the Trashy White Band. So it followed that when the Green Knight's owners finally gave up and closed the restaurant, they converted the space into a lounge and package store, promoted Norma to bar manager, and hired the Trashy White Band to entertain. This is the Green Knight most folks remember. The band's name on the sign out front signaled customers that the place was

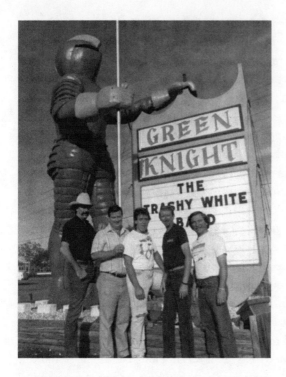

The Green Knight and the
Trashy White Band, Destin,
1970s. *The Destin Log* and
Norma Calhoun.

going to offer something very different from tuxedoed waiters, Grecian urn appetizers, and lobster. The Green Knight was about to become "the partying place of Destin."

"You've got to understand," Norma told the local newspaper years later, in the early 1970s "there was nothing in Destin—no street lights, no street signs, really no city lights, bars were the social thing. People enjoyed the atmosphere of drinking and the fun—we had more of a family party atmosphere." Phil recalls much the same, but with a twist of timing that resulted in two shifts. "At the lounge we usually had the afternoon crowd, [then] about eight o'clock we started to get the nighttime people." The audience to which he "played five, six, seven nights a week" was a diverse bunch—"you would see very rich people with very poor people, fish heads with construction workers"—and since there was not much competition, they all came to the Green Knight. It was, according to Calhoun, "a great place to play." It was also a great place to be played to, as one woman from south Alabama recalled. On a whim she and some friends left after work on Friday and three hours later arrived in Destin about the time the band got into its first set. She remembers the Knight as a classy place, a nice lounge, and recalls how Norma made the group feel "right at home." One girl in the party fell "in love" (or at least "in like") with the drummer, which gave them an excuse to come again and again—not that an excuse was needed.

While the Green Knight evolved into "the partying place of Destin," the Flora-Bama aspired to be *the* partying place on the Alabama coast from the start. But while the Knight had the field to itself, the Bama had competition. Where once travel magazines assured families that the one thing they would not find along Alabama's beaches was a "nest of honky-tonks," by the 1970s travel magazines were telling visitors that if they were looking for entertainment on the Alabama coast they could find it "in one of the many local night spots." Though families were still the backbone of the tourist trade, more and more people were coming to the coast for the things families didn't do—and there were plenty of places to do them. There was the Pink Pony Pub on the beach in the heart of Gulf Shores, next to the Hangout, where college and high school students drank beer bought with fake IDs and danced the night away. There was the Bear Point Marina where in the late 1970s Robert Jones, a writer for *Sports Illustrated*, found a parking lot "jammed with pickups, most of them costly 4-WDs with customized paint jobs." They had been driven there by "skinny, sunburnt men in Levi's and workshirts, with scuffed cowboy boots and baseball caps cocked back on their foreheads to reveal the badge of a farmer, that blanched expanse of skin where the cap has shaded the face." These were men from inland, hardworking, hard-playing men, "half shot with drink" and wearing "the faces of Confederate dead in Mathew Brady photographs." And there were roadhouses like the L.A. Pub and Grub, the Seagull Lounge (better known as the "Dirty Bird"), and the Jolly Ox, where, the story was told, "a good old boy once decked [Kenny] Stabler without warning just to see if he could handle a professional athlete."

Stabler and his friend and fellow pro quarterback Richard Todd, both Alabama natives, were what drew reporters from *Sports Illustrated* and the *New York Times* down to the coast. And when Stabler and Todd weren't "racing boats and trucks and anything else that moves," you found them in places that were air-conditioned, served beer, and had a pool table and jukebox. If the joint served food, all the better. Of the many bars that fit this description, the Flora-Bama was at the top of their list. Stabler and

The Flora-Bama fully formed and before Hurricane Ivan. From Mullet Toss photo display folder in possession of the author.

Todd were bookends for the baby boomer generation. Stabler was born on Christmas Day, 1945. Todd was welcomed into the world in November of 1953. Todd grew up in Mobile. Stabler was from Foley. Both were University of Alabama, Bear Bryant–coached quarterbacks who liked nothing better than "cooling out in the offseason" after a hard year in the NFL. From January to the opening of training camp in July they set the standard for what folks could get away with down there. It was this culture that inspired Howell Raines to christen the coast "the Redneck Riviera," and the moniker would stick.

In the minds of many, Kenny Stabler has become what the Redneck Riviera is all about. Growing up about fifteen miles from Gulf Shores, he hunted, fished, ate what he killed and caught, ate what other folks killed and caught, was a football hero in high school and again in college—except for when he was suspended for "training in beer joints"—an All-Pro quarterback with a Super Bowl ring and a top-dollar home on Ono Island, the gated community within sight of the Flora-Bama. Along the coast he was known for "drinking more beer a day than any four Milwaukeeans [and] boogieing late into the night at roadhouses." In 1978, he told Raines, "I enjoy hanging out with the guys and riding around in pickup trucks, shooting pool and drinking beer." Then he added, "Neither of my wives could understand that."

Nor could those folks who believed that once in the public eye, celebrities should alter their behavior to set a "good example" for those who admire them. Which begs the question, "a good example of what?" Kenny Stabler was a fine example of what people felt the redneck of the Alabama Riviera should be. And in time, living up to that example, that image, would get him into a lot of trouble. But during the summers of the 1970s, before his vacation was over and it was time to go back to work, he and friends such as Richard Todd and "Wickedly Wonderful Wanda," Stabler's lady du jour from up in Robertsdale, lived the life so many wished they could. When a reporter asked if all the stories about him were true, Stabler replied, "I live the way I want to live, and I don't give a damn if anybody likes it or not. I run hard as hell and don't sleep. I'm just here for the beer."

And the beer was at the Flora-Bama.

In the 1970s the Bama had become known as a "good place to get a black eye." Stories of scuffles and fights were plentiful, but the classic remains what became known as the "battle of the Flora-Bama."

It started when Billy Walker—"a fishing captain with the arms of a Russian weight-lifter and the vestige of a Mexican bandit"—got in an argument with another patron over something that happened in the Auburn-Alabama game. The argument turned into a fight and in the struggle the other guy's thumb ended up in Billy Walker's mouth. So he bit it off. Naturally the wounded combatant took Walker to court, and Billy's wife, Lois Gayle, was brought in to testify. Accounts vary as to just what was said, but according to one telling the judge asked Mrs. Walker, "Were you there when Billy Walker bit the man's thumb off?"

"No your Honor," was the reply.

"Then how do you know he bit it off?" the judge asked.

"When I came in he spit it out."

The Flora-Bama was also, according to Stabler, "the best watering hole in the country," and according to many, he should know. And the man who made it so was Joe Gilchrist who, with his partner Pat McClellan, bought the Flora-Bama in 1978—one hundred dollars down (all the money he had) and loans from their friends. In the years that followed the partners turned the Flora-Bama into the landmark it is today.

Adding to the jumble of rooms that were already there, Gilchrist and McClellan eventually created a complex of bars and stages that appeared to have been designed as "summer camp for convivial drunks." There they drew in people as much for the music as for the beer and whiskey. The result was clientele as diverse as found in any establishment along the coast, including the Green Knight. Bankers and bikers, long hairs and short hairs, sorority girls and good old girls, fraternity boys and good old boys, you name it, the Bama had it. Word was that on any given night "you can holler 'Bubba' and fifteen people will respond." In this open, freewheeling atmosphere, things just happened, as they did the night when "a rash of women," energized, uninhibited, and beer bleary, began pulling off their bras and throwing them at people. Some who caught the missiles decided to nail them to the walls for all to see. Later a rope was stretched high across the room and instead of throwing their bras at someone, girls started throwing them up to dangle from the line. Inspired by this, two of the Bama's regular musicians—Rusty McHugh and Mike Fincher—wrote and recorded "I Saw Your Bra Hanging at the Flora-Bama." Some think of it as a love song.

Thus the Flora-Bama became known as the home of the "midnight rambler and honky-tonk rounder" and, in time, it was the place you *had* to visit if you were down on the Alabama coast.

However, Gilchrist and McClellan also cleaned up the Bama's image—just a bit. Although there remains to this day a feeling among some of the more upscale visitors that this is the sort of place where you should wipe off your feet when you *leave*, outlaw attitudes so often associated with redneckery are muted and to most patrons the Flora-Bama functions as a "socially egalitarian demilitarized zone . . . anchored by cold beer, zesty live music, and food good enough that it doesn't scare anybody away." In fact, the food is so good that *Bon Appetit* Magazine listed the Bama as "one of the best over-the-counter restaurants in the country." McClellan, while admitting that they make a special effort to serve fresh seafood, added that the person who reviewed their offerings "must have had a few beers and soaked in the atmosphere, and that's what swayed 'em." And when it comes to providing atmosphere, none would be better than the Bama. Over the years the Flora-Bama would sponsor, promote, and host a variety of events reflecting its redneck reputation (the Annual Interstate Mullet Toss comes to mind), revealing a devotion to civic duty (just about everything would have a charity aspect), and encouraging the creative urges of the talented (as with the Frank Brown International Songwriting Festival). In the process, the Flora-Bama would become an institution. But it would remain a beer joint. A redneck one at that.

Bras hanging from the ceiling of the Flora-Bama. Photograph by the author.

Gilchrist and McClellan of the Flora-Bama, and the Calhouns of the Green Knight, were among the many owners and operators of coastal road-houses and honky-tonks, shrimp shacks and souvenir stands, who did not ignore the basic principles of business, who worked hard to make a profit, but who also had fun doing what they did and felt good about it. While not all could claim a business ethic like the one Gilchrist espoused—"doing well while doing good"—folks who visited their establishments knew they were in it for more than the money. They also knew that if there were no money there would be no Bama and no Knight, so they spent accordingly. It was a mutual agreement that no one had to sign.

However, there was another element working its way through the coastal economy, shaping it into something different from what visitors found at the Knight and at the Bama, and it was exposed at, of all places, a celebrity roast in Foley, a charity fundraiser where the guest of honor was their own Kenny Stabler. Writer Robert Jones was there and recorded it all. Under the Japanese lanterns strung among the trees at the mayor's house, guests moved about to the sound of the bug zappers doing their job, mixing and mingling until they were called to sit down to steaks and shrimp and listen to folks gleefully rake their local hero over the coals. What struck Jones was the "odd contrast" of those attending. One group was made up of "the Foley upper crust, matronly, Rotarian with cash-register eyeballs." The other was "the Stabler gang, raffish, sunburnt, hard of hand and piratical of glance." It was an interesting combination.

Less than a decade later historian Emory Thomas came down to the coast and found a region much changed. Where once there were roadhouses and honky-tonks, shrimp shacks and souvenir shops, mom-and-pop motels and a teenagers' Hangout, he found high-rise condominiums rising, upscale homes under construction, and a new sort of beach booster hard at work. Looking at these promoters, Thomas felt that the two groups Jones found at the Stabler roast "had mated and produced a new generation of raffish Rotarians, pirates with cash register eyeballs, and hard-handed matrons." Lower Alabama had become, as locals would say, "big bidness." The Redneck Riviera had "gone Sun Belt."

And what had caused this transformation?

A hurricane named Frederic.

But before Frederic, there was Eloise.

To get a sense of what these two hurricanes did to the Redneck Riviera, we need to consider once again the larger picture of coastal development. In the early 1970s a transformation began that would signal the decline of the unsophisticated amusements in the Panama City Beach area, open the door for beachfront development along the Destin strip, and even bring newer and bigger buildings to Gulf Shores. The TV show–inspired parks—Petticoat Junction and Tombstone Territory—faded as the shows lost their popularity. Their end was not immediate, but declining attendance meant less money for upkeep, and the shabbier they got the fewer people who came to visit. However, by then the overall economy hardly felt the loss, for in the early 1970s a building boom hit the coast. All of the resort communities were affected, but none more so than Destin. Between 1971 and 1973, low inter-est rates and liberal lending policies put over four thousand single-family homes and condominium units on the drawing board. Similar construction was planned for Panama City Beach, Gulf Shores, and points in between. Even beach villages like Seagrove and Grayton saw new cottage construc-tion, while along recently opened sections of Highway 30-A (the road my grandmother opposed) developers were buying beachfront property and getting construction loans. Significantly, most of what they intended to build was designed for people who wanted something a little more upscale,

Hurricane Eloise damage to the author's family cottage, Seagrove Beach, September 1975. The road in front, the road the author's grandmother opposed, is what will ultimately be Scenic Highway 30-A. Author's collection.

a little more "plush," than what was available a decade before—and they were willing to pay a little more to get it. The "raffish Rotarians" and "hard-handed matrons" were turning their "cash register eyeballs" to the coast.

But their timing wasn't quiet right.

First came the OPEC oil crisis of 1973, with gasless Sundays and talks of rationing. Although the summer season was over along the Redneck Riviera, fewer of the northern visitors, the ones they were beginning to call "snowbirds," made the trip down, so the economy suffered. Then, in 1974, what the oil crisis did not disrupt was undone when the Federal Reserve System's efforts to cool off inflation resulted in higher interest rates and tighter credit. New construction almost came to a halt. Meanwhile, people who had planned to rent their newly purchased condominiums to help pay the mortgage found the rental market depressed and units standing empty. Foreclosures followed. Then some condo owners—at least the ones with good insurance—got help from an unlikely source: Hurricane Eloise.

In September 23, 1975, Eloise slammed into the Florida Coast, a Category 3 storm with winds up to 125 MPH. The eye came ashore between Destin and Panama City—my family likes to think it passed over our place at

Seagrove—and caused damage all along the beach. Most coastal communities experienced hurricane-force winds and property losses. When we finally got back to my grandmother's cottage we found the porch gone and half the roof missing. There was a yellow substance on the walls and it took us a minute to figure out that it was mustard. Someone had left a jar of it on the table, and when the roof came off, the wind picked up the jar and swirled it around, turning the room into a yellow Jackson Pollock painting. Cleaning that up was no fun. However, Eloise did her worst at Panama City Beach, where the newspaper told of "cottages, motels, restaurants, convenience stores, and other beach businesses [that] were strewn across the highway in a tangle of downed power poles, lines, and busted mains." The Hangout, its arcade and its memories, disappeared. The news also reported that "a rush of wind and water tore through the first floor rooms" of the Roundtowner Motor Inn, one of the beach landmarks, "pushing contents out windows and doors. Debris was strewn for hundreds of yards inland, soaked with saltwater and coated with seaweed." Another witness recalled how the Roundtowner "looked like it had been hit by artillery." A short time later the coast was declared a disaster area, and that is what it was.

Eloise also marks the beginning of the end of some of the "amusements" that had once been popular redneck recreation. Already in financial trouble, a few of them, like the once popular Skyride, simply gave it up. Also surrendering were many of the old motels that had given the beach so much of its character. Most had been built on the south side of Highway 98, often on a concrete slab instead of deep-pounded pilings, and when the storm surge washed the sand out from under them their foundations broke and collapsed. That same storm surge destroyed every set of beach stairs between Panama City and Fort Walton, washed away sand far back into the dunes, caused evacuation problems for the many who waited until the last minute to get out, and, many residents claimed, deposited fish on the front porch of some cottages near the water. With the disaster declaration came the National Guard and soon the area was locked down tight—or as tight as it could be. Then slowly property owners trickled back in to assess damages, file insurance claims, and try to find someone who could repair things. Labor and materials were at a premium and fly-by-night operations were everywhere. Aware of this, my father put together a crew, loaded up with plywood and shingles, and headed down from his home about 150 miles inland. Working during the day and sleeping in the rear of the cottage, where the roof was still intact, they made temporary repairs and secured the building until Daddy could find a local professional who could do it right.

Although Eloise passed over Destin, most of the damage was on the bay side of the community. Beachfront rentals reopened quickly and the Destin Chamber of Commerce launched a campaign in the north and in Canada to let snowbirds know that if Panama City was not ready to receive them, the "luckiest fishing village" was open for business. The snowbirds came and rented and, in some cases, bought. Whereas Eloise added to the problems the collapse of the real estate market had caused along Panama City Beach, the storm actually helped Destin recover. In 1976, the year after Eloise, the local newspaper, the *Destin Log*, published a twenty-page supplement that announced that the community was no longer a "condominium graveyard" and listed the units that were on the market. During the next two years over $50 million worth of housing was sold in the Destin area. The village was on its way to becoming a place to go for something other than fishing. The transformation of Destin had begun.

SIX

A Storm Named Frederic

W HAT HURRICANE ELOISE did to the Florida Panhandle pales in comparison to what Hurricane Frederic did to the Alabama coast. It was not that the damage was greater (along the Gulf it was about the same); it was that Frederic drew not only a historic, but also a psychological dividing line in the sand. Since that September day when the storm hit, people along the beaches of Baldwin County have measured time as before and after Frederic.

Orange Beach and Gulf Shores had been hurt by the collapse of the real estate market, but not as badly as Florida, simply because investors were not as hungry for Alabama real estate as they were for developable land in the Panhandle. So condominiums came late to the Baldwin beaches. In the early 1970s a small, two-story complex was built down there. The units sold, even though the sellers had to convince the purchasers that there was nothing wrong with owning only to the center of each of the walls around them and that being governed by a condo association was not an infringement on their personal liberty. Once the papers were signed, the owners did what most condo owners did: stayed in their unit a few weeks out of the year and rented it the rest of the time. And rentals filled up. After years of promoting and hoping, the snowbirds finally came. Attracted by the mild climate and low cost of living, they took up residence in condos, cottages, and motels—especially those with kitchenettes—and in RV parks. Condos and motels were generally newer and better kept. The cottages were, to put it charitably, more rustic. On pilings sunk just deep enough to hold them, they were painted occasionally and patched up as needed. The son of one absentee owner recalled how his father once stopped the car on the way down to the coast to pick up a piece of lumber by the side of the road because it was "just what he needed" to repair the porch. But most of the cottages, condos, and motels located on the water had one thing in common: their builders had cleared the protective dunes and built on the sand. They soon wished they hadn't.

By the late 1970s there were still only fifteen hundred or so year-round residents in Gulf Shores and fewer than that in Orange Beach. However, during the summer more than thirty thousand tourists visited the area—a lot of folks, but few enough to allow the communities to maintain a small-town, friendly atmosphere that out-of-towners, most from small towns themselves, seemed to like. Because so many of the same folks came down at the same time and stayed in the same places year after year, coastal reunions were frequent and it was possible to say, as one Alabama tourist magazine did, "No one is a stranger in Gulf Shores."

This was the Redneck Riviera—a place where visitors and residents "enjoyed ideal beachfront living . . . with gentle surf at their door steps"— or so the brochures said. There was one chain motel, a few mom-and-pop hostelries, a souvenir shop or two, and the "nest of honky-tonks" that weren't supposed to be there but were. There was that first condominium, the Hangout, cottages with absentee owners and homes for the permanent residents, some docks, boats big and small, and an infectious laid-back attitude. You could see signs of progress if you looked hard: a better sewage and water system, a new bridge over the Intracoastal Waterway, improved fire and police protection in Gulf Shores, and close to where the old Sand Castle cottage was located the concrete had been poured for the slab of a new, ten-unit complex, also called Sand Castle, which was to be the first condo development on the beach east of Alabama Highway 59, the road that brought most visitors to the shore. But that would have to wait. Hurricane Frederic would come first.

Ever since Hurricane Camille in 1969, Gulf Coast residents had been paying careful attention to storms. Better warning systems—hurricane hunters, weather satellites, and such—alerted folks to what was happening that September of 1979, as a storm named Frederic soaked the Leeward Islands

The Gulf Shores Hangout before Frederic. Courtesy of the Mobile Press-Register Collection, Doy Leale McCall Rare Book and Manuscript Library, University of South Alabama.

and Puerto Rico, weakened over Cuba, reformed and intensified in the Gulf, then took aim at Alabama. As it got closer the word spread: board up and get out. Thus began what was, at the time, the largest evacuation in Gulf Coast history. Half a million residents from Alabama, Florida, and Mississippi packed what they could and headed inland. The escape routes were not ready for them. Mostly two-lane and rural, the roads quickly became clogged and in some places traffic stopped entirely. Apparently assuming that what brought folks in could take folks out, the states had done little to prepare for such a massive response to the call to leave. Remembering stories from Camille and more recently Eloise, few folks chose to ride it out. Coastal villages became ghost towns. Meanwhile, inland motels filled, upcountry folks opened their homes to the refugees, and communities away from the Gulf set up shelters in schools and churches. There evacuees waited for word from home.

The news was not good. Folks who had stayed had known it was going to be bad just by watching the birds: one resident recalled how gulls "huddled in a triangular shape trying to stand against the wind, only to be knocked over like bowling pins." Then they would "get up, reform in the triangle shape, another bird would take the point and within a few minutes it would start all over again." Just before dawn on September 13, the eye of Frederic made landfall on Dauphin Island. Gulf Shores, some twenty miles to the east, was hit by the northeast side of the storm, the strongest, with 125 MPH sustained winds. Gusts up to 145 MPH were recorded before the gauge

The Gulf Shores
Hangout after Frederic,
1979. Courtesy of the
U.S. Army Corps of
Engineers Collection,
Doy Leale McCall Rare
Book and Manuscript
Library, University of
South Alabama.

blew away. Even worse, Frederic brought with it a fifteen-foot storm surge. Water washed across Pleasure Island, damaging and destroying everything in its path. Beachfront homes were shattered and the debris was carried out into the Gulf and back into the lagoon. Buildings were picked up off their foundations, leaving behind the outlines of what had once been condominiums and motels. As for the birds, looking around after it was over observers reported that "there were not a lot of birds left."

From the air the Gulf Shores Holiday Inn appeared to have sustained minor damage, but on the ground inspectors found that on the first floor there were "only empty cubicles where rooms had been." Gone were the front and back walls, gone were the windows, gone was the furniture. "The motel," a writer from *National Geographic* noted, "resembled an abandoned honeycomb." It was the same up and down the coast. In the motels and condos only a few units survived, and those had been gutted. As for the beach, the dunes that had not been leveled by developers were leveled by the storm. Tons of sand had been taken from the shore and deposited on the beach highway. Most roads, washed out or covered with debris, were impassable. The bridge across the Intracoastal survived, but that was one of the few bright spots in an otherwise dismal picture. Alabama's Redneck Riviera was in ruins.

Then the refugees started coming back. It was not easy. Proof of residence or property ownership was required to get across the Intracoastal, not that

Damage from Frederic, 1979. Courtesy of the U.S. Army Corps of Engineers Collection, Doy Leale McCall Rare Book and Manuscript Library, University of South Alabama.

there was much on the beach side to return to. National Guard troops patrolled the streets and roads and watched for looters, but there were few, for there was not much left to loot. For locals who had thought the coast was overdeveloped before the storm, who had complained of the first condo and the little commercial zone, Frederic "seemed a biblical and logical response" to man's excesses. For others it was a deeply personal tragedy. Sand Castle, the cottage, and those like it were simply "erased" from the beach. A member of the family that owned Sand Castle recalled that it appeared "a tornado must have whipped through; not a piling, not even a dune remained." When he was finally able to get to the site all he could do was dig out "a rusted lamp from the blank beach." The rest of his family's possessions, along with "the wreckage of a thousand other families," floated somewhere out in the Gulf. It was surreal. There were dead fish in the trees and up on the porches of houses that survived. Freshwater lakes were flooded; the lagoon was full of all sorts of debris—power poles, downed wires, refrigerators, stoves, septic tanks, and mattresses. There was no drinking water, no ice, no telephones, and no electricity to run the gasoline pumps even where gas was available. What they had they shared. The owner of the Anchorage nightclub found a butane stove still working, so folks brought food and set up a community restaurant. Hazel's cafe, a fixture in Orange Beach, was able to open and in the days after the storm served meals to over one thousand people—none more grateful than the Guardsmen.

The damage was less extensive in Orange Beach than in Gulf Shores, but it was bad enough. The state park was hit hard, private homes were knocked off their stilts, the Perdido Pass Bridge was put out of commission, and the Flora-Bama was wrecked. Because of the evacuation there was only one coastal casualty, a man who fell out of his boat and drowned near Pensacola. But in the aftermath the emergency room at South Baldwin Hospital treated a number of chainsaw accidents, which occurred when people who had never used chainsaws before tried to clear trees and limbs. Once the coast was declared a disaster area, aid was rushed in and the cleanup soon began. Then came the rebuilding. Then came the developers. Then came the change.

Timing, of course, is everything. People who had lost it all and wondered how they could afford to rebuild discovered that there were people with money (or good credit) who wanted to buy their little parcel of land and would pay well for it. So they sold. Then developers patched the parcels together into bigger parcels, raised construction money, and with that financing raised buildings that, because of the stricter building codes, were "higher and better" than their predecessors. It all seemed to happen so fast. A little over a decade later, in 1992, National Hurricane Center director Robert Sheets testified before Congress about the impact that storms had on the coast and, more important, about the recovery. "Prior to Hurricane Frederic," he told the committee, "there was one condominium on Gulf Shores, Alabama. Most of the homes were single, individual homes behind the sand dunes. Today where there used to be one condominium, there are now at least 104 complexes—not units, complexes—on Gulf Shores, Alabama."

Meanwhile, over to the east, Panama City Beach and Destin, recovered from Eloise, were experiencing similar growth. Federal disaster relief, low interest loans, and a recovering economy surely played a part in this, but what was happening there and eventually all along the coast was that investors and investment opportunities were converging in a perfect storm of economic activity that would redefine the Redneck Riviera. By the 1970s many of the parents of the baby boomers had retired. Houses they'd bought on the GI Bill back in the 1940s and 1950s were paid off, their kids were grown up and away, and the old folks were ready to relax. A goodly number of them decided to do it on the Gulf Coast. Meanwhile, their children were in their thirties and even their forties. Many had carved out careers, were earning good incomes, and were paying mortgages on homes bought when prices were low. They had kids about the same age as they were when their parents brought them to the beach in the 1950s and 1960s, and they wanted to carry on the tradition. Some had disposable income they wanted to invest, and there were developers who were ready and waiting to give them something to invest in.

Every investment situation had its personal twist, its individuality, but the result was usually the same. The investors were a mixed bag. There were retirees from the lower South, looking for condos they could buy, use, and rent to snowbirds. Then there were northern visitors who enjoyed the milder winter weather and low cost, but got tired of renting so they bought a unit to stay in during their season and rent out during the summer. Another group consisted of better-off boomers from the lower South who had come to the coast as children and wanted to recapture those wonderful days of their youth and share the experience with their kids, while picking up a little rental money on the side. Finally, there were boomers from the North who came down to visit the old folks in their "snowbird nest," liked it, and purchased one of their own. The process was simple and the credit was easy. Little down, low payments, long mortgages, rental income, tax breaks—it was investment heaven.

And of course there were the renters. Middle- and lower-middle-class folks, from the deep South in the summer and from the north in the winter. They might not have a financial investment in the coast, but their personal investment bonded them to the beach by ties almost as strong as those who actually owned property there. Down for their two-week vacation, down with the kids, down for family reunions, down to spend a month or two in the RV park, or just down for a weekend to party at the Knight or the Bama, whatever the reason and however they were able to manage it, for the time they were there they considered themselves as much a part of the beach as anyone. And beach folks welcomed them with open arms, or at least some of them did.

This wave of immigrants, transients, and investors had much in common with the tourists and investors who had come down after World War II—much, but not everything. Though just as white, they were a little more affluent, a little better educated, and, at the upper end of the socioeconomic scale, a little more sophisticated than their predecessors. All that notwithstanding, be they summer guests or snowbirds, they came to the coast because they could do things there that they could not do at home—even just avoid the snow.

But the beach was also beginning to attract more folks who could not be called rednecks and would not want to be. One of the first resorts created by and for this group was Pinnacle Port. Begun in the early 1970s, it was nestled between the Gulf and a lake out at the far west end of the Panama City beach strip. When completed the $60 million project would be a world unto itself—upscale condominiums, elaborate landscaping, winding roads, indoor and outdoor pools for the folks who love the beach but don't care for sand and salt water (yes, there are some), tennis, docks, fine dining, a lounge, and even a small store in case a visitor wanted to cook a little something back at the condo or buy a souvenir. About the only thing missing was a place to "juke." If they wanted to do that, visitors would have to go back toward Panama City. Young folks did. The older, more settled ones had a drink at the bar, a nice meal, and maybe a walk on the beach so the little kids (or grandkids) could chase ghost crabs. If the youngsters pestered them enough they might take them to Miracle Strip Park, where the amusements so loved by the less sophisticated were clustered, but otherwise those things were kept comfortably at a distance. The people who came to Pinnacle Port came to the coast for many reasons, but rednecking it up was not one.

Something similar was happening at about the same time just to the east of Destin, where developers were going to work on some two thousand acres of land between the Gulf and the bay that once belonged to Arkansas governor Winthrop Rockefeller. They called their project Sandestin. Promoters claimed that they were out to create a community that was like what Destin was before it was transformed to a tourist destination, one that looked as if it had grown out of a New England fishing village (a nod to the origins of Destin's founders). What they created instead was a sprawling complex of hotels, condominiums, golf courses, town centers, and attractions that were designed for the upscale and affluent. "If you've heard the name 'Redneck

Pinnacle Port, the prototype of gated Gulf Coast resorts. Courtesy of
Bay County Public Library, Panama City, Fla.

Riviera,' take note," the development publicist announced when the site
was up and selling. "Sandestin brings new style to northwest Florida."

The Destin that Sandestin did not want to be was also taking shape. Not
long after the damage from Hurricane Eloise was cleared away, the *Destin
Log* noted that the community was unique because future growth was
unlimited and "plans to handle the growth are virtually nonexistent." It was
as if state and local government were conspiring with developers to turn the
coast over to them. In 1979 the Florida Legislature appropriated $4 million
for the state to buy 1.3 miles of beachfront just east of Destin that belonged
to local landowner Burney Henderson. Community leaders and developers
lobbied against it and Governor Bob Graham vetoed the measure. But the
developers did not get the land they wanted. Henderson held on and waited.

Despite that disappointment, developers were doing just fine. In an
even more development-friendly move the Florida Department of Natural
Resources pushed the "setback line"—the line beyond which no one can
build—closer to the water, which allowed construction on narrow strips
of dune south of Highway 98. In time this would make way for the "wall of
condos" that would line the Destin beaches and cut off inland folks from
the sand and the water. Also, by limiting access to the beach, these developments would drive up beachfront prices for those with money to pay. Where
once a beach cottage was affordable for people like my grandmother and

aunt—a retired state worker and an officer in the military—by the early 1980s these folks were priced out of that market. At the same time, beaches that were once considered open to the public were being declared private by the beachfront motels, condominiums, and homeowners. In 1972, faced with a similar situation, Californian voters approved a measure that declared that "development shall not interfere with public right to access to the sea." Florida made no such declaration, nor did Alabama.

Meanwhile, the Destin real estate market boomed and tourists kept coming, and because of this the Florida Panhandle and the Alabama coast felt less of the impact of the recession of 1981–82 than the rest of the nation. One realtor recalled running an ad in the early 1980s that read, "Termites holding hands is the only reason this house is still standing," and the property sold within twelve hours. Since there was not enough mainland property to satisfy the hunger, Destin area developers began to cast ravenous eyes at Holiday Isle, which most folks considered an undevelopable "sand pile, inhabited by a few birds and surrounded by water." The island protected Destin's fishing fleet. With the Gulf beaches on one side and the harbor on the other, Holiday Isle was a popular destination for teenagers, who boated across for clandestine parties and romantic trysts. I recall more than once looking at the island as our boat left the harbor and thinking, that there is one stretch of beach that can never be developed. The island was too narrow, the sand shifted with every storm—who would risk building there? Little did I know, for in the late 1970s and early 1980s what would be described as a struggle of "genuine epic proportion" would begin over who would control the future of Holiday Isle.

In the 1970s a group of developers bought portions of the island and began trying to get permits for roads and buildings, but without much success. In the meantime storms buffeted the island and offshore sandbars were pushed in to add roughly sixty valuable new acres to the shoreline. Beaches do not stand still; in most cases there is a natural shift of sand from east to west, though storms and tides can alter this significantly. Sand can be eroded and carried out into the Gulf, but sand can also be pushed in and added to existing land by the process of accretion. That happened on Holiday Isle. The question was, whose land was it? The developers who owned the beachfront to which the new land was attached said it was theirs, and in 1981 a group of them sued the state in an effort to get clear title and the right to develop it. They argued that nature can give just as surely as it can take away. The state attorney general, claiming the new land belonged to Florida, threatened to countersue. Meanwhile members of the Okaloosa County Commission argued that the developers must not own the land because they had paid no taxes on it. What followed, according to one observer, was a convoluted tale of "protagonists, front men, surprising twists, unknown ingredients, cover-ups, etc." that would make for a "first rate novel" one day. Finally, development-friendly legislators adjusted the rules so the island infrastructure could be built and condos could be constructed along the shore—a shore that moved with each new storm. The saga of Holiday Isle was far from over.

While developers, the community, and the state were in a tussle over Holiday Isle, folks who lived along the coast were coming to the realization that while county seat politicians were not watching their every move, they were not ignoring them entirely, and the residents didn't like the attention they were getting. When it came to collecting taxes the good old boys in the courthouse made sure the coast paid its fair share, and more. Roughly half of the revenue collected in Walton and Okaloosa counties came from south of Choctawhatchee Bay, but that region got few if any of the services enjoyed by the rest of the county. The tourist who paid the sales taxes and absentee property owners who could not qualify for homestead exemptions did not vote in local elections, so the politicians put the services where the voters were—inland. As early as 1976 there was talk of creating a Special Tax District for south Walton County, with the money to be allocated for increases in police and fire protection and emergency medical assistance, but nothing came of it. A few years later frustrated beach residents seriously considered asking the state to let them secede and create "Dune County." It didn't happen, but the controversy did raise the issue and expose a tension between the two sides of the bay that would only grow with time.

Gulf Shores and Orange Beach had the same problem, though Gulf Shores made up for the county's neglect by incorporating and providing services such as police, water, and sewage on its own. When the national economy dipped in the early 1980s, construction crews in Gulf Shores were kept employed building city buildings—a civic center, city hall, and public library—plus a new post office. Rebuilding the state park after Frederic also created jobs. At the same time the south Baldwin area got its first retirement village/golf community for those who wanted to be near the coast year round. By the middle of the decade Gulf Shores was operating like any small city would. A leash law and a sign ordinance were passed, the community pool was expanded, more paramedics were hired, and a new sewage treatment plant went on line. This last project was particularly important, for one of the reasons Gulf Shores got most of the initial condo development after Frederic was that it had a sewer system that reached down to the beachfront. Moreover, since the beach road was set back one hundred feet or more from the water, there was gulf-front property wide enough to accommodate a large development. In short, Gulf Shores was a developer's dream. Developers built more than condos: commercial real estate boomed. A Winn Dixie supermarket opened a couple of blocks inland and small shops clustered around it. What a writer from *National Geographic* called a "vacation colony" in the days before Frederic was catching the attention of more and more "destination vacation" families who wanted a spot within easy driving distance of home that had amusements enough to occupy their time while they were there. Gulf Shores was becoming that.

The market was hot. Though this was before the days of "flipping"— buying property to resell quickly rather than use—real estate agents were reporting that they "were selling the same piece of property three or four times in one week." But when the buyer who wanted the land got it, the property did not sit vacant. Until 1982, contractors could still use wood pilings and frames for their buildings instead of the more expensive and more time-consuming steel and masonry that would later be required, so small structures—condos, motels, and cottages—could be put up quickly, and they were. Orange Beach soon had its sewer system in place, and in 1981 it got its first condo development, the Breakers. Kenny Stabler bought Unit 12, his jersey number. Because there was so much selling going on, more and more people got into the real estate business. As they did, Gulf Shores and Orange Beach began to experience what other developing coastal communities had experienced before them—a disconnect between what developers and their agents said they were creating and what actually ended up on the ground. In 1980, members of the Kaiser family moved to the coast from upland Baldwin County to open a real estate office. Having grown up "exploring the beaches and back bays of south Baldwin County," one of them told of how he and his siblings wanted to help people "discover the same treasures [they] had found in their childhood." What they did instead was take over the management of Summer House on Romar Beach, one of Gulf Shores' first "upscale condo development projects," leaving one to wonder if purchasers could find in that high-rise the "same treasures" the Kaiser kids had discovered in the "beaches and back bays" when they were younger. Not that it mattered much to the people who bought the condos or rented them from their owners. Exploring beaches and back bays was not high on their list of priorities.

As far as priorities go, getting local government in place was moving up the list kept by some coastal folks. Though most residents loved the tourists and the money they brought in, and though they loved the developers who brought jobs and increased the revenue flow, there were those who were less than pleased with the way the community was changing. So, according to a locally produced history of the region, as a "means for preservation and conservation of a way of life born of pioneers whose lives revolved around the fishing industry," Orange Beach citizens banded together and in 1984, voted to incorporate. But it was too late. That genie was out of the bottle. In fact, in one of those ironic twists, incorporation may have hastened the end of the way of life supporters hoped to preserve. While most incorporation supporters were pleased to have a local police force to control the activities of those whose approach to leisure and labor were associated with redneckery, they found that better infrastructure and better services led to developments that appealed to people who did not come to the coast to preserve an old way of life but to create a new one. As new businesses opened to cater to the upscale, more discerning tourists, old businesses adjusted not just because they wanted to survive but also because they wanted to prosper. For better or for worse, incorporation did not preserve and conserve, at least not the way many of its advocates hoped it would.

Off to the east, Destin also incorporated, but it took two tries to settle the issue. More than most coastal communities (with the exception of Orange Beach), Destin, with its independent captains and crews and its do-it-on-my-own attitude, was leery of government and, especially, the taxes that were needed to run it. So in 1982, when local boosters put the question to a vote, incorporation lost, 1,251 to 796. But in the next two years the tide turned, slightly. In 1983–84, condo sales in Destin doubled to over $200 million and growth reached the point that a moratorium was declared on sewer connections. Destin's own "raffish Rotarians" and "hard-handed matrons" could see development coming to a screeching halt if more was not done to accommodate growth, and they knew that inland interests were reluctant to help the coast, even though it was a cash cow for their projects. So in 1984 a second vote was held and this time incorporation won, barely. Although it would take a while before the city could know for sure just how much property was included within its limits, the vote opened the door for more development, and developers flocked in. The deal was basically this: The city would take tax money generated by the growth and provide its citizens and visitors with a library, a community center, fire and police protection, and water and sewer services. In return, along with the money, developers would provide the city's citizens and visitors with accommodations, recreational shopping, recreational dining, fern bars and water parks, golf courses of the eighteen-hole and putt-putt varieties, resort hotels, and conference centers. Most folks felt it was a good trade-off—most, but not all.

Then there was the beach, which was what most people came for. In 1982, in what would be one of the most significant moves for the future of Destin, the State of Florida finally bought Burney Henderson's 1.3-mile stretch of shoreline and the undeveloped land behind it, for $13.1 million. Illustrating how land value in the area had risen, this parcel was essentially the same one that the state was set to purchase for $4 million in 1979, only to have the plan vetoed by Governor Graham. Three years later Graham's reservations and opposition were apparently overcome, for the deal went through. In the years to come, as a "wall of condos" lined the Destin coast and separated citizens from the shore, the city would have a public beach for inland folks to visit. But will it be enough?

Meanwhile, what was taking place in Fort Walton Beach stood in contrast to what was occurring in Destin, in Panama City Beach, and on the beaches of south Alabama. Although Okaloosa Island had its share of motels, amusements, and condominiums, back in the town itself things were very different. During the 1950s and 1960s, airmen from nearby Eglin Field moved into the city, where houses were cheap and the setting was that of a community instead of a military facility. They liked the town and the people in it, so when they were transferred, as men and women in the armed services regularly were, instead of selling their houses they kept them, fully expecting to return and retire when their tour of duty was over. While away they lived on base and rented their Fort Walton homes to other servicemen and their families. So, when they retired and returned, they came home to a house that was paid for, a low homestead-exempted tax bill, and all the amenities Eglin Air Force Base had to offer. In short, they had it made.

What benefitted these retirees did not necessarily benefit the city of Fort Walton Beach. While communities around them promoted tourism and development as a means to progress and prosperity, residents of the city wanted tourists to stay out on the island, away from them. This was not uncommon. As one observer explained, "Retired people don't want tourism. They don't want the traffic; they don't want any part of this. . . . They don't want the kids, they want to be left alone." Military retirees added an additional twist to the tale. They didn't take part in community affairs. Retirees from the business world came from a culture where executives were expected to join community organizations and participate in their activities; the military had no such expectation of its officers. So when they retired near a base such as Eglin, the base was where they focused their attention. The on-base resources retirees enjoyed, such as the PX, the officers and non-com clubs, the commissary, and the medical facilities, competed with local businesses and limited the revenue the city could raise. Why support building public parks, athletic fields, and swimming pools when you have Eglin's recreational facilities at your disposal?

Therefore, what developed in Fort Walton, and to a lesser degree in the Panama City area around Tyndall Air Force Base and in Pensacola, was a closed community, socially and economically insular, that resisted growth in the 1970s and became downright hostile to it in the 1980s, when Destin was booming. As a result Fort Walton changed little in size, wealth, or attitude during the years when other coastal communities were expanding and changing. It was in Fort Walton that Panhandle developers confronted for the first time an organized "no-growth" movement led by residents who were a far cry from the "pirates with cash register eyeballs" who were calling the shots in other communities. So the developers sought and found opportunities elsewhere. Fort Walton Beach lost businesses while other communities gained them, lost services such as a new hospital, and found itself down the list of places where people with new ideas for making money would settle. Instead it was Mary Esther, the tiny community just to the west of Fort Walton, that offered businesses and developers the support they wanted to settle there and the help they needed to expand. A no-growth, "not in my backyard" philosophy meant that Fort Walton would be largely free of the clutter, congestion, and glitz found in Destin. It also meant that residents of Fort Walton had to drive to the Santa Rosa County Mall in Mary Esther to do much of their shopping.

As for the rest of the coast, between Panama City and Destin the new beach highway 30-A was open, and traffic flowed slowly through Seagrove, around Grayton, through Blue Mountain Beach, to where 30-A connected with U.S. 98. But most of the land along the route was undeveloped, and without county infrastructure support, it was likely to remain so. The local wells supplied communities with often-foul-tasting water (but it made good coffee) and septic tanks were the sewage system. Easy access to undeveloped and unpatrolled stretches of beach opened the way for activities unknown, or at least unreported, in earlier days. Near the eastern end of 30-A the local gay community commandeered a stretch of lonely coast and made it their own. A few hundred yards off the road and hidden from sight by scrub and dunes, it became known variously as the "queer beach" for its homosexual clientele and the "nude beach" for the way most people who came there dressed, or didn't. Heterosexual swimmers and sunbathers were also welcome and many came. Complaints were few and law enforcement generally left well enough alone.

And the weather was good.

For the expanding, growing, developing Redneck Riviera the 1980s was a decade largely free of storms. The only difficult year was 1985, when four hurricanes—Danny, Elena, Juan, and Kate—made themselves known along the coast, but none caused anything close to the damage wrought by Eloise and Frederic. To the contrary, in some places the storms actually built up the beach, and along the shoreline a series of secondary dunes developed in front of the dunes and bluffs that sat inland. Even in Gulf Shores and Destin, where condominiums crowded the water, low dunes with sea oats seemed to pop up and promise that condos would be protected if a real storm approached. Uninterrupted by rough weather, construction continued at a record pace so that by the end of the decade it seemed that the Redneck Riviera was being transformed into something like Miami Beach.

SEVEN

Sorting Out after the Storm

*A*FTER FREDERIC, people along the coast collected themselves, surveyed the scene, and took off in different directions.

In Destin traditional redneckery rocked along despite a controversy created by a song sung by the Trashy White Band that used the "N word" to lament interracial love gone bad. Around the same time, a visionary with a block of undeveloped sand and scrub next door to Seagrove Beach set out to recreate the simple Florida of his youth and ended up creating something else altogether, something that was anything but simple. Meanwhile, over at the repaired and reopened Flora-Bama, singer-songwriter Jimmy Louis suggested that one of the dullest weekends of the year could be livened up a bit by throwing a fish across the state line. He was right.

First, the song.

It was around 1980. I was down at the coast and a buddy who lived there told me we needed to go to Destin and hear the Trashy White Band, so we did. Although I knew of the group, knew that they had helped transform the Green Knight from an aspiring upscale eatery into a top-notch redneck bar, it was the first time I heard them. They were good. But when they launched into what I soon found out was their signature song I was, to put it mildly, taken aback. "She Ran Off (with a Nigger)" was a sad account from the perspective of a man whose wife had left him for a black man. As the slur bounced around the room, I recall looking about to see if there were any black folks in the audience. There weren't. I didn't know at the time, but if all the black residents of Destin had been present, they barely would have filled a table. According to the 1980 census, only four of the town's 3,672 citizens were African Americans. That figure had doubled since 1970, when there were two.

Then, at the end, the singer lamented, "I never shoulda married that black little bitch anyway."

Introspection and irony.

Not what I expected.

The song, like the Redneck Riviera itself, appealed to and repelled people on many levels. But it is unlikely that folks outside Trashy White's circle of fans paid it much mind until early 1982, when the *Pensacola Journal* published an article titled, "Racist Song Lyrics Put Destin Band High on Local Charts." The article caught the attention of civic leaders and caused some to fear that the song might revive a controversy, which at that moment was just settling down. A few months before "She Ran Off" hit the news, a "racist pamphlet" that was circulated by an Okaloosa County deputy sheriff had threatened "to ignite racial tensions" in the area. To calm things down the Florida Human Relations Commission set up a local version of itself and told members to head off trouble when they saw it coming. Hearing of what was going on at the Green Knight, the Okaloosa council met and discussed the matter. However, "unsure if the song would come under their purview," they decided to wait for a formal complaint before taking action. None came. When asked, an African American club owner said he did not think the song would make much of a stir among his clientele. In his opinion it was "just one more gimmick to try to make money." The song was recorded, a few bars put it on their jukeboxes, and that was that until 1989, when the controversy flared again. The owner of a restaurant within earshot of the Green Knight sued to have the song banned, or at least muted, so diners would not hear it. The court refused to intervene, so the band played on. It plays on still.

While the saga of "She Ran Off" played out, a few months before the "racist pamphlet" appeared, a man named Robert Davis dropped in at the office of the *Destin Log* to tell the newspaper about his plans for the eighty-acre parcel of vacant Gulf-front property he owned between Grayton State Park and Seagrove Beach. Now the *Log* had heard development plans before, but what Davis wanted to do was different. Instead of another high-rise, he wanted to build "a village of some 350 homes and various public buildings including a meeting center, restaurants and shops." He told the newspaper that houses in his town would signal "a return to traditional seashore cottage design of yesteryear" and that design, plus the other things he planned, would inspire residents to return to a traditional way of living. He wanted to create what some folks would later call a "down home utopia." It is hard to say just how much of this Davis was able to get across to the reporter that day, for the press seemed more focused on his intent to ask the Walton County Commission to reroute Highway 30-A "so that the road would loop around his property and not through it." With road issues of its own—for Destin, U.S. 98 was both a blessing and a curse—that interest was not surprising. On the other hand it was unlikely that even Robert Davis could have predicted just what would happen to the community he was calling Seaside.

Davis came to his project with a number of advantages. To start with, he owned the land free and clear, having inherited it from his grandfather, one of the founders of Pizitz Department Store in Birmingham. That connection reportedly gave him financial support for his venture, which was important given the state of the economy in the early 1980s. So, without having to go trotting to the bank at every turn, Davis had the leeway to do pretty much what he wanted to do, which was take coastal development in a whole new direction.

Robert Davis was a romantic. He dreamed of recreating the Florida he had known when he came to the beach as a child. He wanted a community of coast-loving folks who lived in cracker cottages, sat on front porches in sweaty splendor, and talked with neighbors who walked by on their way to shop or to swim. He was also a businessman, though a "quixotic" one, with an MBA from Harvard and all that entailed. And he was a "visionary urban planner"—though his talents in this would mature over time with the help of some bright young architects he met while developing "tropical-modern" townhouses in Coconut Grove, near Miami. Stories of Davis and his brain trust sitting around drinking wine and beer and making plans for the future are part of the mythology that grew up with Seaside and how much of it is true depends on who you ask. What is clear is that from these early sessions came the layout for a town with narrow streets and small lots that would force people to interact with each other. Davis and his cadre wanted to create a "real town" populated by real people, and to make all this happen they put together a "building code, with its clear, systematic guidelines for proportions, dimensions, and materials" that they believed would attract schoolteachers and grocers and artists and writers and all sorts of residents who wanted to get "in touch with the simple pleasures in life" instead of "looking at the beach from the window of a condo." Seaside was to be a place where, as one of the early buyers later remarked, everybody would live together and "love each other . . . like back in the old days."

A "hippy-commune" quality permeated the concept, which was based on the idea that anyone who was "handy with tools" could handle most of the work on their houses. Owners were free to do what they wanted with the interior, but Davis and his code enforcers controlled what the house looked like to someone standing in the street. Screened porches, picket fences, and tin roofs were mandatory; construction had to be from materials available in the 1940s or earlier; and colors had to be approved in advance. All this conformity, Davis said, was intended to "convey a sense of time and ease—time for children and parents to grow closer and for families to know each other." The planners did not want "people sealed in an air conditioned refrigerator." They wanted a place where residents could "truly enjoy the indolence of the tropics."

The streets were surfaced with oyster shells, just like in pre-asphalt days, and laid out narrow with connecting footpaths that brought residents to a planned town center. There they would find a grocery, a hardware store, and other shops selling things the residents needed. Included in the plan were a cafe where villagers could gather, a meeting hall/community center, some offices, and a village green where children could romp. There was also talk of a school, a church, and even a cemetery. And of course there was the beach. With Highway 30-A running along the dune line and through the town (the county commission had not approved rerouting) the beachfront was separated from the main community. But as he would so often in years to come, Davis turned a setback into something positive. Apart from "the twin sharecropper cabins" that were hauled in and set up as the Seaside Grill, and Davis's wife's open-air market, the beach side of the road was to remain undeveloped—or at least that was what people who bought into the plan were promised.

No way around it, Seaside was different. Instead of the "instant beach-front high-rises" that were springing up all along the coast, Davis and his friends were out to create what *Time* magazine described as "a genuine town, with shops and lanes and all the unpretentious grace and serendipitous

"Panhandle, c. 1983." One of the first houses built in Seaside, it reflects the town's original "cracker cottage" emphasis. Photograph by the author.

quirks that have always made American small towns so appealing." It was designed to be a place where people of different classes, different incomes, and different occupations would live and work and be happy. If Davis pulled it off, according to *Time*, "Seaside could be the most astounding design achievement of its era and, one might hope, the most influential."

I saw it happen. When my grandmother and my aunt passed away, my father inherited the cottage and together we sat on our deck and watched Davis's "cracker houses on the wrong side of 30-A" rise out of the scrub and palmetto. We really did not know what to make of it—"shack vernac," we heard it called and even Davis admitted, "It's not sleek." But it was not a high-rise, and that made us happy. Some afternoons we would walk down to the Seaside Grill for beer and shrimp. There was a true neighborhood feel to the place. Construction workers from along the coast, people from the village, and folks like us from next door all crowded in there together. It was nice. The first houses were built on the cracker cottage design, just as Davis said they would be—though at the time most of us had no inkling that was his plan. His screened porches were like our screened porches. The picket fences were a bit much and the tin roofs that Seaside would popularize throughout the region had been prohibited by Seagrove's community covenant—too trashy for C. H. McGee, but just the "old Florida" touch Davis wanted. Still, all in all Seaside seemed to fit right in. Then they built the

Seaside Arch, beach pavilion, early 1980s. One of the first designer pavilions
built by the development/community. Courtesy of Bill Wright.

arch—a beach pavilion with steps leading down to the sand. Palladian and
eventually painted an eggshell blue, it looked like something you might find
among Roman ruins, not along the Redneck Riviera. When that appeared
we should have known that whatever Seaside was, it definitely was not
redneck.

While Seaside was taking the coast in one direction, off to the west, at the
point where Florida meets Alabama, the Flora-Bama was heading things in
another. Since Joe Gilchrist and Pat McClellan had taken over, the Bama
had begun featuring more music and putting on more events. It was still a
beach bar, and as good as it ever was. It still offered patrons the diversity
of a biker and banker crowd that welcomed everyone as long as they would
"do-right," and with just the touch of outlaw and sleaze that kept the excitement and the energy level high. But in time Gilchrist, McClellan, and the
regular musicians who entertained there noticed that the last weekend in
April was the deadest weekend in the year. Snowbirds were gone. Spring
Break was over. The summer crowd was yet to arrive. What could they do to
bring folks to the Bama?

So they thought and thought, until Jimmy Louis, one of the musicians,
said, "Let's have a contest." But what sort of a contest? Now at this point the
stories diverge. According to one account Louis had been out west where he
saw competitive cow patty throwing, so he suggested they have a throwing

Throwing the Mullet at the Annual Interstate Mullet Toss, 2010. Photograph by the author.

contest at the Flora-Bama. But what to throw? Someone, probably Louis, said, "Why not a mullet?" The other version of the story, told by Louis himself, was that the idea for the Mullet Toss "just came out of a fit of narcosis. I got stoned one night and thought it up." I've met Jimmy Louis, had a beer with him at Boys Town, the enclave across from the Flora-Bama, where musicians keep trailers and where the sailboat on which Jimmy lives most of the year was docked. And after hearing him tell of how he was lucky to be alive considering all the controlled substances he had ingested, though his memory may have been clouded, I accept his explanation.

Why a mullet?

To some folks, the mullet is a trash fish, a bottom-feeder, a scavenger, and the lowest of the low. Some folks say they aren't even fish at all; they are birds. A Florida court said so.

Michael Swindle in his book *Mulletheads* tells of how, back in the 1920s, three guys were arrested for fishing for mullet without a license, or something like that. They hired a Tampa lawyer named Pat Whitaker to defend them. Whitaker brought in a biologist who sat there and told the judge and jury that only birds have gizzards. This professional opinion was important because judge and jury knew enough about the mullet to know that a mullet has a gizzard as well. Therefore, Whitaker argued, his clients could not be convicted for illegally fishing because a mullet was not a fish, it was a

"Mullet Girls." These women measure the distance the mullet is thrown and make sure all participants follow the rules. Photograph by the author.

bird. Had to be—it had a gizzard. And the jury, faced with this evidence and logic, did the only thing it could and returned a verdict of not guilty. Pat Whitaker went on to a political career that led to the presidency of the Florida state senate. The accused were released and probably went back to catching mullet.

Because they have gizzards, mullet have been said to have mystical powers. Because they are so easy to catch with a cast net, they are popular among folks who fish for the pot. You won't find mullet served at restaurants with white tablecloths, but where they appear on a menu, if the waitress swears they were caught that day, order yourself a "mess." Filleted and fried fresh there is no fish better, and the backbones, fried with the meat left from the filleting, are known as "cracker popsicles." The mullet is the common man's fish, the "rabbit of the ocean" they call it, and it acts the way Riviera rednecks act—together. Mullet school, and sometimes the whole school will leap from the water, turn in midair, and flop back in (unlike most jumping fish, which reenter head first). Scientists have tried to figure out this odd behavior and about all they can come up with is that mullet leap "for the sheer joy of doing it."

So they created the contest.

On the beach, on the Florida side of the line, they set up a registration table. Folks signed in and selected a dead mullet from a bucket of water.

Then the contestant stood within a 10-foot-diameter circle and threw the fish down a 50-foot-wide, 200-foot-long alley and into Alabama—making the Mullet Toss an interstate event. "We are burdened with so many rules in this life," Gilchrist said, "mostly by the government, that we try to keep them to a minimum at the toss." And they did.

1. Stay in the circle.
2. Don't throw out of bounds.
3. No gloves.
4. No sand on the mullet—it has to be slick.
5. Only one throw with each registration.
6. "Mullet girls" will measure the throw, but you must retrieve your fish and put it back in the bucket to be used again.
7. And finally, you can kiss your mullet, but you cannot pour beer into it.

When the day was done the mullet were fed to the seagulls.

Thus, on a slow weekend in 1984, the Flora-Bama Interstate Mullet Toss was born. Beer flowed, fish flew, and the weekend was slow no more.

By the 1980s celebrations had become part of coastal culture. There were shrimp festivals, fishing rodeos, seafood festivals, music festivals—just about anything that could be celebrated was celebrated. An event could be as large and widely known as the Frank Brown International Songwriters Festival, named for the Flora-Bama's legendary night watchman, which drew participants from all over, or as locally focused and simple as the Seagrove Beach Fourth of July Parade. At first the parade was held on the beach with dune buggies participating, but when the road was paved, it moved there. It was purely a community event. After Bloody Marys and Mimosas everybody who wanted to enter gathered at one end of the village. Those who didn't parade stood on the side of the road to cheer. A former majorette who still had her boots and baton led the way, and after traveling the mile to the other end of town everyone adjourned to someone's house for more Bloody Marys and Mimosas and a barbeque.

Next door, Seaside events were equally simple—in the beginning. Even as the first house was being built, "Seaside Saturday" advertised "fresh produce, baked goods, flea market, arts and crafts, shrimp, beer and wine" for those who dropped by. Not everyone who saw this liked it. In the Seaside archives is a letter to Davis from a "Concerned Citizen of Walton County"

Early Seaside construction. The sign, like so much of Seaside, did not reflect the reality of the situation. There were fewer than ten permanent residents, but as far as Seaside was concerned, if you and your family were homeowners, you and your family were residents. Courtesy of Bill Wright.

saying, "The people of Seagrove are justly upset about the 'slung up' market place" and wondering why it could not be "built with a bit more distinction and class . . . something on the order of . . . the gazebo near the Destin East Trailer Park." For what it's worth, my family and I were not among the "concerned"—not yet anyway. But copying trailer park architecture was the farthest thing from Davis's mind. Shortly after a few houses were built, a writer from *Southern Living*, the how-to guide for Dixie boomers seeking to shake off redneck roots, ran an article with pictures taken so that it seemed the town was farther along than it actually was. Intrigued by the story, folks started stopping by. They listened to Davis explain his vision and some bought into it. Others just bought the land.

More publicity followed and Seaside capitalized on it. By 1983 the town had a public relations director who promoted activities that continued to stress Seaside's family focus and its community concern. August brought the Dog Days Festival to benefit the Walton County Search and Rescue Team and a womanless "Mess Seaside Beauty Pageant" to raise money for nearby Bay Elementary School. A Children's Festival was held to support the Coastal Heritage Foundation as well as the Community Benevolent Fund established by the Point Washington Methodist Church. Not everything had a charitable purpose, though. Some things were just for the fun of it. There were a Labor Day regatta, free movies, and an Open Air Bazaar for residents and visitors. But Davis was determined to do more than entertain. He wanted Seaside to become the cultural center of Walton County—a title for which there was not much competition. So there were poetry readings, a Festival of Fine Arts, and the first performance of the Seaside Theater. There were also wine tastings, a croquet tournament, an urban-planning symposium, and a cooking demonstration by food historian John Egerton, who helped those attending get back to their roots by teaching them how to make beaten biscuits and treating Seaside's increasingly sophisticated clientele to a "covered dish meal featuring authentic country ham and all the trimmings." "Authentic"—just like in the "old days."

Davis may have wanted folks at Seaside to enjoy the "indolence of the tropics," but in this frenzy of activity there wasn't much time for indolence. Which really did not matter, for Seaside did not attract the indolent. Nor did it attract the sort of folks Davis had intended to live there. To tell the truth, not many people lived there at all. Most of the folks who attended the goings-on were visitors, renters, who took over the houses the owners had built, paid big bucks for the privilege, and enjoyed all Seaside had to offer. Renting had not been part of the original plan, or at least not high on Davis's list of priorities. A "real town" is not populated by transients. But as more lots were sold, it became apparent, as one of the developer's early investors noted, that Davis was "pissing away his assets." Davis realized this as well and soon began to revise his vision, which wasn't too difficult considering it had been sort of fuzzy from the start. Although selling lots continued to be his main concern, there was also money to be made from running the rental agency and leasing business buildings in the town center. So that is what Davis did. As for permanent residents, as prices rose beyond what could be afforded by the shopkeepers, teachers, artists, and writers that Davis had hoped would live out his dream there, the developer began to shift his attention to the people who could pay the price. Because the recognition Seaside was getting was for urban design and architecture, not for the community and its people, design and style became the focus. Seaside became what Davis said it would be, "a way of life." Only one quite different from what he first envisioned.

A few more articles and an architectural award or two and Davis's "real town" began to be transformed into a tourist attraction. With so many things to do, more and more people came in to do them. They also came to find out if it could really be true. Grown-up baby boomers, the ones the media was calling "yuppies"—young urban professionals—saw Seaside as the cure for what ailed them. Affluent, educated, sophisticated, and for the most part southern, they had worked and hustled and gotten to the top (or were close) and were ready to enjoy it. Then one evening home from the office they picked up *Southern Living* or *Architectural Digest* and read about this town where they could do all those things they could not do at home—leave their cars parked and walk from their house to work to shop to play to be entertained, in ten minutes, with a child in tow. And a beach in the bargain.

So they went to see, rented a house for a week or two, and came away convinced that even if Seaside never became a "real town," the way property value was rising, it was a heck of an investment opportunity—and yuppies loved to invest. So they bought a lot, built a getaway, and gave it a creatively cute name such as Allegro or Toasty Sunset or Frumious Bandersnatch. You don't put names like that to just any house. A named house had to be something special, and these were. Beach bungalows and cracker cottages gave way to larger, more elaborate, more expensive houses, architecturally designed and designer decorated, tin roofed, gingerbreaded with turrets, decks, widow's walks, and porches. In the process Davis lost much of the control he had at the outset, and property owners took over the development of Seaside.

Those of us who watched it from older coastal communities called it "pastel hell," and we weren't alone in our opinion. *Palm Beach* magazine cast a discriminating eye at the community and warned that "one could overdose in Yuppie delight [for] the array of color is like visiting a candy store." Some of Davis's original group even complained of the "populist prettifying" that was taking place. Especially galling was the residents' decision to pave the dusty streets with brick. We set out "building Kansas," one collaborator complained, "but we're getting Oz." However, for renters and owners, Seaside was something else. Here was a place where affluent southerners could indulge their "pastoral urges." The town, with its colorful, whimsical houses, caught the spirit of maturing baby boomers. One of the town's architects later noted, in the "eighties Americans like[d] pretty things," and

Seaside house evolution. Homeowners began to stray from the "cracker cottage" design as the community grew. Photograph by the author.

if nothing else, Seaside was certainly pretty. It was also, as Davis observed in one of his frequent efforts to reconcile what was happening with what he originally wanted, a "horizontal condominium." The design, the plan, and the philosophy were all in place, but where he and his cadre "had *their* plans for life in Seaside," the dreamers found that "Middle America had [plans of] its own." Those plans included buying a lot, building a house, and paying for it with income from rent—just like folks who bought the high-rise condos in Destin, Gulf Shores, and Panama City did.

The fact that Seaside houses were built low—two stories and a widow's walk at the most—made those homeowners natural allies with people from surrounding communities who did not want their beaches taken over by high-rises. As Davis's town was taking shape, down the road, on the eastern side of Seagrove Beach, two multistory condominiums were built—jutting up from the dunes abruptly and towering over their neighbors. From the start the condos ran into problems. Because the Walton County Commission had neglected coastal needs, there wasn't enough water pressure to reach the upper floors, and the local sewage system was inadequate as well. How the developer even got a permit to build was the subject of much speculation. Locals hated the condos. But rather than write a "concerned citizen" letter to the developer, a group of residents made the trip to the county seat at DeFuniak Springs to put their concerns before the government that for so long had ignored them. The county commissioners welcomed them to the meeting, listened to their complaints, and then asked, "What do you want us to do about it?"

"Set a height limit," was the answer.

"Ok," was the reply. "How high?"

This caught the delegation by surprise. They had expected an argument, a delay, anything but immediate action. But with the condos already proving to be more trouble than they were worth, the commissioners saw no reason to let anyone build any more. So members of the board waited for an answer. And, the story goes, one of the protestors shouted out "fifty feet."

And that limit was set.

Development south of the bay would not be allowed to rise above fifty feet, four stories, and though from time to time developers have tried to find ways around the rule, so far they have failed. There would be no wall of condos along what tourist development folks would designate "Scenic Highway 30-A," which would be scenic because, as you drive along it, from time to time you can actually see dunes, sea oats, and the Gulf of Mexico—just like back in the old days.

By offering Walton County developers an alternative to the high-rises that were going up to the east and to the west, Seaside did the folks along Scenic 30-A a service. On the other hand the growing popularity of Seaside as a tourist attraction also had a negative impact on its neighbors. Davis may have wanted a community where folks could sit on their front porches and chat with people passing by, but the traffic going into and out of Seaside was so noisy that people living along the road were driven off their porches and into their cottages, into those "air conditioned refrigerators" that Davis's community vision was designed to discourage.

Seaside changed things in other ways, too.

Back in the 1980s, one of my favorite places to eat was a Cajun restaurant back on Highway 98, a few miles inland from the coast. One night we took some friends, including a couple from Atlanta. The wife from the big city would probably have been happier at a Seaside eatery, but she was a good sport and went along without a complaint. Dressed to the nines in her Land's End cotton sweater and her J. Crew cotton shorts, carrying a handbag that would have cost the lady who waited on us a week's salary, my friend looked around at the caps hanging from the ceiling, at the stuffed

Seagrove Beach, South Walton County's only high-rises. In the distance are the high-rise condos of Panama City Beach. If you turned around, in the distance would be the high-rise condos of Destin. These two condos are the only high-rises in between the two resort cities. Photograph by the author.

alligator, and then at the menu. Our waitress arrived to see what we wanted to drink. All of us ordered whatever was on draft, except the Atlanta lady.

"Do you have chardonnay?" she asked.

The waitress paused, looked perplexed, and then replied, "We don't serve no foreign beer here."

It was a great moment. But it didn't last.

A month or two later I returned for lunch to find a wine list. OK, it was written on chalkboard and said, "We have wine. Red, White, Pink." That was it, but there it was. I could see the future and it wasn't pretty. Soon business began to suffer. So they started serving appetizers, but it didn't help. The place became too trendy for the old crowd but not trendy enough for the new. A year later it closed. Today there is just a vacant lot.

The old landmarks were disappearing. The Blue Room in Destin, where I spent many a happy hour putting a dent in the crustacean population, was gone. Hangouts in Panama City and Gulf Shores had been taken away by hurricanes and not rebuilt. The Green Knight was still there and so was the Flora-Bama. But only one of them would see the twenty-first century.

Playing by Different Rules

Y THE MID-1980S, most counties along the Redneck Riviera had a tourism development council working hard to attract people to their stretch of beach, and the "TDC" stenciled stamp was appearing on everything from park benches to trash cans. Council promotional efforts sent a mixed message to visitors. The stamps, on one hand, suggested order and organization, cleanliness and consistency, safety and security. On the other hand, TDC advertisements that featured pictures of scantily clad young women, spilling out over their bikini tops, and the slogan "When you got it bad, Florida's got it good," suggested something else altogether. Though some critics found the line both "grammatically and morally incorrect," most Riviera visitors had little problem with it either way. The more sophisticated chuckled at it. The less so liked what it promised. Even more to the liking of both groups was another poster, also featuring a buxom young woman, which told folks, "Come to Florida. The Rules Are Different Here."

If nothing else, that was truth in advertising.

Alabama tourism officials could have borrowed the slogan and used it without fear of contradiction, for as has been noted before, no matter the state, when travelers crossed the Intracoastal Waterway and caught a whiff of the salt air, restraint went into neutral and they arrived at the beach knowing they could do things there they could not do, might never do, back home—and get away with it. They could sit on the sand in the sun, empty the cooler while the kids played in the surf, take a nap, and go out in the evening to eat something fried. They could fish in deep water or just float in the Crab Island shallows at the mouth of Choctawhatchee Bay, dive for hermit crabs, play water football, and wait for the ice cream boat to arrive. The options were limited only by the imagination. Meanwhile more-affluent visitors could go to Seaside or Sandestin and for a little while live in a fancy house or condo, eat at upscale restaurants, play tennis or golf or even croquet, drink wine, nibble cheese, and listen to chamber music at sunset. Whatever rules you wanted to follow or break you could follow or break along the Redneck Riviera.

You could also make money.

One of the many attractions of the coast was that the different rules opened the door for dreamers such as Robert Davis as well as for speculators who came down to get rich and get out. A lot of the latter group went to Destin.

Destin's cycle of economic ups and downs was re-created all along the Riviera, and though the rises and falls, the highs and lows, varied with the circumstances, they all came at about the same time and had many of the same consequences. But Destin seemed to come out better than the rest—or worse, depending on how you look at it. As Panama City Beach and its environs recovered from Eloise, Destin expanded to take up the tourist trade PCB could not handle. By the time Panama City Beach was back on track, Orange Beach and Gulf Shores were picking up the pieces left by Frederic, and folks who might have gone there but couldn't looked east and found Destin open for business. Then came the first shots in the Reagan Revolution. Congress passed the president's Economic Recovery Tax Act of 1981 which, among other things, allowed investors to avoid paying taxes by buying rental property. Taxpayers, according to a later *Destin Log* assessment, "took the bait and bought rental property, especially condos." Although the units might bring in little rental income, they "could justify the purchase based on tax benefits alone." Existing rental property was not enough to meet investor demand and the building boom began. The "Destin city bird," the *Log* noted, was not the pelican or the sandpiper, it was the high-rise construction crane.

With the boom came media attention. In 1985, *Good Morning America* did a feature on Destin as one of the "great places to vacation in America." It was great because it had beautiful beaches, deep-sea fishing, amusements, good places to eat, and condominium units to rent at a reasonable price. Where once cottages with kitchens attracted families, now condos, with all the features of luxury apartments, became the rage. A family could rent a condo to fit its size and budget, on or near the beach, with amenities not found even in the newer motels, of which there were not many, for few were being built. Between 1986 and 1999, the number of motel rooms in Okaloosa County and Destin rose 8 percent, from 4,104 to 4,436. During the same period, the number of rental condo units began at 2,088 and rose 111 percent to 4,413—by the end of the twentieth century there were almost as many condos on the rental market as motel rooms. It was much the same along Panama City beaches where during the same period motel units increased 11 percent, from 7,822 to 8,720, while condo units increased 45 percent, from 3,548 to 5,159. Pensacola Beach saw a 205 percent increase in condominium units, but because of the limited-growth views of its leaders and their restrained approach to condo development the actual numbers were relatively low, rising from 520 units in 1986 to 1,588 a little over a decade later.

This growth took place despite the fact that what Congress had given investors to get the boom started was taken away in 1986. Tired of hearing how "fat cats" were making a killing in rental real estate, senators and representatives passed another Tax Reform Act, which eliminated the incentives granted in 1981, and stripped away some earlier incentives as well. What really hurt was that investors could no longer offset write-off rental income with paper losses from the condos they purchased. Throw into this the savings and loan scandal, and soon the *Destin Log* was writing about "ghost condominiums," the products of real estate deals gone bust, leaving investors with nothing but weathered, faded signs bearing "fanciful architectural renderings." "Yep, there's my inheritance," the daughter of a "Destin wheeler-dealer" told a reporter down from Tuscaloosa to survey the scene. "Pointing to a rendering of one of the ghost projects" she sighed, "'nothing more than a pretty picture.'" But the bust was only temporary. Within a year the situation had changed and though she might have lost her money, others moved in and began making theirs.

This was also the time when TDC folks went to work branding what tourists had always called "the beach." Fort Walton Beach and Destin started calling themselves the Emerald Coast, a reference to the blue-green Gulf water that washed their shores. Panama City went its own way, brushing off an old slogan and declaring it had "The World's Most Beautiful Beaches," which it could rightfully claim because some travel publications said it was so. Even though those publications often included Seaside, Seagrove, and Grayton on that list, TDC promoters there simply lumped those together as "The Beaches of South Walton" and added "Emerald Coast" whenever it seemed to fit the advertisement. As for Pensacola, the town liked to call itself "The Western Gate to the Sunshine State," but Pensacola Beach would have none of it. "Pensacola Beach" was enough. Then there were those who wanted to make it more than coastal, so they called the whole region "Florida's Great Northwest." That didn't stick. As for the Alabama beaches, over there the "raffish Rotarians" were happy enough with "Pleasure Island." Although Gulf Shores and Orange Beach were where "Redneck Riviera" was heard first and, of all the coastal resorts, where it will be held to the longest, for some reason TDC folks shied away. Most people who came down didn't seem to care one way or the other. Wherever they went, they were just going to "the beach."

Helping the region through these hard times was the rapid growth of the winter economy, with snowbirds arriving in greater and greater numbers. Again, demographics had a lot to do with this. These were retirees from the north—the Midwest mostly—who had come out of World War II with GI benefits that included low-interest loans for a home and money for an education. They made the best of both, got blue- and white-collar jobs during the 1950s, worked their way up through the ranks, and by the 1980s were ready to spend their pension and Social Security checks in a place where there wasn't any snow. Sprinkled among them were Canadians, who came for the same reasons the others came—climate, proximity, and price. Most snowbirds were comfortably well off, but not rich. They were also active and wanted to do more than sit in the sun and beachcomb. Typically coming as couples, they looked forward to meeting other couples and doing things as a group. They were friendly, sociable, white, and solidly middle class.

The coast needed them, and not just for the money they spent—which was never as much as local businesses wanted (the running joke was that a "Snowbird came down with a double-knit shirt and a $100 bill and didn't change either"). However, what northern visitors spent kept stores open and year-round clerks employed. Restaurants that once closed for the winter continued to operate, and though customers who came for the "early bird specials" and "all-you-can-eat" buffets were not as profitable as the summer trade, the businesses did not have to hire extra help as they did in the summer. Snowbirds were not big spenders, but they did spend, and that was no small matter.

So in the winter, coastal interests and TDC planners, catered to these arrivals from the North. Churches invited them to attend and involved them in activities. City parks and recreation departments registered the guests and helped them find friends from the previous winter. State and province clubs were organized. Community centers sponsored and hosted events—bridge tournaments, bingo nights, dances, and such. Anything to make the guests want to come back next year.

Not everyone welcomed these visitors. Some residents found them rude, pushy, and above all "Yankee." Locals complained that snowbirds drove at a snail's pace and clogged up the streets. They could not understand local accents and slowed the lines at the grocery store. And they were sure they knew a better way to do anything that a southerner was trying to do. As a result, one beach musician branched out and made good money selling bumper stickers that read, "If this is Snowbird

Sign welcoming "snowbirds" to Gulf Shores, 1974. Courtesy of the Mobile Press-Register Collection, Doy Leale McCall Rare Book and Manuscript Library, University of South Alabama.

Season, why can't we shoot 'em." But on the whole, snowbirds were a lot like everyone else, and being that, they fit right in—so long as they didn't talk.

And between the snowbird season and summer there was Spring Break.

Although this student rite of spring had been growing in popularity since the 1950s, in the 1980s Gulf Coast promoters launched the campaign that would, in time, make Spring Break on the Redneck Riviera a rival to Breaks in Fort Lauderdale and Daytona. Because southern schools let their students loose to come to the beach at different times, a bigger Spring Break crowd promised to fill coastal coffers for a month or more. The first of them began to arrive in mid-March, about the time the snowbirds began to leave. Some students even took the last week of their grandparents' rented "snowbird nest" and made it their headquarters. That was just the beginning. They kept coming, in wave after wave, spending money, having fun, and causing trouble until after Easter. Meanwhile rival sites—Fort Lauderdale and Daytona—decided to crack down on Breakers and discourage local businesses from catering to them. That opened the door for Panama City Beach to become the center for the annual ritual of sun, suds, and sex. Gulf Shores, Orange Beach, and Destin did their part, but nothing could match PCB for offering the young and hormonal all the wet-T-shirt contests and cold beer they could handle. Memories of this rite of passage are legion but are usually told only after assurances that no names will be mentioned.

The Vietnam War made it difficult to justify sending an eighteen-year-old off to fight and possibly die while at the same time treating him or her as less than an adult here at home. So states lowered the drinking age to eighteen. Those who enjoyed this extended privilege remember the change as significant, but others—law enforcement mostly—say things really did not change that much. The unofficial drinking age on the coast had always been eighteen. Bars and liquor stores did not report a dramatic increase in sales. The only businesses that really felt the impact of the lower drinking age were those that made fake IDs.

Motel and condo owners were of a mixed mind about Spring Break. Although the money was good and it helped to keep profits up and staff employed in the dead weeks between winter and summer visitors, some of that profit was lost in the clean up. One motel owner pointed to his establishment and told a reporter, "Every fire extinguisher in these rooms is gone," stolen. Students, he complained, "break chairs, they break bottles, and [they break] telephones." Another owner told of hearing a disturbance and going to the room and finding "kids so drunk" that they "had ripped the door off the refrigerator" and packed it full of "lemonade and Scotch and beer." Even though most students did not cause this much damage, incidents such as these presented owners with a dilemma. Should they refuse to rent to students? Some did just that and rented only to people over the age of twenty-five unless younger renters were accompanied by their parents. They made less money than they might have otherwise but kept losses from damages to a minimum. Many who allowed students required a hefty deposit, charged a higher rent, and hoped they would come out ahead. As would be so often the case along the Redneck Riviera, most owners took as much money as they could get and hoped for the best.

For other beach businesses, Spring Break marked the opening of the summer selling season after the slow snowbird months. Alvin's Island,

Students on Spring Break, Panama City Beach, circa 1980. Courtesy of Bay County Public Library, Panama City, Fla.

which had evolved from a five-and-ten-cent store back in the 1950s, set the pattern for beachwear establishments that sold everything from bathing suits to shark-tooth jewelry. Summer was their season. It was also the season for the T-shirt, airbrush, auto tags, daiquiris-to-go, beer-by-the-cup, hangover breakfast, lunch-on-the-run, hippy head shops (in the 1960s), and all the other stores, dives, entertainments, and amusements that served beach folks during the day. Same with the clubs and cafes—the hot and cool spots where the young and the restless hung out after the sun went down. As more and more condos rented out in the summer, beach services became big business and the college boys who set up chairs and umbrellas earned more than money. Owners gave their chair guys distinctive T-shirts, which girls coveted. Soon it became known along the coast that to get one of the shirts, a young lady was expected to provide certain, shall we say, "favors."

And in the background music was playing.

But what music? Cultural historian Stephen Whitfield contends that unlike the beach music in California, "a Florida sound never developed." But what about Jimmy Buffett? While most would agree with Florida scholar Gary Mormino that more than any other singer, Buffett, who grew up in Mobile, "incorporated the 'flip-flops' lifestyle of the Florida Keys in his records" most would also agree that Buffett "achieved more commercial success than cultural influence." Along the Redneck Riviera, Buffett songs from the 1970s and 1980s—"Rag Top Day," "Pascagoula Run," "Great Filling Station Holdup"—convey the feel of the time and place. But not long after these were recorded, his "Gulf and Western" music took on a decided Caribbean flavor. Still, Buffett occasionally returns to his roots, and his 2006 song "Bama Breeze" is figured to be a tribute to the Flora-Bama. So they continue to love him along the coast, and would welcome him like a long-lost friend if he returned, even though everybody figures he has moved on. But back in the 1980s the biggest problem Buffett had making his mark along the Alabama-Florida coast was that he wasn't there. So instead of Jimmy Buffett creating the sound of the Redneck Riviera, it came from the pickers and singers at places like the Green Knight, Michelle Lynn's, and the Flora-Bama, a sound that Ken Wells, a chronicler of "beer culture in America" calls "trailer park rock."

Phil Calhoun and the Trashy White Band singing "She Ran Off" and such represented the rougher, deeper pitched, outlaw side of the scene. On the lighter, more laid-back side were the songs of Flora-Bama regulars "Rusty and Mike" (McHugh and Fincher) whose antisocial, antiestablishment repertoire included "I Never Knew a Bitch Could Eat So Much," which recalled a surprising date, "White People Party" poking fun at the upscale and their "Caucasian Occasions," and "Po' Ass People," which celebrated the joy of being just that. Though Rusty and Mike, Phil Calhoun, and other local "stars" never made it as big as Buffett, their songs are of the time and the people and the place. If there is a Redneck Riviera sound, they have it.

Their authenticity came from the fact that they weren't just visitors— the Riviera was home. Musicians who played and sang along the coast also held down full-time or part-time day jobs. They knew their audience well because they lived and worked with them. This was especially true for most of the musicians at the Flora-Bama. When some Bama music makers needed a place to stay, Joe Gilchrist let them pull in trailers and put them on a piece of property he owned across the road from the bar—they didn't have cars, Gilchrist recalled, and "most couldn't be trusted to drive anyway." There on an expensive piece of real estate along the Old River side of the island, within sight of the mansions of Ono Island, the squatters created

Boys Town. As one of them mused, it was a place that enabled "just a few of us old hippies and people who work across the street [to] get to live down here and enjoy life like the millionaires," while over on Ono "millionaire folks [were] staring at poor folks" who were drinking beer, partying after hours, singing, and occasionally sleeping. Other regulars lived nearby so the Bama and Boys Town became the center of what amounted to a musicians' colony. There they lived the life they sang about.

Jimmy Louis—the same Jimmy Louis who came up with the idea of the Mullet Toss—was singing in a Fort Walton bar where Joe Gilchrist heard him and watched him "moon" an unappreciative audience. Thinking, "We need that guy at the Flora-Bama," Gilchrist offered him a job and Louis took it. A few days later Louis hitchhiked over and went on stage. He eventually bought a sailboat and docked it a few miles away at Pirate's Cove, where he cleaned and repaired other boats when he wasn't singing at the Bama or sailing to the Bahamas, which he did every winter. Generally recognized as a first-class talent, Louis turned down recording contracts to keep doing what he was doing. When asked just what that was, he replied, "I'm in the music business. I love music, but I hate the business." So he sang and sailed and scraped boats, saying, "It's what I do." Besides, he added, "I've had money a few times in my life and all it did was confuse me."

It is hard to have a good time when you are confused, so folks at the Flora-Bama avoided confusion whenever possible. Bama patrons appreciated the unconfused simplicity and directness that came from the bandstand when Rusty and Mike cut loose with "Why Don't You Get Yourself a Room" or "She Put a Louisiana Liplock on my Alabama Pork Chop." Jimmy Buffett's Parrot Heads may sing along with "Why Don't We Get Drunk and Screw," but Rusty's female fans, the famous "Lolas," were up on the floor for "Wild Ass Women," and it is hard to find a sing-along better than Jay Hawkins' rendition of "Dead Armadillo."

One particular song by Mike and Rusty—"Down and Out in Paradise"—catches life lived at the end of the social ladder that the TDC folks did not want tourists to know about. When Rusty first got to Florida, as he told it, he hung out in Destin, behind the Marlborough Motel, down close to the docks. Times were tough, jobs were scarce, and food was in short supply. For entertainment he would watch the charter boats return from a day on the deep. The captains displayed their customers' catch for all to see and so the mighty fisher-folks could take pictures. Then the deck hands filleted the fish, packed the ice chests, and threw the backbones into the water for the crabs. Rusty noticed "there was a lot of meat on those backbones," so when the captain, crew, customers, and onlookers were gone, he hopped into the water, knocked off the crabs, and pretty soon he was "dining on backbones in the gumbo." During his time in Destin he got to know some of the girls who worked at the Whiskey Barn—"They would give us their mistakes, you know, whiskey mistakes, and this, that, and the other," he says—and they would tell him, "'Rusty, don't run off, in a while you can walk me home.'" Free fish and free whiskey and free affection—"down and out in paradise." So when he moved over to the Flora-Bama he just "scuffed up the past and put it all together," and wrote the song.

While singers and songwriters were writing their own rules and creating their own sound, others were promoting a coastal economy that often played by rules of its own. By the late 1980s the economy had stabilized, most of the effects of the savings and loan crisis had passed, interest rates were coming down, and developers were developing again. And upscale was the word. Golf courses with patio homes lining the fairway were appearing here and there—buy a lot, have your plans approved by an "architectural review committee," and you were good to go. The influence of Seaside was apparent as more "communities" appeared on the drawing board with bricked streets, wooden houses painted pretty colors, picket fences, and tin roofs. Many of these were gated, which Seaside, to its credit, was not.

But just because there was no gate, did not mean that Seaside was open to everyone. A victim of its own success, Seaside grew rapidly and as it did, the price of lots skyrocketed. When condos down the coast in Destin were having a hard time attracting buyers, the value of land in Seaside "surged" and lots that would have sold for fifteen thousand dollars in 1982 were selling for forty thousand dollars or more six years later. People who were paying this kind of money for sand and scrub were not about to put a cracker cottage on their investment. So the houses grew larger, more elaborate, and more expensive. This changed the population of Davis's creation and as the population changed, so did the creation itself. At the outset Davis and his collaborators talked at length about wanting "this community to be affordable for starving artists and people who have to work for a living"—OK, the starving part was probably a little over the top, but they really believed (or

Evolution of Seaside. More houses, bigger houses, closer together.
Photograph by the author.

at least hoped) that Seaside residents would be "a mixture of people." To
have a real community the Davis team realized they needed to "integrate
several strata of society." So they planned to bring in "lower income, singles
and [the] elderly [who] could live in apartments above stores or in 'outbuild-
ings,'" little "mother-in-law" cottages similar to what had been provided for
maids in Seagrove.

That simply didn't happen. Davis admitted later that he "had exces-
sive faith in building topology, in the power of architecture" to create the
community he wanted. Instead, another force, scarcity, shaped Seaside. It
turned out, he reflected, "this place is more desirable than we ever dreamed
it would be, and less common." So prices went up and up. This had two direct
effects. First, *Palm Beach* magazine noted, it "eased out the younger, more
middle-class buyer, opening the Tiffany glass doors for doctors, lawyers,
architects, bankers, preservationists, collectors and two-paycheck Yuppies."
But it also meant that the few garage apartments, granny flats, and similar
rentals that these upscale owners built were not going to be rented to students or workers or snowbirds at prices they could afford. If these owners
were going to allow folks to come in and spend time in and around their
homes, those renters were going to have to pay top dollar to do it.

And they did. Seaside, despite its imitators, was so unusual that many people wanted to visit and were willing to pay the price to do so. As a result, the rental program, which was almost an afterthought in the original scheme, became a critical ingredient in Seaside's financial success. Davis wasn't the only one to benefit financially: When some owners signed up with the Seaside rental agency they found their homes so popular that it was difficult for them to schedule time for themselves. In addition, the rental program brought in visitors who bought things in the Seaside shops which operators leased from Davis, another source of income that was only incidental at the start. And while all this was a cash cow for Davis, it was no small benefit to the investors. In the early 1990s a Seaside committee report noted, "Most of Seaside's rental homeowners rely upon revenues generated through rental activity . . . as a critical means of covering some, most, or all of the cost of their investment. Rental income, for the majority of Seaside homeowners, was and is the element that makes our investment possible."

No wonder that renters, when they arrived at their "cottages," found waiting in the refrigerator "a bottle of excellent French wine and a basket containing croissants, butter, jam, and Colombian coffee." These folks were paying for the best and owners wanted to make sure they went away happy and came back again.

Seaside seemed to have contracted "affluenza"—a disease that journal-ists found in other parts of the state where "prestigious communities exude luxury and privilege but also signal disturbing signs of vulgarity laced with antisocial overtones." Where once Seaside was to be a residential commu-nity served by a small grocery, a small hardware store, and a neighborhood cafe, by the end of the town's first decade the grocery was specializing in gourmet foods and wines and more kinds of olive oil than most folks knew existed, all for the recreational cook who wanted to show off his or her skills in the high-tech kitchen back at the rented "cottage." For those who favored recreational eating without having to deal with the preparation, the neigh-borhood cafe had morphed into an award-winning restaurant, while other, less formal (and less expensive) eateries had opened around the town cen-ter–village green. As for the hardware store, it was no longer a place where the handyman could get a hammer and nails. Instead it was a boutique to "provide Seaside homeowners with home furnishings that exemplified the 'Seaside Style'"—a "mini–general store where customers could find items ranging from bathtub faucets to Egyptian cotton sheets." It also featured "exciting and rare home décor items" so the renter could take a little "Seaside Style" back to their homes to remind them of the good time they had (and show off to friends).

Seaside was a lot of things to a lot of people, but redneck it was not. And yet, when a writer from *Travel and Leisure* came down to do a story on renting at Seaside and asked Davis to recommend a restaurant outside the village, he picked Chapman's, an unadorned, concrete-block cafe back on the bay where, he said, "the mullet, if caught that day, is a local delicacy." It is safe to assume that in the early days Davis ate at Chapman's and at another favorite back-bay eatery, Nick's (whose cook was invited to the Jimmy Carter White House to teach the chef there how to fry shrimp). But the story is told that when Davis dined at Nick's he took his own butter in which to dip his steamed crabs, rather than eat the "margarine/olio concoction" served there.

It is impossible to say how many people tried Chapman's on Davis's recommendation. Most folks who rented in Seaside stayed in Seaside, and during the summer, the "high season," Seaside took on the character of an exclusive, upscale summer camp, through which campers passed on a weekly basis to play sports, swim, eat, drink, go to the beach, or just relax with a book, which could be bought from Sundog, Seaside's own bookstore. Tying the community together—and as much a Seaside signature as the tin roofs and picket fences—were the streets, those brick streets that owners, tired of dust when it was dry and potholes when it rained, had wanted and paid for themselves. There was another benefit: because the streets were narrow and the houses were close to the road, few people turned in to sightsee, and for those who did, Davis observed that "the rumble of bricks under their tires [caused them to] instinctively slow down." So "children bike freely on the streets, people saunter along on their way to the beach, and nobody seem[s] concerned about being run over." If anything in the new Seaside captured at least the spirit of the old, it may have been the effect of the streets. Not that any of the changes in houses and community seemed to concern Davis. "The fact that Seaside strayed from its original idea doesn't bother me greatly," he told a *Palm Beach* writer in 1988. "People invest themselves here. They take pride in ownership. And if they have the money for central air, wicker furniture and expensive antiques, why deprive themselves of these luxuries." But still there were some who noticed that in the heat of the evening, rather than sitting on the porch talking to people passing by, folks were inside where it was cool. Instead of the sound of voices in the streets, you heard the sound of air conditioners.

Seaside sold investors on the idea that one's own home in a community close to the beach was the best place to put one's money. Seaside also convinced investors that they could earn money by renting their property through the town rental agency, for a fee, and Seaside would keep up the property for them, for another fee. The people who rented the houses would shop at Seaside shops and dine in Seaside restaurants, which the operators leased from Seaside—and Seaside, of course, was Robert Davis.

But not everyone shared Davis's communitarian vision, though some, such as the developers of Tannin Village on the Alabama coast, gave it a shot, at least visually. In Destin and Panama City, in Gulf Shores and Orange Beach, and to a lesser extent in Gulf Breeze across the bay from Pensacola, developers with less land but with financial backing decided that up was the way to go, so they set out to convince investors that most of the things that Davis offered—individual ownership, rental income, maintenance, and such—could be found in a high-rise condominium. There would be little of the "community" of Seaside, but there would also be fewer rules and regulations. And there would be a beach view. So even as Seaside was building and evolving, condominium developments, increasingly larger and taller, were going up, and as the market recovered, they were selling. On one side of them was the beach, in effect closed off from inland access. On the other side was a highway—be it Thomas Drive or Front Beach Road in Panama City Beach, Highway 98 through Destin, or Perdido Beach Boulevard in Orange Beach. And across the road were stores and shops and amusements and restaurants, which were about all the community folks in the condos would get or wanted. Stuck in between the high-rises, sometimes shaded by them, was the occasional motel, a holdout from that earlier era, waiting for someone to rent a room or for a developer to buy it up, tear it down, and put up another condo.

Roads brought people in, but they also presented a problem. In Destin, U.S. 98 ran right through the property that was purchased from Burney Henderson and turned into Henderson State Park. People who wanted to restore and preserve the natural beauty of the land wanted the highway closed and traffic routed to the bypass being built north of the town and away from the beach. Groups from Okaloosa and Walton counties, however,

Alabama Gulf Coast condos. A similar picture could be taken at Destin or Panama City Beach. Photograph by the author.

wanted to keep the route open for easier access to the coast and its attractions. The argument went on until 1989 when the county agreed to the closing and a hunk of old Florida was saved. While one road was blocked, others were opening or widening, and the tourists were coming south. When I-10 was completed and U.S. 231 down from Dothan, Alabama, was widened to four lanes, Panama City Beach become second only to Walt Disney World as Florida's drive-to destination. Plans were also made to siphon some of this tourist trade to Destin, and in 1994 the Mid-Bay Bridge opened across Choctawhatchee Bay to bring travelers down to connect to the rerouted and rapidly developing U.S. 98/Emerald Coast Parkway with its giant water park for the tourists, its giant Wal-Mart for the locals, an outlet center, and a Hooters.

Bringing the people in was one thing, but moving them about when they got there was something else, and the traffic problem would only get worse as the coast became more popular. In time it became general knowledge that anyone wanting to get somewhere fast had best stay off Front Beach Road and Thomas Drive during Spring Break, Perdido Beach Boulevard when the Mullet Toss was going on, and Scenic Highway 30-A around Seaside any time during the summer. Bottlenecks were many, gridlock was frequent, and at night around the clubs people found it easier to walk to where they were going than drive. This led Panama City Beach to make drunk walking illegal. That's correct, it was against the law to walk on the right-of-way in that fair city if you were under the influence. But party people made rules of their own, and if they saw the police approaching they hopped into the nearest car, whether they knew the driver or not—a good way to meet folks. Or better yet, they jumped into the back of a pickup truck, of which there were many, while they got their IDs ready in case the officer asked. If partying hard was an element of redneckery, on Panama City Beach the Riviera was rocking.

Back in Destin, in the old town area, things were a little calmer. Boats continued to leave the docks at dawn and come back with their catch in the evening. But even down at the harbor, the crush of commerce had arrived. In among the tackle shops, the dive stores, and the places where you could get a shrimp sandwich and a beer, more upscale bars and restaurants appeared, some with patios overlooking the water, and for the first time there were complaints that the place smelled like fish. Not the aroma the well-appointed and fashionably attired wanted with their Pina Colada and crab dip. But the folks who worked the boats, who also smelled like fish, did not go to those places. They went to bars like the Green Knight, a little inland but a world away from tourists who were encouraging developers to remake the coast in their upscale image.

But the Green Knight had fallen on hard times—not the lounge, though it was not the "go to" place it once had been, but the statue, the landmark that folks used to measure distance to and from other points. It was in danger. The storms of 1985 damaged the arm that held the spear, but locals took up a collection and the arm was replaced. Then in January, 1989, a report came over the Associated Press wire that plans were in the works to tear down both the Knight and "his seedy lounge" and replace them with "a Spanish-Mediterranean style, super up-scale" development featuring boutiques and specialty shops. By that time, the Knight wasn't even green anymore. Sun and rain and storms had turned him into the Aqua Knight and while he still looked seaward, condos blocked his view of the Gulf. Though he held his ground, spear ready, with a portable sign at his feet announcing the liquor specials, it was obvious that, new development or no, the Knight's days were numbered.

Some folks said they should move the statue to the pass where the Gulf meets the bay and set him down overlooking the harbor—"the Colossus of Destin."

It would have been fitting.

But it didn't happen.

Storms and Sand, BOBOs and Snowbirds

*I*N THE 1990S prosperity returned.

The Redneck Riviera has always attracted the affluent, but they were always in the minority and they usually kept discretely to themselves. In the 1980s they began to come out a bit—out of Sandestin, Pinnacle Port, Ono Island, and of course Seaside—but for the most part they remained isolated in upscale resorts or along golf courses. They did not rub shoulders (or anything else) with the common herd unless it was during one of those occasional slumming expeditions they organized to the Green Knight, the Flora-Bama, or a similar watering hole. It was not that they were openly snobby, most were too well bred for that. They just did not mingle with the masses much. Which was OK with the masses.

Meanwhile the ever indefatigable and optimistic real estate interests along the coast—well entrenched in the tourist development councils—sold the beach to ready buyers. Property values, which had gone flat for a while, rebounded, and in 1991 a *Destin Log* columnist asked his readers, "What recession?" However, as property on the Gulf became more and more expensive, what had happened in Seaside began to happen in Destin, Panama City Beach, and on the Alabama coast. People who worked in the motels, ran the condos, set up beach chairs, waited tables, and did all those things that made life easy for those who came to the beach to be served were priced out of the housing market. Some who worked in Destin went across the bridge to Fort Walton Beach and found homes and apartments they could afford. Seaside workers rented in Seagrove Beach if they could find places to rent, or went back across Highway 98 and even across the bay. Panama City Beach had a better supply of affordable rental property, but it was a shrinking market. Increasingly the morning and afternoon traffic across the bay and Intracoastal Waterway bridges began to look like traffic in the cities that tourists came to the beach to escape. And woe be to the unlucky visitor whose drive to or from the coast coincided with the daily exodus. On holiday weekends—Memorial Day, Fourth of July, Labor Day—there were honest-to-God traffic jams.

Meanwhile, more and more was built in which service industry workers were needed, and prices continued to rise. The high-rise condominium was being crowned king in Destin, Panama City Beach, and Gulf Shores, but even south Walton County, where height was restricted, was not suffering for development dollars. Newly inaugurated *Coastal Living* magazine, which aspired to be for the beach cottage and condo owner what *Southern Living* was for the suburbanite, reported that "for miles along the Florida Panhandle coast, you can see sprightly gabled houses here and there, inspired by the celebrated neo-traditional resort town of Seaside—but without the town." The "Seasiding" of the coast spread to Alabama where, with the help of some of the same people who belonged to Robert Davis's planning group, an Orange Beach developer set out to create the Village of Tannin. Smaller than Seaside—sixty acres to Seaside's eighty—the project was based on the Seaside-inspired (or at least exploited) concept that was being called the New Urbanism. Tannin consisted of 150 tightly compacted lots connected to a planned town center by narrow streets and alleys. People in the village could park their cars and walk about, just as they could in the Davis development. Lots in Tannin did not sell as rapidly as lots had in Seaside, but property values rose steadily and because the building code was more flexible than Seaside's, Tannin's developers and investors believed that in time there would be "an amazing array of architecture" in the village. Even before the town center was built, there was a "waiting list for events wanting to be on the square." The future looked bright for the Village of Tannin.

It is difficult to overstate the power some developers had over the direction of coastal development at that time, but anyone who doubts should consider the case of "Odom's curve."

In the early 1990s, Joe Odom was one of Destin's rising young real estate magnets. At the top of his development list was a piece of land located on the north side of what had been Highway 98, before the road was closed through Henderson Park and traffic was routed to a new Highway 98, built inland. Old Highway 98, renamed Scenic Highway 98, served as a county-maintained access road for people living along the beach. On his land Odom wanted to build Destiny by the Sea, a neighborhood of top-of-the-line homes he would sell at top-of-the-line prices. The only problem was location—not the location of the development, but the location of Scenic Highway 98, which ran between his development and the beach. Odom knew that the sort of folks who would buy into his neighborhood would not want to cross hot asphalt, dodging traffic, to get to the shore. Not a very dignified way for dignified people to reach the development's main attraction. But Odom had a plan. He would get the county to reroute the road around his property. This would put traffic to the north of and away from Destiny and give his investors unobstructed access to sand and surf.

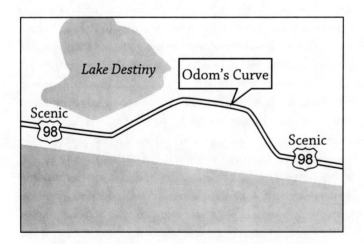

Rerouting highways is the stuff of which developer dreams are made. C. H. McGee wanted the county to route the beach road north of Seagrove. Van Ness Butler wanted the road to bypass Grayton. Robert Davis wanted Scenic Highway 30-A to take the same route that McGee had proposed. And Joe Odom wanted Scenic Highway 98 to run around Destiny by the Sea. McGee and Davis failed. Butler had clout in the courthouse and got his way. So did Odom. Jay Odom was close friends with the chairman of the Okaloosa County Commission and rising political star Ray Sansom. So, despite screams of protest, with Sansom's help he got the rerouting approved. Neighbors were outraged. "I don't think any developer, no matter who he is, has the right to move a road," a resident of a subdivision into which the rerouted traffic flowed told the *Destin Log*. The right? Probably not. The power? Some do. Joe Odom did. And the curve, which is there to this day, testifies to the fact.

Meanwhile, as Joe Odom and Ray Sansom moved on to bigger things, others were moving on as well. Moving, but moving slowly, for traffic was piling up.

In the early 1990s work began on the Mid-Bay Bridge connecting Destin's soon to be completed Emerald Coast Parkway (the rerouted Highway 98) to the mainland and the tourists coming down. At the same time Sandestin announced a $60 million expansion and Silver Sands Factory Outlet opened to create a bottleneck where the parkway meets Scenic Highway 98 and Sandestin. Back in Destin things were bad and getting worse. The Emerald Coast Parkway may have taken traffic off the beach route east of the town, but U.S. 98 still ran through the heart of Destin and during the tourist season the village was choked with cars. Early in 1996 the *Atlanta Journal-Constitution* sent a reporter down for a midwinter look at what was becoming a favorite destination for tourists from the Georgia capital. U.S. 98, he reported, was an "unsightly jumble of billboards, fast-food restaurants, gift shops, neon signs and utility poles." What was once a lucky little fishing village was a mess.

The reporter also found locals who wanted to do something about it. In December 1995, the Destin Chamber of Commerce sponsored a seven-day planning session to discuss the town's future. Hundreds came and, "fed up with snarled traffic, dismayed by the town's rundown look [and] fearful that development might make condo canyons out of the few remaining open stretches of the beach, residents began drawing a line in the sand." Some said "the town's welcome mat [had] been too inviting." Others blamed "poor planning, weak zoning and a willingness by local leaders to approve almost any new project." All wanted "to keep Destin . . . well, livable." But how? Suggestions ranged from "transforming the highway into a heavily land-scaped avenue with tasteful signs and businesses with facades that complement one another" to "bicycle lanes, better [land]scaping to make walking more pleasant and possibly even public trams that would whisk groups of people from place to place and cut down traffic." All sorts of ideas were bandied about—a mile-long boardwalk along the city's harbor, water taxies, underground utilities, and restrictions on high-rise buildings. Most are being bandied about still.

Over further east the situation was much the same, though community concern was considerably less. A writer for the *Beach-Bay News* complained, "Today the Panama City Beach strip could serve as a model of how not to develop a natural resource." Thanks to the "garish collection of T-shirt shops, goofy golf, water rides, arcades, and fast food restaurants amid a sea of asphalt . . . the gorgeous beach has been mugged and gagged, left nearly invisible from the highway." Which was a shame, for with the "bumper-to-bumper traffic," drivers forced to slow down could have enjoyed the coastal scenery, if there had been any to enjoy. But instead of at least discussing alternatives, like the folks in Destin were doing, the folks who governed Panama City Beach and their TDC allies responded by inviting more of the same.

However, one change was evident. As condos rose along the coast and more affluent folks mingled with the less sophisticated, Panama City Beach became, according to former police chief Lee Sullivan, a "kinder, gentler" place. When he joined the force as an officer in 1971, Sullivan recalled, he "worked more stabbings, shootings, throat-cuttings, and murders out here." If "there was a car that was parked on the side of the road you'd better go ahead and pop the trunk because somebody was dead." Six years later, when he became chief, the crowd was changing and so were the emergencies to which the police responded. Instead of stabbings, shootings, and throat-cuttings, Sullivan's officers were called out to investigate tourists "drowning in the Gulf" or "being run over on the side of the road."

Over on the Alabama coast, Gulf Shores, which travel columnist Starr Smith wrote was once "a slightly unsophisticated but promising holiday resort town that did not quite shape up to the Florida scene," was doing its best to overtake Destin and Panama City Beach in tackiness if in nothing else. Coming down on Highway 59 from Foley, visitors longing for sand dunes and sea oats were assaulted with "an unbroken string of billboards . . . hawk[ing] beaches, golf courses, water slides and zoos." The closer they came to the coast, the worse it got until finally the highway ended at the beach. From there, either way they turned they faced a jumble of motels and condos, souvenir shops and cafes, attractions and amusements, all clustered along the strip with no evidence of either planning or zoning—or, some would say, good taste.

Permanent residents were not that impressed either, but most were not inclined to do anything about it. Like residents of other resort towns, they complained about traffic and the lines at the grocery stores, but they liked the conveniences that were built for the tourists. Citizens of Gulf Shores and Orange Beach were a practical bunch. They knew, as one put it, that the "economy is oiled almost entirely by the coconut-scented visitors who parade around in skimpy attire, clutching bright-colored beach toys and their room keys." Tourists might charter boats and fish, they might hit the bars so they could drink and boogie the night away, or they might just relax on the beach, eat a nice meal at a local restaurant, and turn in early, but whatever they did, most locals wanted the visitors to enjoy themselves. "The tourists," a resident acknowledged, "by and large provide our quality of living." Pleasure Island had become just that, an island for pleasure.

Only the little beaches like Seagrove and Grayton, sheltered from high-rise development by height restrictions and still under the control of individual cottage owners, seemed immune to the development that was engulfing the bigger coastal towns. With its population too small to support much new commercial activity, Seagrove's growth consisted mainly of expanding the existing stores, as in the case of the Village Market, which opened a cafe in the back and turned the front into a slightly upscale convenience store and T-shirt shop—a real convenience store and gas station opened down the road, close to the two lonely high-rises that remained to symbolize what local opposition had stopped. Later a small strip mall was shoehorned in, and by the end of the decade a couple of other restaurants were added. The new establishments were all very low key, all very tasteful, and in some cases very expensive.

As for Grayton, in one of the most spectacular transformations along the coast, Belgian-born Oli Petit and his brother Philippe turned the old

Red Bar & Picolo's (formerly Butler's Store) interior, Grayton Beach.
Photograph by the author.

Butler store into the Red Bar & Picolo's Restaurant. Although the building held fond memories of the days when it was the community center and
teenage hangout, over the years the place had fallen on hard times. The Petit
brothers revived it, started serving food that was not typically "Gulf Coast,"
added décor that was anything but roadhouse, and eventually brought in
jazz and blues musicians whose repertoire was as far from the trailer park
rock as possible. Around the Red Bar a few other upscale beach boutiques
and cafes opened, but not many, for commercial space was limited. Grayton,
closed in by state parks to the east and west and by the Gulf to the south,
could only grow north, out to Scenic 30-A, and it was there that most of the
commercial development occurred. As for the village, it remained largely
a tightly packed collection of cottages, some dating back decades, that
together looked like the sort of community Robert Davis remembered from
his childhood and intended Seaside to become, only it didn't.

Along the coast the distinction between those who embraced redneckery
and those who rejected it was becoming clearer. *New York Times* writer Peter
Applebome, noticed it while doing research for his book *Dixie Rising: How
the South Is Shaping American Values, Politics, and Culture*. Driving along the

Florida Panhandle in the 1990s, he saw attractions and accessories created for the people McGee and Butler and Davis did not want in their villages. At a "squat yellow tourist emporium" that advertised "Factory Outlet, Concrete Souvenirs" on one sign and "Bumble Bee Realty" on another, he found "yard art without end"—flamingos, dolphins, Buddhas, faithful black lawn jockeys, and frogs of every description from "derby-wearing Irish" amphibians to "raffish stud-muffin" toads, all spread out under fluttering Georgia state flags bearing the in-your-face Confederate battle flag, which he concluded was more appealing to the "emporium" clientele than the "prosaic Florida one" with its "muted Confederate design." Looking over these treasures he drew the conclusion drawn by so many—"They don't call the panhandle L.A.—Lower Alabama—for nothing."

Then he drove a little further and found just the opposite, "the relentlessly tasteful *Architectural Digest* dreamland of Seaside, the instant Dixie Cape Cod of cobblestone streets, white picket fences, widow's walks, languorous front porches, and New England cottages in Bermuda pastel shades of pink, yellow, and blue where platoons of Atlanta lawyers and squadrons of Birmingham doctors' wives alight each summer to eat designer corn chips with peach melba salsa, drink pina coladas, and take seaside yoga classes."

No concrete yard art in sight.

Comparing the two—the emporium and Seaside—Applebome concluded that "in the South these days, it always helps not to be too sure you know where you are." One was the Redneck Riviera, one wasn't; one was Lower Alabama, one wasn't; one was "Dixie Rising," the other . . . ?

And peopling Seaside were visitors (and a few residents) that one commentator compared to the people David Brooks described in *BOBOS in Paradise: The New Upper Class and How They Got There*. Where Emory Thomas had noticed the coupling that produced the "raffish Rotarians, pirates with cash-register eyeballs, and hard-handed matrons," Brooks found that a mating of 1990s corporate America with the counterculture of the 1960s had given birth to "BOBOS—Bourgeois Bohemians." These were the well-bred, well-educated, well-careered, well-off "better sort" who were environmentally aware, intellectually stimulated, health conscious, kid friendly, and family oriented. They lived in what Brooks called "Latte Towns," affluent communities, often in magnificent natural settings where they could have trendy shops, gourmet bread stores, organic groceries, and of course a Starbucks. BOBOS considered it vulgar to spend thirty thousand dollars on a jacked-up four-by-four truck with Jeff Gordon's number on the window and a bumper sticker reading, "If you ain't from Dixie you ain't for shit," and they would never spend one thousand dollars on a wide-screen TV on which to watch the race. However they found it acceptable, indeed commendable, to spend the same money on a top-of-the-line hybrid SUV with a high safety rating, on which they proudly displayed stickers announcing their support of the Sierra Club and the name of their children's expensive private school. And it would be far better to take the TV money and put it into a slate bathroom with a water-conserving toilet. Here were the "best" of the baby boomers—affluent, acquisitive, self-absorbed, and socially progressive. Having grown up proper and privileged, Brooks observed, they set aside "the sixties-era things that were fun and of interest to teenagers, like Free Love, and retained all the things that might be of interest to middle-aged hypochondriacs, like whole grains." Their world, like the world of yard-art folks, was defined by consumption, but in their world people wore natural fabrics, ate natural foods, played natural sports (that required simple but expensive equipment), and supported natural causes—like saving the rain forest, which was conveniently someplace else.

Was Brooks being too harsh? Am I? Perhaps. They weren't bad folks. They simply had an outlook of their own. And they came to the coast, like so many before them, to find that perfect place where they could do what they could not do at home. Or, in the case of many of them, do what they did where they came from, but in a place where everything was a little more exotic, more exclusive, a little more convenient, and full of people just like themselves, people for whom yard art was a museum-quality replica statue of St. Francis tucked back in the foliage just off the patio. For the southern BOBOS, the Lexus driving, latte sipping, Republican voting, Bourgeois Bohemians from Buckhead (in Atlanta), Mountain Brook (outside Birmingham), and similar enclaves around the region, they could find it all at Seaside—including the statue of the saint.

In addition to being a beach home for BOBOS, Seaside suggested an alternative, some say a solution, to the sort of growth that was taking place in Destin, in Panama City Beach, and along the Alabama coast. But Seaside was not, could not be, for everyone. So even as Seaside was growing and evolving, citizens in other towns were trying to find their own ways to better manage growth or, in some places, stop it all together. This effort took many forms. Setting up coastal chambers of commerce and business associations were the first steps, and local leaders such as Davis and Joe Gilchrist over at the Flora-Bama were active in their respective movements. On Pleasure Island the Alabama Gulf Coast Convention and Visitors Bureau was organized to help Orange Beach and Gulf Shores work together on common problems, but having separate governments made cooperation between the two cities difficult, and the bureau often found itself doing little more than adding another level of bureaucracy.

Other communities held meetings to discuss development issues, draft reports, and adopt comprehensive plans. However, efforts to limit growth usually came in the form of emergency measures rather than serious long-range planning. Despite all the talk of managing growth along U.S. 98 through Destin, nothing was done until traffic became so bad that in 1996 the city called a temporary halt to development along the highway. A few months later the traffic flow was reassessed and development resumed. It took a lawsuit by a local "civic activist" to defeat a proposed sixteen-story condominium that was to be built in the middle of a neighborhood of single-family homes. That it took a court order to force the city to obey its own zoning regulations revealed at least part of the problem. No-growth sounded nice in theory, but for those whose livelihood (and bottom line) depended on growth, the courts were meddling where they shouldn't. As the mate on a charter boat told me as we sailed into Destin Harbor and I pointed out the condos and hotels crowding down to the water, more accommodations meant "more people to fish."

The most successful no-growth effort, however, was the one undertaken by Fort Walton Beach. By the time Destin began to boom, Fort Walton had settled into being a community that offered few activities like dining and entertainment to people who were not connected to the military. Not that locals cared. Fort Walton's downtown may have dried up, but there were still Okaloosa Island amusements and beyond that Destin, the very thing they did not want their city to be. So the residents of Fort Walton Beach remained comfortably in their retirement neighborhoods, and when they did go out they drove to another town. For Fort Walton Beach, no-growth meant just that—no growth.

Meanwhile, "progress" was taking its toll. In 1992, the Green Knight bar closed its doors. The next year the statue was finally taken down and moved to a place called Bernie B's Green Knight Inn on Okaloosa Island. Norma and Phil Calhoun were asked to run it, but they turned it down. "We just didn't feel we were Fort Walton Beach people," Norma told the press. It was a wise decision. Fort Walton Beach people didn't take to the Knight, and a year later Bernie B's closed. They tried to move the Knight again, but by then the steel frame had rusted out and it broke apart. After so many years "standing through storms and everything," Calhoun reflected, "that was the one battle he couldn't fight, those trips up and down 98." As for the old location, developers promised to "deliver to that corner a new, modern-day landmark the city can be proud of." They didn't.

It is doubtful that the Green Knight could have survived in its rusted-out state even if it had not been moved, for the year after the statue was finally taken down the Gulf Coast was hit by two hurricanes, either of which might have done him in. Late on the morning of August 3, 1995, Hurricane Erin came ashore near Pensacola. A Category 2 storm, its strongest winds, approximately one hundred miles per hour, were felt around Fort Walton Beach. Low-lying areas were flooded and there was some wind damage, but in light of what was to come, Hurricane Erin was a minor blow. As everyone along the coast knows, the severity of a storm is measured by what it does to *you*, not what it does to the guy down the beach. That is why what came next remains firmly fixed in my memory.

Two months after Erin, on October 4, Hurricane Opal slammed into the Florida Panhandle. Every walkover, every set of stairs from Panama City Beach to Destin was washed away. Up on the bluff, high above the storm surge, Seaside's award-winning beach pavilions lost roofs and attachments, but in the village Robert Davis's building code proved its worth. Back from the beach there was little damage, but things were different where the land was low. Water fifteen feet deep surged into Grayton Beach, flooding the town. Scenic 30-A was breached more than once, and the further west you went, the worse the damage was. Opal did to Destin and Fort Walton what Eloise did to Panama City. Destin's docks were badly damaged and across the harbor on Holiday Isle "whole houses simply disappeared." On the west side of the pass, the section of U.S. 98 that ran through Eglin Air Force Base property was broken in some places and covered with sand in others. The storm surge swept across Okaloosa Island, pushing water three to nine feet deep into homes. The Gulfarium, Fort Walton Beach's "tourism show," was so badly damaged that it would remain closed for six months. When the storm had passed evacuees were brought over to the island by bus to survey the damage but were not allowed to get out and poke about. The National

Damage to the beach and dunes after Hurricane Opal. The storm eroded the beach down to the dark sand. At the time this photo was taken, rebuilding had begun but only one staircase was back in place. Photograph by the author.

Guard had its hands full protecting the island from looters who came across in boats and even on surfboards. As for the beach itself, where there was a bluff the waves cut deep into it, exposing dark sand, stumps of ancient forests, and in one case the remains of a shipwreck, including the eighteenth-century brass spikes that had once held the timbers together. In undeveloped areas the dunes, some nearly twenty feet high, were washed flat.

Buildings built or improved after Eloise and Frederic were better constructed and generally survived, some with paint sandblasted away, some with windows blown out, some with the first floor flooded, and some with little damage at all. Many older, weaker structures were lost, and many of those left standing had to be torn down, which opened new property for development, just as Frederic had on the Alabama coast. Looking at the devastation, Navarre Beach developer and homeowner Bill Pullum tried to put the best face he could on the situation. "If there's any bright spot," he said, "it's maybe that many of the older buildings that were less attractive and less able to withstand storms are gone, so Navarre Beach will be cleaner and better." If you wanted cleaner and better, he was right. If you came to the coast seeking that old way of life that Robert Davis sought to recreate at

Seaside, you were out of luck. The area had undergone, as one survivor later observed, "involuntary urban renewal."

Anyone who wanted to see what involuntary urban renewal could lead to had only to look at how Gulf Shores and Orange Beach had responded to Hurricane Frederic.

Depending on whom you ask, by the mid-1990s, Gulf Shores was either paradise or paradise lost. The town's website (a fairly advanced publicity tool at the time) boasted that it offered "all the waterside recreation imaginable" for those who liked that sort of thing. For those who preferred to spend time "on shore [there were] beach boutiques, seafood restaurants, condominiums, hotels and beach houses [that] provide quality products, services, and accommodations." It was, according to one travel writer, "a blissful vacation Xanadu which embraces every form of a holiday agenda" and above all has "friendly and glowing people who love their island and like to show it off." Not everyone saw it that way. A writer for the *Arizona Republican* came through town and reported to readers that "the beach, called the 'Redneck Riviera,' is glaring white. Along its length, high-rise motels line the ocean and the sand is covered with beach towels and sunbathers. Colorful umbrellas and colorless lifeguards dot the shore, and there is a Captain's Table restaurant every half block." He was not impressed.

Orange Beach was even worse, at least in the eyes of people who lived out on the Fort Morgan Peninsula. Hurricane Frederic did not damage development along the road to Fort Morgan because there wasn't any to speak of. When poststorm development did come, it consisted mainly of beach houses on pilings tucked in between the large plots of state and federally protected land that took up nearly half of the peninsula. Some folks were reluctant to build on the beach there because a mile or so offshore were oil-drilling platforms, which cluttered the view. Others loved it because there were no high-rises and when one was proposed in the late 1990s, locals rose in protest. Their rallying cry—"Don't Let Fort Morgan Become Another Orange Beach."

So what did Orange Beach have that offended the Fort Morgan folks? Well, it had the Phoenix I, II, III, and so on (seven in total by 1999)—a string of condos, the largest of which, when seen "between the darkness and dense fog" looked to one critic "like a giant wall, its 14-story frame out of focus and its 247 patios just blurry squares in the night." Although there were still stretches of beach where cottages on stilts sat perched above the sand, the Phoenix complex so dominated the scene that nothing else seemed to matter. It was the pride and joy of developer Tommy Robinson. "It gets me right here," he told a reporter from the *Birmingham News* as he "slapped his fist to his heart." "'When I look at this, I think, "This is something that somebody else must have done." I can't believe I did this.'" Others couldn't believe it either, but they didn't share Robinson's enthusiasm. John Dindo, a marine scientist and president of the Alabama Coastal Foundation, called what was happening to Pleasure Island "the New Jerseyization of the Gulf Coast" and complained that what "was a village" had been "turned into a concrete jungle."

However, that "concrete jungle" and the coast around it had, by the end of the century, become Alabama's No.1 tourist attraction. There were eleven thousand condo and hotel units open and another two thousand "in the works." It was reported that "in Orange Beach and Gulf Shores vacation rentals and seasonal homes outnumbered year-round dwellings 3–1." It was just like it had always been only there was more of it. Lower South families still saved up all year for that week at the beach. The more fortunate and affluent bought vacation homes or condos, and some retired there. But if you walked out on the beach on a summer day you saw the difference. Fifty years ago it would have been you and a few others strolling along. In the last decade of the twentieth century, on any given summer day it was estimated that "as many as 100,000 people may be frolicking on the beach." This was what made cash registers ring along the rest of Alabama's Redneck Riviera, but it was exactly what the folks on Fort Morgan Road did not want.

All of this development threatened the one thing that made the area attractive—the beach. As buildings inched closer and closer to the water the warning went out to "all Alabamians who enjoy the sound of the surf, the smell of salt in the air and the feel of sand beneath their feet" that the beach, the "linchpin of the coastal economy," was in danger. Eroded by even minimal hurricanes, such as Danny in 1997 and Georges the next year, and deprived of sand by dredging to keep shipping channels open, the beach between the Gulf and the buildings was so narrow in some places that people walking the beach at high tide ended up wading in the water. Close construction also meant that the beach had little room to rebound after storms, and though there was not another Frederic during the last years of the decade, smaller tropical systems accelerated erosion and added to the problem. The Alabama Department of Environmental Management issued new construction standards designed to force developers to do more to protect the beach and laid down rules that prohibited the rebuilding of storm-damaged structures that had been built too near the shore. The agency also required large condo complexes to build boardwalks and plant sea oats to protect the dunes. Tommy Robinson, the proud developer of the Phoenix towers, bought into the plan. Preserving the beach, he told the press, "preserves the future. And when you preserve the future, you can still make money." It was good business, no doubt about it. That was the bottom line.

Meanwhile, there were residents along the coast whose concerns went beyond shrinking beaches and "canyons of concrete." These were the folks for whom winter was once a welcomed relief from the crush of tourists who filled the condos and crowded the beaches, a time when the coast was once again theirs. Even though locals knew where summer visitors hung out and could avoid them if they wanted to, they still looked forward to the cold weather break. But as snowbirds arrived in greater and greater numbers, that changed. Snowbirds were different. They came down to live like the locals lived, shop where locals shopped, and eat where locals ate, so in winter lines at the grocery stores, gas stations, and home-cooking cafes got longer and longer. Certainly they were an economic boom to businesses, but to many regular folks they were an irritant. Everyone seemed to have "snowbird stories"—the pushy northerner arguing with the clerk and tying up the checkout line, the elderly man who stops traffic as he and his wife try to decide whether or not they should switch lanes, and the impossibility of getting a decent tee time at the golf course.

So locals struck back. In the spring of 1997, some of the "friendly and glowing people who love[d] their island and like[d] to show it off" announced they had had enough. Flyers appeared on the windows of cars with out-of-state tags that were parked at shopping centers, in condo lots, and along the streets in Gulf Shores and Orange Beach. Put there by a group calling itself the Coalition of Permanent Residents, the bulletins announced that their organization would seek the passage of a twenty-dollar monthly "vexation tax" that would be levied on every snowbird that came down to the coast, a fee to compensate for "the mental anguish and frustrations encountered every day by permanent residents [trying] to get to their appointed rounds." City fathers and tourist officials recoiled at the idea and assured winter visitors that no such levy was even being considered, but the point of the proposal was not lost on snowbirds, who let it be known that if they were not welcome on Pleasure Island, there were other places they could go. Others thought the whole thing was silly and really did not worry about "what one fool with a typewriter and somewhat poor grasp of grammar says." Nevertheless the chambers of commerce and their welcoming committees doubled their efforts to make the visitors happy and instead of driving off the offenders from the North, the effect was just the opposite. The Coalition of Permanent Residents, if it was ever a real coalition at all, faded from the scene.

TEN

Trouble in Paradise

*T*HE FLORIDA PANHANDLE moved quickly to repair what Opal had done and in the spring of 1996, word went out that even though some places, such as Holiday Isle and Okaloosa Island, were still recovering, on the mainland there were rooms aplenty for those who wanted to visit the coast, and even some beachfront locations were accepting reservations. Popular Destin Harbor restaurants were open again, the docks had been rebuilt, the fleet was back on line, and the fish were biting. However, TDC officials issued "a word of warning for beach lovers. Come prepared for a visual shock." All along the shore of Okaloosa and Walton County "Opal devastated the beach and dune system," and the sugar-white sand that had once moved Dr. Stephen Leatherman, the famous "Dr. Beach," to rank the beaches from Panama City to Pensacola among "America's best," were gray and, to some folks, ugly. But just as the manmade environment was being repaired, the beach was getting its share of restorative care. In some places, the Florida Department of Environmental Protection issued emergency permits to allow sand to be brought in to rebuild the dunes. Some property owners planted sea oats and other natural vegetation to hold the sand in place. Others just tossed treetops and broken bushes where the sand had been washed away, figuring that in time new sand would blow in and cover the trash.

In the wake of the storm an issue arose that put a new wrinkle in the old debate over who owns the beach. On one hand

Panama City Beach after Hurricane Opal. Courtesy of Bay County Public Library, Panama City, Fla.

the people who made their living off the tourist trade understood that no matter what other amusements a resort might offer, the beach was what attracted most visitors to visit and most residents to reside. Therefore, it made good economic sense for local and state governments to help rebuild the beach if for no other reason than the economy depended on it. But where would government get the money? From taxes levied on citizens of community and county and state? And if a particular stretch of the beach were restored—"renourished" came to be the preferred word—with public money, the public should have access to it. Right?

But on the other hand, if a person owned beachfront property and did not want the "public" making themselves at home in what the landowner considered his back yard, could the landowner opt out, refuse the renourishment, and keep their property eroded and "private"? Geologists who studied beach movement pointed out that even if property owners refused new sand, the renourished beach next door would likely wash over to them anyway. Scientists also pointed out that if the beach were not rebuilt evenly, a gap in the shoreline would open the beach to more erosion and endanger adjacent property when another storm hit. Then someone pointed out that without the beach to slow or stop the storm surge, property along the coast was more likely to be damaged, and to cover their losses private insurance companies would raise rates on everyone, even those who did not live in harm's way. Or beachfront owners would turn to the recently created state insurance agency, which would take more from the public pot to cover people who refused to renourish their beaches. Ultimately the taxpayer would get the bill.

It was a quandary.

And as in any quandary, people addressed the matter as best suited them, if they could. Where beach towns were incorporated, local governments sought state and federal help and beaches were renourished, though some beachfront owners grumbled at the possibility that the built-up beach might not belong to them. Where there were no towns, counties stepped in to apply for grants and make repairs. Seaside, as one might expect, turned restoration into a community project. Since Seaside's beach belonged to the town, nearly one hundred homeowners got out and planted more than five thousand sea oat plugs along "their" rebuilt bluff and "their" dune line. But Seaside, as everyone knew, was not like the rest of the coast.

In 1997, after the storm damage was repaired, Seaside's uniqueness was recognized once again when award-winning Hollywood film director Peter Weir announced that he wanted to use Seaside as the location for *The Truman Show*. The movie was to be about a man who lives in a town that is actually the set of a TV show, but he doesn't know it. Truman Burbank is the unwitting star of a twenty-four-hour reality series, without the reality. All of the people in his life are actors under the control of a demonic director who determines who does what, when, and where.

Seaside was cast in a starring role. Apart from some new facades on the town center buildings and a pile of rocks on the beach to create a jetty, the town was allowed to be what it was, a carefully laid-out village that could have been a movie set, but wasn't. A few local folks, including the Davises, appeared briefly in the film, which added to the excitement generated by the arrival of stars such as Jim Carrey, and soon "actor sightings" were reported at restaurants in nearby communities. The filming went well, everyone cooperated, and then the Hollywood crew all went home to put it together. Then they brought it back, and on June 3, 1998, a special screening was held at the United Artists Theater in Fort Walton Beach, followed by an "elegant black tie Gala at the Seaside Lyceum." It was, according to a special edition of the *Seaside Times* (the village's adjective-prone

Truman House. Originally named "Kaleidoscope," this Seaside house was selected as the home for the principle character in *The Truman Show*, so naturally it was renamed. A comparison with the early "cracker cottages" reveals how Seaside architecture evolved. Photograph by the author.

newspaper), an opportunity for "the Emerald Coast and Seaside to strut their stuff." And they did.

Then came the second-guessing, for those watching the film soon realized that Seaside was not only a star of the film, it was a villain. Seaside came across, in the words of one reviewer, "as a Stepford community where everything and everyone is perfect—and fake." Seaside ("Seahaven" in the movie) was where Truman was trapped, surrounded by lies and unable to escape. Seahaven had been created to enable Truman to make money for everyone else; product placement was the rule by which the director produced commercialism-dictated perfection. Soon once-proud Seaside investors were asking themselves whether or not "millions of moviegoers [would] see their home as paradise on earth or as the poster town for disingenuous cuteness." Even Robert Davis, who some uncharitably compared to the devious director in the film, was beginning to have second thoughts about the production. Seaside's "founder" (the term "developer" had been quietly dropped from references to the man who started it all) revealed that he had almost turned the project down because there "was a risk, a big risk, that all the prejudices about Seaside could be confirmed." Yet those prejudices were what attracted director Weir to the town. He liked Seaside because it looked fake, and to drive home the point he set to "tarting it up" by getting rid of real trees and "replacing them with plastic topiary"—much to the founder's dismay. But the reaction was not entirely negative. The movie was well received and Paul Goldberger of the *New Yorker* pointed out that despite all the comparison of Davis's community to Truman's "saccharine-coated jail," Seaside was "a serious place" and therefore, it was "different, in the end, than Seahaven." "The brilliance of Seaside," Goldberger wrote, "is that it knows just how far to push cuteness and then it stops."

Robert Davis knew when to stop. He also knew how to use something like *The Truman Show* to clarify and advance his still-evolving dream for Seaside. As Seaside became more popular, more upscale, and more financially successful, it began to attract what its founder described as "increasingly cosmopolitan southerners." These investors were impressed by the money they could make from renting their homes and by the appreciating value of their property. The other aspects of Davis's dream and the New Urbanism movement it inspired were important to the homeowners only if those elements made their investment profitable. To ensure this, they wanted more control over what was increasingly "their" town. They gained control through the creation of a town council that, in effect, took governing the community out of Davis's hands. However, the founder retained his vision of a "real town" with all the institutions such towns should have. And because he owned most of the commercial property, he could and did write into leasing agreements provisions that had shopkeepers contributing to cultural events through the Seaside Institute. This became the vehicle for the many and varied programs put on to entertain and enlighten homeowners, renters, and folks from surrounding communities who drove in to see and do and buy. Though some critics accused Davis of forcing businesses to subsidize his dream, as long as the dream brought in customers, no one complained very loudly.

Seaside was becoming what Davis called a "holiday town," a resort like those he had studied while at the American Academy in Rome as a recipient of the Rome Prize Fellowship in Urban Planning and Design. Over there he saw towns where people could act out, if only briefly, what life would be like if they actually lived there, which of course is what people have always done at the beach. What did it matter that Seaside offered latte and Italian ices instead of beer and pickled eggs, the Florida Ballet instead of the Trashy White Band, croquet instead of crabbing, and a couple of wine-tasting festivals in the bargain? This was what the sort of folks Seaside attracted wanted the coast to be, so it was what Seaside gave them. Robert Davis wanted "to make Seaside a place where the art of life is enhanced by surroundings which are full of both art and life." Even his critics had to admit he was doing that.

Yet Davis would not abandon his plan to make Seaside more than a resort. With the money he received for allowing *The Truman Show* to be filmed in the village he underwrote the creation of the Seaside Neighborhood School, a middle school whose opening coincided, not coincidently, with Davis's son's reaching middle-school age. One of Florida's first charter schools, it was able to operate independent of most state regulations, and to all but the most careful observer appeared to be an elite private school. With support from the community and money from the state, the school offered a unique educational experience for the handful of children who actually lived in the town and kids from neighboring communities who were lucky enough to get in.

If a town needed a school in order to be "real," it also needed a church, and Davis was on top of that as well. Early in the life of the community a retired pastor living in Seagrove held Sunday services on the Seaside deck overlooking the Gulf, which locals and visitors attended as the mood struck. Finally, in the fall of 1999, ground was broken for the Seaside Interfaith Chapel, and by the following spring a gleaming white Upjohn-influenced church sat on a lot at the rear of the community. Looking at it from my secular perspective I wondered aloud to my wife just how residents and visitors would respond to this. What sort of minister would be hired? What sort of services would be held? Her response, drawn from years of experience with the uses to which churches are put, assured me that those were minor matters, for the purpose of the Seaside Interfaith Chapel was to provide a venue for weddings when the now popular and often crowded beach was unavailable. She was right, of course. There was good money in the marrying game, just as there was in whatever else Seaside offered.

Not everything Davis proposed was accepted. When he laid out plans for a small graveyard next to the church, "as traditional town churches have always had until recently" it was roundly rejected. The founder might "remember with affection the tranquil church graveyards of the towns in which we grew up" but homeowners in whose neighborhood the cemetery would be located did not share the feeling. The idea that because they came to Seaside with parents and grandparents in life, they might want to come to visit them in death, was not particularly appealing to the living. So the idea was shelved.

Meanwhile, Seaside prospered. When receipts were totaled at the end of its first decade the little town without a gate or a high-rise had brought in over $4 million in rentals from visitors, who spent nearly $7 million in the shops and restaurants. The assessed value of the partially built community was $54 million and in 1992 alone forty-three new homes were built. Seaside was big business and getting bigger.

What it comes down to is that while many homeowners did not buy into Robert Davis's dream of a real town, or a holiday town, or even a laboratory for New Urbanism, they did buy into the fact that those who invested in it made a tidy profit, and in that sense they were very like investors who were putting their money into condos elsewhere along the coast. The difference was that Seaside's image was so important to its livelihood that even those who were less than enthusiastic about Davis's "dream" were not about to let anyone take potshots at the place. So it was not surprising that when a writer for the *Wall Street Journal* was mildly critical in an article headlined "Despite Acclaim, Town of Seaside Fails to Become a Cozy Community," homeowners and merchants responded to assure readers that even though the population was transitory, in Seaside, "community spirit reigns." What also reigned was organization, governance, and a sort of upper-crust social-ism in which everybody chipped in (not always voluntarily) to things that Davis (mostly) and the town council (at times reluctantly) considered the common good—the Seaside Institute with its varied programs, the summer evening concerts and movies, and all those other activities that contrib-uted to "surroundings full of art and life." Still, the *Wall Street Journal* had a point. Seaside was not a town in the traditional sense, but rather "a specu-lative resort community." At the same time, the *Journal* admitted, Seaside was "not like those identical units around a golf course or stacked up at the beach." Seaside was different, and the difference mattered.

There was, however, one way in which Seaside was like other resorts along the Redneck Riviera—it was, the *Journal* reported, "populated mostly by southerners." But there, once again, was how Seaside was different. Not many folks buying and renting condos could say that they were attracted to those places because "the nineteenth-century atmosphere . . . reminds them of quieter times in Tennessee or Alabama," because the last thing you would find in the Phoenix towers and others like them was nineteenth-century atmosphere. If it was Davis's goal to create a space where people could get back to a simpler era and reconnect with family and friends, for some of the visitors he had pulled it off. Seaside was a stage on which actors—either tourists or residents—acted out the parts the community let them assume, resident redneck not being one. So in that sense, Seaside was Seahaven and, stretching the analogy, Davis was the director, and on a summer weekend the town was "jammed" with actors dressed, a reporter from the New Orleans *Times-Picayune* wrote, "like Gap ads."

Though the visitor from New Orleans felt Seaside "might benefit from sticking in a couple of ticky tacky restaurant shacks, some things that don't quite fit," that was not what Seaside was about. Davis could, and did, suggest that a little "mess" might not be a bad idea—"real towns are 'messy,'" he once observed—but the BOBOS who were Seaside's natural clientele, did not pay what they paid for a "mess." Coming from the Big Easy, the writer logically would think a town like Seaside "could do with a dose of attitude like the guys who flip burgers and grill amberjack for sandwiches at the Grayton Corner Café down the highway in Grayton Beach." Unlike the intense, solicitous, polite, and perky people who ran the Seaside shops, the guys working in Grayton "claim to shut the café when the surf's up." Seaside merchants would never consider such a thing. Close and a customer might be disappointed, or the store might miss a sale.

If you had to draw a distinction between Seaside and its neighbors, Seagrove and Grayton, that would be it—"attitude." The three communities were full of southerners—though the definition of "South" had broadened to include states as far away as Oklahoma and Kentucky. Most of the visitors, like the residents, were well to do and in outlook solidly bourgeois. The architecture of the neighbors, like the architecture of Seaside, defined and shaped the outlook of people who lived there or visited. As Seagrove and Grayton grew, houses were added that could have easily fit in at Seaside. In Seagrove a couple of three-to-four-story condos were squeezed in, and off to the east a developer built expensive homes, put a gate at the entrance, and sold exclusion to ready customers. But at the heart of the older communities were individual cottages, some still bearing the stamp of C. H. McGee's original design. As eclectic as their owners, they failed to fit any particular category other than utilitarian. Some newer ones were built as tall as the rules allowed, with apartments on every floor they opened to renters. Some even added small swimming pools, another reminder that many folks came to the coast for something other than salt water and sand. And on any given evening in the summer or during various holidays, you could see neighbors walking to Seaside from Seagrove, or driving in from Grayton, to enjoy what Davis's community was, then returning to what it wasn't. For the folks in Seagrove and Grayton, a little bit of Seaside was nice, but a little bit was all they wanted.

In the 1990s, many Southerners who caught the dot-com bubble before it burst made money and spent it on the coast. In 1996, *Southern Living* conducted an informal survey of the "most popular family vacation destinations" and Destin came in third, behind Walt Disney World and Myrtle Beach, an indication of the growing popularity of the "lucky fishing village" with the magazine's sophisticated readership. For the less sophisticated there was what was left of Panama City Beach's amusements but even those were disappearing fast. In the mid-1990s the land on which once sat Petticoat Junction was cleared to make way for an Applebee's restaurant and a new Wal-Mart. Similar sites suffered a similar fate. In their

Club La Vela sign, Panama City Beach. Photograph by the author.

place came a new type of amusement venue, offering not "family" entertainment fit for children but activities designed for an older crowd—teenagers, college kids, and young singles who came down to the beach to party and spend. Destin had Fudpucker's with its volleyball tournament. And on Panama City Beach there was Pineapple Willy's, Spinnaker, and Club La Vela, the "largest nightclub in the USA," with contests that did not include "find the needle in the flour." They had theme rooms, a pool, and the parentally reassuring Darkroom designed just for teens, "featuring the hip-hop, booty and Top 40 groove you love to dance to"—no ID required. Better than a Ferris wheel or a haunted house any day.

For the older folks, the aging baby boomers whose kids were at the clubs, there were more mellow activities. In the summer of 1995, the old Long Beach Hangout was remembered with a party at the Boardwalk Beach

Resort. Those attending dressed in 1950s clothes, danced 1950s dances, and generally had a good time. A few years later developers pulled down what was left of Long Beach and replaced it with a row of high-rise condos. All they kept was the name. Nostalgia was also the theme at the Flora-Bama, where during the winter locals and snowbirds skipped Wednesday night prayer meeting at the local Baptist church and accepted the invitation to bring "a covered dish to share with old and new friends" and "do it with us on the line." Happy-hour drinks were cheap, the music was familiar, and there were door prizes. The good times rolled, gently.

By the end of the twentieth century the Redneck Riviera had become big enough and varied enough to offer something for those who wanted the old as well as those who sought out the new. Although the Gulf Shores website admitted things had changed, the Tourist Development Council tried to put change in perspective. "Today," the TDC boasted, "visitors cross the Canal via a five-lane, high-rise bridge," and though "the skyline is a bit more crowded" (a classic understatement) those arriving can "still enjoy the same family resort atmosphere, the same glowing sunsets, the same mild weather and the same beautiful beaches. Some things never change."

Growth, however, had many drawbacks. In 1998, Alabama and Florida were among the six states named "Beach Bums" by the Natural Resources Defense Council for failing to regularly monitor water quality and notify the public of beach pollution. Both states protested the findings, claiming they did monitor the beaches and arguing that the study did not fully consider what was being done to ensure public safety, but the report did call attention to how the rapid expansion of coastal communities had put a strain on waste treatment plants and increased the amount of polluted runoff that was getting into the Gulf. The next year the crush of tourists on the Fourth of July overwhelmed Orange Beach's sewers, forcing the city to expand the system, but that would take time, and in the meantime water quality suffered. Planning ahead was not a characteristic of coastal communities, and in one particular instance a lack of foresight by the Orange Beach City council led to a decision regretted again and again. In the fall of 1999, the city fathers turned down a chance to purchase a twenty-six-acre plot that sat on both sides of the beach highway and included a stretch of undeveloped shoreline. They should have done it. Though the price was steep, $20.6 million, developers would later pay a lot more for it. And Orange Beach would be without its own beach.

Although there were still people on Pleasure Island who could recall "when a beach trip meant pitching a tent and building a fire," who remembered when the Alabama coast was "a wide ribbon of open sand, with dunes so tall that local children would clamber to the top and roll down to the shore," and who could tell of the time when fishermen's nets "were the threads that bound the community, not just quaint restaurant décor," those days were gone. In their place was a tourist industry that pumped over $1 billion into the Baldwin County economy in 1997, at the time a fifth of the state's tourist total. Some 22 percent of Alabama's tourist-related jobs were in Baldwin County and there local governments survived on lodging and sales taxes. And yet, despite all this growth, the Alabama coast remained remarkably balanced—about one-third of the property was commercial, another third was in private residential, and the remaining third—Gulf State Park, Fort Morgan, and Bon Secour National Wildlife Refuge—belonged to the public. It could have been worse.

Despite all the changes wrought by the tourist boom of the 1990s, most locals loved, or at least tolerated, the visitors for one simple reason—they meant jobs. What developed was a tourist economy in which the demand for workers increased dramatically. During the last two decades of the twentieth century the service-based income in Destin-dominated Okaloosa County increased 760 percent. Add to this the ever-increasing construction going on in the county and unemployment all but disappeared. Destin was not alone, except for the mainland areas of Fort Walton Beach where no-growth was still the word, the call went out—if you wanted a job, go to the coast.

And if you wanted good employees, skilled and unskilled, who would work hard and cheap and on whom you could depend, you needed someone in your company who could speak Spanish. During the 1990s the occasional Latino worker who picked up odd jobs on the coast was joined by what some saw as an "invasion" of immigrants from Mexico and other Central American countries, come north to find work. Some came to earn money to send to families back home, others came to stay and become American citizens; some arrived with the necessary papers to qualify them for work in the States, some came illegally. Whatever their intentions and status, when they got here they found jobs in the booming coastal economy.

The result could have been predicted. Redneck Riviera racism that had gone largely untested because the black population was so small now came out of the closet and concentrated its fury on people whose skin was brown and whose language was different. Maybe fury isn't the right word, for there was none of the violence that was once unleashed against African Americans in other parts of the South. Instead there were oft-heard complaints that the immigrants were overwhelming social services, especially emergency rooms in local hospitals; that they were dangerous, unlicensed, and uninsured on the highways; and that the places where they lived—inland cheap motels, cottages, and in some cases tents and travel trailers—were overcrowded, dirty breeding grounds for all sorts of illegal activities—especially drugs, because "everyone knows" that Latinos have "connections" south of the border. Even when studies showed that the illegals, whose numbers were always greater in fiction than in fact, paid a significant portion of their income in local and state sales taxes, and that they contributed to the economy in a variety of other ways, the feeling that these workers were taking advantage of our country and its traditional tolerance for immigrants was evident.

There was even talk of devising ways to discourage Hispanic workers from taking jobs along the coast—the Destin City Council voted to ban tent living in residential zones—but it was evident that without them the construction industry would suffer. Meanwhile, in the tradition of immigrants throughout our history, many Latinos opened businesses of their own. A region that had few if any Mexican restaurants soon had scores. Small family grocery stores opened to sell back-home products to away-from-home people. Soon there appeared among the many construction trash bins some painted in bright colors and labeled with a Hispanic name followed by "Co." Before the 1990s were over it seemed that every leaf blower, lawn mower, trash collector, trim carpenter, brick layer, and roofer was Latino. Like it or not, and many locals didn't, the coastal economy depended on these workers.

One of the places where this dependence was most evident was on a hunk of south Walton County real estate that St. Joe Paper Company decided to develop. St. Joe had been a player, some would say "the" player, in Florida politics for most of the twentieth century. Part of the Du Pont empire, under the direction of the legendary Edward Ball, St. Joe's holdings eventually included paper and pulp mills, railroads, banks, a telephone company, at least one city, a number of state legislators, a governor or two, a United States senator, and more Florida land than the state of Delaware. In the Panhandle alone, St. Joe owned over one million acres, which included around 250 miles along bays and streams, plus parcels that together totaled 5 miles of undeveloped beaches. Part of this property was located behind and encircling Seaside and Seagrove Beach. For some time rumors about the future of the land had circulated. This was where C. H. McGee had wanted Highway 30-A to go, around his town. Robert Davis reportedly had the same idea when Seaside was on the drawing board. Later it was rumored that Davis wanted to buy some of the land so Seaside could expand. About the only thing that was consistent about this speculation was that St. Joe had other plans for the property—though no one was quite sure what they were.

Rumor mongers and speculators soon got their answer. In the 1980s and 1990s St. Joe began divesting itself of its manufacturing and utilities operations and focused instead on developing its vast real estate holdings. So it was not long before the company decided to do something with land it owned next to Seaside. It was a nice piece of property. Starting at the road that carried visitors in from Highway 98 to Seagrove Beach, it doglegged off to the west behind Seagrove and Seaside, and ended up crossing Highway 30-A and hitting the beach between Davis's town and Grayton State Park. Containing just under five hundred acres it could hold five Seasides with land to spare, but what St. Joe wanted to build was not Seaside. Instead, St. Joe teamed with the real estate development giant Arvida, and brought in the people who had developed the Walt Disney Company's Celebration community near Orlando. These planners were told to take the land, which included some fourteen hundred feet of beachfront, and turn it into a community of neighborhoods connected by trails, boardwalks, and roads, where houses would not be squeezed together as they were in Seaside, where nearly half the land would be left to open spaces and preservation areas, where there would be a beach club, a tennis club, and a boathouse on the lake that separated the development from the state park. There would also be a sixty-room inn, plus shops and restaurants and all the amenities someone who would pay nearly $200,000 for the least expensive lot in the place would expect. (The most expensive was listed at $525,000 in the "2000 Initial Release." A couple of years later that would be considered a bargain.) When all the lots were sold and all the homes were built, there would be over one thousand residences in what St. Joe was calling WaterColor.

There was a certain irony in St. Joe's decision to bring in the Disney team to develop WaterColor. The story is told that when Walt Disney was looking for land for what would become Disney World, he contacted Edward Ball to arrange a meeting so the two men could talk about Disney purchasing some of St. Joe's property. Ball, who was known for his cantankerous personality and single-minded focus on his company and its many investments, had never heard of Disney. So he had the Californian checked out and did not like what he learned. When Disney called back, Ball reportedly dismissed him with a curt "we don't deal with carnival people." Now Ball was dead and the people running St. Joe knew what Disney was.

The company and the developers also knew that WaterColor was not going to be another Seaside. None of that New Urbanism for those folks. Although the houses would reveal a Seaside influence, a travel writer who visited once the development was up and running, noted how there was "none of the plastic/Stepford Wives feel of Seaside . . . [and] none of the pastel, freaky colors." WaterColor reflected more of the natural environment than Seaside. With everything "in earth and water tones" the community tended to "blend and flow instead of leap out at you." Indeed, it was reported that the first permanent employees hired by the developer were a landscape architect and horticulturist. This calculated divergence from the Seaside plan created a certain tension between these neighboring communities. There would be no connecting roads between the two, though eventually openings would be added to the dividing fence so residents and visitors could walk or bike from one to the other. Though the evidence is only anecdotal, it seems likely that more people wandered over from WaterColor to Seaside than traveled the other way, for Seaside always had something going on. When one of the WaterColor sales people let it slip that they considered Seaside "our historic district," Robert Davis reportedly was not particularly pleased, but the truth was that Seaside contained many precedents WaterColor followed and many it avoided. For the folks who bought into WaterColor, Seaside was a nice place to visit, but they wouldn't want to live there.

Although WaterColor got started at a time when the local economy was slowing and when sales along the coast were sluggish, it did well for some of the same reasons Seaside got off to a good start—St. Joe, like Davis, owned the land, and St. Joe, even more than Davis, had the money to support it. And, returning to the point made a few a pages back, neither WaterColor nor the down-the-beach developments of WaterSound, Rosemary Beach, and the others that would soon line Scenic Highway 30-A, could have gotten off the ground as well as they did if there had been no Hispanic workers. The building boom that took off in the late 1990s was the result of baby boomer affluence, cheap credit, liberal lending, favorable tax policies, and available labor. Take out any one of these factors and the boom would have been less than it was.

Away from the construction and the yard care and the places where folks worked hard and cheap, the accent heard was not Spanish, it was southern. Just as it had been since people had begun coming to the beach, the majority who arrived on the Redneck Riviera to visit or buy were from the South. In 1999, the research firm Claritas did a study of tourism on the Florida Panhandle and found that Alabama sent more travelers to that coast than any other state and Birmingham provided more visitors, proportionally, that any other U.S. city. Atlanta, being bigger, sent more in actual numbers, but with Mobile, Montgomery, and Huntsville also in the top ten, Alabama led the way. Noting this, the *Birmingham News* suggested that "thanks to property purchases and an all-out tourism assault" on Sandestin and the beaches along 30-A "Walton County may as well be flying the Alabama state flag." These were the folks that the new wave of development between Destin and Panama City sought to attract. While Seaside promoters talked a great deal about tradition, WaterColor and similar resorts were traditional as well. However, the tradition they followed was that of the status-defining enclaves on the north side of Atlanta and the south side of Birmingham, which were home to Dixie's new elites. These were WaterColor's target buyers, and even as the first lots were being sold the sales office was amassing a database that was heavy with zip codes from those and similar suburbs. Prohibited from building high-rise condos by the county's height restriction, but having been shown by Seaside that there was money to be made in single-family homes and town center conveniences, St. Joe and the others set out to get the most they could from their property, and they did.

Although WaterColor and the others ran rental services to help some homeowners pay the mortgage, developers were finding that more and more people were buying true second homes there, places they could come for a long weekend, a week, or even a summer. Critical to their ability to stay down for longer than a vacation was the advent of the Internet, which allowed homeowners to bring their businesses with them. Once again, Seaside led the way in this. From the beginning Davis talked about people living in his community and commuting to work first via telephone and fax, and later by the World Wide Web. Davis had always promoted this as a way to make his community "real," and though few people actually ran businesses from their homes, it was a way for homeowners in Seaside to spend more time in their houses. The same was true for WaterColor, WaterSound, Grayton Beach, Seagrove, and all along the coast.

Upscale renters increasingly expected all the comforts of home. For a while they were content with a TV. Then they wanted cable or a satellite dish and a VCR or DVD player. By the turn of the century a high-speed Internet connection was becoming a must for the upscale renter. WaterColor also brought in other conveniences for its homeowners and people from neighboring communities. Seaside's little market could not supply all the needs of grocery shoppers, unless all they wanted was a variety of olive oils. For staples families had to make the trek to Panama City or Destin. But with WaterColor came a big-chain grocery store and a liquor store to supply the basic needs of the beach communities. Located on the connecting road, they were convenient to people both inland and on the coast. The grocery was so popular that locals soon learned not to shop there on Sunday, the traditional day for the new wave of renters to come in.

And naturally, there was a golf course. Noting that championship golf attracted visitors and investors to Sandestin, St. Joe developed a golf and residential resort at Cane Creek, not far from WaterColor and WaterSound. It caught on quickly and lots sold on the average for more than $400,000. Cane Creek and similar developments were based on a simple, well-known fact—not everyone comes to the beach to go to the beach. Where once Panama City–type amusements entertained the less-than-sophisticated southerners who liked the coastal environment but did not like sand and salt water, now Sandestin and Cane Creek and Shark's Tooth west of Panama City Beach awaited Dixie's country club–joining, white tablecloth–dining, poolside drink–sipping upper crust for whom sand and surf were for the kids, not the grownups.

But not everyone bought into the golf resort idea. Shark's Tooth was a Greg "The Shark" Norman–designed course that was the centerpiece of the Wild Heron golf community. The course and resort were planned to curve around the north side of Lake Powell, across from Camp Helen State Park, the site of the old Avondale Mills employee camp. But the developers did not own all the land. One small plot belonged to the Fleming family from Geneva, Alabama, who bought it in the 1930s, built a cabin, and dug a well from which a windmill pumped water. The cabin was still there, still used by the Fleming clan, and the windmill could be seen from the highway bridge, though most folks sped by without noticing. Wild Heron wanted the Fleming land, which would have fit nicely into the scheme of fairways and greens, but the Flemings did not want to be part of a golf course. The developers came to them with a number of different proposals and strategies that they hoped would eventually force the family to come on board. The Flemings were not interested. Wild Heron kept pressing. The Flemings held out. The developers thought the family was trying to run up the price. They did not understand that the price was not the point. The family simply wanted to keep its land and keep it the way it was. So Wild Heron started playing hardball. The company resurveyed the land lines to try to establish claim to more of the Fleming property, it cut off the family's land access to their cabin, it even threatened to take the family to court. Nothing worked. Finally, Wild Heron and the Flemings called an uneasy truce. The land, the cabin, and all those memories stayed in the family. Today, if you slow down as you cross the bridge and look off to the north, across the lake, you can see the windmill. A symbol of a family's defiance—and its victory.

ELEVEN

Taming the Redneck Riviera

S HORTLY AFTER THE 1978 Howell Raines *New York Times* article gave the Redneck Riviera national exposure, concerns that the nickname might bring negative publicity to the region prompted a member of the Gulf Shores City Council to introduce a resolution condemning the label. It was voted down. Mayor Mixon Jones, one of the three real estate developers who served on the council and an opponent of the measure, explained his vote this way: "No, sir," he told a writer from *Sports Illustrated*, "we don't think the publicity [from the Raines article] was all that bad. . . . We believe that any publicity helps—good or bad—just so they spell our name right."

That may have been the prevailing attitude then, but in the years that followed, as chambers of commerce and tourist development councils sought to attract more upscale, affluent visitors, boosters tried to distance their beaches from the name and the image it conjured up. For the most part they succeeded, and by the turn of the century a travel writer for the *Montgomery Advertiser* passed over the "fortunately short-lived sobriquet 'Redneck Riviera'" with little comment, while *Golf & Travel* announced that down in south Baldwin County the "Redneck Riviera [is] no more." As if to confirm this transformation, in 2002 Panama City Beach tourist promoters came up with a new slogan—"White Sand, White Wine, White Necks."

In their efforts to put the region's redneck past behind them, advocates of the upscale had little interest in preserving what was left of the old. Besides, forgetting the past and embracing the future had always been what the coast was about. In the fall of 2000, the Panama City newspaper noted, "With only minute amounts of undeveloped beachfront property left . . . a new trend is afoot to demolish small, decades-old properties and build taller and much denser buildings in their place." The old Gulf Crest Motel, whose "Holiday Inn rip-off neon sign" was a landmark on Panama City Beach not unlike the Green Knight in Destin, was one of the first to go. In its place they built what was the tallest building on the beach, for a little while at least.

Even the older residential communities showed little enthusiasm for clinging to what used to be. In the early 1990s Robert Davis and Van Ness Butler were, according to Davis, "almost tarred and feathered" when they "made a proposal for a historic district" in Grayton Beach that included a plan for managing "the conservation and development" of the village. Davis and Butler backed off, and in the years that followed, Grayton's dirt streets were paved, "monster houses" were built in and among the older cottages, and more restaurants and shops opened, including one with grounds designed to replicate, or at least resemble, Monet's garden at Giverny—a far cry from Ross Allen's Jungle Show, which once packed them in at Panama City Beach.

But modern tourists did not come to the beach to savor the old. Back in the 1990s a visitor to Grayton wrote in the American Airlines publication *American Way* of her visit to what was "once referred to as the Redneck Riviera" and rented a "cabin" which was, as she described it, plenty redneck for her. The "cabin" was "actually a small house made from large cement blocks, with a puzzle of rooms behind plastic sliding doors"—not the accommodations she had expected. But she did find "several museum-quality paint-by-numbers renderings, and a Fifties kitchen with an eating bar and an electric stove the size of a Cadillac," where the "trained chef" in their party was able to whip up a gourmet meal. Things were made better by Seaside being close and by the fact that the beach at Grayton deserved its reputation as one of the nation's best.

Had she returned to Grayton a decade later she likely would have been happier, for Grayton had changed. In 2008, the *New York Times* "discovered" the village and told readers how what was once "a low-key spit of sand that offers nothing but houses and beach" had become a "haven" for folks

Lee beach cottage, Grayton Beach, Florida. Built in 1926 and purchased by Ethel Lee of Montgomery, Alabama, in 1938 for $350, it has been the family retreat ever since. Despite the development around it, the Lee cottage has remained largely unchanged. It was featured in *Coastal Living*, December/January 2011. Photograph by the author.

like the employee-benefit consultant out of New Orleans who happily paid $500,000 for a three-bedroom getaway tucked in among the "clutch of old-style cottages and waterfront homes on stilts," and the nuclear-fuel broker from Atlanta who got his retreat for $800,000—both bargains considering the average house there was reportedly selling for $1.6 million. What attracted these folks and convinced them to lay out the money for a place so far from home? By 2008, Grayton Beach had the Red Bar where you could eat well and listen to live jazz, a "funky inn" where people "looking for something that's totally unique" could find it, places for the recreational shopper and two real estate offices that could guide visitors to accommodations that did not harken back to times past. Grayton Beach, it seemed, had struck that happy balance. It "is not aristocratic," a homeowner from Atlanta told the reporter. "You don't shave and you don't wear socks. . . . There are no high-rises and it has that old, cottagey charm to it." It also had a "wild beachiness" and, though "upscale for sure," pulled upscale off "in an unfussy, down-to-earth way that residents relish." "I don't like those suburbs they build at the beach," the Atlantan said. "I just want the beach." At Grayton they got the beach, and a lot more.

When Grayton folks mentioned "suburbs at the beach" they were talking about their neighbors, those "neat, pastel-colored hamlets with windswept names like Rosemary Beach, WaterColor and Seaside," places that the *New York Times* pointed out were "popular for their locations and resort-style amenities." Once Robert Davis might have chafed at the suggestion that the town he was creating should be included in that list, but by the time the New York reporter arrived Seaside's founder had accommodated himself to the fact that what he had built did not turn out quite the way he planned. That said, there was no denying that later developments—even WaterColor and its counterpart, WaterSound—were influenced by Seaside, as were similar communities along the coast. The companies that created those resorts were not as caught up in modern urban design theories as Davis, who had gone on to become the chairman of the Congress of the New Urbanism. They were content to let Seaside serve as "a living laboratory" where the principles the theorists were preaching could be put into practice. What they admired and copied were the ways Davis made money. Meanwhile, the man who started it all packed up his family and moved to San Francisco where the Congress of New Urbanism was based, leaving his town to be run by the homeowners. He kept a residence in Seaside, returning every so often to play the role of town founder and deny rumors that he planned to sell out and leave for good. Meanwhile Seaside continued to do what it was comfortable doing and be what it had become.

But of all the things Seaside accomplished, the one that no other resort quite matched was the family emphasis that permeated the community. Since those early days after World War II, "family" is what the coast has been all about. Even as condos got taller and entertainment became more sophisticated or sleazy (take your pick), families continued to come to the coast for the beach and for the amusements. Seaside had the beach. As for amusements, there were sports, camps, plays, movies, and a host of other well-designed, well-organized activities that kids and grown-ups could enjoy. And there was Seaside itself, where on any given day a pedestrian ran a greater risk of being hit by a kid on a bicycle than by an adult driving an automobile. Once, speaking of his son, Davis reflected on the "charmed life" the boy led, getting off the bus with friends and having run of the village—not as the scion of the founder, but as a child in a safe environment.

Other resorts tried to match Seaside in this. WaterColor came close. As for condominiums, they didn't have a chance.

What all this development did, in addition to bringing in conveniences that before had been an inconvenient drive away, was inspire some coastal communities to organize things better than they had been organized in the past, which in turn inspired a few residents to resist the civilizing influences they came to the coast to escape. For example, when Seaside and Grayton paved their streets, some residents of Seagrove Beach decided it should do the same. Others in the community objected, and from the controversy FOOS—Friends of Old Seagrove— came into being. Ironically, the two sides were inspired by the same thing—a desire to preserve what used to be. For the street pavers, the important thing was that it was their street and they could pave it or not as they chose—to them, personal independence was what Seagrove was all about. For the dirt road advocates, paved streets threatened the character of the community, not to mention some

Seaside Arch pavilion, with children's bikes ridden from a cottage to the beach. Photograph by the author.

of the trees that gave the village its name, and community trumps individuality any day. In the end the organization proved to be more organization than most folks wanted. Interest waned and FOOS withered away, leaving Seagrove with some streets paved, some streets not, and some folks wondering what all the fuss was about in the first place.

Then there was the parade.

You will recall that every Fourth of July folks from Seagrove paraded. Before Highway 30-A was paved locals drove beach buggies along the shore and on the dirt roads. Alcohol was always involved. Blacktop made the parade better. It allowed folks to meander the mile from one end of the village to the other, where sometimes Seagrove's paraders were met by a similar group from Grayton. Sometimes not. Again, alcohol was always involved. For a few years during the 1980s a group of catamaran enthusiasts put together an Independence Day race—the Rags to Riches Regatta. One year the boats would begin at Seagrove, sail to Grayton, turn around and return to Seagrove. The next year they started at Grayton, went to Seagrove, and then back to where they began. No one could remember which community was "rags" and which was "riches," and except for the contestants and their fans, no one ever knew who won. But the T-shirts were really neat and alcohol was always involved.

Then, a few years after Seaside was founded, Davis's village decided to take part in the parade. Then they took it over. Organized it. And the next thing those of us who had participated in earlier parades knew, what had once been a community activity became a celebration of commercialism. There were store-sponsored floats, a band, and (since the coast had finally gotten its own county commissioner) a stray politician or two. Year after year it got worse—or better, if you are the tourist development type. Merchants entered more floats, church groups with their own product to market joined in, more politicians appeared, and every scoundrel in the bunch was a patriot. On and on the extravaganza came, stretching the entire length of the town, until it arrived and collected itself at the Seaside village green where there were speeches, music, food, festivities, and prizes, all neatly choreographed to bleed out any suggestion of spontaneity.

Instead of being what it once was, the Redneck Riviera had become big enough, diverse enough, to be whatever visitors wanted it to be. And with careful planning tourists could have a week or two of fun, with no surprises to disrupt their serenity. If a family wanted to come down and bond at the beach they could rent a three-to-five-bedroom condo, depending on the size of the group, in a high-rise with a Gulf view, just an elevator ride from the surf. For those who did not like sand and salt water there was the pool (indoor or outdoor), the fitness center, the tennis courts, the Jacuzzi, and, not too far away, golf. For those wanting something more residential, less "touristy," there were houses in Grayton, Seagrove, and similar communities that rental agencies handled for the owners and which allowed visitors to pretend, for a little while at least, that they actually lived there. In between were places like WaterColor, which quickly became "a luxurious, all-amenities available development that combines hotel-level service with homes, shops, markets, gardens, golfing, biking trails and other comforts into a seamless whole." One travel writer took his "hippie-chick bohemian" wife with him to the St. Joe resort and though she usually "distains planned developments as unnatural and fake," she came away impressed. "You know," she told him, "I've seen how the other half lives, and I could get used to this."

As for the half that didn't live that way, well, anyone who wandered inland looking for a golf course (as one writer did) could still find "good ol' boys in pickups [cruising] the piney back roads . . . , roaring past low brick houses with open carports, trailers selling fireworks, and more small, red-brick churches than can possibly have congregations," but by then "those bad-boy princes of the bayous seem[ed] like caricatures of folk mythology" to the outsider. "Their world," the golfer reported, "has been bypassed by the shiny new malls and . . . the new four-lane highway designed to zip cars from I-10 down to the beach." "Heck," he observed, "in these sadly evolved times, even the Pink Pony has a Web Site."

Not that Sean Daws, from out on Fort Morgan Road, needed to check the Internet to find out where to go. Interviewed in the spring of 2001, by *Birmingham News* reporter Thomas Spencer for an article to be titled "Less Redneck, More Riviera," Daws came across as one of those "bad-boy princes of the bayous" who were as endangered as any federally protected species. Standing by the "General Lee," his "genuine imitation souped-up Dukes of Hazzard Dodge Charger" complete with horn that played "Dixie," Daws looked out over the yard of his "bayside cabin" at the collection of "vehicles that sit in various states of de- or reconstruction," and wondered how what "used to be called the Redneck Riviera" had come to this. For Daws the coast was "becoming a foreign land" where people listen to hip-hop instead of Lynyrd Skynyrd and "dress like gangstas or *GQ* models." The last time he cranked up the General Lee's horn and played "Dixie" he was pulled over for violating the local noise ordinance. "I guess rednecks aren't popular any-more," he told Spencer. "I'm out of place here just about."

The Fort Morgan peninsula still had clusters of beach cottages on stilts far from the conveniences of civilization. There were still a few "plastic-tabled, non-arugula, fried seafood dives" that catered to people who came to the coast for "sun, sand, surf, and lazy, no-cares, no-rules, beer-drinking loafing," and Daws could still fish in what amounted to his back yard. But he couldn't explore the dunes and beaches as he once had. New property owners were possessive, and his sort of folks could not wander about for fear that "somebody is going to yell at you for coming across their lawn." To make matters worse he said, "they're paving all the roads in Baldwin

County," leaving no place for him and friends to kick up dust. "The whole atmosphere has changed," he told Spencer. And it had. All along the coast that he used to roam, places were popping up where the affluent and sophisticated could find the "Epicurean flavor [and] amenities" they sought. There they could enjoy a meal at a "Bass Ale-on-tap-Asian-calamari-serving highfaluting restaurant" and later visit a "French-manicure-Swedish-massage-spa." Daws was right, he was "out of place here just about."

However, if tourists wanted a little taste of redneckery, and many did, the person at the front desk or at the rental agency could tell you how to get to a local establishment that served cold beer, raw oysters, boiled shrimp, fried mullet, and atmosphere. Some places marketed and sold refined redneckery, packaged like the T-shirts you could get in their gift shops. Others didn't. Without forcing the issue the Flora-Bama successfully upheld its reputation as "ground zero on the Redneck Riviera." On any given evening anyone who wanted a rare experience to tell about when they returned to their full-time day job—who wanted to mingle with bikers, bankers, students, shrimpers, and anyone else who enjoyed sitting under bras hanging from the rafters, listening to trailer park music, drinking a little more than they should, and eating something steamed or slimy—could drop in at the Bama and not be disappointed.

All along the coast were local versions of the Flora-Bama, conveniently located close enough for resort folks to visit but far enough away not to cause concern among the classy and socially conservative. Despite all the stories about redneck revelry, it wasn't what drew the affluent and sophisticated to the coast. They were down for what the promoters promised—the "beautiful beaches, fine restaurants, luxurious hotels, and many other attractions to entertain them." They wanted, according to the impressed travel writer and his equally impressed wife, what resorts like WaterColor offered: a place "for folks who like to get away from their day-to-day grind, but still want to maintain a certain level of civility and decorum in their vacation plans—in other words, the tools needed to make a proper martini or to open a bottle of fine cabernet." If they did not want the Redneck Riviera, it was easy enough to avoid it.

Of all of the upscale developments coming on line at the start of the new century one of the most interesting was La Borgata, a resort community designed on the Seaside-WaterColor model that in 2006 was laid out on a divot of sand west of Panama City Beach. It would be a place, the press release announced, where people could "remember when"—without being too specific on just when "when" was. La Borgata, with promised "resort-level amenities and conveniences" and a cutesy name—Italian for "the little village"—really did not sound much different from other new resorts until you read down the report and discovered that the investor whose name was being put up front was none other than Alan Jackson, country music star and running buddy of Jimmy Buffett. On top of that, the company behind the venture was headquartered in Enterprise-by-gum-Alabama, down in the southeast corner of the state and the home of many of the folks who made the Redneck Riviera what it was, or used to be. And as if that were not enough to cause some to hope that the "when" to be remembered might have more to do with the "something tall and strong" Jackson and Buffett sang about in "It's 5 O'clock Somewhere" than with a "proper martini" and "fine cabernet," another spokesman for the company was Nashville great George Jones, "Ol' Possum" himself. Was this the revival of the Redneck Riviera? Or the last nail in its coffin? Time would tell.

What was evident was that amid all the publicity for the upscale and sophisticated, all the *Southern Living* and *Coastal Living* and Sunday travel sections picturing new resorts with date palm–lined avenues leading to supersized copies of St. Croix or St. Thomas or St. Whatever, folks still went to the Gulf Coast looking for what a writer for the Associated Press called a "beach with attitude." But it speaks volumes that his search began with a visit to the Alabama Gulf Coast Convention and Visitors Bureau. Although the person at the desk assured the reporter that at the Flora-Bama—"our five star road house"—a visitor would find attitude aplenty, it was almost as if the Bama had become a caricature of itself, at least in the minds of TDC folks. Around the same time another reporter traveled up and down the coast, from Gulf Shores to Panama City Beach, trying hard to ferret out places where the Stabler gang might have hung out in their prime, places "for those afraid that today's fun-lovers are spending all their time at wine-tastings." It was a worthy effort, but the list compiled includes the Howl at the Moon piano bar on Okaloosa Island, Bud and Alley's in Seaside, and Club La Vela in Panama City Beach (popular with the "halter top and span-dex set")—places you wouldn't expect to find the General Lee parked out-side. For the "pirate who's already looked at 50," the writer recommended LuLu's Sunset Grill, on the Intracoastal Waterway in Gulf Shores, where Jimmy Buffett's sister served up good food and acoustic music so as "not to disturb the birds that flock to the wetlands there." But the most redneck thing found at LuLu's was "redneck caviar"—a "mixture of black beans, onions, peppers and seasonings, served on a cracker." Living on the wild side for the acid-reflux set.

Not only did it seem that the Gulf Coast was working hard to shake off its redneck past, it was also trying to be as inoffensive as possible. Though calling it a "beach with attitude" suggested otherwise, the truth was that for the chamber of commerce and TDC folks who were running things, "attitude" was fine so long as your attitude did not interfere with people having a good time and merchants making money. Which is why the folks who put on the National Shrimp Festival down at Gulf Shores moved the Jesus First Ministries and its Christian music stage to a "little-used" part of the grounds and later "cut it out entirely."

Jesus First Ministries was just one of many religious groups that became more active along the coast as the twentieth century entered its last decades. Evangelical ministries from cities such as Birmingham and Atlanta moved to the beach because, as one "missionary" put it, "that was where the sin was." Efforts to reach the hellbound came in different forms. One big church from north Alabama brought down scores of students to live in a church-leased motel, work in carefully chosen local stores to pay for room and board, and spend their "free" time wandering up and down the shore talking about Jesus to anyone who would listen. For some it was a calling. For others it was a way to spend the summer in the sun. For the committed, it was putting Christian faith into action. For the rest, there was the satisfaction of doing something worthwhile. But witnessing on the beach was not easy. Some of the young evangelists were disillusioned at the patriarchal nature of some of the enterprises and complained that in assignments and tasks men always seemed to be given preference over the women. And then there were the difficulties beach evangelists faced trying to bring the message to those they felt needed it. "It was pretty hard," one said, "to witness to someone who is drinking a beer and wearing a thong."

Jesus First Ministries was part of this coastal evangelical movement. Founded in the early 1990s, according to its director it "served as a haven for homeless beach kids, a life-changer for alcoholics, a gathering place for Christian youths sharing the message of salvation, or just a refuge for people who need counseling or prayer." The organization had taken part in the Shrimp Festival for years and once won second place for its float in the festival parade. But as early as 1995, a member of the Jesus First board (who was also a member of the Gulf Shores Chamber of Commerce, which put on the festival), noticed something was different. "That year," he told the *Mobile Press-Register*, "it seemed they put golden handcuffs on us, really tightened down. We couldn't pass out tracts or witness to people; we had to stay in our area."

But even in their "area" the folks from Jesus First were causing problems—at least for some. There were complaints that the ministry engaged in "too much high-profile proselytizing on the beach" and that there were violations of the festival's "no one can come down and pass out literature" policy, which chamber representatives said was designed to keep down litter. The owner of the building that the ministry rented also owned commercial property around it, and many of those establishments served alcohol. Although none of the businesses complained about Jesus First, "a couple of customers" approached members of the ministry to object to activities that kept them from "having a good time." Others observed that Jesus First was simply "out of place." The chamber tried to solve the problem by moving Jesus First's "Christian music area" to a location "off the beaten path so those who might be offended could steer clear," but complaints continued. It came to a head in 1998, when the building's owner terminated the ministry's lease. When she took over the building, the owner told the press, "Jesus First was primarily a retail business" selling T-shirts and Christian music. But over time "they became strictly an outreach." And while "outreach is a wonderful thing," she added, it was "not the kind of business we want on the beach." So the termination "was strictly a business decision."

And no doubt it was. Although members of the chamber talked of complaints of "altar calls, preaching and love offerings" and expressed a "fear of litigation" if they favored one group over another, it all came down to dollars and cents. As the owner of the property that had been the ministry's headquarters put it, "I want to have businesses who draw tourists to the beach, and outreach just didn't fit in with what we were trying to do down there." Most members of the chamber likely agreed. Apparently so did Jesus First. After years of "criticism and opposition from business leaders who . . . viewed their methods of sharing the 'Good News' as incompatible with good times," the ministry's board voted to disband. Although there was talk of the very litigation that chamber members had feared, Jesus First decided "that legal action was not the answer." The chamber, no doubt, breathed a sigh of relief.

In the end, however, some supporters of Jesus First believed the ministry had won. About a month after it lost its lease and moved, Hurricane Georges tore into the beach and destroyed the building they had just vacated. "Well, you see what happened," said one of the chamber's critics. "You don't kick God out." Many members of the organization were not quite ready to consider Georges to be God punishing those who opposed the ministry, but there was an understandable feeling among members that by getting them off the beach "the Lord was protecting [them]." In the end, the damaged building was torn down and in its place the property owner opened a parking lot for Fat Tuesday's restaurant and bar and the T-Bonz steakhouse, two businesses that "fit in."

Jesus First was not the only beach business being closed down. Slowly and surely, one by one, amusements that had entertained the southerners who made the Redneck Riviera what it was shut their gates and dismantled their attractions. Newer, bigger, and more luxurious hotels and motels and condos were being built, and the people who rented or bought them were not the sort of people who wanted to spend a day and evening wandering from ride to ride along the carnival-like midways and from game to game at the "penny arcades." Chamber of commerce business leaders welcomed this "change in the caliber of tourist" even though, as one of them put it, "I don't think you'll have quite the beachy atmosphere" the coast once had. He was right. But as the old gave way to the new, one thing seemed as permanent as the beach itself: the Miracle Strip Amusement Park on Panama City Beach endured for a few years into the twenty-first century. Then, after "several unprofitable summers" brought on by declining attendance, lawsuits, rising taxes, and rising fuel costs, owner Billy Lark announced that the park would shut down after Labor Day, 2004. It was a blow to the people who as children, teens, and parents had ridden the "fastest roller coaster in the world," who had visited the arcade and gotten the fortune-telling chicken to tell them whether or not the girl they just took on the Zoom Flume would be "the one," and when the answer was "yes" had taken her to snuggle in the Abominable Sno'Man. So they came back one more time, even some of the married couples who had met there. They rode the rides one more time and bought a piece of memorabilia at the silent auction, and when the gates shut for the last time and the lights went out, they were sad.

Miracle Strip Amusement Park at the height of its popularity in the 1970s and 1980s.
Courtesy of Bay County Public Library, Panama City, Fla.

Aerial view of the eastern edge of Seaside with part of WaterColor. WaterColor appears in the upper portion of the picture, Seaside's Neighborhood School in the lower right, and the Seaside Chapel in the center. Photograph by the author. Airplane flown by Peter Horn.

Meanwhile, the upscaling continued, and as it did Panhandle tourist development councils, not content with the moniker "Emerald Coast," or even the "Panhandle," went on another name shopping spree. Unable to come up with anything themselves, one of their critics told me, the TDC folks laid out sixty thousand dollars to "some Hotlanta city wizards to find out why anyone would come to the Redneck Riviera." What the taxpayers got in return was "an answer delivered in an expensive mayonnaise jar" full of sugary white sand. Visitors didn't come for the amusements, or recreational eating, or recreational shopping, or to get drunk and shake their booty. They came for "The Beach."

Sixty thousand dollars to tell TDC people, who are supposed to be on top of these things, that visitors come to the beach for the beach. So naturally the TDC people set to work to get folks to call the beach "The Beach." Local government in Walton County voted to designate U.S. 331, which carried tourists down to the coast, as "The Beach Highway." Coastal Vision 3000, a private promotional organization that was created to, among other things, "enhance the branding of the region and to bring more people to the beaches," started a campaign to "promote the beach area extending from Escambia County to Franklin County as a region under the 'brand identity' of 'THE Beach.'" Reaction was, well, mixed, but Coastal Vision 3000 was not deterred. Made up of "a coalition of major players on the local business scene," it pushed ahead. Calling their beach "The Beach" might be "a little arrogant," said the chairman of the group's founding committee, but, he added, "I don't know of another beach in this country that can back it up the way we can."

Not everyone felt the same. The local press reported that some people were upset because "the term left no room for local identities" of which there were many. Some folks who "had lived down here more than a decade" found The Beach "a little confusing and even downright upsetting." Other places along Florida's long coastline were quick to point out that it was not just arrogant, but inaccurate for the Panhandle to call itself *the* beach because there were so many beaches—on the Atlantic at Daytona, Fort Lauderdale, and Miami, plus others on the Gulf at Longboat Key, Siesta Key, and Sanibel Island—that were just as famous and as "beachy" as anything along the Redneck Riviera. The Panhandle may have some beaches, but it was not "The Beach."

Aerial view of Seagrove (right), Seaside (left), and WaterColor (inland). Note the density of Seaside and WaterColor. Seaside Chapel stands out on the left. The author's house is in the center, one lot in from the beach. Photograph by the author. Airplane flown by Peter Horn.

Coastal Vision 3000 pressed on. It added "marketing tools to identify 'the Beach' as 'Northwest Florida's Gulf Coast,'" and even came up with an official slogan for the campaign—"A way of life that can change yours."

Folks outside the loop of tourist development found the whole thing amusing and a bit silly, but Coastal Vision 3000 was serious. Part of their marketing push was to get an airline interested in the area because the sort of tourists and investors they wanted to attract were the sort of tourists and investors who wanted to fly, not drive. That led naturally to talk about a regional airport that could accommodate a major airline. This naturally aroused the interest of the St. Joe Company, a member and major contributor to the organization. St. Joe had land. St. Joe had money. And St. Joe had WaterColor and WaterSound to sell to folks who would just love to fly in. However, Coastal Vision members knew that potential visitors needed to be told what the region was and why they would want to go there. Central Florida's brand was a mouse. The Panhandle's brand would be The Beach.

TWELVE

Making Money "Going Wild"

*I*F ANY ONE THING seemed to fly in the face of TDC efforts to present "The Beach" as a family-friendly, affluent-attracting playground for the settled-yet-sophisticated, it was Spring Break. During those few weeks in March and April all the plans to create an upscale image were seemingly set aside as local businesses and chambers of commerce concentrated on turning a profit. In no place was this more apparent than at Panama City Beach, and it was there, around the turn of the century, that it got out of hand.

First, a little history.

By the 1980s, going to Florida for Spring Break was more popular than ever. Meanwhile, according to *Time* magazine, many south Florida communities, tired of rowdy kids and the turmoil they caused, "began to question why the heck they had invited such unruly houseguests in the first place." For Fort Lauderdale, 1985 was the last straw. When nearly four hundred thousand students descended on the town, local officials responded with stricter laws against public drunkenness and the mayor went on ABC's *Good Morning America* to tell students that they were no longer welcome. Daytona Beach offered itself as the new Spring Break capital, a title MTV confirmed in 1986, when it aired its first Spring Break special from that location. But Daytona Beach soon regretted that decision, and by the end of the decade city fathers were discouraging students from spending their holiday there. So students, at least the more affluent ones, began seeking out more exotic places, such as Cancun, for their spring romp. Meanwhile, others looked for a place closer to home, a place they could party with friends, a place they could afford, a place that wanted them. They found Panama City Beach.

Panama City Beach promoters knew, or at least should have known, what they were getting into when they decided to offer their town as Daytona's replacement. The American Medical Association (AMA) had recently issued a Spring Break warning about "binge-drinking and risky sexual behavior" among young adults who took off for the coast. In particular the AMA expressed concern over young women who were known for their "prebreak anorexic challenges" and for "documented promiscuity" once they arrived at their destination. Even though the drinking age had been raised back to twenty-one by the National Minimum Drinking Age Act of 1984, AMA records revealed that binge-drinking and risky behavior continued. Some universities even went so far as to distribute "safe break bags," which contained "sunscreen, condoms, and a sexual-assault manual." No matter where the students went, trouble followed.

However, Panama City Beach promoters also knew the size of what *Time* was calling a "lusty young demographic" and the money it could bring to their community. In the 1990s, as states began to lengthen the school year and August lost a couple of vacation weeks, Panhandle tourism flattened and businesses along the Gulf Coast began looking for ways to recoup summer losses. They quickly focused on Spring Break. Thus began the promotion that would, in a short time, turn Panama City Beach into the most popular Spring Break destination in the nation. It would also turn the community into one of the most watched and studied. Reacting to the AMA warning, researchers from the University of Wisconsin–Stout surveyed some eight hundred students in Panama City Beach during Spring break 1995 to determine just what attracted them to the coast and what they were doing when they got there. The results disturbed parents, intrigued their college-age children, and told local promoters what they needed to do to attract these free-spending customers.

Approaching students as they sat on the beach, hung out in beachfront bars, or lay around the pools at popular hotels, researchers asked their subjects about their backgrounds, why they came to this particular beach, and about their drinking, drug use, and sexual activity. Granting that there would be some lying, the results nevertheless painted a clear picture of

Spring Break and its participants. They chose Panama City Beach because it had a "good party reputation," which they planned to do nothing to diminish. And alcohol was the fuel that fed the fire. Three out of four of the young men surveyed said they got drunk at least once a day while they were down. Forty-three percent of the women were daily drunks. One in five men said they never sobered up at all. On the average, young men consumed eighteen drinks each day, while the women consumed ten. Half the men said they drank till they were unconscious or threw up at least once while they were down. The women were more restrained—only 40 percent puked or passed out. If the weather was warm, they were on the beach by 10:00 in the morning with a keg of beer and a bottle of whiskey. If it was cold, they took the party inside.

The survey revealed "a clinically dangerous level of drinking" that put an end to the old assumption that experimenting with alcohol during Spring Break was just "harmless fun." Interviewed by the Associated Press, the head of the research team reflected on the findings: "If you are a parent and your college-age son said to you, 'Well, Dad I am going down for spring break,' you would think 'Well, in my day I went, [had] a few drinks here and there. No big deal.' You might approve of it." Yet, he said, "by the same token, would you tell your son, 'Well, son, here's a bottle of Jack Daniels. Let me see how quickly you finish it and by the time you are passed out, I will go buy another one and come right back.'" That, he suggested, was happening in Panama City Beach.

As for sex and drugs, student responses brought no more comfort to parents. About 32 percent of the students surveyed said they used marijuana during Spring Break and over half said that they used drugs more at the beach than back at school. And drugs were readily available. Fifty-two percent said they had been offered a controlled substance during their vacation but, in one of the few bright spots in the survey, only 3 percent said they had tried a new drug. The old, time-honored stereotype of drunken fraternity men proved true. Those belonging to a fraternity got drunk more than "independents," and nearly twice as many "brothers" used marijuana than students outside the Greek world.

Then there was sex. Twenty-one percent of the men said that they had sex with a new partner during Spring Break. If a guy had someone waiting for him at home he was twice as likely to go to bed with someone he did not know than the guy who came to the beach free from "previous attachments." By their own admission, of those who had sex on Spring Break only 57 percent always used a condom, while 43 percent said they used a condom "sometimes." The numbers were about the same for women as for men, which left a lot to chance.

But Spring Break was more than sex, drugs, and liquor—although liquor seemed to always be involved, even when student "mischief" only included soap suds in a hotel fountain, filling the hotel pool with patio furniture, and running about playing "squirt gun war" among the cars stalled in traffic along Front Beach Road. That thoroughfare, described as "twelve miles of motels, liquor stores, fast-food restaurants, bars, arcades, miniature golf courses and adult tattoo and body-piercing shops," was as important to the visitors as the big clubs with the DJs and the beer specials. Students wandered along this strip, in and out among the gridlocked cars, talking with other students, meeting new folks, and drinking, even though it was illegal to consume alcohol on the right-of-way. The same congestion that turned students into pedestrians also made it difficult for the police to enforce whatever laws the students were breaking. So they turned Front Beach Road into a twelve-mile party.

The police controlled things as best they could and hoped that the weather turned nasty so students would stay in the rooms and drink there rather than take themselves and their liquor to the beach or the streets. But even when it got overcast and rainy, as it did along the coast in March, students were able to create chaos, as they did over in Gulf Shores, where what went on in Florida was duplicated, though on a smaller scale. Although in 1990, Gulf Shores sent out the word that it would not "tolerate rowdies," the "rowdies" came anyway. A couple of years after the Panama City Beach survey the *Mobile Press-Register* reported that in Gulf Shores over a twelve-hour period, police reported arresting twelve minors for public drunkenness and possession of alcohol. Minors were not the only problem. Police were also called to break up loud parties and alcohol-related fights, and students were arrested for crimes that ranged from indecent exposure to criminal mischief and DWI. "Everybody's drunk," one patrolman told the press, "and they get caught when they start getting stupid." In the "getting stupid" category was the "slingshot," a three-man contraption that enabled students to stand on the balcony of a condo and fire water balloons into the traffic on the road down below—funny until it was your car that got hit. Some students shot eggs instead of balloons, which for the victim was less funny still.

But not everyone saw Spring Break in the same light. Though city officials along the coast complained of what it cost their towns in time and
resources, the folks who ran the chambers of commerce were of a different
mind. Although they admitted that the youngsters were a lot of trouble, by
1995, the Spring Break season in Florida and Alabama was attracting some
five hundred thousand students and generating over one billion dollars for
the local economy. Tourist development officers loved it and wanted more.
As late as 1999, Panama City Beach had no item in its budget for marketing
Spring Break. In 2003, local leaders set aside four hundred thousand dollars
to sell spring in the city. It worked. In a few years, spending during the seven
weeks of Spring Break would represent one-third of Panama City Beach's
yearly revenue. As Florida historian, the ever insightful Gary Mormino
observed, "Spring Break is to Florida beach cities what Mephistopheles was
to Faust: a great deal, if you don't mind the downside."

The downside was why members of the Baptist Student Union and the
Campus Crusade for Christ descended on the coast during Spring Break to
feed students pancakes, offer them beach games such as volleyball, invite
them to listen to Christian music instead of rap, and give "revelers . . . a little
reminder of [their] mortality." Organized as "Beach Reach" the purpose was
to preach "without getting pushy" and suggest that self-restraint should
not be "something they left at home." Some students accepted the food—
as students always do. Some students stayed on to play and listen—"it's
nice to meet good people" one burned-out breaker said. And though no poll
was taken to reveal just how successful the evangelists were, the number of
people who dropped by their blue and white striped tent revealed that many
appreciated the food and the effort.

Nevertheless, you did not have to look far to find the historical continuity between the folks and forces that created the Redneck Riviera and the
Spring Breakers who arrived in the 1990s to enjoy it. Like those who came
before them, these students were down to do what they could not get away
with at home. Moreover, Spring Break at Panama City and Gulf Shores was
still, for the most part, a southern party, so another link with the past was
forged. Students on Spring Break at the turn of the century were the latest
in a line that culturally and sometimes literally stretched back to grandparents and even great-grandparents who came to the coast after World War II
to get away from the pressures of home and work. From there the genealogy
followed a path through students in the 1950s and 1960s who visited the

beaches, danced at the Hangouts, drank beer on the sand, met and mingled on warm spring nights, and went home to Birmingham and Atlanta and Jackson and points around and between with stories to tell. Their children followed them to party at the Green Knight and the Flora-Bama, dance to the Trashy White Band, sing along with Rusty and Mike, and really put the redneck into the Riviera. It was all in the family genes. And though the older ones might read of the recent goings on, shake their heads and click their tongues and say they would have never done such, they would have, and deep down they knew it.

These were their children.

What may have disturbed parents and grandparents most about Spring Break was not the drinking or the sex, or even the drugs, but how drinking, sex, and drugs became marketing tools to attract students to the beach—and how readily students responded. Once again, Panama City Beach stands out as an example of what "pirates with cash register eyeballs" could do if allowed to do it. At the end of the century the Florida town set up a committee just to promote Spring Break and promote it they did. And so it followed that one dark, damp, cold winter day a student opened his campus newspaper and out fell a slick, colorful insert which, when unfolded, revealed a poster of a bikini-clad young lady suggesting that if "your classes have you stressed out, burnt out, studied out" then "the solution [is] Spring Break Out 2000 Panama City Beach Florida." It was a masterful piece of advertising, created for and by the Panama City Beach Convention and Visitors Bureau. Though aimed mainly at the college-age male, promoters knew that "where the boys are" was also a draw for the girls, so they loaded up the poster with promises that appealed to both.

"GPA stands for Great Party Action." A tamer portion of one of the posters sent to lure students to Spring Break at Panama City Beach. Author's collection.

In good Florida fashion, businesses told customers of all the wonders that awaited them.

With key words in bold, this is what the poster said:

We Have 27 Miles Of Sugary White Beaches and Emerald Green Water so you can **Party Out.** More Than 18,000 Rooms So You Can **Chill Out.** Award Winning Restaurants So You Can **Pig Out.** Monster Supper Clubs So You Can Blow Out [it was not clear why "Blow Out" was not in bold]. Live Entertainment and Concerts so You Can **Rock Out.** Nationally Sponsored Bikini Contests so You Can **Play Out** Your Spring Break Fantasies In A Warm and User Friendly Destination That Knows What **Spring Break Is All About.**

"**Play Out** Your Spring Break Fantasies." What more could a winter-weary college student want?

Well, how about a Break Out 2000 Party Package?

For prices starting just under thirty dollars a student could purchase a Gold Pass Club Card that entitled the bearer to "no cover and free beer at 2 clubs every day" plus "free cover charge to Club La Vela." La Vela, which advertised itself as the "largest nightclub in the USA," hosted "pool side contests all day [and] super parties all night." There, with your card, you could get "over 30 hours of free beer each week." Throw into the mix free pizza, free T-shirts, and student discounts at a variety of local stores, and the stressed out, burned out, studied out were hooked. In the days that followed, the hits almost overwhelmed the promoters' "killer website."

Not everyone approved of the advertisement. Some members of the Bay County Tourist Development Council and the Panama City Beach Convention and Visitors Bureau opposed spending their money on printing and distributing the posters. They found the bikini-clad model "distasteful and unnecessary," an interesting position in a town where taste, especially in the use of sex to promote tourism, had seldom been an issue. Critics also argued that "the long-range success of this beach cannot be based on spring break," but it was the short-term success that supporters had in mind, so critics were outvoted. As far as Russ Smith, co-chairman of the Convention and Visitors Bureau's marketing committee, was concerned, the poster was "as clean as it can be and still attract the attention of college students." Attuned to his target audience, Smith told critics, "There is no reason to advertise for spring break and make it some type of family milk-and-cook-ies piece." And of course, he was right.

Rolling Stone said so.

Coincidental with the circulation of the poster *Rolling Stone*, the maga-zine for the young and the hip, came out with its Spring Break 2000 issue and among "the hottest places to go" was Panama City Beach. The PCB mar-keting folks had done their work well.

The *Rolling Stone* piece caught the flavor of what was by then "America's biggest spring-break destination," a perpetual party where, despite the availability of "rave drinks" and drugs, "most of the 500,000 kids in town seem more interested in the local aphrodisiacs: beer and oysters"—they were their parents' children. The magazine also provided a snapshot of what Spring Break in Panama City Beach was like at the opening of the new millennium.

If nothing else, *Rolling Stone* was trying to be helpful. Want a cheap break-fast, hit the All-American Diner buffet. A cheap lunch could be had at the Cajun Inn, while the best cure for a hangover was the hash at Corams' Steak and Eggs. The bars, dance floors, open-air decks, and stages for bikini and wet-T-shirt contests at Spinnaker and Club La Vela got the usual nod, and "once you're well stimulated, try Sharkey's which gained fame a few years back for its faux-sex contest that looked a hell of a lot like the real thing"—a trial of skill that required participants to "form as many sexual positions as possible within sixty seconds." "Cheap and hip hotels" were recommended, "midnight skinny-dipping" was encouraged, and breakers were told they should sample the "local cocktail," hunch punch: "one and you're done." And if you were conscious and hungry, the Wal-Mart Supercenter was the best place for a "3 AM Oreo run." As for the "Best Beach Characters," *Rolling Stone* gave the nod to the evangelical Christians—the "Bible thumpers . . . saving souls in sin city. Give them credit for trying."

And who were you likely to meet? The "typical" Panama City Beach Spring Break girl, according to *Rolling Stone*, was "junior education major from Auburn," who blew off mid-terms to leave school early, checked into the Holiday Inn Sunspree Resort and a short time later appeared wearing an Abercrombie and Fitch tank top and Oakleys, ready to cruise the clubs in hopes of finding that special someone who would make her the "trophy wife" she longed to be. When she returned home she would notice the rose tattoo on her ankle and go get a pregnancy test. As for the "typical" guy, he would be down from Michigan State where he majored in electrical engineering. Wearing swim trunks by Nike and a Panama City Beach T-shirt, he wandered the beach, where he developed [an] "inferiority complex" comparing himself to the muscle-bound Spring Breakers from southern schools. He spent his time drinking, hanging around, and ogling "bare chests of the best looking women he's ever seen." He did not get laid.

Only a veteran can testify to the accuracy of the magazine's assessment, but one bit did ring true—the Michigan State guy could have been there. Thanks to a combination of proximity and promotion, Panama City Beach was becoming increasingly popular with Spring Breakers from the North, and though *Rolling Stone* reported seeing a T-shirt bearing a Confederate flag logo and the words "Like Hell I'll Forget," any residual redneckery of that old, damn-the-Yankee-to-hell variety was rarely evident. There were fights, "incidents" the newspapers liked to call them, but they were usually over girls, and alcohol was always involved. Regional differences were not a big deal.

The only visitors who might have clashed over such differences were high school students, of whom there were more than a few down on the coast for what was also their Spring Break. They were the ones who caused the police the most trouble. As Lee Sullivan, the former police chief and later mayor of Panama City Beach, pointed out, "college students have something invested . . . they really can't afford to have a criminal record that would impede their futures" so they are more careful. High school students, on the other hand, don't think that far ahead. With a fake ID and a Gold Pass Club Card they were good to go, and so they went. And some of them ended up in jail. Some of them ended up worse. Jim King, a paramedic in Panama City, knew how bad it could be. He had seen people hit with full beer cans thrown from the upper stories; he saved "a fifteen-year old girl [who] was so drunk that minutes after we got to her she went into respiratory arrest"; he treated students with second-degree sunburn, "blisters all over . . . almost like they've been in a fire"; and when asked if the "kids ever puke on you" he replied, "all the time." King had also picked up the bodies of students who fell from a high-rise when they tried to "crab" from balcony to balcony—"trying to impress some good-looking honey. . . . I've seen them dead; I've seen them maimed for life. My job's not for everyone."

Fortunately, most of the incidents did not require King's attention. Reinforced with units from the Florida Highway Patrol, local law enforcement knew what to expect and were ready. "We act like assholes," a member of the city's no-nonsense Tactical Street Crime Unit told *Rolling Stone*. "It's our job. . . . [We'll arrest you] and when the cells are overcrowded, you'll be handcuffed to a metal rail." And "assholes" they were, especially when the charges were serious—DWI and drugs and assaults. However most of the crimes committed by students—underage drinking, creating a disturbance, criminal mischief, indecent exposure—were misdemeanors, so rather than throw the violator in jail or cuff him or her to a rail, the officer gave the student a summons to appear in court on a later date. Of course, some wouldn't appear. They'd go home and the case would remain open. Then, years later, when they tried to get into the military or get a job or get some sort of a clearance they would discover they still had charges against them in Panama City Beach. Settling these was expensive and troublesome, for both the lawbreaker and the law, so to move things more swiftly and efficiently state attorney Jim Appleman set up the Spring Break Court.

Spring Break Court was not created to deal with felonies. Appleman wanted to take care of "the normal peeing on the side of the highway, walking down the beach with a drink in your hand, sharing a six pack with your underage buddies"—minor infractions that clogged up the system. In the new process, when a student was arrested he or she would be cited and told to show up for court at 8:00 the next morning. And in the violators would come, high school students, college kids (with the Southeastern Conference well represented), a smattering of visitors from colleges further North (for either a fear of southern justice or better manners apparently restrained Yankee visitors), and a few good old boys and girls without institutional affiliations, come to town to see what all the fuss was about. The judge would give them the choice—a $250 fine or put on an orange vest and give the city six hours of community service. Most chose to serve the community and later that morning they went to work picking up the trash that they had helped scatter about the day before. When they were done, their record was purged, and they went back to doing what they had been doing before—but usually with a little more care. Of course, some never showed up at all. And when they didn't officers went out to the hotels and motels where they were registered, names and addresses in hand, to locate their rooms, wake them up, and haul them off to jail for "failure to appear." That was more serious. The fines were higher and there was a night of jail in the bargain—not the memory they came to the coast to create.

In an interesting aside, *Rolling Stone* added that for those Spring Breakers who were not attracted to the wonders of Panama City Beach, there was Destin, "which once harbored a solid influx of Spring-Break revelers," but since "has lost some of its panache to Panama City." What Destin had to offer, in addition to a few harbor eateries and some scaled-down clubs, was fishing. Whoever wrote the piece knew enough about the place to explain that the "100-fathom curve" offshore attracted everything from bottom feeders to trophy-size billfish, so if fishing was what you wanted, Destin was the place to go. Then, in a nod to the magazine's upscale and affluent readership, the author suggested that rather than venture out on a "party boat" that carried forty or so "hopefuls," fisher-folk should "charter a boat that accepts no more than six people." Though more expensive, "this ensures that you'll receive decent tackle and assistance, and spend less time avoiding the seasick patron next to you." What the author did not mention were any of the bars where charter captains and crew hung out, or the seafood dives where fried and raw were the order of the day. Instead, "before you blast out of town," the writer advised readers, "hit the deck of the Fudpucker's on the beach for a rummy cocktail." If the Trashy White Band was in town, it didn't make the list.

In comparison to what was going on in Panama City Beach and to the attention that community was receiving, Gulf Shores and Orange Beach were nothing short of peaceful. Students came in. The Pink Pony and the Flora-Bama were full and fun, crop dusters were taken out of winter storage so they could drag banners across the sky advertising specials at one place or another, jet skis zoomed across the water, the water slides and miniature golf courses were full. Yes, there was underage drinking. Yes, the traffic was horrible at times. Yes, students cavorted as students always do. Even a few of them "ran amok." But media attention was directed elsewhere. Even the *Birmingham News*, which could always be counted on for a good Gulf Shores Spring Break story, sent its reporting team to Panama City Beach. And why? Largely because in one of those rare moments of "raffish Rotarian" restraint, Pleasure Island promoters had not put out the welcome mat the way Panama City Beach had.

Despite the controversy and the criticism, Spring Break Out 2000 was a financial success, and since the bottom line was, well, the bottom line, the Panama City Beach Convention and Visitors Bureau decided to do it again in 2001. So out went another insert, and soon stressed and shivering students were being told come to Panama City Beach to work on their GPA ("Great Party Action"). Although there was no bikini-clad lass on the poster, the number of "specials" that were advertised more than made up for that omission. The list went on and on: one package included "free cover at La Vela," another let you "Gorge on all the food and drink you can handle for just $15 a day . . . [including] free beer from 10 a.m. to 6 p.m. EVERY DAY," or you could go to the Sandpiper Beacon for the "World's largest & longest keg party, Wet T-Shirt Contest and Wet Jockey Short Contest." And to no one's surprise, half a million answered the call.

So the CVB put out another for 2002, and in an apparent effort to improve on the already successful formula, local establishments added specials that included "all the beer you can handle for $5" and "booze cruises," which sent liquored-up students out on boats in the bay or the Gulf. That was too much for the American Medical Association. In a conference call with reporters around the country the organization's chairman-elect took Panama City Beach to task for its role in changing Spring Break from "an innocent respite from academics" to an event "marred with alcohol-related deaths and injuries and sexual assaults." One can argue just how "innocent" earlier "respites" had been, but the AMA had a point. Hoping to reverse this trend the physicians "strongly recommended" that local businesses stop promotions that encourage students to do the very things the AMA deemed dangerous. Although the Panama City promoters might be making money, the organization warned that doing it by promoting "binge and underage drinking" resulted in a social and physical cost far greater than the monetary profit.

Panama City Beach's excesses caught the attention of some who had no intention of asking local businesses to do anything other than what they were doing. Joe Francis, creator of the popular video series *Girls Gone Wild* heard of the goings on along the Gulf Coast and concluded that a "wide open" Panhandle community was a perfect location for his Spring Break taping. Now it is unlikely that anyone reading this book does not know about *Girls Gone Wild,* but just in case, in theory the enterprise works like this: Francis and his crew would arrive at a location where young women are known to "go wild." When the young women did, Francis and crew filmed them—topless, bottomless, and often engaging in sexually suggestive (and for some, sexually stimulating) activities. Francis claimed that he was careful to confirm that all of the girls he filmed were over the age of eighteen and had them sign a waiver saying they agree to the filming and to their "naughty bits" being shown and sold in the video.

Half-naked, thoroughly drunken women getting their pictures taken down along the coast was nothing new. Spring Break reports often included accounts of guys who walked along the beach with disposable cameras, offering "Mardi Gras–style beads for a peek of flesh" and a picture. Francis surely figured he could do the same. What the creator of *Girls Gone Wild* did not realize was that things were changing along the coast. Panama City Beach mayor Lee Sullivan, the former police chief, had begun trying to clean up the town's "once-tawdry image," and as far as he was concerned, what Francis was planning would "go counter" to that effort. Local police had already cracked down and arrested some amateur photographers and their "models" for doing what they did on a public beach, but apparently the *Girls Gone Wild* team figured that in the land of contests that involved "wet T-shirts" and "wet jockey shorts" the line between what was legal and what was not was blurred and easily crossed.

So it should have come as no surprise that Joe Francis would think Panama City Beach was just the place for him to do what he wanted to do.

He did not figure on Mayor Sullivan.

Panama City Beach was indeed cleaning up its act. Reacting to the AMA criticism of its promotional activities, the Spring Break 2003 advertisement highlighted concerts, great disc jockeys, lazy river rides, jet skiing, and parasailing instead of "booze cruises" and keg parties. It urged students to drink responsibly and advised those who went clubbing, "If you came with a friend, leave with that friend . . . call a cab . . . refuse a drink of any kind from a stranger . . . [and] realize that drinking laws will be enforced." The president and chief executive officer of the tourist bureau set the tone. "We hope that students will take a minute to realize that their safety and fun depends on the decisions they make throughout spring break," he told the press. It wasn't "milk and cookies" they were selling, but neither was it "free beer from 10 a.m. to 6 p.m. EVERY DAY."

It was not as if Francis and *Girls Gone Wild* had not been warned. As soon as word got out that the operation might come to Panama City Beach Sullivan announced, "[If] girls go wild they'll also go to jail and so will those who take videos of them baring it all." Reminding the press of his efforts to improve the town's image, Sullivan added, "We're trying to have a good resort and a good tourism business." What Joe Francis was bringing in was not something the mayor wanted his community "subjected to."

Francis and his crew arrived amid even more "hoopla" than was "usual" even for them. What followed played out like this, more or less: Girls went wild and were filmed, just as they had at other times and in other places. Then the father of one that had been filmed with another in a steamy shower scene contacted the sheriff's office and reported that his daughter was a minor. The sheriff's office got in touch with Sullivan and the mayor brought the hammer down. Arrested and charged with more than seventy counts that included "racketeering, drug trafficking, prostitution and promoting the sexual performance of children," Francis and company were hauled off to jail, his Ferrari and private jet were confiscated, and officers collected some 175 hours of video recordings of Spring Break parties, footage that "prosecutors say . . . contains alleged minors performing sex acts."

When Francis got out on bail, he sued Bay County and everyone involved in his arrest, claiming that his First Amendment rights were violated, and into the courts it went. You almost need a map to follow what happened after that. All but six of the criminal charges were thrown out because of a "flawed search warrant," but before Francis could deal with what charges remained the two girls in the shower scene, both seventeen, plus five other women, sued Girls Gone Wild for "emotional distress." This landed Francis back in jail and eventually led to contempt charges for not properly participating in court-ordered mediation. Out on bail again, he was slapped with a criminal contempt order for failing to show up on time when he was ordered back to Florida. He settled the lawsuit with the girls and made bail, but before he could leave the jail, guards found prescription pills and money in his cell. The next thing Francis knew he was facing criminal charges for bringing contraband into a detention facility. Bail was denied because he had "impugned the integrity of the judicial process," and he likely would be there still had he not been transferred to Nevada to face tax evasion charges.

Just about everybody left behind in Florida agrees that through it all the man behind Girls Gone Wild was his own worst enemy. State attorney Jim Appleman, who was close to the case in its initial phase, felt that by announcing that Panama City Beach "was wide open and he was going to do what he wanted to do" Francis was daring the mayor to stop him, and Sullivan was not the sort of person to run from a dare. From the moment he arrived, Joe Francis was a "marked" man. While not completely disagreeing with Appleman, Sullivan says it was Francis's "arrogance and bad judgment," his "cavalier attitude," and his "obvious disdain" for authority that got him into trouble. Joe Francis did himself no favors by ranting on about "corrupt city officials," the "evil" and "vengeful" "Nazis" and "cockroaches," who he claimed were "pissed off at me for asserting my First Amendment rights against them." Once out of Florida, Francis had a website set up to present his side of the story. He also went on the Fox News Channel to tell lawyer and talk show host Greta Van Susteren how he had been wronged by the mayor and the rest.

Sullivan, as you would expect, would have none of it. To the mayor, Joe Francis was nothing but "a soft porn director" who "gets young women to expose themselves and has it on a video and sells it to men who can't function without that encouragement." The constitutional argument was just an after-the-fact excuse. What really happened, according to Sullivan, was that Francis came down to what he thought was "Gooberville" and "we rained on his parade." When he left, "Panama City Beach did not have the allure [it had] before he got here."

Reflecting on the events and the controversy, talk show host Van Susteren brought it all into focus. It had become "a grudge match," she said. "Joe has poked a stick in the eyes of the prosecutors" and they are "messing with him" in return. And they were. For despite all the upscale condos, the clubs, the fern bars, and the white-tablecloth restaurants, one principle of the Redneck Riviera remained intact—mess with me and I'm gonna mess back.

And as if this were not enough, there was Snoop Dogg.

The rapper, whom Francis allegedly described as a "bitch magnet," came down with the *Girls Gone Wild* crew to film *Girls Gone Wild: Doggy Style* and was arrested for luring two underage girls to take off their tops in exchange for marijuana and Ecstasy. In response Snoop filed an affidavit saying the girls voluntarily exposed themselves. But by then Snoop was having a change of heart, at least as far as his association with Joe Francis was concerned. Surveying the situation the "bitch magnet" cut his ties with Francis because *Girls Gone Wild* was discriminating against African Americans. "If you notice," he told the Associated Press, "there hasn't been no girls [of color] at all on none of those tapes. That ain't cool, because white girls ain't the only hos that get wild." He told the press that black and Hispanic "hos" have been "complaining to me like crazy" and to answer their complaints he was thinking of producing his own line of videos. That, he concluded, would "bring some flavor to the table."

Not exactly what the advocates of affirmative action had in mind.

And thus it ended, not with bang, but with a whimper.

Joe Francis was gone and reportedly would rather stay in a Nevada jail than return to Panama City Beach to face the charges that remained. Girls might still go wild on the coast, but not in Francis videos.

Local Convention and Visitors Bureau folks toned down their Spring Break promotions. There would be no more mail-outs to colleges advertising all the booze, sex, and rock and roll anyone could want, but a partnership worked out with MTV would assure local businesses that students would know that Panama City Beach was "the premier Spring Break 'place to be' for the country's college crowd."

"Arrested? Call Appleman." This sign near the Panama City clubs offers legal aid to those who need it. Photograph by the author.

Lee Sullivan eventually ran for state representative, lost, and became a local Fox News talk show host. From that platform he continued "refining Gooberville" and exploring ways to "have good business without an overabundance [of] debauchery."

Jim Appleman retired from his position as state attorney, went into private practice, and has used his experience to become the "Spring Break Lawyer"—as attested to by billboards strategically located around town, advising students, "Arrested? Call Appleman."

The official chosen to review the 175 hours of tapes confiscated from Francis's tour bus watched them all and reportedly told his wife that he never wanted to see a bare breast again.

And the students?

They kept returning.

Always young, always happy, always a little stupid, always looking to do things they could not do back home.

Just like those who had come before them.

THIRTEEN

Selling the Redneck Riviera

PANAMA CITY BEACH may have wanted to refine its image—"there is a difference between 'having' spring break and 'being' spring break" Mayor Sullivan pointed out—but local businesses did not want to refine away any of the $300 million that Spring Break brought in. "To walk away from that level of revenue," the president and CEO of the city's Convention and Visitors Bureau noted, "is not a prudent decision." And if nothing else, those folks were "prudent." So they cheered and patted themselves on their collective backs when Joe Francis was run out of town, and then they returned to the business of hosing down T-shirt clad women, holding bikini contests, and, with the help of MTV, spreading the word that there was still a party going on. As a result, little really changed. The kids kept coming, they kept spending, and "raffish Rotarians" kept loving it.

One example can serve for all.

According to "Spring Break lawyer" Jim Appleman (and he should know), despite the city's promises to curb student excesses, the "Wal-Mart on the beach sells more beer than any other establishment in the U.S. during the months of April, May, and June." He had been there and seen "four guys with four shopping carts [in which] they have got ten to twelve cases of beer wheeling them out the door." To keep up with demand the store had "a truck that is coming there constantly" and

One of the old Panama City Beach motels still in operation. Photograph by the author.

there were "refrigerated semis in the back that sit full of beer." From the trucks to the students was a short trip. Business as usual.

However, there was concern in some quarters, not about what the students were doing but about changes on the beach that might prevent them from doing it. In addition to being drawn to Panama City Beach by its "good party reputation," in years past students liked the town because of cheap accommodations such as the Majestic Motel and Resort, which for years was "symbolic of the laid-back, no frills style" those early Spring Breakers sought. Advertising the "cheapest rooms" on the beach, the Majestic, with its onsite bar, its clutter, its noise and lack of rules and regulations, was firmly fixed in the memories of many—if they could remember anything at all. But in 2002, it was announced that the Majestic was coming down and a "pricy condo" was going up. City officials, who were striving to "undo their town's honky-tonk image through ordinances limiting garish signs, adult businesses and tattoo parlors," applauded the decision, but some business owners expressed concern that this would reduce the ranks of Spring Breakers. If, as expected, the number of hotel and motel rooms declined from about nine thousand in 2003 to around forty-four hundred in 2007, where would the students stay?

In condos!

There were, and always would be, students who came to Spring Break on the cheap, who sought out places like the Majestic for thirty-five dollars a night, or who just slept in their cars or on the beach. But by the 1990s a new breed of Spring Breakers were coming to the coast. Like their parents, whose credit card they carried, they came looking for something more upscale and sophisticated than the Majestic or a backseat or a tent. Driving down in "personality" cars—SUVs that had never been off-road, cute convertibles bought for Daddy's little princess, cars that made a statement about attitude and affluence—they arrived with more money and high expectations and were willing to spend the former to achieve the latter. So they rented a condo. It was what they wanted and, more importantly, what they were used to. As any campus housing director would have told you, the days of two-to-a-room-gang-shower-down-the-hall dormitories were over. Modern students wanted their space and amenities, and they (or their parents) were willing to pay a bit more for these luxuries. Renting a two-to-three bedroom condo with a small group was more like the life they lived in their dorm suite or apartment back at college. They came to the beach to party, not to slum. And if they happened to meet that "special someone" they would surely rather invite him or her back to a designer-decorated condo than to a "low rent rendezvous" like the Majestic. Condos were "chick magnets." Motel rooms, well, weren't.

But it wasn't the loss of student guests filling in the "dead season" between snowbirds and the summer crowd that doomed the small motels. Nor was it the low interest rates that allowed developers to borrow and build cheaply, or even the "general gentrification of the beach" that took place in the 1990s and spilled over into the twenty-first century. All of those mattered, but what mattered most was that as the new century opened, property values were on the rise and motel owners were being offered more for their establishments than they ever dreamed they could get—so they took it. "The beach ain't going to be the same no more," a cleaning lady at the Majestic told a reporter. "But it's progress."

Yes it was.

And it was happening all along the coast.

Late in the 1990s the *Mobile Press-Register* wrote of the "Invasion of the Condos" on the Fort Morgan peninsula, where rezoning for density and height had become an issue. In Gulf Shores and Orange Beach it was much the same. All along Pleasure Island developers were gobbling up land and building on it. As one resident put it, the "genie was out of the bottle."

Over on the Panhandle, Destin was no better. Writer Rick Bragg traveled U.S. 98 in 1999 and was appalled at what he saw. "Concrete condominiums, as imposing as anything in Miami or Fort Lauderdale, line the beach front on both sides of this paradise, blocking views of the Gulf [while] tower cranes in the distance promise more." Destin was once "the world's luckiest fishing village" but, Bragg wrote, "now the village is gone, at least the village that older people remember," and "the fishing is no longer so lucky." Real estate folk didn't seem to care. They were "turning sand into money," and lots of it. By 2000, around 86 percent of Destin's land area was built on and developers were looking at the rest with "cash register eyeballs." Sales of condos doubled from the year before, as the Florida Panhandle became "a playground of the new, fat economy." It seemed that the boom that had been building since the mid-nineties would go on forever.

So, even as they bemoaned what they were losing, Destin residents like charter boat captain Michael Beaubien admitted, "We knew we weren't going to keep this beauty secret for a long time." But, he reflected, "how could we put a fence around us and say, 'No, get out'?" Yet even as they accepted what their village was becoming, they were not entirely happy with the people who were making it so. Condo owners who visited a couple of weeks a year and rented out their units the rest of the time had no connection to the town. "Instead of accepting our heritage of a small town," one resident complained, "they just want to change it"—which was one of the things that differentiated this group of interlopers from those who came before them. The people who visited the beach after World War II and their children and even their children's children came to enjoy the coast for what it was, and what it was wasn't: home. But among the new invaders were upscale investors who wanted what they had at the coast "to be just like where they came from." They wanted to remake the Redneck Riviera in their own image, an image that, at least as they saw it, was anything but redneck.

So it was, all along the coast. "It's kind of heartbreaking to see it turn into concrete," reflected Dewey Destin, great-great-grandson of the town's founder and namesake. "There are more jobs and the properties are worth more money," he acknowledged, but he lamented that the growth had hurt the local fishery, made the water dirtier, and clogged roads with traffic.

"But," he added, "this is what you get when you exchange nature for economic well-being." And the economy was doing well, especially the real estate market. In 1990, there were 194 new condo units sold in the Destin–Fort Walton area. In 1997, that number reached 937—with prices ranging from $300,000 to $1.4 million. "We have been discovered," county commissioner Nick Nicholson told Bragg. And they had.

And not just Destin and not just condos. Along Highway 30-A in south Walton County, new upscale developments appeared. Using some of the same New Urbanism concepts as Seaside—a town center, public spaces, and everything within walking distance with a baby in tow—they each added a particular touch that made each unique. On the east end of the highway was Rosemary Beach, built where folks who lived alternate lifestyles and wore few if any clothes once frolicked. Rosemary was the first, but soon others followed—Alys Beach and WaterSound—crowding out the small clusters of low-rise condos and faux-Seaside houses that were built after the road was paved but before the new and affluent came to change things. One can only imagine what a visitor in the 1990s must have thought of the seventies-era log cabin resort tackily tucked in among it all. How much longer could that last?

Longer, it seems, than the goats that once grazed on Ono Island.

On the Alabama coast, Ono set the standard for upscale and exclusive. Because it was located hard against the Florida line, when island development began in the 1970s the first residents were cut from pretty much the same cloth as those on the mainland. One of the early owners selected his lot, he said, because it was "right straight north of the Flora-Bama" and from there he could "get a pair of binoculars and see [whether] the Baptist or Methodists [were] going in." However, the island developed rapidly and soon the waterfront lots were filled with big, expensive houses with big, expensive boats tied to the docks. It became "the" address for many of Alabama's elite (Kenny Stabler owned a home there). Though inland there were older homes that were more modest than the ones you could see from the mainland, Ono Island's reputation for isolating the rich and famous from the common herd spread. Accessible by water or by the gated bridge, Ono Island was, in effect, an unincorporated, self-governing community of permanent and part-time residents unencumbered by and generally unconcerned with things other folks did. It was Alabama's version of Seaside, but without all the New Urbanist theories and with a gate.

Then the weather turned.

In recent years there had been hurricanes, tropical storms, rain events, and such all along the coast. There had been wind damage and beach erosion. Storm surges had washed out roads and washed away structures on the water. But there had been nothing like Frederic or even Opal. So residents knew that time was running against them and in September, 2004, time ran out.

Folks along the coast watched Hurricane Ivan as it battered Granada and Jamaica, drifted into the Gulf, grew to a Category 5, 160 MPH wind monster and turned north. On Monday, September 13, people in coastal areas were told to evacuate. Then, as the storm approached Alabama, Governor Bob Riley ordered everyone who lived in Mobile and Baldwin counties, south of Interstate 10, to get out. Roads heading inland became one-way, and for the first time all lanes of Interstate 65 were northbound. Along the coast, from New Orleans to Panama City, residents heeded the warnings and soon an estimated two million people were on the move. At 3:00 on the morning of September 16, Ivan's eye came ashore at Gulf Shores. Although it had weakened to a Category 3 storm, the surge drove water across Pleasure Island and into the bayou behind. Then the storm tracked into Alabama, taking hurricane-force winds far into the state and leaving thousands without electricity. In the weeks that followed, power company crews from all over the Southeast arrived to help repair the damage.

Returning evacuees found roads washed away, roofs gone, docks and piers splintered, boats washed up on shore, signs down, and damage everywhere. The National Guard patrolled round the clock. Governor Riley made the Gulf Shores United Methodist Church his headquarters and from there state relief efforts were coordinated with those of the Red Cross, the Salvation Army, and FEMA, the Federal Emergency Management Agency that many on the coast felt made thing worse instead of better. A team from the Southern Baptist Association arrived with green shirts and chain saws to help clear trees that seemed to be down everywhere. Some people said it was Frederic all over again, but it wasn't. One of the differences apparent to those who had survived that storm a quarter of a century before was that government aid and insurance companies got there quicker and were better organized—especially the insurance companies. More property was destroyed and damaged by Ivan than by Frederic because there was more down there to damage and destroy. The insurance companies understood

Beach after Hurricane Ivan. The author's cousin Benny sits on a piece of a deck that washed in. Photograph by Martha Hauptman.

this and were anxious to find out just how bad it was for their customers and their stockholders. They did not like what they found.

One of those customers was the Flora-Bama. The storm surge gutted the ground floor, which included the main bar with its bras and decorated bathroom stalls. The wall of water swept across the road and pushed the trailers, shacks, and the gazebo of Boys Town into Old River. And when the water subsided the sand remained. Soon word spread east and west and inland that the Flora-Bama was hurt, maybe even beyond repair. The *Mobile Press-Register* reported that "beach bums from Apalachicola to Atmore were clutching their beers in fear." The future of the most famous bar on the coast was in doubt.

But the Bama was not finished. Owners Gilchrist and McClellan resolved to "renovate the Flora-Bama in such a way that after a couple of drinks, it will all feel the same." There would be some changes: for example, the main bar would be bigger—"it was getting a little cramped" anyway, Gilchrist told reporters. Otherwise the owners promised that the rebuilt Bama, with its warren of rooms, would be true to "the style, structure, and mystique of the pre-Ivan Flora-Bama for generations to come." All this involved putting back into the Bama as much of the memorabilia and graffiti-covered walls and stalls as they could. This, the owners told their friends, would "be tricky" because in spite of the damage, people kept coming to drink and party, so the Bama was "as busy as ever." But Gilchrist and McClellan were sure they could work around it.

One of the things they had to work around was the Frank Brown International Songwriters Festival. Sponsored by the Bama and held mostly on its premises, the festival had become a much anticipated November event. Scheduled after the last warm-weather visitors were gone but before the snowbirds arrive, like the Mullet Toss in April the festival pumped life into what were some of the deadest weeks on the coast. Named after the Bama's legendary night watchman, it attracted the known and not-so-known, the successful and the wannabes, who came because the Bama was a place where they could play their music, not someone else's, to appreciative audiences. There was a moment after Ivan when some talked of postponing the festival for a year, but the coastal community rallied around the bar and the songwriters. New venues were set up along the beach, accommodations opened up for the artists, and working together they pulled it off.

The biggest hurdle the Flora-Bama had to overcome may have been the Escambia County Board of Adjustments, which had to be convinced to approve the variances the Bama needed to build back like it was. After a lot of arguing and jumping through bureaucratic hoops, the board finally agreed to allow the rebuilding. With the papers signed, Gilchrist and McClellan set out to prove once again that they knew how to turn just about anything into a party—and do a little charitable fund-raising in the process. On a warm Saturday in April, 2005, the week before mullets were scheduled to be tossed, "hundreds of domestic-beer clutching" fans of the Flora-Bama gathered to watch the Mullet Man Triathlon, a charity event, after which McClellan and Gilchrist handed out bricks salvaged from the bar, numbered and certified and signed in exchange for a donation to an organization called Rebuild Northwest Florida, which was helping folks who lost homes in the storm. Then Gilchrist ceremoniously unscrewed the address numbers to use in the new Flora-Bama, made a little speech saying "goodbye to our old building," and then stepped aside. Then a typical Flora-Bama crowd—"bikers, southern belles, vacationing business people, triathlon participants, wealthy owners of neighboring condos, news crews, construction workers, firefighters"—joined a "kilt-wearing man" in singing

The Flora-Bama rebuilt after Ivan. Despite the damage and the loss of so many of the features of the place (restroom wall autographs and most of the original bras hanging from the ceiling), new bras were tossed, and customers claim that the restored Bama is just as much fun as the old. Photograph by the author.

"Amazing Grace" and watched as a John Deere excavator knocked down what was left of the Flora-Bama.

There were some tears, but most were certain that the Last Great American Roadhouse would come back better than ever. "We're going to make it as ugly as possible," Phillip Harter, told the press. Harter, a Bama bartender for nearly twenty years and a temporary worker for FEMA until the bar opened again, summed up the mood of most: "A couple of big parties, and it'll be back to normal." He was right.

Hurricane season 2005 started out badly for the Redneck Riviera when Hurricane Dennis came ashore west of Pensacola in July, but it was a minimal storm and though there were evacuations and damage Dennis was no Ivan. Nor was it a Katrina, which hit New Orleans in late August and erased for most Americans the memories of the storms that had previously pounded Pleasure Island and the Panhandle. That suited the Alabama Gulf Coast Convention and Visitors Bureau just fine. Concerned that a fear of hurricanes would discourage tourists from coming down, the president of the bureau went before the city councils of Orange Beach and Gulf Shores and asked that in the future references to "hurricanes" in public statements be replaced by the phrase "tropical occurrences." A consultant had been brought in to advise them how to calm public fears and the consultant suggested the substitution. "Consumers have short memories," the consultant told them, "so don't keep reminding them." Of course the "H-word" did not disappear, but neither did the tourists.

And neither did the investors. In the wake of Hurricane Ivan came another "perfect storm" of economic activity brought on by a collision of investors, money, and projects. In stories that sounded a lot like those written after Frederic, newspapers reported that "many property owners, instead of fixing damage caused by the hurricane, took the opportunity [to] sell their land, pocketing their insurance proceeds to boot"—a double payback on their investment. With a variety of loans available and regulatory oversight insignificant, developers found it "easier to get financing for $1 million-a-pop condos than $100-a-night hotel rooms," so the money poured into condos. At the same time real estate analysts were noting that "aging baby boomers [were seeking] second homes on which to spend their increasingly disposable incomes" and that "these demographic and market changes [had] spurred an increase in condominium sales." Between 1993 and 2003, following trends like those over in Destin and Panama City Beach, the number of condo units on the Alabama coast doubled from seven thousand to fourteen thousand, and that number was expected to double again by 2008. Meanwhile, prices kept going up. Even with Ivan and Dennis, the median price of a condo in 2004 was $203,200, nearly a 17 percent increase over the year before. In six months beachfront property, if you could find it, went from $70,000 a foot to $1 million or more. John Brett of Brett-Robinson Company, one of the largest real estate developers on the coast, loved it. "I feel like we're in an emerging market here. A lot of growth potential," he said, "as long as the market holds."

In 2004 the market seemed to be holding pretty well. Along Scenic Highway 30-A, in south Walton County, where a fifty-foot height restriction kept high-rise condos out, no one in real estate was suffering. In 2003 the average cost of a second home there was $587,000, and in places like Grayton Beach and Seaside homes were selling for well over $2 million. With prices like that it was hardly surprising that in Walton and neighboring Okaloosa County home construction increased 575 percent in 2004. But another perfect storm was brewing, one caused by inflated prices, low lending standards, easily circumvented zoning laws, and good old-fashioned greed.

A lot of people wanted property near the Gulf and demand was outrunning supply. So to get more units on a relatively small amount of land, developers proposed to go up, higher and higher. But even communities like Gulf Shores, Orange Beach, and Destin had limitations on height and over in Panama City Beach a politician with a no-growth platform ran for mayor—and won—so "higher and higher" had its opponents. Then in a move that would make any coastal chamber of commerce proud, Orange Beach mayor Steve Russo led the city council to approve an arrangement that allowed developers to build what they wanted to build as long as they would reward the city in return—Destin adopted a "tier" system that accomplished the same thing. Rewards for the city included valuable beachfront, infrastructure improvements, and other concessions that, in time would include pledges of around $100 million in property and services. The practice was called "bribery" by those who opposed it and "good business" by those who didn't. What it meant was that if a developer could "show benefits to justify the City Council's deviations from development standards" then the city council could approve the deviations. And who judged whether or not the benefits justified the deviations? Why the city council.

Since it was illegal in Alabama for a county or municipality to charge developers a standard "impact fee," as is done in other states, city leaders simply refused to rezone property for the development if they felt the public benefits weren't sufficient to justify the arrangement. Developers did not seem to mind, publicly at least, and Larry Wireman, of the most successful developers on the beach, may have spoken for most of them when he said, "I don't think they're being unfair at all." If the developer is "going to burden [city infrastructure], I think you should try to do something good for the city" in return. Maybe so, but it was a system ripe for exploitation, and there were rumors of money being passed under the table before a vote was taken. Then, in 2006, Mayor Russo and a local real estate developer were indicted and later convicted on federal criminal corruption charges that involved a land scheme that netted the mayor $400,000 in return for services rendered.

The Orange Beach arrangement may have gotten the mayor in trouble, but it also made a lot of folks rich. As developers got permission to build, people who owned the property that developers wanted to develop were in an enviable position. If they played their cards right, held out until the right moment, they got top dollar for their parcel. However, those living next door were not particularly happy with their neighbor's good fortune, especially if it meant that their property would soon be shaded by condos. So into the city council meeting they went to protest that the high-rises going up beside them would "eventually lead to [their] property being surrounded by condo towers, diminishing its serenity," and destroying their way of life. Mayor Russo and many on the council were not particularly impressed with their argument and in one observation, the irony of which would become evident when his corruption case went to trial, Russo expressed his belief that those folks who were trying to "preserve this single-family residential area" only wanted to get the same sort of money their neighbors had gotten. "I don't think," he told the group, "it's right [to hold up a project] until they get enough zeros."

But the real money was not in selling the land. It was in selling the condos. Or better yet, selling condos-to-be. In the first decade of the twenty-first century a whole new breed of "raffish . . . hard-handed . . . pirates" focused their "cash register eyeballs" on the coast and before they were done, "flipping" had become the new way to make money, lots of money, and make it fast.

"Flipping," quite simply, was a variation on the old and time-honored practice of buying low and selling high. But in what came to be called the "condo game," investors with access to credit and connections with real estate agents who could handle the deal were able to buy a condominium that existed only on paper, then sell it quickly, at a tidy profit, before a single nail was nailed or a yard of concrete poured. This selling and reselling—flipping—created such a demand for condos that more and more beachfront homes and motels were bought at higher and higher prices, knocked down, and replaced with massive condominiums, such as the two three-hundred-foot towers of Larry Wireman's Turquoise Place. Although that project was not scheduled to be completed for two years, in the summer of 2004, units went on the market at prices starting at $1 million. And they sold—in some cases, more than once.

According to real estate agent Bob Shallow, the strategy employed by flippers was to buy a high-priced condo, built or planned, with little of their own money invested, and then sell it as quickly as possible. Twenty percent was the usual down payment, but with the right connections the investor could cover the required 20 percent for as little as 1 percent of the money up front. Then the investor would turn around and sell to a ready buyer, make a tidy profit, pay off what he owed the bank and agent, and then walk away with thousands of dollars, while the new buyer went looking for someone to whom the unit could be sold. Shallow, one of the most successful agents on the coast, gathered a cadre of investors he could steer to condos ripe for flipping. He called his group the Dolphin Club after Flipper, the TV dolphin.

Bob Shallow and Orange Beach were not unique. All along the coast agents and flippers lined up to make money fast, but they weren't the only ones. Flipping was part of what *Time* magazine called a national "raucous obsession with real estate" that produced popular TV shows like *Flip This House* and created the housing bubble that lifted the economy after the tech crash of the 1990s dragged it down. However there were those who warned that "the same psychology of greed" that burst the tech bubble could burst this one as well. No one wanted to listen to such "buzz-kill talk." They would rather hear people like Shallow describe how they were working in what was "without a doubt the best market ever" and they believed Shallow when he said "nowhere in the country [was] it so stable and flush" as it was along the Gulf Coast. Such assurances—bolstered by stories of condos selling two, three, and even four times before anyone actually got a key to the unit, with everyone involved making money—were more than enough to keep the profit minded in the game. Besides, if the buyers disappeared and the selling stopped, the owners would still have a condo to use or rent and an interest-only loan they could afford until the market turned around. Or, the more unscrupulous among them understood that with only a few thousand dollars of their own money in the scheme, they could just walk away and leave the bank or the developer holding the bag.

Not that anyone thought that would ever happen. Agents and developers with some sense of history argued that the boom and bust of the early 1980s was the result of a "false market" that collapsed amid concerns over double-digit mortgage rates and fears that changes in the tax code would discontinue deductions for interest paid on second homes. But in 2004, they assured (that word again) investors that the demand for second homes was a real one and market forces would keep that demand high. Then they reminded the cautious that back in 1991, the forty-eight-unit Surfside Shores condo on Pleasure Island went on the market for an average per-unit price of about $95,000. All units were sold within four months. In January 2003, sixty-six units of the twenty-six-story Island Tower, not far from Surfside Shores, went on preconstruction sale for an average of around $430,000. They were gone in less than an hour. Eighteen months later, though Island Tower was still under construction, units were reselling at an average price of more than $700,000. Better get in while the getting in was good, agents and developers advised.

Condominiums were not the only real estate that flippers flipped. In coastal counties, Walton in particular, where height limitations were actually enforced, more single-family, second-home developments appeared—some gated, some not—and though the turnover was not as rapid as in the "condo game," resales were frequent and a lot of money changed hands.

How much money? In 2004, the *Mobile Press-Register* traced the brief history of units 103 and 407 in the Caribe Resort Condominiums in Orange Beach. In May of 2002, a woman from Point Clear, Alabama, bought unit 103, a completed three-bedroom, three-bath condo, for $295,000. The next day she sold it to a Louisiana couple for $380,000. It may have been a prearranged deal, but whether it was or wasn't, the seller made $85,000 in less than twenty-four hours. Four months later the Louisiana couple sold it to another Louisiana couple for $475,000 and made $95,000. Good work if you can get it. As for unit 407, in May of 2002, at its initial offering, two Gulf Shores women bought it for $399,000. A year later they sold it to an Orange Beach couple for $640,000. A few months later those owners sold 407 to a partnership registered in Georgia but apparently controlled by a prominent family in Atmore, Alabama, for $735,000. "In less than two years," the *Press-Register* noted, "unit 407 increased in value by 84 percent."

Of course there were people who were concerned by this rapid rise in prices. Some warned that it could not go on forever. Because so many of the buyers were speculators who never intended to occupy what they were buying, some predicted that sooner or later the market was "going to have a problem." They knew that speculators do not hold on to property. They have to turn it over fast. If there is not someone to buy it, rent it, live in it, or use it as a second home, the whole house of cards would collapse, which is what happened.

Late in 2007, the condo game began to unravel. Though most folks did not think of the ever-rising prices along the Gulf Coast as part of a worldwide speculative bubble in real estate, that was what it was. When risky loans were exposed and overinflated asset prices began to fall, the bubble burst. Far away from the Redneck Riviera the failure of financial institutions like Lehman Brothers sent shock waves through the real estate market and overnight, or so it seemed to developers and buyers, the days of easy credit were over. "Investiculators"—as the high rollers, the in-quick and out-quicker take-the-money-and-run folks were called—were left with property they could not sell and debts they could not pay. Foreclosures mounted. "The flippers," one real estate agent observed, "have flopped."

It was not a pretty sight. I know; I saw it.

In Destin, where an Orange Beach–like tier system was created that allowed developers to build higher and bigger in exchange for something that would benefit the public, more and more condominiums went up. And as in Orange Beach, when the credit dried up the buyers went away. By the summer of 2008, finished projects sat empty, unfinished projects remained unfinished, and banks owned a lot of real estate they didn't want and couldn't sell. Riding along Destin's "concrete canyon corridor of condominiums" the "For Sale" signs were everywhere. Foreclosure announcements filled a whole section of the local newspaper, testimonies in print of hopes that had vanished and dreams that would never come true. Back when the boom was at its peak one real estate agent told a reporter, "The last time I heard so much talk about easy money was right before the bubble burst on tech stocks." But not to worry, the agent said, for "with condos, unlike the stock market, you won't wake up in the morning and lose half your value." Well, maybe not half, but as real estate went into a free fall, people who found that they owed more on a condo than it was worth knew they were in trouble.

It was much the same further down the coast. Just west of Panama City Beach, La Borgata, Alan Jackson's much-touted "residential, family oriented" development, sat empty and forlorn. Sand blew from the houseless lots and covered paved streets on which no cars traveled. Underground utility connections stuck up from the soil like so many trees that had been planted and had died, leaving only the trunks. And someone—a vandal with a sense of irony or a disgruntled investor—had slipped in and changed the name on the sign to read "La Forgata."

Further west, where once everyone was building, the hammers and saws were silent and the lilting sounds of Spanish were no longer heard. No one was working. "Hard times," in the words of a local writer: "'For Sale' and 'For Lease' signs rise like tombstones from the white sand and tawny sea grass that line Walton County Road 30-A, which winds through more than a dozen exclusive, resort communities." The area was attracting fewer tourists and those who did come spent less. Local businesses were hurting. Which ones survived depended largely on "how long they have been around." Older establishments, restaurants, fish markets, and grocery stores would make it, even though some cafes that had enjoyed year-round business were moving back to the "traditional business model" and closing in the winter. Retail and service industries, the ones that depended on discretionary spending, might not make it.

Even deep-pocketed developers such as the St. Joe Company saw sales decline and the planned expansion of WaterColor was delayed. Nearby, at its sister development, WaterSound, lots sat empty, ponds were only half full, and landscaping had been deferred. But nowhere was the impact of the downturn more evident than at Nature Walk, a gated community nestled in between St. Joe's land, Seagrove Beach, and a state forest. Developers had taken this perfect location and put in winding streets, bike and walking trails, board walks and bridges, parks with ponds and benches, a pool and cabana—all a homeowner could want. At the entrance they built a welcome center with tall windows to let in the light and high ceilings to give potential buyers a sense of space and freedom. Landscaped with plants native to the area, the center suggested what homeowners could do with the lot they bought, if they bought one, but no one did.

Timing, they say, is everything, and for Nature Walk the timing was bad. Opening just as the recession hit, its owners could not sell the lots and could not pay the bank what they owed it. Soon the welcome center closed and the people who were there to welcome customers went to another job, if they could find one. The gate was locked. A sign was erected telling anyone who might wander by which financial institution now owned it. The wooden bridges cracked and splintered in the sun. Weeds grew out of cracks in the streets and sidewalks. Trash collected on the paths. And a small cluster of display homes, built to show customers what they could have if they bought in, sat half-finished and empty, doors open for anyone who wandered by, but not even vandals came through. Nature was taking over Nature Walk.

All along the Redneck Riviera, realtors still on the job but barely hanging on reflected on what had happened, on how "out of control" the market had been only a short time before. They recalled how in those heady days of Dolphin Clubs and flippers, "We actually saw 'seller's remorse,' where the sellers felt that they could have gotten more for their property if they had waited." That was "quite a switch from what we are seeing today," real

SELLING THE REDNECK RIVIERA 227

estate veteran John Cook told a reporter who was putting together the 2008 Progress Edition for the *Destin Log*. Instead of sellers who were remorseful for not waiting, there were "sellers willing to do almost anything to unload a property." The good old days were just that—good and old. "I am certain," Cook added, "that we will never see such a sight again in our lifetimes."

Maybe so. But along the Gulf Coast, few people really believed that anything could last long—even if it were good, but especially if it were bad.

FOURTEEN

"Where Nature Did Its Best"

I'VE ALWAYS FOUND IT more than a little ironic that C. H.
McGee chose "where nature did its best" to entice people to
come to Seagrove Beach and despoil it. But McGee was no different from the other developers who were attracted to the
natural beauty of the Redneck Riviera and, once there, set
about erasing as much of it as they could.

When Peter Bos arrived in Destin in 1972, only a few years
out of Cornell School of Hotel Administration and "searching
for development opportunities," he looked at the harbor and
declared it "the singularly most beautiful piece of property"
he had ever seen. For the next thirty years Bos built a career
in the area. He took over and expanded Sandestin Golf and
Beach Resort, developed marinas, built an upscale shopping
mall that he called Destin Commons, and created Legendary
Inc., a family of companies that gave him an interest in just
about every sort of business on the coast. Among the properties he developed was HarborWalk Village, a collection
of shops and restaurants anchored by the Emerald Grande
Towers, "Destin's only full-service resort." Emerald Grande, in
all its buff and burgundy glory, sat at the foot of the Destin
Bridge, squarely in the middle of that "singularly most beautiful piece of property" that caught his eye in 1972, dwarfing the
docks and dominating everything.

Bos's Legendary operations may have been what Dewey
Destin was referring to when he talked about "what you get

Emerald Grande dominating Destin Harbor, 2009. Photograph by the author.

when you exchange nature for economic well-being." However, it must be said that Bos was no worse, and in some cases was better, than most when it came to preserving and protecting natural surroundings, though he did so in that well-established Florida tradition of making nature conform to what developers wanted it to be—whether what they wanted it to be was "natural" or not. The Emerald Grande was just that: grand, and colorful, and gaudy, and well appointed, and opulent (what else could you call a counter-top made of marble that the brochure boasted came from the same quarry that supplied the Paris Opera House?), and overwhelming—so tall that in some seasons it shaded parts of old Destin from dawn to dusk, like a sun-dial. So it was no surprise that Bos's creation had more than its share of we-want-our-village-as-it-used-to-be critics. But Destin city manager Greg Kisela would have none of it. "Whether or not you like Emerald Grande," he told the local press, "it has to be successful, because the harbor is our ticket. It is our past and our future."

The harbor was also where old and new Destin collided, and often both sides came out the worse for it. From the harbor the working charter boats went out in the morning and to the harbor they returned with fish on ice and gulls following behind. As the harbor developed, trendy restaurants came in and built decks where patrons could sit and eat and drink and watch the drama of the docks as the day's catch was displayed and filleted. But some people on the restaurant decks eating and drinking and watching complained of the smell and of the noise, as though they thought fish would not smell fishy and gulls would quietly wait their turn for the heads and tails and backbones the deckhands threw into the water. So to cut down on the smell, clean up the harbor, and attract fewer birds, deckhands were told not to throw out the heads and tails and backbones for the crabs and gulls, but save them till the next day, when the smelly mess could be carried out and thrown into the Gulf to feed the fishes waiting there. One more inconvenience for the captains and crews, one more bit of old Destin that visitors would never know, fewer crabs under the docks, and, if there were a latter-day Rusty McHugh around, fewer backbones for the gumbo.

But nature was known to take revenge on those who pushed her too far. Build where you shouldn't and a storm will get you, cut down trees or dig up vegetation and the soil will wash away, foul the water and there will be none for drinking or swimming, go into the Gulf when and where you shouldn't and there could be trouble.

For some folks the Gulf was trouble anyway. Those who came to the beach to play on the sand and in the surf loved it. Others didn't. Salt water burned their eyes, sand made them itch and chafe, seaweed got into their swimsuits, jellyfish stung them, red tide clogged their sinuses, and there were sharks. Those people sat by the pool and enjoyed the sun, played golf, shopped, ate, and then went home to tell folks how great the "beach" was. In some regards the nonbeachloving beachgoers had a point. At times the beach could be less than what the tourist development councils advertised. Yes the Gulf was salty, the sand was sandy, and the water wasn't always clear, especially in early summer if there was a June grass invasion. The slimy stuff would appear offshore one morning, a dark patch that slowly drifted in to foul swimming areas and turned the surf into a green soup, until it washed up on shore to rot and stink. Year-round and summer-long residents complained like everyone else, but they knew that what collected on the coast would anchor the sand that eventually covered it and help the beach withstand future storms. They laughed when Seaside, to keep its beach clean for its homeowners and guests, scraped up the grass, for they knew that when September gales battered the shore, Seaside's beach would erode more than its neighbors—and they were right. But if you were down for the one week that you had saved for, planned for, longed for, green slimy water and stinky beaches were not part of the package you ordered.

Then there were sea creatures, such as jellyfish that appeared in the water to sting tourists and convince little children that the pool was where they should play. No telling how many of the people who like the coast but don't like the beach feel the way they do because at an early age they were stung and never forgot it.

And there were sharks.

Everyone knew, or should have known, that sharks were out there. The Gulf was their home. A tourist could, and often did, stand on the balcony of their upper-floor condo, look out at the clear, emerald green water and see the long, slim cylinders, lined up like submerged logs, between the first and second sandbar, about one hundred or so yards out. They could watch swimmers unknowingly approach and could see the cylinders, alive now, with a gentle motion of the tail, ease away, for most of the time sharks were no more interested in swimmers than swimmers were in sharks. However, over the years, as more people came to the beach, more people invaded the sharks' habitat, and the chance of an encounter increased.

Then, in the summer of 2005, a shark attacked and killed a fourteen-year-old girl off Miramar Beach in Walton County, just east of Destin. Two days later a sixteen-year-old boy was attacked and badly bitten when he was fishing in waist-deep water off Cape San Blas down the coast from Panama City. In both cases there were extenuating circumstances—the girl was around two hundred yards off shore and the shiny jewelry she was wearing may have attracted her attacker. The boy was reeling in a fish and the struggling catch may have drawn the shark to him. But for the families of the children, extenuating circumstances did not matter. After those incidents helicopters began flying along the coast looking for sharks and when they saw them, the pilot circled round to let folks along the beach know. The precaution worked. Reports of shark attacks declined, and when they did, flights were cut back until they were needed again—which for someone might be too late.

Then there were the mice.

As early as 1984, the *Mobile Press-Register* reported that down on the coast some "condo developers had to deal with controversies over construction on the sand dune line and the plight of the nearly extinct beach mouse."

At that point it is unlikely that many people knew there was such a thing as a beach mouse, much less that it was "nearly extinct." So when "federal officials moved in to rescue the mouse from the bulldozers and managed to remove a few of the nocturnal creatures" before site preparation began, most folks thought that was a reasonable solution. However, the next year the Alabama Beach Mouse was put on the federal endangered species list. Soon after that it was joined by the Perdido Beach Mouse, and the stage was set for future conflicts. No longer would it be acceptable to simply rescue the beach mice from the bulldozers—if you could catch them. The rodent was federally protected, which meant its habitat, the place where builders wanted to build, was protected as well.

Although some who had seen the mice described them as "precious little animals," scientists considered beach mice important for more than their aesthetic appeal. Researchers pointed to the mouse's "dwindling population as a signal of the decline of the Gulf coast's natural environment." As long as there were mice around to "emerge from the sand dunes at night to munch on sea oats" and scatter the seeds, it meant that the coastal ecosystem was healthy and the natural balance was in place. The loss of the beach mouse habitat and the subsequent loss of the beach mice meant "the entire coastal ecosystem has moved closer to death."

So the battle line was drawn. On one side were environmentalists who wanted to save the mouse and with it the natural beach. On the other side were developers who either couldn't have cared less about the mouse or felt they had done all that could be reasonably expected to protect the rodent and its habitat and intended to do no more.

In the late 1990s the environmentalists got an ally. Out on Fort Morgan Road residents and vacation cottage owners rose in protest when they learned of plans for the Beach Club, a "massive" development that, according to the *Mobile Press-Register*, was "being built untouched by local zoning." These folks joined with the Sierra Club and Friends of the Earth and together they sued the U.S. Fish and Wildlife Service and the Department of the Interior on the grounds that the permit granted to developers violated the Endangered Species Act and threatened the habitat of the beach mouse. "Condominiums are not in short supply on the Alabama coast," environmentalists and their supporters argued, "but native species are." To the dismay of developers, a federal judge agreed, more or less. In June 2002, the judge ruled that the permit to build had been granted without a full assessment of the impact the development would have on the beach mouse habitat. Though there were appeals, the immediate effect was that at least one developer stopped developing.

Down on the other end of Pleasure Island another controversy was brewing, and the mouse was about to find itself at the center of this one as well. Now there are few things that the folks who put the "redneck" in the Redneck Riviera valued more than their boats. Whether built for speed or fishing or both, whether used on the Intracoastal Waterway, taken back into the creeks and marshes, or powered out into the Gulf, the boats were lovingly maintained and treated with respect. But boats need water, and since most owners did not have a dock of their own, they depended on public ramps—the common man's marina.

Beach Mouse habitat sign, Fort Morgan Road, Alabama. Photograph by the author.

The Orange Beach public ramp was especially popular. However, parking was limited, so when the weather warmed and boaters arrived, trucks and trailers spilled out of the lot and onto the shoulders of the road. Neighbors complained about the noise and the traffic. Boaters complained about the inconvenience. But the city had a solution: at the east end of the town Orange Beach owned a vacant plot of waterfront land with access to the pass that led into the Gulf. It was just big enough for a ramp, a parking lot, and restroom facilities. So the city decided to build a second ramp there, and in the summer of 2007, officials unveiled their plans.

It seemed a perfect solution. Only it wasn't—at least not to owners of upscale condos nearby and to the folks with homes on Ono Island, which was right across from the proposed ramp. They protested to the city council that the noise from the rednecks and their boats would take away from their peace and tranquility and spoil their quality of life. The city council was aware that most condo and Ono owners were not residents (and therefore did not vote), whereas many of the boaters lived in town, so plans for the ramp went ahead.

Opponents tried another tactic—stop the ramp to save the beach mouse. If a mouse could halt work on the Fort Morgan development, the opposition reasoned, it could stop the Orange Beach ramp.

Although the folks on Ono and in the condos had previously shown little if any interest in saving the beach mouse, overnight they became advocates for the endangered rodent. To help them in their crusade they brought in environmentalists who they were sure would be their allies. Only they weren't. When environmentalists appeared before the city council they testified that while the property was prime beach mouse habitat, building a ramp *wouldn't* endanger any mice because there were no beach mice where the ramp was to be built. Surprised but undeterred, the condo/Ono alliance announced that since the place was so perfect for a mouse colony, they would catch some mice at another location and turn them loose on the proposed site. This had been done in the past, when beach mice were taken from Gulf State Park and used to repopulate public lands over the line in Florida. Why not do it again?

Because, said the environmentalists, the feral cats would eat them, just as feral cats had eaten the mice that once were there. The mice couldn't be restored until the cats were gone.

Feral cats had been a problem for native species for some time, but this particular cat population had a specific origin. A while back someone had pointed out to the person planning a condo nearby that he might have trouble getting the necessary permits because there were beach mice on the property. Not to worry, said the developer. He went down to the local animal shelter, adopted some cats, and turned them loose. That solved the beach mouse problem and put a cat problem in its place.

In time some local women started feeding the cats (being out of mice to eat, they were hungry). These women were as determined to protect the cats as environmentalists were determined to protect the mice. Hoping to satisfy the cat feeders, the condo/Ono coalition hired a professional trapper to humanely trap the cats, move them to another location, and open the land for the mice. But when the trapper trapped a cat that was not feral, the owner was outraged, and the controversy continued.

It continues still. As yet, no ramp has been built.

Meanwhile, off to the east, along the "Beaches of South Walton" another clash between environmentalists and beachgoers was brewing, this one over toys, tents, and turtles.

Sea turtles of various types—green turtles, leatherbacks, and loggerheads—had been coming ashore since forever, from late spring through summer, to lay their eggs. Not many people ever saw them. They came ashore at night, struggled across the sand to the selected spot, dug their nests, deposited their burden, covered it over, and returned to the Gulf. The next day you could see the trails they had left, and if you knew where to look you could find the eggs, soft and rubbery and just the right size for a rolling-race down the dunes, a game beach children played years ago, before they knew any better. The turtles faced other dangers as well. Residents recall being on the beach at night and occasionally seeing a nesting turtle. Then, hearing a rustling among the sea oats in the dunes, they shined their flashlight toward the sound and saw the glow of eyes—raccoons, lined up waiting for their feast.

And there were the toys, tents, and chairs. If a turtle came on shore and bumped into an obstruction while seeking a place to nest, she might get discouraged, turn around, and go back into the Gulf where she would deposit her eggs to be eaten or to rot. And there were lights. As the coast developed and added brightly lit motels and amusements, people began seeing tiny, perfectly formed turtle hatchlings, smashed flat on the highway, run over as they crawled toward the glow they thought was the moon over the Gulf, which instinct said would guide them to the water. Heading into the Gulf could be dangerous as well. Between nest and water there were ghost crabs and birds, while waiting in the waves were all sorts of creatures who just loved to eat little turtles.

So the U.S. Fish and Wildlife Service and the National Marine Fisheries Service recommended that sea turtles be put on the endangered species list. But even before the listing, there were folks along the Gulf who wanted to protect the turtles, and they settled on a two-part mission. First, something needed to be done to give the nesting turtles an unobstructed beach, and second, the lights that attracted hatchlings inland needed to be dimmed or extinguished. Both proposals ran directly counter to long-standing beach traditions.

First, the unobstructed beach.

Turtle nesting season and the summer tourist season were the same. For years it had been customary for beachgoers to carry a lot of "stuff" to the beach and leave it there overnight to be used the next day. They would put up a tent or umbrella and surround it with chairs, toys, and coolers, creating a kind of outdoor rumpus room. At the end of the day, rather than take their stuff back up the stairs and over the dunes to the place where they would spend the night, they left it. No one ever stole it. The worst that might happen would be that someone would borrow a chair to watch the moon rise, and those folks would usually put it back where they found it. It was an honor system and generally it worked. At the end of the day some folks would take down the tent in case a storm came up and pile the stuff neatly inside the frame, but others would just leave everything scattered about. Why worry? There wasn't much happening on the beach at night. Unless you were a turtle.

For turtles, night was a busy time. As early as 1995, environmentalists along the Redneck Riviera were telling anyone who would listen that the stuff left on the beach was getting in the way of turtle nesting and threatening the survival of the species. So naturally talk began about requiring people who brought stuff to the beach to take it off the beach at night.

Some people didn't like that. Taking stuff away was difficult, inconvenient, and just not the way things had been done all these years. One local noted that maybe it would be best for the breed if the turtles that were too dumb to find a way around a tent pole or chair were weeded out, while the turtles that could figure out the problem survived—survival of the fittest would make the species stronger. But "turtle people," as the less zealous called the more zealous, would have none of that. The debate raged, more or less, until 2007, when the "turtle people," who were by then organized as TurtleWatch, got the Walton County Tourist Development Council to begin a campaign called "remove it or lose it." This tactic seemed to satisfy federal requirements to protect an endangered species, but the effort upset folks who did not want to leave their stuff on the beach at sunset and come down the next morning to find it gone.

Now to be fair, sheriff's deputies who were sent out to enforce the new code did not take the stuff away at first. Instead they tagged it with a warning telling owners that if anything interfering with "beach maintenance, nesting turtles, or emergency vehicles" was left on the beach another night, code enforcers would take the stuff away the next day. Many folks, not believing this could happen, tore up the tag and left their stuff. When they returned in the morning, the beach was clean. According to David Sell, TDC beach management director, "the first year (2007), it was unbelievable. We were removing a dumpster a day." Word got out and the next year "it was about a dumpster every three or four days." But with no way to recover what was lost, tourists and those who rented to them were angry and ready to go to court.

Meanwhile, the county commission got into the act and passed an ordinance that was supposed to fill a legal loophole and put more authority behind enforcement. The ordinance said, in effect, that you had to have a permit to leave things on the beach overnight, but even with a permit if what you left would "obstruct, hinder, or otherwise impede" evening activities by government employees or turtles, your stuff would be removed. The county commissioners were convinced that this revision addressed all objections.

The county commissioners were wrong.

When code enforcers came onto the beach that was claimed by Edgewater Condominiums and took away some items there, the condo filed suit. As far as Edgewater's condo association president was concerned the code was "part of a growing trend toward over regulation by the county" and she and the association's attorney complained of the "growing encroachment" of the county on private land. The condo argued that requiring a permit to keep items on what it claimed was condo property was "unconstitutional" and wondered why the county required permits when the EPA and the Corps of Engineers did not. Meanwhile, regular folks who did not want to lug their stuff home every night began pulling it back and putting it under the county maintained stairs leading down to the beach. They figured that if the stairs did not obstruct the turtles or vehicles on official business, the stuff under the stairs wouldn't obstruct them either. The signs that appeared at access points to the beach told beachgoers how to get to the beach, where to throw their trash, the dangers they faced in the water, the things they could not do on the beach, and whom to thank for all this information. What the signs did not tell beachgoers was that they could not store their stuff under the stairs, so beachgoers figured that they could.

Turned out they couldn't. Enforcers carted it off anyway.

As the controversy swirled around them the county commissioners voted to change the in-your-face "Remove It or Lose It" slogan to the kinder, gentler "Leave No Trace." However the friendlier name did not change the enforcement and those who got their stuff taken away by the dawn's early light were not happy.

In the summer of 2008, all this came to a head, when what seemed like half of the town of Puckett, Mississippi—"home of three hundred wonderful people and a few old grouches"—made their annual trek to the beach. They rented houses and condos and settled in for a week of fun in the sun.

Beachgoers from Puckett, Mississippi, with assorted friends, summer 2009.
Photograph by Walter Lydick.

In class and character Puckettians were direct descendents of the people who came to the coast after the Second World War and for whom, rightly or not, the Redneck Riviera was named. As they had in years past, they covered the sand with all manner of obstructions—tents and coolers and chairs and toys—and left them overnight. The county enforcement folks came, picked up the Puckett stuff and carried it away. Irate phone calls followed and as the threats never to return cascaded upon the folks who were just doing their jobs and the officials who told them to do it, county commissioners and TDC planners began to wonder how they could get out of the mess they were in.

The mess got worse. A new sheriff took office and announced that "he did not see enforcement of county ordinances as a proper role for sheriff's office personnel" who had their hands full with the crimes that he felt were more important than tagging tents. Then word spread that if you had some old busted coolers and broken chairs, just pile them on the beach and the county would take them away for free. In the midst of all of this, someone went down after the enforcers completed their morning rounds and took pictures of the ruts made by the vehicles they drove along the beach to pick up the stuff. The pictures were published in the local newspaper, with a caption pointing out that the ruts were so deep that they were a bigger obstruction to nesting turtles than tents and toys.

Critics had a field day. They gleefully noted that in an effort to kowtow to the federal government (a major sin in some coastal quarters) and make the "turtle people" happy, county commissioners had passed an ordinance that made matters worse for everyone and everything. The Walton County regulations told folks that they could not leave their stuff on the beach overnight because it would obstruct emergency vehicles that seldom came to the beach at night. The rules said folks could not leave their stuff on the beach overnight because it might hinder beach maintenance even though no one came out to maintain the beach in the dark. The county sent out enforcement vehicles that made ruts that were bigger hazards to turtles than they stuff they came to carry away. It was ridiculous. Everyone lost. Even the turtles.

Now no one was for killing turtles. (Even my friend who volunteered to eat at any restaurant that would serve turtle soup was kidding—I think.) However, to opponents of the ordinances this was just one more case of government trying to prevent people from enjoying the sand and the water the way they always had. These dissenters held to a fundamental belief, nurtured by years of uninterrupted activity, that the beach belonged to everyone, which meant that it belonged to no one—not turtles, not mice, not condos or hotels, not the guy who claims to own beachfront property, and most of all, not to the government. To these folks, they themselves were as much a part of the natural environment as sea oats and dunes, so to limit their activities or cause them inconvenience just for the sake of a turtle or two—well, it wasn't right. And when a condo successfully sued the county for coming on its "private" beach and confiscating a volleyball net, and was allowed to keep the net up, longtime beachgoers wondered who would sue the county on their behalf.

The answer, of course, was "no one," so while the sheriff's department and the TDC's beach maintenance crews argued over whose responsibility it was to tag and confiscate the stuff, beachgoers adapted to the new rules. Seeing that at the end of the day the businesses that rented out umbrellas and chairs to the more affluent tourists folded up their stuff and took it back to the foot of the dunes and away from the county stairs, the not-so-affluent who brought their own chairs and umbrellas concluded that if they did the same whoever was sent out to make ruts and confiscate would leave their stuff alone. And it worked. The beach maintenance folks who greeted the dawn doing what they were told to do must have thought that it was a logical compromise. Besides, the enforcers and the enforced are cut pretty much from the same cloth. Just a bunch of hardworking, decent folks, some trying to have some fun, some trying to make a living, neither wanting to cause the other any trouble.

As for the turtle people, they pointed out, with some logic, that "it does not make a difference to a sea turtle whether it is private or public property, it is their sea turtle nesting habitat" and they will try to use it. As for the "pull it back" compromise, they pointed out that sea turtles nest "anywhere on the beach—not just to the toe of the dune," so even leaving stuff that far back "seemed like a bad practice."

Maybe it was, but before long the argument shifted once again and protecting the turtles became more than a matter of toys and tents on the beach.

In July 2008, the *Panama City News Herald* reported that the "Bay County Tourist Development Council adopted a draft ordinance restricting man-made lighting along the beach to protect endangered turtle hatchlings."

As has already been pointed out, for years anyone paying attention knew that turtle hatchlings emerged from eggs and sand, saw the city lights, and headed inland, where they were flattened as they tried to cross the road. But now the federal government, with the Endangered Species Act in hand, was telling counties and communities that if local governments wouldn't adopt appropriate lighting standards then the U.S. Army Corps of Engineers would stop helping rebuild storm-damaged beaches. This caught the officials between a rock and a hard place. The beach was their moneymaker. It was what drew most tourists to the coast. After the storms of 2004 and 2005, they needed the Corps to keep the strand wide and pretty. Although the U.S. Fish and Wildlife Service assured beachfront residents that while "lighting is one of the greatest threats to sea turtles on land [it] is the easiest and most affordable to correct," folks living and working on the coast were not so sure. Retrofitting or removing the hotel, motel, condo, and parking lot lights for the sake of turtles promised to be troublesome, expensive, and an enforcement nightmare. But it had to be done.

So the Bay County TDC drew up an ordinance—eleven pages of rules, regulations, suggestions, and exceptions. The U.S. Fish and Wildlife Service made changes, and when those were accepted, the federal agency endorsed it. Then it went to the Panama City Beach City Council and the county commission, where it was debated as "a work in progress" and finally passed. But even though TurtleWatch got a government grant to purchase "sea turtle lights" and distribute them free to beachfront property owners, replacing prohibited lights was slow going. That too was a work in progress.

The debate over turtles, tents, toys, and lights was yet another example of what was becoming an increasingly common complaint along the coast—that the overregulation of individuals and institutions was spoiling the beach for everyone. It was what citizens who opposed the incorporation of Gulf Shores, Destin, Panama City Beach, and points in between had predicted would happen, and now they were saying "we told you so." But it was the price those who favored incorporation were willing to pay for police protection, street maintenance, water, sewers, and schools—all those things that attracted businesses and buyers, tourists and investors. The line between the two positions was becoming clear, and both sides were spoiling for a fight.

FIFTEEN

Stumbling into the Future

I T ALL HAPPENED SO FAST.

In the summer of 2001, David L. Langford of the Associated Press traveled down to the Alabama Gulf Coast and returned to confirm the existence of what Fodor's *Gulf South* guidebook called "the Barrier Island Republic." Created by a keg-party coup in the late 1970s, "when a group of hard-partying locals seceded from the United States," this "beach with attitude" existed in secret, without government, without taxes, without politicians, without anything but an "official bird . . . the sea-gull, the flying rat of the coast." The "republic's" only purpose was to "let people know that [its citizens] weren't willing to succumb to condo-fixation."

Less than a decade later the very thing barrier islanders "weren't willing to succumb to" had pulled off a countercoup, taken over their republic, and driven the hard-partying into a few coastal enclaves such as the Flora-Bama, or inland to places such as Bennie's Redneck Rendezvous. But even at the Bama the partying was controlled and calculated so as not to lose its appeal to lower-middle-aged good old boys with beer bellies and good old girls with too much makeup and too few clothes. All along the Riviera it was much the same. Redneckery—that lean, mean, hard of hand and piratical of glance redneckery— was in retreat.

But it was not dead.

Over in Destin, Norma and Phil Calhoun had given it a transfusion, transplanted an organ or two, and kept it going.

With their old venues closed Norma and Phil opened their own, Calhoun's Pub and Grub, in a strip mall up the hill and across the road from Destin's Gulf-front condos. Norma ran the bar and restaurant, Phil and the Trashy White Band entertained. And when he wasn't leading the group (and the audience) in old favorites such as "She Ran Off" and "All American Redneck," Phil was singing gospel. There is a picture on the wall of him with his preacher's wife, which she complained wasn't really big enough. Behind the bar, next to the telephone, a sign answered that often-asked question— "WWJD—what would Jesus do?" "Jesus," the sign reads, "would slap the shit out of you."

If you drop by one afternoon you can have a beer with a little of what is left of old Destin. After the boats have brought in their charters and catches, after the fish are filleted and packed, after the deck is cleaned and the tackle readied for the next day, some of the captains and deckhands slip past the tourist bars and boutiques that line the harbor and drive over to Calhoun's. Even though Norma doesn't mind if they bring their sweaty, bait-stained selves inside, they are gentlemen, so they sit at the patio bar to cuss and discuss whether or how the people who made Destin the "world's luckiest little fishing village" are going to survive. The real estate market collapse and subsequent recession took its toll on recreational fishermen as it did on everyone else. Before the crash they could earn enough in eight to nine months so that with a few odd jobs they could get themselves and their families through the winter. After the crash customers who once chartered them for twelve-hour trips cut back to half that length. And with construction at a standstill good winter jobs were few. Deckhand Steve Brown told the *Destin Log* in November 2008 that he had recently "done everything from delivering pizzas to throwing a paper route, to remodeling jobs" but there just wasn't much off-season work. Some boat owners borrowed to get through, while others such as Captain Bud Miller got a commercial fishing license so in the winter he could "keep fishing just to pay the monthly bills." Miller knew the Gulf in winter was cold and rough and sometimes dangerous, but as he told the *Log* in the fall of 2008, you "have to go out when buyers buy." It came down to either taking "a butt whipping at sea or a butt whipping at the bank."

Mighty fishermen with Captain Mike and Mate "Groovy" after a day on *The Huntress*, Destin. Photograph in author's collection.

There was also the "butt whipping" fishermen were getting from state and federal bureaucracies. "When I first started out," one captain told the press, "I had four documents . . . a captain's license, a state commercial fishing sticker, a radio license, and documentation for the boat with the federal government." That was it. "Now I have to have eighteen documents" just to get out of the harbor, he said.

Rules and regulations followed them to sea.

Since the 1980s, the National Marine Fisheries Service (NMFS) had surveyed what recreational fishermen caught. The agency used this information to set quotas on what could be brought in the next year. Red snapper being the most popular fish, NMFS naturally focused its attention there. When computer models suggested that red snapper stocks were running low, the NMFS sent out the word that recreational fishermen could catch only so many pounds of red snapper a year. In 2007 fishermen exceeded the quota. NMFS set another quota and in 2008 recreational fishermen topped it again. Frustrated NMFS took another tack. It reduced the snapper season from 122 days to 74 days and the per-person limit from four fish per day to two. If poundage kept increasing, NMFS warned, the season would be shortened to 51 days.

Now how, you might ask, despite these restrictions, did recreational fisherfolk continue to go over the limit by so many pounds? The answer was simple. If you can keep only two fish, you keep the biggest. So you go out, catch a nice snapper, and if it meets the length required, you put it in the live well or on ice and keep fishing. You catch another snapper and into the well or the cooler it goes. Having reached the two-fish limit, do you stop? Of course not. You are out there to fish, so you do. And if you catch a larger snapper you put it on ice and throw out the smaller one, which by now might be stunned or dead. Either way, Flipper usually gets dinner. That's right. Bottled-nosed dolphins, the most intelligent mammals next to man (and some think smarter than the NMFS rule makers), have figured out that if they follow the boats an easy meal awaits.

See what is happening? Recreational fishermen keep exceeding their poundage quotas because they only bring in the bigger fish. Smaller snapper are thrown back but how many survive is questionable. You would think the snapper population would continue to decline as a result, but no. In the fall of 2009, snapper stocks had grown to the point that the NMFS official in charge of snapper regulations announced that "it looks like to me we have ended the over fishing in the Gulf of Mexico as a whole." But what about the computer models and snapper surveys? Well, according to a study done for the congressional committee that oversees the NMFS, the survey on which red snapper quotas were based was "fatally flawed." Yet, the regulations remained in place and "they" were thinking about adding more.

So in February 2010, over four thousand charter boat captains, fishermen, and friends from all over the country descended on Washington to protest restrictions that had put their livelihoods and the fishing-tourist industry in danger. Wearing T-shirts and carrying signs that read "I FISH! I VOTE!," they met with politicians who said they got the message. Maybe they did. But if they didn't, and if a better snapper survey was not developed and the quota system was not changed, soon Orange Beach would no longer be able to advertise itself as America's "Red Snapper Capital" and the luck of the world's luckiest little fishing village would have run out.

Nourished beach and rebuilt dunes. In time, as promised, the dark sand did turn white.
Photograph by the author.

But even though a lot of people come to Destin, Orange Beach, and points around and between to go out into deep water and catch big fish, the main attraction along the Redneck Riviera was what it had always been—the beach. The beach was the reason condominiums and communities crowded the shoreline. If there had been no beach to look out on, no beach to sit on, no beach to play on, there would have been no real estate market to collapse. Yet year after year, storm after storm, in many places the sand for which the Redneck Riviera was famous was disappearing.

Panama City Beach had long since resolved to do something about it. After so much sand was washed away by Hurricane Opal in 1995, local officials decided to undertake "an aggressive beach nourishment project aimed at curbing erosion." Finished in April of 1999, the program dredged 7.25 million cubic yards of sand from the Gulf and added it to the shore, created new dunes and made the beach look better than it had before the storm. There was the usual grumbling about cost, and some people who owned beach-front property wondered aloud if rebuilding what they considered their yards with public money made their yards public beach. For the moment, however, Panama City Beach and its immediate neighbors seemed pleased with the results.

Walton County had the same problem and sought the same solution. Hit hard by Opal and later storms, in 2003, Walton officials began talking with their Destin counterparts about nourishing (or renourishing, the terms were often used to mean the same thing) a county-line straddling stretch of beach that had been declared "critically eroded" by the Florida Department of Environmental Protection. As it turned out, nourishing the coast it shared with Walton County was the least of Destin's problems. Although the eye of Hurricane Ivan came ashore one hundred miles to the west, that September 2004 storm tore up beaches all the way to Destin, where Holiday Isle was especially hard hit. Some 250 homes were so badly damaged that building inspectors declared them uninhabitable. As for the beach, in some places it virtually disappeared. The next year Hurricane Dennis took more sand, leaving beachfront decks and boardwalks at the island's condo complexes in danger of toppling into the water. Restoration and nourishment efforts soon began, only to be halted when a dead sea turtle was found and reported. By the time work resumed, more sand had been lost.

In the opinion of many, the people who built and bought on Holiday Isle were only getting what they deserved. Dewey Destin, scion of the founding family and a town councilman to boot, told a reporter from the *New York Times* that for years "people didn't build over there, because only a fool would live over there, because hurricanes would wash whatever you build away." But during the development boom of the 1980s, beachfront was beachfront, so developers developed and people bought and the storms came to prove Dewey Destin right. But "I told you so" was no comfort to residents of Destin Pointe, a Holiday Isle "neighborhood" of cottages and condos. They began to press local, state, and federal governments for a comprehensive program to restore the whole shoreline. At first folks seemed to think it was a good idea. Then, to the surprise of Destin officials, some beachfront property owners said no.

Why would beachfront property owners oppose the rebuilding of their beaches? Because, as one of the leaders of the opposition put it, if Destin or Florida or even Washington adds one hundred feet of sand to your piece of the eroded coast, "you no longer own waterfront property, you own public beachfront property." And opposition property owners did not want the public frolicking between their homes and the Gulf.

As far as the nourishment opponents were concerned, the public had been nuisance enough. Tourists had spilled over from a public beach nearby,

Holiday Isle, across from Destin Harbor. Photograph by the author.

ignored "Private Beach" signs, and set up umbrellas and tents wherever they chose. In one case a couple staged a "barefoot wedding" just outside an owner's back door. In another, an owner discovered some of the "public" happily enjoying his hot tub. According to yet another owner, when he told the "public" they were on "private" property, they asked, "How in the world can you own the beach?" The answer he gave "through an awful lot of hard work"—did not satisfy the trespassers.

You can understand why interlopers felt that way. Along the Redneck Riviera the visiting public had long believed that the beach belonged to everyone. When that "right" was infringed upon by people who said the beach was theirs, those who felt violated struck back. In the summer of 2004, a public outcry arose after police told a longtime tourist that he had to get off a condo-claimed beach in an area that he had been visiting since childhood. Seeing it as a "them vs. us" situation, the evicted told the *New York Times* that he was not going to let "people from up North who bought condos" get away with it. So he recruited some members of the local Jimmy Buffett "Parrot Head" club and staged a beach sit-in. Always afraid of bad publicity, local officials got the police to back off a bit, but the battle line was drawn. On one side were beachfront owners who felt they were being "demonized" for wanting to "live the American dream," while on the other were beachgoers who argued that the owners were unfairly denying a similar dream-fulfillment to them.

Although both Florida and Alabama have long traditions of protecting private property, there is also a legal principle that holds that traditional or customary use can transcend property rights. There are also cases in which the public interests can be deemed greater than those of private ownership. So naturally the two sides—those who wanted to nourish and those who didn't—went to court. And when the Supreme Court of Florida declared that restoring critically eroded beaches was in the public interest and therefore legal, the work went ahead. As the sand was brought in, an appeal headed for the U.S. Supreme Court.

Where restoration and nourishment took place, it was generally regarded as a success, at least by those doing the restoring and nourishing. After getting the go-ahead from the Florida Supreme Court a Destin–Walton County partnership went to work and in 2008, their project was selected as one of the nation's best restored beaches. But time was running out for Holiday Isle. On Labor Day 2008, Hurricane Gustav came ashore in Louisiana. Although Destin only got tropical storm–force winds, the winds drove waves against island condo sea walls and did $300,000 worth of damage. When it was over, visitors and owners could fish off the decks where they once sat and looked at the beach. If another storm came those decks would be in the water, and everyone knew that sooner or later another storm would come.

Meanwhile the controversy grew. Nourishment opponents looked out on the sand being brought in and complained that it was too brown. Officials replied that the sand met prescribed standards and that it would get whiter as a result of "the sun and the natural erosion from the grains of sand rubbing against one another." Opponents were not satisfied and soon the spirited and acrimonious debate shifted to the local newspaper, where articles and letters to the editor generated an online commentary war. Writers with monikers like "Destinite," "No2Politicians," "sand bug," and "scubaqueen" whaled away at one another, each claiming they had science, the law, and moral integrity on their side, and that their opponents were either a bunch of land-grabbing socialists or liberty-hating "sand fascists." In addition to beach nourishment and sand color they argued over taxes, fees, insurance rates—just about anything local, state, or federal government did that they did not like. Only when the U.S. Supreme Court agreed to hear the nourishment case did the two sides quiet down, a bit.

The theme of not-from-around-here elites conspiring to keep good old boys and girls away from traditional party places was echoed and even amplified over in Alabama, where a movement was afoot to build an upscale hotel and convention center in Gulf State Park, the state's public, and affordable, beach playground. Now state tourist officials had long lamented the lack of first-rate convention facilities down on the coast. Although Gulf State Park had a 144-room hotel, a restaurant, an auditorium, and a few meeting rooms, the facilities were spartan at best. So really big meetings went elsewhere and state tourist officials had to bear the shame of seeing some of Alabama's wealthiest and most politically powerful companies holding their annual gatherings in other places, such as Sandestin. Chambers of commerce and TDCs in Orange Beach and Gulf Shores were upset as well, for conventions bring in business for everyone. Then Hurricane Ivan came along and wrecked the state park hotel. In the aftermath Alabama governor Bob Riley came up with what the Associated Press reported as "a plan to build an upscale park hotel in a partnership between Auburn University and Atlanta-based West Paces Hotel Group." According to the governor's office no state funds or park bonds would be spent on the project.

The plan appeared to be good for everyone. The state would get a $100 million 350-unit, six- or seven-story hotel and convention center that would accommodate up to two thousand people. Auburn would get an on-the-job-training facility for its "hospitality industry" students and a lot of good publicity. Orange Beach and Gulf Shores would get more tourists. And the West Paces Hotel Group, which would oversee design, construction, and operation, would make a tidy profit. Even the tiniest mammal stood to win: according to Branett Lawley, state conservation commissioner, "to protect beach mouse habitat, the complex would be set back farther from the beach than the current hotel."

Nothing was left out—except the "public."

As the condos rose in Gulf Shores and Orange Beach, places for the less affluent families became fewer and fewer. Soon Gulf State Park, with its inexpensive rooms and cabins, was one of the few beachfront resorts still catering to those folks. Ivan had taken the hotel away and damaged the cabins. And now the state wanted to build something that the "average Alabamian" could not afford—or at least that was what former state conservation commissioner Charley Grimsley warned was happening.

Grimsley was not the only one upset with the plan. The Alabama State Employees Association and the Alabama Education Association both had concerns about the use of student workers and the leasing arrangement, but their protests did not resonate with the general public the way Charley Grimsley's did. The former commissioner came out claiming that the governor was taking "the most treasured piece of public land in Alabama . . . away from the people to build a four-star Ritz-Carlton-style hotel, complete with luxurious spas fit for a king." With his populist blood boiling, Grimsley went on to charge that "because most Alabamians cannot afford to be pampered and pedicured in a four-star hotel," only the wealthy would benefit. It was another case of "the rich getting richer and the poor getting poorer."

So they all went to court and the Alabama Supreme Court ruled, without dissent, that the leasing arrangement violated state law. Grimsley saw it as a victory for the people. "Long after I'm gone," he told the *Mobile Press-Register*, "I want the poorest man in Alabama to be able to take his children and grandchildren to the beach at Gulf State Park, fill their hands with sand and proudly tell them [that] the Gulf State Park beach will belong to them, their children and their grandchildren forever." Meanwhile, Governor Riley and his allies went to work to convince the legislature to call for a referendum on a constitutional amendment to make the plan legal. It hasn't happened yet, but that doesn't mean it won't.

Then there was Peek's Motel. Peek's was a Panama City Beach landmark. Pinkish, plebian, low-rise, and proud, it sat in the middle of the condo canyon, a reminder of a time when the beach was lined with family-owned, family-operated accommodations to which families returned, year after year, for their seasonal week at the beach. It was a place for reunions with other families from other places, a place to recharge batteries, a simple, clean, inexpensive on-the-beach-near-the-amusements fifty-four-unit paradise where respectable rednecks could enjoy their Riviera. Like so many similar places, Peek's was started by a couple of Alabamians, James and Florence Peek, who came down from Montgomery in 1953 to begin a new life on the coast. They built a successful business, grew old, and in the mid-1990s their son, Jerry, took over. Despite competition from more upscale condos and hotels, Peek's continued to do well.

About the time Jerry Peek became the operator the real estate market took off, and as it did the land under his beachfront motel became more and more valuable. Offers came in, but unlike his neighbors, Peek did not sell. Some said he simply did not want to give up what his family had worked so hard to build, some said he loved the business and did not want to leave it,

Peek's Motel, Panama City Beach. Peek's was one of the last family-style motels on the beach, victims of rising land values and increasing tax assessments. Photograph by the author.

others said he was waiting for a better offer, but whatever the reason, Jerry Peek held on.

Peek's clientele were what the owner called "old school." They were blue-collar folks, who stayed with him because he charged $109 to $119 a night in season and because they didn't "want to go up 21 floors to get to their room." Like their parents and grandparents who kept Peek's in business over the years, modern guests worked in mills and factories, shops and stores, and when the recession hit many had their hours cut or, in some cases, lost their jobs. For those in the latter situation there were no more vacations at the beach. Between 2006 and 2009, Peek estimated that business declined 30 percent.

Even as his income was going down, Peek's taxes were going up. In 2001, the motel was assessed at $1,157,258—the first time it broke the million dollar mark. His taxes were $16,791. Over the next seven years, as property around him was bought for big bucks, the value of Peek's beachfront grew. In 2006, the tax assessor said the motel and the land on which it sat was worth $2.16 million. By 2008, the figure was set at $5.98 million—a jump of 517 percent in seven years.

As the value of the property climbed, so did the taxes. But with revenue falling, Jerry Peek could not keep up payments, and by the summer of 2009 he owed more than $166,000 in back taxes. If he did not come up with the money on his own, Peek would either have to take out a mortgage, the property's first since the 1950s, or lose the motel. "It's reaching the point," he told the *Panama City News Herald*, "where I'm about to throw some tea in the bay."

Peek was not alone. Between 2008 and 2009, Bay County's delinquent tax rolls increased by 25 percent. When the list of delinquent taxpayers was published, it took up seventy-six pages of newsprint. All along the Panhandle there were folks who were also "about to throw some tea in the bay." Not that the feeling was anything new. Even before "Tea Party" protestors took to the streets and airwaves, there existed along the Redneck Riviera an attitude that held that the region had all the rules and regulations, government and governing that it needed—probably more—and that taxes were only one element in what many residents and visitors saw as a vast bureaucratic "conspiracy" to keep people from doing what they came to the beach to do. The warning was first raised when municipalities began to incorporate, and from that time forward some argued that local government had become an instrument used by the few to dictate to the many—or to put it more precisely, an instrument of "them" to dictate to "me."

As long as there had been a coast, people had come to it to get away from the institutions and attitudes that restricted them back where they came from, and as long as coastal restrictions were minimal they were happy. Some came to visit, some came to live, and some came just to do business, but in any case, most took comfort in the fact that county governments and the authority they wielded were inland and away. Though there were inconveniences and difficulties, the freedom from surveillance and scrutiny more than made up for what was missing. But as coastal populations grew, the need for things like sewers, water, sanitation, roads, hospitals, and police and fire protection became important, particularly to community leaders who wanted to civilize the shore and make it attractive for free-spending tourists and deep-pocketed investors. So the beach interests pressed for and got coastal representatives on the county commission, pressed for and got their communities incorporated, pressed for and got what inland municipalities had—and with those benefits came the politicians and bureaucrats, the taxes and the tensions.

Then the grumbling began—by many some of the time, by some most of the time, and by a few all of the time. At the core of each complaint was that fundamental conviction—which had been the conviction of beach visitors and beach residents as long as they had visited and resided—that being on the coast gave them certain exemptions from the social, economic, and political restraints placed on everyone else. Whether it had to do with sand or sex or turtles or tents or lights or liquor, each believed that the way it should be done was the way he or she wanted to do it, and each went forward armed with the conviction that the views he or she held should be shared by everyone. Folks down there might cooperate, but only until they disagreed. Compromise was rare, a lasting consensus impossible. Contention was the rule, courtesy the exception, and no one was his brother's keeper unless his brother had something someone wanted to keep. To make matters worse, in almost every disagreement, everyone involved usually had at least a smidgen of right and reason on his or her side. In these disputes, government was seen as an agent for either good or evil, depending on whom government supported; politicians were usually considered corrupt or incompetent or both unless they agreed with you; tourist promoters and developers were either selling paradise for a pot of porridge or making the economy hum; and environmentalists were either saving our coast one mouse at a time or threatening the livelihood of the most noble of God's creations—the human race. Righteous indignation was their mother's milk, everybody was put-upon by someone else, and "my way" was the American way. When controversies erupted, as they did with studied regularity, all involved went into battle secure in the knowledge that the Lord of Hosts and the Constitution of the United States were their allies.

While this was going on, there were also folks doing what Floridians had always done—looking on the bright side. In the *Destin Log's* 2008 Progress Edition local real estate analysts said, "We've already hit the bottom and we're just bumping along there for a short time, giving everyone who wants to get 'lucky' the opportunity to make their move." While the *Log* did not think there would be a repeat of "the late lamented housing boom" for decades, if ever, it did predict that because Destin and other coastal communities were "drive-to destinations, recovery [would] likely be faster than many other resort markets." Over in Gulf Shores "lucky investors" were snapping up foreclosed units for one-half to one-third of the original price.

It looked good, until you realized how many condos and houses were still on the market.

It was difficult to paint a rosy picture when foreclosures were frequent and business was so bad that restaurants that had been operating year-round cut back to the traditional practice of closing in the winter. With tax revenue reduced, there was less money for schools, streets, and law enforcement. To add to coastal woes, in the summer of 2008, gas prices rose to four dollars a gallon in some places, making it more expensive to drive to the "drive-to destinations." Yet despite it all, the coast remained the place to go for folks from the lower South, and taxable lodging revenue from the 2008 summer season was only slightly down from hurricane-recovered, record-setting 2007. So there was hope.

Hope was what the *Northwest Florida Daily News* was peddling in June 2008, when it told readers that "with economic news from Washington and Wall Street sounding gloomier every day, with homes sales plunging and 'bed tax' revenue sputtering, business interests along the Emerald Coast could stand some cheering up." The way to get happy, the paper said, was "to listen to Peter Bos."

Since his arrival back in the 1970s, Peter Bos had become, according to the *Daily News*, "this area's highest profile developer." His projects were among those that transformed Destin from "a sleepy fishing village" to one of Florida's most visited spots, so naturally he had his detractors. But when he spoke people listened, which was what the *Daily News* editorial board did that summer when Bos laid out "what he [saw] in the region's future." Peter Bos expected (or at least hoped) that "a surge of 'increasingly affluent' folks" would soon arrive on the coast to revive and sustain the economy, but only if the coast had the "first-class amenities" they wanted and demanded. "Businesses that meet these people's expectations will thrive," he told the board, no doubt counting his Destin Commons shopping center and Emerald Grande/Harbor Walk resort in that category.

These "increasingly affluent" folks, Bos said, fell into two groups: "white-collar business people" who could pack up their computers, vacation in Destin, and "still maintain vital contacts"; and retiring baby boomers who would "be drawn to locales with unspoiled beaches and abundant recreation"—"You aren't gonna retire in Montgomery if you can help it," he said. The boomers would be flush because those "reliable frugal Americans who endured the Great Depression and scrimped and saved, [were] dying—and leaving money to their children." By Bos's estimate "seven trillion dollars [was] changing hands," and he wanted Destin to get its share.

Still, some things had to happen before the "increasingly affluent" arrived in numbers sufficient to fuel recovery. At the top of the list was the completion of the international airport that at the time had just cleared its final environmental and legal hurdles and on which construction was about to begin. It was to be located north of Panama City on land donated by St. Joe Corporation, and the *New York Times* was not alone in believing that the airport was "more of a real estate project than an effort to address a pressing transportation problem." However, Bos and others like him seemed unconcerned that St. Joe owned most of the developable land around the airport and that if things fell its way it might make millions in the deal—that was the way things were always done down there. For tourist development councils an international airport meant that the Redneck Riviera would be a fly-to destination for the "increasingly affluent" they wanted to attract. Down they would come from suburban enclaves too far away for driving. Upon arriving, they'd be greeted and shuttled in comfort to WaterColor, WaterSound, Seaside, Sandestin, and the Emerald Grande, where they would find all the "first-class amenities" they expected.

Whether upscale or downscale, the economy on the Redneck Riviera depended on tourists, and so it followed that as real estate struggled to recover from the crash, in 2009 tourist development councils unveiled new marketing campaigns to bring in visitors. Walton County launched a $1 million effort to attract tourists during the months between snowbird season and summer, and all along the coast other groups followed suit. However, in Panama City Beach this effort revealed a division between two groups: TDC officials who wanted to replace the city's "Spring Break Party" image with one more family focused, and those businesses for which Spring Break often spelled the difference between profit and loss when the year's receipts were totaled up. When the TDC dropped its arrangement with twenty-four-hour college campus cable network MTVU—a "deal with the Devil" one local restaurateur called it—a co-op of beach businesses began making plans for a campaign to create a "buzz" on college campuses with promises of "weekly celebrity appearances" by cultural icons such as Paris Hilton and Kim Kardashian.

However, everyone knew that the debate was less about good taste than about money. Although the Panama City Beach TDC had dropped MTVU it reportedly "beefed up public relations efforts with college campuses with social marketing such as Facebook" to make sure that PCB remained the place to go on Spring Break. Many in the business community did not believe it would work. Chad Hart, owner of Inertia Tours, which sold Spring Break packages, figured that "in a few years, revenue [would] be down in March" and the city would begin to reconsider what it had done. "It's a really stupid thing to do business-wise," he told the press. The city, however, went ahead with its plans (minus Hilton and Kardashian), and though the final figures are not in yet, if the traffic jams on Front Beach Road and Thomas Drive were any indication, Spring Break 2010 at Panama City Beach was a roaring success.

Destin, however, used Panama City Beach as an example of what it did not want its Spring Break to be. Reacting to accounts of a Spring Break "simulated sex" promotion by a local club, the *Walton Sun* asked, "Do we really want to emulate Panama City Beach?" The paper warned the community that even though making money had long been what the coast was all about, this sort of business "encourages a type of behavior that is neither desirable nor entertaining." So it followed, not surprisingly, that instead of going after MTV, Destin hosted the Weather Channel.

It was not the first time that "adult" entertainment had caused the *Sun* and other area newspapers to remind readers that such establishments and activities were accompanied by the "drunkenness, the drugs, the obvious sexual overtones and outright displays [that] lead to a degradation of family values, property destruction, crime and personal injuries." In the winter of 2008, an Atlanta strip-club operator sought a license for topless dancing in a Destin club. His request was denied because city ordinances only allowed nude dancing in an industrial zone out near the airport. What followed was a furor that involved residents of neighborhoods near the club, ministers, the business community, local citizens, good old boys who wanted to see girls dance half-naked, and lawyers for both sides. Suits were filed, mediation was ordered, and meetings were held. Finally a settlement was reached, and by the end of 2010, Destin would have a topless bar where such establishments were supposed to be—out in the industrial zone near the airport. It was "going to be a first-class establishment," the owner told the *Daily News*.

However, in some places Spring Break was moving away from the PCB and Pleasure Island condos and into smaller resort communities where boom-built minimansions sat empty and inviting. What occurred was a natural collision between the desire of students to get to the coast for their holiday, the desire of parents to keep their little darlings away from dens of sin such as Club La Vela, the desire of rental agencies to increase bookings, and the desire of owners to get extra cash to pay the mortgage and keep the wolf away from the door. Together these forces resulted in a new source of income in hard times and a veritable youth invasion of quiet communities such as Seaside, Rosemary Beach, Seagrove, and Grayton. House parties, so popular in the 1950s and 1960s, were revived, though in most cases today's owners required adult supervision and high security deposits. It was a kinder, gentler Spring Break for the kids, who got to sit out on the beach, meet and hang out with other kids, and stay up late in the relative confines of the community. But sometimes, late at night the silence was shattered by the "noxious activities [and] offensive noises" C. H. McGee's covenant had outlawed. Neighbors complained to the sheriff and the rental agent, and eviction often followed. Subsequently, Walton County passed a noise ordinance—another rule.

Although the impact of the recession was seen everywhere, the coast at the end of the first decade of the century was creeping toward recovery. The housing market was still stagnant, and rental bookings were still down, but the snowbirds arrived on schedule—not as many as before, but enough to keep condos and motels and RV parks from standing empty. As a result of the economic downturn, more visitors from the North stopped along Pleasure Island and the Panhandle instead of going farther south, where it was warmer but more expensive. Another positive sign for some was that in the spring of 2009, the *Destin Log* announced that "student workers [were] back on the radar" as businesses began looking for part-time spring and summer help. True, students provided cheap labor and as such might have been one more indication of the tourist industry cutting costs, but for some observers it brought back memories of their student days when they worked on and around the beach for enough money to play the summer away.

The recession seemed to inspire in many people a nostalgia of sorts, a longing for better times past, and looking back through rose-tinted glasses, some saw a way to make money off memories. In the spring of 2008, just as the housing market was coming unraveled, a group of investors opened the Hangout in Gulf Shores. A modern reincarnation of the popular gathering spot of "pre-condo days," it was created to "pay tribute to the original, open air Hangout that graced the Gulf Shores beach scene in the late 1950s and early 1960s." With lots of memorabilia scattered around and a large screen to show "nostalgic beach movies," it was designed to appeal to the baby boomers who remembered the old and would enjoy the new. It was also up to date just enough, the owners hoped, to attract a younger crowd who would keep the place rocking well after the boomers were in bed.

The owners had considered building a condo, but either through foresight or luck they had decided "the market needed entertainment," so they had avoided the condo crash. How well entertainment will do remains to be seen, but because folks come to the coast to be entertained, it is a good bet that the Hangout will do OK. Besides, it is part of a larger commercial venture inspired by the Envision Gulf Shores Plan, one of those "let's figure out the future" projects coastal promoters love so. This one originally envisioned turning the four blocks at the town's main intersection into a "walking district around the public beach and develop [there] retail, restaurants, residential space, and public parking." With money tight, most of the project was put on hold, but the Hangout was a good start.

Still, the most nostalgic place on Pleasure Island, maybe on the whole Redneck Riviera, was the Flora-Bama. Rebuilt and rocking, it remains a touchstone for generations of beachgoers. And its celebrations—the Polar Bear Dip, the Frank Brown Festival, and the others—restored and rejuvenated old-timers and newcomers alike. And every April, fish are still thrown and beer is drunk—over one three-day period contestants and spectators at the Mullet Toss downed over 4,000 cases, which comes out to nearly 100,000 twelve-ounce cups of beer, enough to muddle and modify many a memory, and carry the middle-aged back to when they were twenty-one.

Gilchrist also rebuilt Boys Town, or at least brought in new trailers, and he repaired the dock so Jimmy Louis could sail in and stay awhile.

It wasn't what it used to be, but it was close enough.

SIXTEEN

Who Wants a Beach That Is Oily?

S O WE GET BACK to where it all began, back to the beach, to what the *Miami Herald* called Florida's "signature attraction." Even if there were no golf, no amusements, no recreational eating or shopping, no fishing, no Flora-Bamas, no Seasides or Sandestins, folks would still come to Florida for the beach. And if tourist industry figures are to be believed, the beach is also why they come to south Alabama.

However, as we have seen more than once, some folks figured that they had the right to keep people off the part of the "attraction" they claimed was theirs. Others contended that they couldn't, not legally anyway. So it followed that late in 2009, a case was argued before the U.S. Supreme Court that promised to determine, once and for all, whether or not an individual could "own" the beach and, by owning it could bar others from it. If the Court decided such private ownership was not permitted, then the state's "signature attraction" belonged to the public, and the state could maintain it for public use.

The whole thing focused on "nourishment"—the rebuilding of eroded beaches by the state. The process was not new. Back in 1922, New York's Coney Island was washing away so officials pumped in sand to enhance the shore. Since that time there had been over three hundred major beach nourishments around the country. Not surprisingly, Florida, with its 825 miles of coastline, had the most of these projects—140. Thirty-five of Florida's sixty-seven counties used taxpayer money to build up their beaches. And under Florida law, a beach created with public money belongs to the public.

Some folks had no problem with this. Down the coast, near St. Petersburg, the city manager of Belleair Beach told the *St. Petersburg Times* that residents there "love beach renourishment." Living near some of the most heavily eroded and frequently nourished beaches in the country, residents of Belleair and their neighbors agreed with local realtors that beaches not only protected beachfront property, they increased its value. Better to have "a big, wide beach behind you, instead of having water coming right up to the seawall," one real estate agent noted. However, there was a catch. According to state senator Dennis Jones, who represented the stretch of the coast where Bellaire Beach was located, "if the public pays to restore a beach, they should have the right to access it." Jones, who got the nickname "Mr. Sandman" for his ongoing efforts to nourish the beaches in his district, saw it as a quid pro quo arrangement. The state enhances and protects beachfront property at public expense, and in return beachfront property owners allow the public access to the state-created beach.

However, there were some beachfront property owners who said they would rather "opt out" of nourishment and have a private beach, even if it was eroded, than have a beach that was broad, wide, and public. But it was not that simple. Beachfront owners received public support in ways that went beyond nourishment. Most had their property insured under state and federal programs that were subsidized by taxpayers. Nourishment supporters accused owners of wanting to reject the very thing that not only protected their property but also kept insurance premiums at least a little lower for the folks subsidizing them. Then there was the matter of state- and federal-built roads and bridges that had allowed developers to develop beaches that homeowners now claimed were private. In other words, it could be argued, and was argued, that the public made it possible for beachfront owners to live on the beach and therefore the public had a right to sit on the sand, nourished or not.

But was opting out even possible? The beach moved and engineers said that if one owner nourished and that owner's neighbor did not, sand from the rebuilt beach would eventually drift next door. As a result the unnourished owner got public sand from the nourished neighbor. The "opt-out" replied that this was part of the natural process, however the public was

Seaside's nourished beach after Hurricane Opal. Initially homeowners were told that there would be no residential construction south of Scenic Highway 30-A, but like so much of Seaside's initial plan, that changed. Photograph by the author.

quick to point out that nature had been altered by nourishment and the unnourished were benefitting from it.

Then there was the question of protecting the coast as a whole, which Florida claimed was its responsibility. An opt-out beach leaves an eroded gap in the nourished shoreline, and while that space might be filled in by the natural movement of the sand, it might also accelerate erosion for neighbors. So it would seem that it was the duty of the state to maintain something of a regular shoreline so everyone would be protected, and therefore opting out could not be allowed. But if no one were allowed to opt out, and if the government nourished the beach and declared it public, would beachfront owners be due compensation for what was "taken" from them—their beachfront? Most observers agreed that the state did not have the money to buy up the beaches of Florida, even if taxpayers wanted it to, and many did not. The cost of restoring alone was at times hotly debated—inland politicians argued that their constituents should not have to pay to protect and insure places where people should have never built in the first place—Destin's Holiday Isle, for example. The state's buying the beach was not an option.

Then there was the legal principle of "customary use," which held that beaches that had been customarily, traditionally used by the public long before there were beachfront owners to claim them could be used by the public still. Did Florida beaches fall into this category?

It was, most everyone agreed, a mess. Most everyone also agreed that if it was resolved in favor of the beachfront owners who wanted to opt out, everything from property values to insurance rates to the state's $65 billion tourist industry would be affected. As Senator Jones summed it up, ending the beach nourishment program would "have a crippling effect on Florida's economy." Even so, opt-out beachfront owners and their supporters argued that the very idea that a state could "take" private property for whatever reason, to protect whatever interests, without just compensation for the owners, violated what they felt was one of the most fundamental rights of American citizens—the right to own property, protect that property, and use that property as they saw fit.

With compromise out of the question, a judicial decision appeared the only way to resolve these differences, or to at least declare that one side was "right" and the other "wrong," that one "wins" and the other "loses." So the case of six Destin beachfront property owners went before the U.S. Supreme Court, where eight justices listened to attorneys argue that the plaintiffs' property rights should extend all the way to the water, or at least the mean high-tide line, no matter who pumped sand onto the shore. (Justice John Paul Stevens, who owned a condo in Fort Lauderdale, sat this one out.) Those attorneys contended that back in 2003, when Destin, Walton County, and the state added sand to create a seventy-five-foot-wide public beach, the state took away their clients' "ability to own, possess and exclude persons" from what they claimed was theirs. As a result "commercial vendors" were setting up on land that their clients should be able to control. As one of the owners put it, the case was about "heavy-handed government actions that eliminated private property rights without either consent or compensation."

Lawyers for the state argued that the state's responsibility for protecting the public and its resources justified nourishment, that a nourished beach paid for by the public should be open to the public, and that the principle of "customary usage" allowed people to use the beach whether it was nourished or not. They also pointed out that if the Court ruled for the property owners "we'd be in the position of paying private property owners to put sand back in their yards." In the questioning that followed, Justice Antonin Scalia raised the point that rather than "taking" from the property owners, the state was actually giving the owners something and wondered if the additional beach and the protection it afforded might be "sufficient compensation" for what the owners claimed was "taken." Other justices asked the lawyers questions about who owns the sand that accumulates naturally and whether the state could build a beach just to attract students on Spring Break.

And when the day was done, the justices went into their chambers and the two sides waited for a ruling.

Meanwhile, back down on the Gulf, nature was not waiting. Beaches on the western end of Holiday Isle were washing away. For home and condo owners there, nourishment was not an issue. They wanted sand and wanted it so desperately that the strings attached did not matter. Their argument was not with the government or the public it represented. Their argument was with property owners across the pass on Okaloosa Island. At issue was the question of where the sand to nourish the eroded beach should come from and who should pay the bill.

As we have seen, for years the Gulf side of Holiday Isle, across from Destin Harbor, had had problems with erosion. The issue became critical in 2009 when Tropical Storm Claudette took away so much sand that Florida governor Charlie Crist visited Destin, surveyed the damage, and declared, "We've got to have some beach reconstruction, that's very clear to me." But saying was one thing, acting was another, and before the city could get the necessary permits and approvals, a second tropical storm, Ida, hit. Ida washed away more sand, eroded foundations, and caused some structures to collapse. Conservative estimates set the cost of the damages at $500,000. "This shouldn't have happened," a member of a Holiday Isle homeowners association told the press. "We've never had any beach restoration down here, and until we do we'll just keep getting beat up by storm after storm."

A plan to restore and nourish Destin (including Holiday Isle) and Okaloosa Island beaches was in the works when some Okaloosa Island homeowners who didn't want to participate filed suit. Their position was much like that of the opt-out beachfront owners in Destin, but they were also upset about the quality and color of the sand being brought in and felt the special assessment levied on beachfront owners to pay a portion of the $20 million project was unfairly calculated. Moreover, as far as the Okaloosa litigants were concerned, their beach did not need nourishing, so they wanted their island to be taken out of the restoration plan.

It was true that Okaloosa Island did not have the erosion problems being experienced by Holiday Isle. According to one homeowner there, Tropical Storm Ida actually added beach to their property. As far as they were concerned, Holiday Isle should solve its own problem. And what a problem it was. According to one estimate it would take a line of dump trucks eighty-five miles long to carry the 200,000 to 300,000 cubic yards of sand needed to restore the island beaches. That was a lot of trucks, which would mean a lot of noise and a lot of congestion—a lot of all the things people came to the beach to avoid. Wasn't there a better way? many wanted to know.

There was: the sand could be pumped in.

As luck would have it, at that very moment the U.S. Army Corps of Engineers was getting ready to dredge the pass between Holiday Isle and Okaloosa Island, the pass that led into Destin's famous harbor. Since most coastal engineers believed that the beaches migrated from east to west, the sand in the pass had washed in from eroded Holiday Isle. So Holiday Isle folks suggested, why not put the sand back. The pass would be cleared, Holiday Isle would be renourished, and the cost would be considerably less than anticipated. It looked like a win-win situation for everyone.

Of course it wasn't. Even though those involved weren't traditional rednecks, the good old boy and girl belief that "what is mine is mine and you'd better not mess with it" still permeated the region. Residents of Okaloosa Island, already upset over the cost and execution of nourishing plans, rose in protest. The sand in the pass might have come from Holiday Isle, they said, but it had been heading for Okaloosa Island before jetties and the pass cut it off. Okaloosa Island may have enough sand now, they argued, but there was nothing to guarantee that it would in the future. Therefore, the dredged sand should be placed on Okaloosa Island, where it was going, instead of Holiday Isle, from whence it came. The Okaloosa point was simple—if Holiday Isle got Okaloosa sand then one day Okaloosa would erode and need nourishment, which they were on record opposing. As one Okaloosa resident put it, "Holiday Isle's scheme to fix their homes involves destroying ours."

Meanwhile, there was a pass that needed to be dredged, and unless it was, and soon, shoals would build up and Destin's fishing boats would not be able to get out into the Gulf. Some saw this as an unfortunate consequence of the controversy. Others understood that it was part of the strategy by Okaloosa homeowners to get the sand put where they wanted it put. Until they got their way the Okaloosa group talked of "holding the harbor hostage" with lawsuit after lawsuit. It was another mess, but for the moment at least it was a local mess. However, if the U.S. Supreme Court ruled in favor of beachfront property owners in the Destin case, the Okaloosa Island–Holiday Isle controversy would become part of the bigger picture.

Then there was Seaside, where the question of beach ownership and access turned into a controversy uniquely its own. And why not, for Seaside was unique. A gated community without gates, upscale and exclusive, yet welcoming to all. A good neighbor to those next door who came and went in and out of Seaside almost as if they lived there. Folks from Seagrove and WaterColor walked from their beach to Seaside's beach, then up Seaside's stairs to Seaside's shops. They biked or rode golf carts into the town center to attend concerts and eat at the restaurants and cafes. They liked Seaside. Then in the spring of 2007, signs appeared on the beach boundaries between Seaside and Seagrove on the east and between Seaside and WaterColor on the west. PRIVATE they read, NO PUBLIC ACCESS. In smaller print was added, "Pavilion Use and Beach Access Strictly Limited to Homeowners and their Guests." And at the bottom, in bold letters again, it warned SECURITY ENFORCED. Similar signs appeared at the roadside entries to Seaside's beach walkovers. The community had cordoned off its beach with signs.

Seaside signs denying neighbors unrestricted access to the town and its beach. This is a much-less-intrusive announcement than the one that first appeared—it does not block the street. Photograph by the author.

Signs also appeared in the middle of streets leading from Highway 30-A into Seaside's neighborhoods warning those who came in for wine tastings and such that there was "No Event Parking" there. If they could not find a place in the town center, and there weren't many, they would need to go somewhere else. So they spilled over next door, into Seagrove's streets, yards, and driveways. To add insult to injury, Seaside put up signs where the dirt streets of Seagrove met the brick streets of Seaside, telling Seagrove residents that the golf carts they rode about in were not welcome. With that the isolation was complete—or as complete as the sign makers could make it.

Seagrove residents responded with signs of their own. Handmade, colorful, and inviting (Seaside's were professionally done and threatening), they read: "WELCOME to SEAGROVE, Golf Carts Allowed, Public Beach Access." It was not so much that Seagrove wanted Seaside's excess, but rather that Seagrove wanted folks to know which community was friendly "Old Florida" and which wasn't. There was no mistaking the point.

Some people in Seaside were not happy with their town's signs, and Susan Vallee, the managing editor of the *Seaside Times*, was one. The *Times*, the community's in-house newspaper, generally avoided controversy. Most of its newsprint was devoted to praising the town and its founder, promoting and reporting events, and providing space for advertisers. In the *Times*, Seaside was a happy place, a Truman-esque place where nothing could go wrong. So it must have come as a surprise when above the fold of the "Holiday 2007" issue was the headline "Welcome to Seaside . . . or Not."

Vallee could see how event parking inconvenienced Seaside homeowners and renters (how prohibiting parking in Seaside inconvenienced neighbors was not mentioned) and she could even see a reason for the signs at entries to the beach, though she found them "distracting from the beauty of the walkovers" and thought it was "a shame" that they were there. What really got to her were the signs on the beach, the signs telling neighbors that they were no longer welcome to walk along the shore into Seaside, maybe to have lunch or visit shops. It wasn't the aesthetics of the signs, it was the message, a message she found "to be downright rude." Besides, she added, "Seaside is, by its definition, a New Urbanist town, an open and inviting community," and these signs ran counter to that intent.

But more than that—and here what Seaside had become, indeed what the coast had become, kicked in—it wasn't good for business. "We depend on tourism to live and to help us maintain the property values of our homes" she wrote. "If the tourists disappear then we are in trouble." "Calling security on people walking to the beach with their families is a dangerous precedent" because "day-trippers" not only buy from Seaside stores and shops and eat at Seaside cafes, they become renters and homeowners. Excluding people was "not what we're about here." She ended by urging "the Town Council and the rest of Seaside's decision makers" to find a compromise that would "welcome guests and ensure that homeowners and renters" would have a place on the beach. "Seaside," she reminded readers, "is just too special a place to resort to lowly 'No Trespassing' signs." It was a ringing reaffirmation of the position taken by TDC officials all along the coast. Even where the beach was "private," and Seaside could make as good a claim as any for the beach "belonging" to the community, even where there had been no nourishment by the state (and Seaside's beach was not part of the Walton County/Destin nourishment effort), relegating visitors to that small portion of the coast that the state "owned" would not be good for the region's image. And in the tourist business, image is everything.

Seaside's "decision makers" got the message—or messages.

They learned that the community was not free to do whatever it wanted without regard to its neighbors or anyone else when the Walton County Fire Marshall removed the "private street" signs located at the entries to the village. It was not that Walton County particularly wanted golf carts and automobiles driving into the neighborhoods, it was that no one, not even the "decision makers" of Seaside, could put "obstructions in the streets" that would hinder emergency and fire vehicles. As for the signs limiting access to the beach, they disappeared as quickly, as quietly, and as unceremoniously as they had appeared. In Seaside the question of "who owns the beach" was settled, and the message to the outside world was clear: Seaside owns it, but you are welcome to use it. Just be nice.

Not much chance of such a compromise happening in Destin. Over there it had gone too far, and the United States Supreme Court was going to have to settle the matter.

Then while the litigants waited, on April 20, 2010, a bubble of methane gas escaped from a British Petroleum oil well off the Louisiana coast, shot up the drill column, expanded rapidly, broke through seals and barriers, and exploded. Eleven people died as the Deepwater Horizon rig burned and sank. Oil began pouring into the Gulf. Local responses were many and varied, and almost all were angry. "Boycott BP" some said. Others wanted to stop all offshore drilling. And there was the uncomfortable reminder that someday, somehow, alternative forms of energy would have to be found, and one day something other than gasoline would fuel the cars carrying vacationers to the Redneck Rivera. Environmentalists and people whose livelihood depended on shrimp and oysters argued that the marshes should be protected first, because if the oil got into the swamp and grass, efforts to get it out would destroy the very thing they were in there to save. The

Deepwater Horizon/BP oil rig ablaze. Courtesy of the U.S. Coast Guard.

beach, on the other hand, could be cleaned up much more easily. This made perfectly good sense if seafood was your industry, but if your economy depended on tourism, protecting the beaches and cleaning up the water offshore was as important, if not more important, than making sure oyster beds were safe. Tourism and real estate employed more people and brought in more money than the shrimpers, oystermen, and even recreational fishing. If resources became scarce, money ran short, and a choice had to be made between beach and marshes, the debate would get mean and messy.

But in the first weeks after the spill, no one had to choose. BP assured the federal government and the feds assured the coast that the company could plug the well and, according to its CEO, Tony Hayward, the impact would be "very, very modest." So in mid-May the Hangout Music Festival in Gulf Shores went on as scheduled, with the Zac Brown Band singing "Toes"—"I got my toes in the water, my ass in the sand, not a worry in the world, a cold beer in my hand"—which was fast becoming the latest Redneck Riviera anthem. When it rained the last day the promoters threw the gates open and let everyone in free. And there was no oil on the beach. Meanwhile, people were cutting their hair and shaving their pets, stuffing the clippings into panty hose, and sending the bundles down to soak up the spill. Over in Walton County local officials approved a plan to buy bales of hay to scatter across oil-slick water to stop the plumes before they came ashore. At Calhoun's Pub and Grub the Fishermen for Christ evangelical group met to discuss options and take things to the Lord in prayer. Everyone wanted to do something. Everyone wanted something done.

BP's initial efforts failed to stop the leak and as more oil poured into the Gulf, concern mounted. Adding to the anxiety was the growing realization that what had caused the crisis and what it would take to set it right flew in the face of deeply held beliefs common to the coast. Over the years Baldwin County and the Florida Panhandle stood out as some of the most conservative sections of their states, if "conservative" meant believing that lower taxes would limit government and a limited government would leave citizens alone to make money and live well. Now all but the most libertarian had to face the fact that the oil rig disaster might have been prevented if the federal government had enforced drilling regulations and requirements, and if a private company, in this case BP, had not been allowed to put the public at risk for profit. Most unsettling of all was the growing conviction that it would be the taxpayer, the one who voted for limited government to save money, who would ultimately pick up the tab for the cleanup, and it would be the local economy, not BP, that would suffer. So, remaining as true to their core beliefs as the situation allowed, locals demanded that the ones responsible for what had taken place make it right, and do so with little inconvenience or cost to themselves. However, because they all knew that was not going to happen, they vented their populist anger against Big Oil for creating the catastrophe, against the federal government for not preventing it, and against the Obama administration for not making BP stop the flow of oil and clean it up.

What troubled locals most, according to a poll taken by the *Destin Log*, was that because of the spill the popular "perception" of the region would suffer, and the change in perception would "damage the area's tourism market." Which returns us, once again, to the single most important thing for which tourists came to the coast—the beach. Readers of the *Log* worried about how Destin would be perceived as a tourist destination, but also high on the list of things they feared the oil would do was "mar [the] crystal white beaches for years to come."

Because "The Beach" was what they were.

Give credit to the consultants hired to come up with a name—a brand—for the product, for they came up with the right one. The region wasn't the Panhandle, or Florida's Great North West, or the Emerald Coast, or even the Redneck Riviera. It was The Beach. Even if tourist development councils, county commissioners, and city councils had never passed resolutions and renamed highways, it would have been The Beach. So when it was announced that the first new international airport in the United States in more than a decade, the one built on St. Joe land just north of Panama City, would be named Northwest Florida Beaches International, few were surprised.

Naturally BP tried to calm coastal fears. It also tried to limit its liability, for if it was found that the blowout was caused by company negligence, under the Clean Water Act it could be fined up to $4,300 for every barrel of oil that poured into the Gulf. Shortly after the explosion a spokesman said that only about one thousand gallons a day was going into the water. Then the company upped the estimate to five thousand gallons, and the CEO, who had said the damage would be "modest," took the statement back and apologized. By Memorial Day, the official beginning of the summer season, scientists were saying that the spill might be ten times that much, though it was hard to tell because the pictures of oil spewing into the Gulf provided by BP were poorly focused and fuzzy. Still, from what scientists could see, enough oil was flowing into the water and drifting toward shore that if it continued the spill might become the worst environmental disaster in U.S. history. It was so bad that they were not even calling it a disaster anymore; it was a catastrophe.

Almost immediately the finger pointing began. Each of the private companies involved with the rig—Transocean, which owned it; British Petroleum, which leased it; and Halliburton, which was supposed to plug the well—blamed the other for the blowout. Democrats blamed the Bush administration for letting members of Minerals Management Service, which was supposed to be regulating offshore drilling, get literally and figuratively in bed with folks from Big Oil. The agency had "a culture of substance abuse and promiscuity" one report read. When it was revealed that offshore drilling facilities had proceeded without the proper permits and were not inspected regularly, the head of MMS resigned, not that it made much difference to people whose livelihoods depended on clean water and a clean beach.

The Obama administration did not fare much better. Even the "ragin' Cajun," James Carville, the yellowest of Yellow Dog Democrats, gave the president a thumbs-down for his response to the crisis. Although Obama accepted responsibility for what the government did and did not do, most agreed that he should have been less trusting of assurances from oil companies that they knew what to do if there was a blowout.

Days passed, then weeks, and as BP, the EPA, the Coast Guard, and the White House bumbled along with no clear strategy, locals became increasingly frustrated. Those trying to help by sending down hair-filled panty hose to soak up the oil were told to stop because the homemade sponges weren't effective. The Florida Department of Environmental Protection tested Walton County's hay-spreading plan and told the county that it would not work either—the hay would not absorb the oil and would create a bigger mess to clean up. The county responded that it would rather have a bigger mess offshore than have the oil come in and spoil their "pristine beaches." Locals applauded this defiance until the widely believed rumor got out that the hay was being supplied by a relative of a retired county official. Then some had second thoughts.

BP's plans to stop the leak—Top Hat, Junk Shot, and Top Kill, which columnist Ron Hart said sounded "like rejected titles of Bruce Willis movies"—failed, and by early June the company was down to its last resort. Engineers planned to cut off the pipe, cap it, and draw the oil up to a waiting tanker. This had not been tried before because if it failed, even more oil would be released into the Gulf. It worked to a point. Cutting the pipe and capping it reduced the flow, but did not stop it. That would only happen if relief wells were successfully drilled, and no one would know if such drilling had succeeded until August—over two months into hurricane season.

Meanwhile, as tar balls and oil plumes drifted closer, tourists cancelled reservations and over the usually crowded Memorial Day weekend, rental property sat empty and the lines at restaurants were short. The worry spread. When Alabama governor Bob Riley told the press that if the oil came ashore the 2010 tourist season would be lost, he was talking about a disaster for more than the coast. Thirty-five percent of Alabama's tourist income came from its beach counties and the recession-battered state would be hard pressed to replace that revenue. Florida's Panhandle counties were threatened the same way. Tourist taxes and property assessments supported everything from schools to sewers. Property value had fallen dramatically when the housing bubble burst, and if revenue from tourism was also lost, critical services would have to be reduced. It was an environmental crisis with far-reaching economic consequences.

Whose fault was it? Increasingly the evidence pointed to BP. In the decades since the last major oil spill, oil companies such as BP made enormous profits, which they put back into drilling technology instead of developing ways to deal with a blowout. When the CEO of BP acknowledged, "We did not have the tools you want in your tool box," he admitted the choice they had made. Still, he wasn't telling coastal folks anything that they did not already know.

As BP struggled with the public relations nightmare created by the spill, a deep gloom settled on the region. Sick jokes like "soon they will be offering specials on preblackened shrimp at the Flora-Bama" fell flat, and when FOX News, usually considered the source of all wisdom down there, did a story that suggested that the oil had already arrived on Gulf beaches when it had not, the Destin Area Chamber of Commerce roared "what the hell" and demanded the reporter apologize. "The national media's mass hysteria has given us a media crisis, not an oil crisis," a chamber spokesman said.

Of course, there was an oil crisis and soon even the most positive promoters were hard pressed to deny it. Florida launched a come-on-down "The Coast is Clear" campaign, paid for by BP, for at the time the coast was, but tourists interviewed over the Memorial Day weekend told the press that they had come down because it might be the last time they could see the beach as it should be. Though BP promised to clean up any oil and "restore the shoreline to its original state," folks there were increasingly skeptical. The *Destin Log*'s ongoing poll revealed a shift in opinion as residents grew less concerned that the perception of the spill would keep tourists away and more worried about the impact the spill would have on wildlife, the ecosystem, and the beaches. They knew, instinctively, that what made the coast a place where people wanted to live, where tourists wanted to visit, and where investors wanted to invest was in danger.

Following the progress, or lack of it, day after day, local folks could not help but wonder when and if anyone would take charge and get things done. "Discombobulated," was the way the mayor of Orange Beach described the response to the crisis. People down there wanted to work, they needed to work, and there were plenty of jobs that needed to be done, but BP was not hiring, at least not hiring locals. Governor Bob Riley, visiting the coast,

Signs warning beachgoers of oil in the sand and the water. Photograph by the author.

told the press, "Every person I saw tending boom was from the state of Maine." Those in charge promised to do better but it seemed everyone had to check with someone else before a decision could be made. On June 4, it was reported that there were 1,150 boats available to help protect Alabama and the Panhandle, but only 112 were trained and activated. No skimmers, just promises. There were booms, but no one to put them out. And the bad news kept coming in. When tar balls were found on Pensacola Beach, the executive director of the Santa Rosa Island Authority contacted BP and asked for the cleanup crews that had been promised. Two days later, still no crews. And back at Gulf Shores signs appeared along the tide line: "*HEALTH ADVISORY*—PUBLIC IS ADVISED NOT TO SWIM THESE WATERS DUE TO THE PRESENCE OF OIL RELATED CHEMICALS."

Headlines in the *Anniston Star* announced the "Wrecked Riviera."

As frustration with BP grew, the Florida attorney general called for a greater federal role in the cleanup, only to discover that Washington's role was limited by its own rules. Under the Oil Pollution Act of 1990 cleanup was supposed to be handled through a Joint Unified Incident Command that included, of course, the oil companies. This put BP in a position to shape the response in its favor, and it did. At the same time it was becoming clear that the company had withheld information on the size of the spill in an effort, it was widely believed, to limit its own liability. Meanwhile, folks along the coast were caught in a bureaucratic tangle. They would have preferred to

Local opinion of BP, tacked to the wall of a Destin Harbor bar.
Photograph by the author.

clean up the oil as it came ashore and submit vouchers for BP to pay. "When it comes to taking care of beaches," Escambia County Commission chairman Grover Robinson told the press, "That's something we know how to do." But the law would not let them just go out, do it, and get reimbursed. They had to go through the Unified Command and BP. Frustrated, some citizens began wishing aloud that FEMA was in charge. And when coastal folk began wanting FEMA back you knew things were bad.

Response was painfully slow. Never a favorite along the coast, President Obama alienated locals with his measured reaction to the situation and his seeming lack of righteous indignation at what happened. They called him "No Drama Obama" and wondered if anyone in Washington really appreciated their situation. Movie director Spike Lee, dismayed at the president's cool approach to the crisis, advised Obama, "If there's any time to go off, this is it," but "going off" was not this president's style. Still, some progress was detected. Finally, fifty days after the well blew, "qualified community responders" were being hired from unemployment rolls, trained, and paid eighteen to twenty dollars an hour to clean up the oil when it came ashore. However, because most of the oil was still off the Louisiana coast, that was where most of the effort was concentrated. Alabama and Florida felt slighted, and they were.

As the oil calculator on the *Destin Log's* online site rolled over the 35 billion gallon mark—nearly eight hundred times what BP first "estimated" the spill to be—readers learned that "ankle-deep, mousse-like oil" had reached the Alabama-Florida line. That same day, June 10, the *Mobile Press-Register* reported that the boom laid out to block the oil from coming through Perdido Pass and into the inland bays, bayous, and marshes had failed, and lumps of petroleum were coming in. "There goes my flounder fishing," observed a resident of Bear Point. He saw the oil about midmorning on June 9 and called the Unified Command in Mobile; four hours later he was still waiting for someone to come check. As he waited, BP announced yet another plan, a mechanical system of sliding screens that would close off the pass. The state would build it, BP would pay for it, and it could be ready in three weeks. But by then it might be too late. "A Chinese fire-drill" the Orange Beach mayor called it. His constituents agreed.

So they cancelled fishing events well into September, while a group organized as Seizebp.org began to demand that the government seize all BP's assets and place them in a trust to pay for losses along the Gulf. At about the same time, Florida pulled its "Coast Is Clear" ad campaign because the coast wasn't clear—or at least soon wouldn't be. TDC organizations along the Redneck Riviera began an effort (paid for by BP) to promote other coastal activities—golf, relaxing by the pool, recreational shopping and eating, and bird watching (no mention of cleaning them first). An impassioned plea from Gulf Shores celebrity and restaurateur Lucy "LuLu" Buffett urged folks not to cancel reservations but come on down for what "might be one of the most memorable vacations you will have." As she was writing, brother Jimmy was over on Pensacola beach at the opening of his new, 162-room Margaritaville Hotel, built on a site that was cleared by Hurricane Ivan in 2004. Though the timing could not have been worse, what Buffett built reflected a new approach to development that came out of the condo crash a few years earlier. Coastal developers, unable to get financing for more condos when the market was saturated with foreclosures, found investors willing to put money into motels and hotels that would not depend on individual buyers and would not encourage speculation and flipping. Margaritaville Hotel fit neatly into that trend.

"This will pass," Buffett said as he walked along the beach with Governor Charlie Crist, and there was a belief, or hope, among them all that it would. And when it did, if it did, Buffett's hotel would be ready. Before the oil started washing ashore, ever-optimistic real estate agents were telling inland folks about great bargains in the condo market and chambers of commerce were touting moderately priced hotels and motels. This shift in customer base suggested, according to one Gulf Shores broker, "the return of more traditional clients, rather than investors." Adding that "Baldwin's coastline has always been a blue-collar vacation spot," he saw evidence that those folks were returning again. Or at least they were until the oil approached. Not even rednecks wanted an oily beach and oily water. If the coast was not clear, they would go somewhere else.

And what would become of the Redneck Riviera?

SEVENTEEN

The Last Summer

O N JUNE 17, the United States Supreme Court handed down its decision in *Stop the Beach Renourishment, Inc. v. Florida Department of Environmental Protection et al.*, and the city of Destin, along with a lot of folks in the tourist industry, breathed a sigh of relief. The court held that the state could rebuild beaches, that rebuilt beaches were public, and that beachfront homeowners were not due compensation for what they claimed was "taken" from them.

But no one danced in the street with joy or jumped from the Destin Bridge in despair. Except for the beachfront folks who sued, city officials, the TDC, and a handful of people who had wanted the case to be all about property rights and "judicial taking," nobody seemed to give a rip. Apart from the short Associated Press story that was expanded to reflect local views and an editorial or two, Panhandle newspapers had surprisingly little comment on the subject. A few days after the decision, one of the litigants wrote a column in the *Destin Log* arguing, more or less, that because his beach had not been nourished and probably would not be for a while, his beach was still private—the picture of the author, tuxedoed and smiling, seemed to underscore the difference between those who claimed to own the beach and the ones they wanted to exclude, the difference between upper crust and lower. The comments that appeared with the online column showed little sympathy for him or his cause, but few bothered to comment.

When compared to the acrimonious debate that preceded the decision, the response was a near-deafening silence. Some locals suggested that the city should sue the ones who had filed the original suit so taxpayers could recover some portion of what had been spent winning the case. Others asked if the private beach owners were going to allow cleanup crews to trespass on their sand to get the oil when it washed ashore. Then, a few weeks later, the county agreed to leave the beach claimed by the column writer's condominium out of the coming restoration project, a move some felt might have prevented all this controversy at the outset. The agreement still had to be approved by an administrative judge but with that compromise, for the moment at least, things settled down.

As for the good old boys and good old girls who had wandered the beaches as if they were their own, the decision (if they knew there was one) had little impact on their lives, so they paid it no mind. What they wondered, along with everyone else, was whether or not the folks who were supposed to be in charge would clean up the beach so they could wander it again. Oil was already washing up on Okaloosa Island and it was almost into Destin Pass and the bay. Oil was also threatening to halt the dredging of the pass and the nourishing of Holiday Isle. Although the antinourishment folks hinted at more litigation, most figured that the highest court had spoken and that was that.

Four days later, on June 21, more than sixty days after the blowout, I loaded my family and Libby the Lab for our annual trip to Seagrove Beach. My mood was somber. During the week before the trip, I had followed news that had become increasingly depressing and bizarre. Someone had finally got hold of BP's 582-page regional spill plan for the Gulf and discovered that among the "sensitive biological resources" that the company was going to protect were walruses, sea otters, sea lions, and seals. Signing off on this assessment was a "national wildlife expert" who just happened to have died four years before the plan was submitted, not that it mattered to the Minerals Management Service. Apparently unconcerned with logic or facts, MMS approved the plan, which explained, finally, why BP didn't have a clue what to do when the well blew.

In a sardonic attempt to look on the bright side, someone observed that if BP could reanimate the dead, and get the deceased to sign this "dumb-assed report," restoring the Gulf Coast should be a piece of cake.

Oil-fouled Pensacola Beach. Redneck Riviera beaches from Gulf Shores to Pensacola were hit hard. The farther east and away from the spill the beach was, the less the damage. Courtesy of U.S. Air Force. Photograph by Tech. Sgt. Emily F. Alley.

Things were not going well for BP. Its stock lost nearly half its value as word circulated that the federal government was pressuring the company not to pay dividends until the damage to coastal economy and ecology was paid in full. Then, on day fifty-four of the spill, as BP once again upped the estimate of how much oil was flowing into the Gulf, state and local officials in Alabama issued an order that only vessels working on containment and cleanup could go through boom-protected Perdido Pass. Some locals on WaveRunners had been jumping the booms like they jumped waves in the Gulf. Unfortunately, sometimes they landed on what they were trying to jump, damaged the barrier, and let the oil in. So the governor and Pleasure Island leaders closed the pass to all recreational boat traffic, including charter boats going out. With that, fishing from the "Red Snapper Capital of the World" ceased. What government regulations on size and number had threatened, BP and the blown well accomplished. For the foreseeable future, fishermen were out of business.

Frustration continued to grow. Even as the passes into the bays and marshes were being closed, counties along Florida's Redneck Riviera began demanding that they be allowed "to secede from the unified command of the oil-spill response and declare independence from everything but BP's money." According to the *Destin Log* local officials wanted "BP out of the decision loop." Since the Unified Command seemed incapable of keeping the counties informed of the progress of the oil, the counties wanted to set up their own warning system. They wanted to deploy booms to protect their beaches and bays without having to wait for the Coast Guard to tell them it was OK. They wanted to build their own berms when and where they felt the need. They wanted to try their own ideas and do what had worked in the past without having to seek permission from anyone. True, they were only making a request, but in it was the implied threat that they were going to do it anyway and they dared the government to stop them and BP not to pay.

Getting BP to pay was not a sure thing. As the first fingers of oil washed up on Orange Beach protesters gathered at Perdido Pass to listen to environmentalists familiar with Exxon's response to the Alaska oil spill tell Alabamians to expect BP "to break every promise it is not forced to keep." A "testy" letter from the Coast Guard to BP's chief operating officer telling him to pick up the pace of containment in anticipation of the president's imminent arrival on the coast was greeted with skepticism by folks who wanted the pace picked up no matter who came down from Washington. A lady who owned a condo out on the Fort Morgan peninsula and rented it most of the year was getting cancellations. So she called the BP Spill Service, and during "two very long and complicated telephone calls" she learned that to file a claim she had to give them her "life history, SS#, tax returns, etc." When one guy on the phone "assured [her] that all the info would be secure," it was all she could do not to say, "But this is BP! How secure can anything be?"

As cancellations at Gulf Shores and Orange Beach increased, over to the east, where the oil had not reached, chambers of commerce and tourist development councils were telling folks looking for a summer getaway that on their beaches "Serenity is now more attainable than ever" and more affordable than it had been in years. Seafood restaurants near the coast reported doing a booming business as locals anticipated the price of everything from the Gulf would be going up and they wanted to get in one more taste before it did. Then, to add perhaps even more urgency to the message, on June 12, a storage tank that had been on the Deepwater Horizon rig washed up on Panama City Beach, fifty-four days after the rig had exploded. If debris from the explosion could make it, the oil could not be far behind.

Finally, BP seemed to be getting the message. Complaints of the half-hearted and ineffectual measures taken to protect the Alabama coast brought more pressure from the White House. The company responded by hiring private boats, "Vessels of Opportunity" they called them, to go out into the Gulf to look for oil and skim it when they could. BP also stationed a two-hundred-ton freighter off Destin to serve as a decontamination station to clean boats coming in from the toxic waters. Most of the Vessels of Opportunity came from the coastal fishing fleets, and the money helped cover some of the cost of lost charters. All this was well and good, but still folks wondered why more than fifty days had passed before the company launched this full assault.

Others knew why. The oil giant was in the middle of a public relations disaster that threatened it as surely as the environmental crisis threatened the coast. Efforts to muzzle the press and keep workers from talking to reporters made little difference as the oil washed up. The underwater oil plume that BP so long denied even existed was real and rolling in. Once scientists finally got the information they needed, the estimated flow into the Gulf rose to 2.6 million gallons a day. The "modest" impact so cavalierly talked about proved to be catastrophic instead. CEO Tony Hayward became the poster child for how to make a bad situation worse. The company's upbeat commercials assuring everyone that it would "make this right" were greeted with hoots of derision, and *Miami Herald* columnist Carl Hiaasen wrote that BP's effort reminded him of a scene from the movie *Animal House* in which a smooth-talking fraternity man explained to the pledge whose brother's car he had just destroyed—"You f***** up. You trusted us. Hey, make the best of it."

Making the best of it was getting harder and harder. For a number of years my buddy Mark and I had taken our sons fishing on the *Huntress* out of Destin. We were scheduled to go out again on June 30. But on June 15, day fifty-seven of the spill, I got an e-mail from Captain Mike. "The reports of oil were not good," he wrote. "It's now four miles off beach." And not just sheen, he said. "I'm talking the real deal big thick ugly mass." He and his mate "Groovy" were "going to try and fish till they shut us down," but no one knew how long that would be. That same morning the lead story in the *New York Times* ran with the headline "Efforts to Repel Gulf Oil Spill

Are Described as Chaotic." The article was mostly about Louisiana, but it could have been about Gulf Shores, Orange Beach, Pensacola, or Destin, for according to National Oceanic and Atmospheric Administration there were more miles of "potentially beached oil" along the Redneck Riviera than along the marshes of the Pelican State.

That was all the Okaloosa County commissioners could take. Tired of having to go through the maze of federal and state regulations and having to wait on BP to provide the support they requested, the commissioners voted unanimously to strike out on their own. "We made the decision legislatively to break the law if necessary," Chairman Wayne Harris told the press. "We will do whatever it takes to protect our county's waterways and we're prepared to go to jail to do it." With that they budgeted $200,000 to add additional protection to the pass into Choctawhatchee Bay and dared folks at the state Emergency Operations Center in Tallahassee and the Unified Command in Mobile to do anything to stop them. In a room packed with angry people, the commissioners told the BP and Coast Guard representatives present that while they would continue to cooperate with the various state and federal agencies, they wanted to "send a loud and clear message" that they wanted their requests acted on immediately. When Martha LaGuardia, commander of the Coast Guard, expressed sympathy but told them that "moving ideas and plans through the chain of command was the proper way to do things," the commission would have none of it. Fed up with the chain of command, Harris told LaGuardia, "We've played the game. We're done playing the game." Citizens, who had long considered county commissioners just a bunch of upcountry good old boys who couldn't care less about the coast, applauded.

Ever since the well had blown, ideas for what to do next had been coming in to BP and the Unified Command, where most languished. Someone proposed that rather than fine BP for violating the Clean Water Act and having the money go to EPA, this revenue should be used to pay people to "prospect" for the tar balls along the beach and be paid when they turned in what they collected. But turning folks into "prospectors" did not get far. Neither did the idea of turning loose oil-eating microbes and letting them gobble up the spill. What did catch BP's attention was a machine developed by a company funded by actor Kevin Costner that used centrifuge processing technology to separate oil and water. Now you might have thought that an oil company, drilling underwater, would have already tested and approved something like that, but given BP's record for being prepared, it was considered by some remarkable that it took the company only one month to agree to purchase six of the machines for testing and another month to announce to the world how "excited" the oil giant was about the plan. Some cynics said that Costner's testifying before Congress about the lack of interest BP had shown in schemes like his might have had something to do with BP's decision. But even when the company agreed to buy and deploy thirty-two of the machines, it would be August before enough of them were in place to make a difference. By then nearly four months would have been lost.

Meanwhile, President Obama showed up at Tacky Jack's in Orange Beach, where he ate something fried, drank sweet tea (no beer), and got an idea of what was happening to the Alabama coast. From the restaurant he could see efforts to protect the pass from incoming oil, could see the charter fleet sitting idle, and could see places at the entrance to Cotton Bayou that were already stained by the spill. The president talked to folks, most of whom had voted for the other guy, had his picture taken, and then headed out to the meetings that locals hoped would be more productive than what had taken place so far. Along his route, people waved flags and gawked. A few held up signs. One read "You have two ears. Use them." Those two ears got filled the next day when the president met with people who wanted him to do more than listen. They wanted action.

They did not get it. That night the president spoke to the nation and when he was done folks along the coast were still wondering just what he was going to do about the oil. The idea that this crisis would give the nation the opportunity to finally develop a comprehensive energy policy was not going to save birds and fish and the beach. President Obama may have been looking at the big picture, but even his supporters on the coast, what few there were, were disappointed. "He still doesn't get it," an old friend and loyal Democrat living down there wrote me not long after the president finished talking. "Yes cleaner energy is spiffy. It's a political issue. Let it go for now." However, she continued, "we want our damn water cleaned up. Now. What we have down here is a cluster fuck. We want a plan with objectives and specific knowledge of what will be done to achieve those objectives. We want SOMEBODY to have the authority to make a decision in a matter of hours, not months. We've had enough meetings to make an academic administrator envious. Now go to work."

Going to work was what they were doing over in Destin. After the county commissioners voted to strike out alone if their plans got held up in red tape, the Florida Department of Environmental Protection quickly approved all the outstanding permits, and plans to block the pass and keep the oil out of the bay went ahead. Because of this rapid response, local officials continued to seek permission for strategies such as a stronger boom system, which had finally been approved by the Unified Command to put in place at Perdido Pass, but if permission was not forthcoming then they were prepared to go ahead and ask forgiveness later. Although reports varied, oil was said to be as close as two miles off shore, hovering, waiting for the wind to push it in. Everyone seemed willing to help. There were volunteers aplenty and developer Peter Bos told the commission that he could get them barges to block the pass. Around 80 percent of the charter boats had signed up as Vessels of Opportunity, but a few kept fishing. Still, they knew, or at least feared, there wasn't much time left. Boats were going out "back-to-back-to-back," one captain reported. "We're trying to get it done, before life as we know it is over."

About the only thing coastal folks liked about the president's speech was when he spoke of BP's "recklessness" and renewed his promise that "we will make BP pay for the damages their company has caused." So they waited to hear what came out of the closed door meeting scheduled for the next day, the first (critics noted) direct encounter between the president and BP executives in the fifty-eight days since the well blew out.

What came out sounded good—a $20 billion escrow fund to guarantee that BP would pay what it promised to pay and what the law required. But there was still the gnawing fear that the money would be too difficult for working folks to get and would be slow in coming for everyone. Riviera residents wanted something done for them and to the people responsible. They liked the idea, floated by Louisiana congressman Joseph Cao, who told BP executives at a house committee meeting that rather than resign, they should do what "in the Asian culture we do." Rep Cao, a Vietnamese-American Republican, suggested, "We just give you a knife and ask you to commit hari-kari." Filet knives the fishermen weren't using anymore would work just fine.

All of this was on my mind as we approached Seagrove. What had been planned as a quiet summer, revising this manuscript and writing up reaction to the U.S. Supreme Court ruling in the Destin nourishment case, had turned out anything but that. I was in a foul mood driving down. Traffic did not improve my attitude: there wasn't any. At least not the old kind—lines of SUVs with kids inside and bikes on the rack trying to pass RVs driven by retirees from Indiana. My mood darkened.

We got to the bay, the landmark that told us we were almost to the beach, the place where we always roll down the windows to smell the Gulf. What would I smell this time? I wasn't sure. Almost kept 'em up. But I didn't. And it hit me—salt air with a delicate bouquet of decaying marsh grass. Wonderful. We arrived at the house and saw people riding bikes, walking, jogging, just like last year and the year before. So we walked across the road and stood on the bluff, looking out over the Gulf—no slick, no sheen, no slime. Emerald green near the shore, darker further out, green again at the sandbar, then dark blue on to the horizon. There were lots of people on the beach, a few in the water. Cleanup crews walked along the tide line, picking up what had washed in. You could spot 'em. They were the ones wearing long pants. And moving slowly—it was hot.

My mood improved. I even began to appreciate the efforts of some friends to find humor in the situation. And the absurdity of it all—according to one who sat in on some of the BP meetings, "the acronyms specific to the oil spill seem to have been conceptualized by some adolescent boy." "Surface Cleanup Assessment Technique" becomes "SCAT." "Cell on Wheels" is "COW." And, the best yet, "Tarball Underwater Recovery Device" is transformed into "TURD." It was, a friend wrote, a "surreal experience . . . sitting in a conference room filled . . . with stern expressions while agency officials discussed how the SCAT teams were communicating via COW about the TURDs." It was hard "to keep a straight face while I scanned the room for a hidden camera and Alan Funt!"

Then there was fishing.

News reports from Louisiana dwelled on how the oil was threatening a culture, a way of life. It was no less for the fishermen along the Redneck Riviera. The oil was depleting the oxygen in the water. As it did the fish fled. There were reports of schools of fish swimming east as if they were being "herded." What could not move that fast—the shrimp, oysters, minnows, and such—died. The captains and mates wondered when they would ever fish deep water again. My son and I wondered the same thing.

But there was still the shore. We could fish the surf. For as the oil depleted the oxygen out in the Gulf, some of the fleeing fish came in and schooled in the shallows. Not all of these were welcomed. Just in time for the thirty-fifth anniversary of the movie *Jaws*, a number of sharks, big and small, were seen off the Alabama coast. As the oil pushed them toward us my son speculated that we might catch one. I hoped we wouldn't.

Even after three months, it was still difficult to get clear information about what was going on. Crews hired by BP were told if they even acknowledged someone from the media "with a wave or a nod they [would] be fired on the spot." When a boat full of newsfolk pulled alongside one of the decontamination ships the members of the crew working for BP "scrambled below and hid." The media complained about being shut out, but to little avail. "You can understand why," the wife of the ship's captain told me. "Who would want the press interfering with efforts to save the Gulf walrus?"

Meanwhile BP CEO Tony Hayward, the one who promised to "make this right," went back to England to watch his yacht race off the Isle of Wight. Folks on the coast, whose boats were docked and tethered, were not pleased. More than a few offered to loan CEO Tony a knife. Haywood was not the only BP executive to rile up residents of the Riviera. BP chairman Carl-Henric Svanberg, a Swede whose English needed polishing along with Hayward's PR skills, told the press that BP was not one of those "greedy companies." "We care about the small people," he said. The response to that was predictable. There was outrage and there was disgust, but there was also the reaction from folks like Orange Beach mayor Tony Kennon, who laughed and said, "They can call me anything they want. . . . Just write the check and send it to us."

As the spill spread along the Redneck Riviera, folks began to consider its impact on other cultural aspects of the region. What would happen if Spring Breakers did not return to Panama City Beach, if mullet no longer flew at the Flora-Bama, if no one came to redneck it up with the Trashy White Band? And what would happen to the folks who sold shrimp from the back of their pickups? Over the years I often bought fresh shrimp, heads on, from shrimpers who were part of a network of independent operators who considered their association with the government an adversarial relationship. They would take part of their catch and sell it directly to the customer—no middle man. The customer paid in cash and the IRS never knew.

Now this time-honored tradition of not reporting on-the-side income was about to come back to haunt them. As the waters they once fished were closed, as their boats became Vessels of Opportunity working for BP, there was no longer any out-of-the-truck-bed selling to go unreported. How could they apply to BP for what they had lost when there was no record of their having had it? BP was paying, when it paid, lost income based on calculations created by someone who didn't fish who was trying to figure out what folks earned who did. And naturally, the calculators used reported income as the basis for their calculations. Unreported income was not taken into consideration. Yet that unreported income was often what determined the difference between "just scraping by" and "doing well." So what could they do? How could they convince BP that they made more than what they reported to the government? Who kept records of unreported income? And even if they did, by reporting it to BP, would they be opening themselves to an inquiry by the "gub'ment" and maybe a bill for back taxes? It was a dilemma.

Meanwhile, there were more protests. The biggest and best organized was Hands Across the Sands, which was begun by Dave Rauschkolb, owner of a beachside restaurant at Seaside, as a protest against plans to allow drilling off the Florida coast. On June 26, sympathetic coastal residents stood on shore and joined hands in a silent statement that was impressive in its dignity but questionable in its effectiveness. Cynics, and there were many, pointed out that some protesters arrived in gas guzzling SUVs and left the motor running to keep the air conditioner going while they made their stand against the policies that gave them the gas to burn. Others noted that despite the impact that the spill was having on the coast, this was a political, rather than an environmental problem, and until the hand-holders came up with a political solution, it would be business as usual for the oil industry.

It was too much for some. In Orange Beach Captain Allen Kruse signed his boat the *Rookie* on as a Vessel of Opportunity. It seemed the only thing he could do. Tightened restrictions on catch, a shorter snapper season, all the forms to fill out just to fish, and then the oil spill—all of it had taken its toll. He went to the BP training meeting, listened to what his new line of work would be, returned to the *Rookie*, sent his crew on an errand, and climbed up on the flying bridge—that was when they heard the "pop." Returning, the crew found him dead of a self-inflicted gunshot wound. Years before, Kruse and his twin brother had agreed that when they died they wanted friends to spread their ashes in the creeks and coves around Orange Beach, in the places where a younger brother's ashes had been spread. But his friends couldn't carry out his wishes because of the oil.

Another casualty was optimism. Even in the worst of times that was the one thing to which folks along the Redneck Riviera continued to cling. Now optimism was fading fast. Local promoters tried to perk people up with free concerts. Taking some of the money BP had given to revive tourism, Okaloosa County officials brought in Kenny Loggins and the Doobie Brothers for a "Rock the Beach" extravaganza. The weather cooperated, thousands attended, and the effort was judged a success.

Over on the Alabama coast they had even bigger plans. Jimmy Buffett was coming home.

On June 21, 2010, the *Mobile Press-Register* announced that on July 1, Jimmy was going to do a free concert in Gulf Shores to promote tourism. With him would be Kenny Chesney, the Zac Brown Band, and some others. For those who could not make it, or could not get one of the thirty-five thousand tickets that would be "given away," "Jimmy Buffett and his Friends Live from the Gulf Coast" would be broadcast on CMT. Alabama governor Bob Riley applauded the plan and promised that the state tourism development department would pick up some of the production tab—causing a few folks to wonder why BP wasn't paying for it all. Still, it seemed like a great idea and everyone was happy.

Until they tried to get tickets.

Within minutes of the tickets becoming available online, they were gone. A short time later some appeared for sale on eBay and the anger grew. There was no shortage of theories about what had happened: the tickets went to scalpers, the tickets went to out-of-towners, the computers threw out local requests, and so on and so on. Promoters fought hard to explain that there was no conspiracy to exclude people who lived on the coast; that a third of the tickets had gone to local hotels, motels, and condos to offer as incentives for people who would come down and stay a while; and that the rest went to fans on a first-come, first-served basis. The demand was just too great.

So the ticketless began making plans to watch it on TV. The city of Foley announced it would put up a big screen outdoors and invite everyone to the party. "Making the best of the situation" was becoming the alternative to optimism. One cafe owner was telling folks, "Come see the worst manmade disaster in history."

Then they cancelled the concert. Delayed it, actually. With Hurricane Alex churning the water off Mexico and sending swells crashing onto Gulf

Jimmy Buffett concert on the Alabama coast after the spill. Courtesy of the *Mobile Press-Register*.

beaches it was decided that the weather was just too uncertain so promoters put it off until July 11. This sent those with tickets—those who offered tickets as part of a rental package and those who had changed vacation plans to come down and boogie on the beach—scrambling to figure out what to do next. Meanwhile, Buffett dropped in unannounced at his sister's restaurant and played a two-hour set for an audience that word-of-mouth swelled to around two thousand—mostly locals, along with some concert ticket holders who had come down despite the cancellation and were glad they had. At a time when meaningless gestures had become common on the coast, this one meant a lot—even to those who only heard about it the next day.

Meanwhile, everyone watched the weather, watched the water, watched the shoreline, and waited. BP's damage control efforts weren't helping a bit, but there was general agreement that the folks doing the hot, thankless job of cleaning up the oil when it came ashore were performing up to expectations—though in some cases those expectations were not very high. Trying to finish this book while in Seagrove, I would begin my day with online reading of the latest reports of how far the oil had drifted. Then I would take Libby the Lab down to run on the beach while I checked to see if anything had come ashore. It was a deathwatch of sorts, waiting for the inevitable but trying to do what could be done before it came. Turtle Watch people began moving eggs from identified nests and transporting them to the East Coast, far from the oil. Turtles that hatched from the eggs that remained would have to get over the ruts created by cleanup crew vehicles and get by the beach stuff that overworked beach patrollers were no longer taking up and carrying off, and if they made it, the water would probably kill them anyway. And to the water they would go, because the turtle light regulations were working, so at night the beach was dark.

With prime fishing areas closed by the federal government the Destin Swordfish Tournament was cancelled. However, more out of hope than conviction, officials from the Destin Fishing Rodeo announced that for the sixty-second straight year the event would be held in October as scheduled. "We're not going to let some silly little oil spill ruin our history," one of the rodeo board members told the press. Another member added, "If you don't go forward, it could put this town in a state of shock." Come October, he said, "there will be dead fish . . . on the docks." But the effort to revive the region's flagging optimism fell flat. Though most agreed that it would be a shame to cancel the rodeo so far in advance, they noted that the charter boats that signed up with BP would not be able to take part. There were others who wondered if the "dead fish on the docks" would be those caught or some that washed up. Cynicism was taking the place of optimism.

With all this happening my family and I settled in at Seagrove to wait for the Fourth of July. The beach was clean, thanks to the crews that picked up trash as well as bits of tar. The water was sort of nasty with seaweed churned up by the recent storm, but the wind was offshore and easterly so if there was oil out there, and reports said there was, it was being held back. We were ready.

July third. By 10:00 a.m. the beach was filling up with tents and umbrellas. By noon it seemed like half of Puckett, Mississippi, was there, returned for their annual outing. Word spread among the better-bred that the Puckettians were the riff-raff from Gulf Shores, come to our beach to escape the oil. Apparently the better-bred had not been around the year before or the years before that, or if they were they weren't paying attention, for people like the Puckettians were enjoying the beach long before the upscale arrived.

Since there was no oil, local boaters held the revived Rags to Riches Regatta and once again the catamarans sailed back and forth between Seagrove and Grayton until someone was declared a winner. I watched from the beach and wondered how Tony Hayward's yacht would do against this

Tents on the beach, Fourth of July weekend, 2010. Although there were fewer tourists after the oil spill, the hardcore kept coming. Photograph by Walter Lydick.

competition. A fireworks display was promised for the evening, just as in the past, so we kept watching for the barge that was usually towed offshore and used as the platform for the pyrotechnic extravaganza. None appeared; BP had leased all the barges. This year, the fireworks would be launched from shore.

On July Fourth, they held the parade. There were the usual politicians and the usual businesses, but no church floats because it was Sunday.

That night we sat out in front of the house, in lawn chairs, drinking beer and talking to people as they walked by on their way to Seaside for dinner or a concert or something. The contrast between the two groups was, one might say, striking. There was our contingent of lower South people, friends and family, adults and children, descendents of the folks who founded the Redneck Riviera so long ago and gave it to us as our birthright, our heritage, telling stories of how it used to be and concluding that if it got any better we couldn't stand it. And there was their contingent, the ones walking by, dressed like Abercrombie and Fitch models, going to Seaside to see and be seen and probably glad we weren't going with them.

Fourth of July Parade, Seagrove Beach. Although businesses and politicians are still parading, there are more and more community groups and collected individuals like the Margarita MeMaws. Photograph by the author.

A couple of days after America's independence was celebrated the folks from Puckett went back to Mississippi, home to jobs and responsibilities. There were crops to harvest, lesson plans to write, online courses to finish, stores to stock, kids to get ready for school. The Puckettians had to ease back into being farmers, teachers, firefighters, state troopers, school administrators, nurses, secretaries, and students. For most, it was an easy transition, for even though they might have done things at the beach that they normally would not do, they remained what they were before they had arrived—good, decent, hardworking folks, the kind that have always come to the coast for a break from the routine that they know will be waiting when they return home.

A week later BP took off the well cap that was siphoning some of the spill, and while Jimmy Buffett played his delayed concert and gave the coast a much-needed psychological lift, oil gushed full force into the Gulf. But the beach where Buffett played was clean and the folks who watched it on CMT saw what local business leaders wanted them to see—white sand, sparkling water, rolling surf. When Buffett added the line "It's all BP's fault" to his signature song, "Margaritaville" the crowd cheered. When he closed with new lyrics to an old favorite and sang "I hope that I'm around to see, when the coast is clear," some cried.

On July 14, BP got the new cap on the well and after eighty-five days and over 180 million gallons, oil no longer flowed into the Gulf. It was not a permanent solution. That would come when a relief well plugged the hole. But it was better than what had been before.

About the time the Puckettians left, the Beach Issue of *Florida Travel and Life* appeared online. It announced that the coast along Highway 30-A, Walton County's stretch of the Redneck Riviera, was the "Pearl of the Panhandle," the place where visitors should go for "southern hospitality in a trendy setting." Pearl of the Panhandle. Another name to add to the list.

But when the magazine described the "ethos of 30-A" and told of the "anyone-can-do-it activities" being done down there, it did not chronicle the sort of "anyone-can-do-it" doings done by the folks who first came down to visit the coast. *Florida Travel and Life* was not writing about the Redneck Riviera but about what the region's "raffish Rotarians, pirates with cash register eyeballs, and hard-handed matrons" wanted readers to believe the Redneck Riviera had become. The article focused on places like Rosemary Beach, Seaside, and WaterColor, places with neat yards, picket fences, front porches, and color coded cottages, places where the successful and sophisticated come to enjoy the fruits of their labors.

During the years covered by this book the sort of people who visited the Gulf Coast changed, and the coast changed with them. Beach promoters, sensitive to popular tastes and trends, created attractions and events designed to appeal to those who were coming and to those they wanted to come. Visitors arrived looking to have fun in an exotic setting where the rules were different. But as people changed, so did the rules. Where earlier tourists were loose and laid back, the newer ones demanded order, organization, and in some cases an investment opportunity. They got all of these. Politicians, prosperity, class, culture, and commercialism combined to stifle spontaneity and turn much of the Redneck Riviera into a playground for the affluent, the intense, and the opportunistic.

Much of it, but not all. In some cases, redneckery remained, to the distress of many who wanted it otherwise.

Although local boosters applauded the idea of BP-underwritten free concerts featuring mainstream music makers, they wanted concerts that would show the rest of the country that the beach was open for business and the business of the beach was good clean fun. However, when it was announced that Lynyrd Skynyrd, whose song "Free Bird" has been called "the redneck national anthem," was coming to Okaloosa Island, the reaction was different. A Skynyrd concert, one critic wrote, would attract people who were not good for the region's image or its economy. "Every toothless redneck from a hundred miles," the writer complained, would "bring in [their] own Busch and Natty Lite and food," set up lawn chairs, groove to "Sweet Home Alabama," and then leave. The only way for local businesses to make any money would be to "open a cheap cigarette and Confederate bandana shop."

Despite these misgivings, and despite some rain, the concert went off without a hitch. The crowd that collected there looked a lot like the one that had gathered to hear Jimmy Buffett over in Gulf Shores. And the people at both were not unlike the people who had always slipped down to the Redneck Riviera. They were the children, and in some cases the grandchildren, of beachgoers who over the years came to the coast to swim, fish, ride rides at the amusement parks, dance at the Hangouts, listen to the Trashy White Band at the Green Knight, and throw mullet at the Flora-Bama.

As for the folks who weren't there, the ones who stayed comfortable and secure in condos and gated communities, they missed a good time.

Acknowledgments

FIRST I WOULD LIKE to thank Jacksonville State University and its Eminent Scholar program for the support given me over the years. President William A. Meehan, Vice President for Academic and Student Affairs Dr. Rebecca Turner, and Dean of Arts and Sciences J. Earl Wade have been sources of encouragement. The faculty of the Department of History and Foreign Languages and able secretaries Lisa Green and Audrey Smelley were helpful and patient. I also owe a debt of gratitude to graduate assistants Loren Girman DiBiase, Clay Wisner, Blake Wilhelm, and Maggie Hutchinson for all their work; and to Professor Miriam Hill for help with maps. And a big thank you to the folks at the *Anniston Star* who supported me in so many ways.

Suzanne, my wife, has been with me and this book from start to finish. She has listened to stories (and been in a few), she has read, edited, gently criticized, and warned, "I don't think I'd include that if I were you." She is my rock in a weary land.

Our children, Will and Anna, have spent summers and school breaks on the coast from the time they were born, and it is their natural habitat. Watching them grow up on the beach, adapt to the sun and sand and salt water, catch blue crabs on the bay and ghost crabs by flashlight at night, learn to shuck and eat raw oysters, and make friends with the environment has made me more aware of what a wonderful place the

Redneck Riviera is and how lucky we are to be part of it. Thank you Grandma Minnie and Aunt Sarah for building the cottage and passing it on to Daddy. Thank you Daddy and Mama for turning it over to us.

From the time when I had nothing but a book title, up until now, Nicole Mitchell of the University of Georgia Press has encouraged me, prodded me, and kept telling me that she wanted the book, until she finally got it. Then she went above and beyond the call of director-duty to help me put the manuscript into its final form. She is a treasure.

I also wish to express my thanks to Sydney Dupre, John McLeod, and Jon Davies of the University of Georgia Press and especially to copy editor Molly Thompson for her patience and her attention to detail and consistency.

Bunches of folks contributed to this effort in one way or another, and trying to list them all would run the risk of leaving someone out. But I am going to try anyway.

Jim and Lyra and Bob and Dawn got me started. Ed and Jane, Brad and Vivian, Susie and Gilbert, Mark and Lauren, and Gerald and Lee kept me going. We lost Bob, so he, Jim, and I never got to open that beach bar—"Two Professors and a One-Eared Trucker." Too bad. It would have been a winner. We also lost Vivian, who added that touch of Okie redneck to the Riviera. With these folks I drank a lot of beer, ate from the Gulf, sat on the beach, watched the moon rise, and planned for the future, which I guess is now.

And there were the veterans of the fishing and poker trips over Spring Break—Bob, Brad and his dad, John, Ed and Ted, Ed, Hugh, Richard, Jim, and O.C. Oh, the stories we could tell.

After I moved from Georgia to Alabama, a new flow of friends began making the trek to the cottage that was now ours. Chris and Kim, David and Allison, Jim and Suzanne, Mark and Dana, Steve and Kelly, Bill and Beth, and Aimee and Rance. Suzanne and I had children by then, so having kids to bring along upped our friends' chances of being invited. So their children came—the Cravens (Drew, Anna Katherine, Courtney, and Caroline), Maggie Cox, the Sides (Clarke, Luke, and Anna), the Hullers (Adam, Scott, Paige, and Kellie), Maddie Murray, the Meehans (Drew, Will, and Carol Grace), and Aubrey Kirk. And there were more children—Peyton, Bethany, Hudson, Hannah, Rebecka, Farrah, Taylor, Drew, and Sammy, plus the Jacksonville First United Church Youth Group and their brave chaperones. They entertained us. Some even cleaned up after themselves.

Family came as well. My oldest daughter, Kelly, along with husband Jamie and son Andy; sister-in-law Ellen with Arnie, Grace, and Olivia; brother-in-law Gary with Laurie, Garrison, Ansley, and Troy (and various friends); Nathan and Rebecca; and Mama Lucy.

Then there is cousin Benny, like a brother to me, a Mississippi law enforcement officer and movie star (see *Ghosts of Mississippi*) whose Mama (Aunt Anne, my Daddy's baby sister) lives next door to our Seagrove place. Benny is at his best sitting in his Mama's driveway on a warm summer evening, drinking beer while his daughter Leanna (a Mississippi State cheerleader) tries to comb out his ponytail and his other daughter, Sarah (captain in the Air Force), tells sister how to do it. He talks with people walking by on their way to some event at Seaside, and the sight is a study in contrasts. As long as Benny is alive and well, so is redneckery.

There are Bob and Genie from Puckett, Mississippi. Bob, who fights fires, Genie, who can teach just about any kid who wanders into the Puckett Attendance Center, and their children—Beth Ann (who can bale hay, sell anything you got on eBay, and drop a deer at two hundred yards), Hollis (who is cutting a swath through Ole Miss), and Mary Jo, the baby, who used to bite herself and blame her sisters. Their beach house is near ours, and they and the rest of the Bentons and Huffs are as good as it is ever gonna get.

And the people lucky enough to live down there—Aunt Anne, Cobb, Fred and Kat, Peter and Susan, Didon, Barbara, Bill, the Drewes, Rebecca of the Red Bar, George who owns the Village Market, Anne who works there and everywhere else, and the Whites who own Sundog Books in Seaside, the best beach bookstore on the coast. And those who have vacation homes nearby, the Lydicks, Johnsons, Tuckers, Hannahs, Williams, Joneses, Harrises, Woodall/Thompsons, and Yerby/McDaniels. On down the coast, on Lake Powell, are the Flemings—John, Carrie, Alex, and Carson. And back up in Birmingham are Ernie and Trisha, who used to live back in the grove. Great folks all.

Four "beach ladies" read parts of the book in its various stages. Margaret Long of Orange Beach was a constant source of insight and information, as was Karen Triplett Grant of Panama City Beach. Both are longtime residents and know what went on down there—and why. Kathleen Deyo Blais from Baldwin County offered suggestions and stories, and Cam Payne of

Fort Morgan (by way of Anniston) was a great help with that part of the coast.

I am also indebted to William Hatfield, editor of the *Destin Log*, and to Debbie Wheeler, who writes for the *Walton Sun*.

Others who wrote me and let me interview them (on the record) are thanked in the "Essay on Sources." You were terrific.

Alfred Rivers, a friend and classmate from high school days, showed me the letter his father wrote from Hawaii, longing for Gulf Shores. That gave me the opening I needed. Ora Wills of Pensacola, historian and poet, offered her insight into the history of African Americans in that area, and put me on the path to finding out about Johnson Beach, which I never would have discovered if J. Earle Bowden, journalist and historian, had not told me of Mrs. Wills and how to find her. Thanks to Paula Triplett Bailey for the pictures of Trip's.

And my Daddy, my brother Bill, Uncle Canoy, Ken, Joan, and Arabella— thanks for the memories.

Essay on Sources

THIS BOOK is the result of years of research and writing that began with a short piece, "Seasided," that was published in the *Atlanta Journal-Constitution*, October 9, 1994, and culminated with an essay in the spring 2010 issue of *Southern Cultures*. Titled "The Rise and Decline of the Redneck Riviera: The Northern Rim of the Gulf Coast since World War II," the *Southern Cultures* piece covered the Mississippi coast and Dauphin Island, which are not included here. Though the Mississippi coast is equal in redneckery to any place on the Gulf, it contains economic, cultural, and demographic elements that set it apart from its neighbors to the east. So it was decided to save that area for another day—and likely another historian. The same factors led to the decision to leave Alabama's Dauphin Island out as well. I would like to thank Jacksonville State University and its Eminent Scholar program for support in the research and writing.

Rather than providing formal citation notes, I have chosen to identify the principal sources used in this study in the form of the essay you are reading. The chapter-by-chapter breakdown that follows this essay should enable readers to tie specific sources to the story being told. The difficulty of documenting this book in a more traditional way comes from the fact that so much of it is based on my own experiences. In 1954 my grandmother bought property in Seagrove Beach, Florida, midway between Panama City and Destin. Two years later she built a "cottage" there. For over half a century that has been my home away from home. My account of my family's early days there, "Florida Room: From 'Redneck Riviera' to 'Emerald Coast': A Personal History of a Piece of the Florida Panhandle," was published in the *Florida Historical Quarterly* 81 (Winter 2003): 316–22.

At roughly the same time I also published "Developing the Panhandle: Seagrove Beach, Seaside, Watercolor, and the Florida Tourist Tradition," in *Southern Journeys: Tourism, History, and Culture in the Modern South*, ed. Richard D. Starnes (Tuscaloosa: University of Alabama Press, 2003). That essay was an expansion and elaboration of an earlier piece, "Seaside, Florida: Robert Davis and the Quest for Community," which was published in *Atlanta History* in the fall of 1998.

Although I had this close connection to the Florida Panhandle, the mere fact that I grew up in south Alabama, around one hundred miles north of Mobile, made Gulf Shores and Orange Beach close and convenient for my friends and me. So it was that through high school and college I traveled there frequently and developed a fondness for those communities and those people that continues to this day. If you have never tossed a mullet at the Flora-Bama, well, you should.

Over the years I have published pieces on coastal doings in the *Atlanta Journal-Constitution*, the *Birmingham News*, the *Mobile Press-Register*, and the *Anniston Star*, where I am a weekly columnist. Writing these has kept me abreast of what was going on down there and allowed me to discuss the evolution of the region with people whose thoughts and observations are incorporated into this essay and detailed in the book.

Some of the richest resources for the study of the Gulf Coast are local newspapers, many of which, happily, are now found online. Though most are shameless boosters of their economies, they also reflect the thoughts and, in some cases, the memories of people who made their communities what they were and are. In particular the *Destin Log* created the Destin History Project in connection with its 2008 and 2009 Progress Editions. These are on its website and are valuable to any researcher. Add to these a host of local studies by local people and you have a core of commentary from which to work. Among these are Patricia H. Bonkemeyer, ed., *Once Upon an Island, as Told to and Collected by the Gulf Shores Woman's Club* (Foley, Ala.: Underwood Printing, 1955); *From Cottages to Condos,* compiled and written by the Gulf Shores Woman's Club (Foley, Ala.: Underwood Printing, 1955); Margaret Childress Long and Michael D. Shipler, *The Best Place to Be: The Story of Orange Beach, Alabama* (Bay Minette, Ala.: Leedon Art, 2002); *The Way We Were: Recollections of South Walton Pioneers* (Santa Rosa Beach, Fla.: South Walton Three Arts Alliance, 1997); and *Of Days Gone By: Reflections of South Walton County, Florida* (Santa Rosa Beach, Fla.: South Walton Three Arts Alliance, 1999). Images of the early development of Pensacola Beach and the areas around it can be found in Deborah J. Dunlap, Betty Ann Copeland Johnson, and Tracey L. Martin, *Remember When: A Pictorial Journey of Gulf Breeze* (Pensacola, Fla.: Bayshore Publishing, 2002).

For a thorough analysis of the development of Florida there is none better than Gary R. Mormino, *Land of Sunshine, State of Dreams: A Social History of Modern Florida* (Gainesville: University Presses of Florida, 2005). A good account of the sort of people and attitudes that drifted down to the Gulf Coast from inland Florida is Diane Roberts, *Dream State: Eight Generations of Swamp Lawyers, Conquistadores, Confederate Daughters, Banana Republics, and Other Florida Wildlife* (New York: Free Press, 2004). See also Tracy J. Revels, *Sunshine Paradise: A History of Florida Tourism* (Gainesville: University Press of Florida, 2011). For a closer look at the Alabama coast's Baldwin County context see O. Lawrence Burnett Jr., *Coastal Kingdom: A History of Baldwin County, Alabama* (Baltimore: PublishAmerica, 2006). The Gulf Coast during World War II is covered in Allen Cronenberg, *Forth to the Mighty Conflict: Alabama and World War II* (Tuscaloosa: University of Alabama Press, 1995).

Howell Raines's classic piece "Todd and Stabler Offseason Game: Living It Up on 'Redneck Riviera,'" appeared in the *New York Times*, June 21, 1978. It was followed by William Oscar Johnson, "The Key to the Case Is Missing," *Sports Illustrated*, April 23, 1979, online from the *SI* Vault, and Robert F. Jones, "Getting Nowhere Fast," *Sports Illustrated*, September 19, 1979, 88–102. Add to these Ken Stabler and Barry Stainback, *Snake: The Candid Autobiography of Football's Most Outrageous Renegade* (Garden City, N.Y.: Doubleday and Company, 1986), and you will get a good idea of what Alabama's Redneck Riviera was in its heyday. Emory Thomas's commentary on the situation a decade later, *Travels to Hallowed Ground: A Historian's Journey to the American Civil War* (Columbia: University of South Carolina Press, 1987), is dead on target. For comments on the coast at the start of World War II see *Alabama: A Guide to the Deep South* (1941), reprinted as *The WPA Guide to 1930s Alabama* (Tuscaloosa: University of Alabama Press, 2000), and *Florida: A Guide to the Southernmost State*, Federal Writers' Project of the Work Projects Administration for the State of Florida (New York: Oxford University Press, 1939). The "Covenant for Property Located at Seagrove Beach, Florida, between C. H. McGee and Minnie E. Jackson," which lays out McGee's plan for his community, was filed April 21, 1955, in Walton County, Florida. A copy is in my possession.

Other sources that have helped me clarify my thoughts about the evolution of the region are Sunny David, "Condo Mania," *Pelican*, June 15, 2004; Matt Dellinger, "The Terrible Opportunity: How a Crisis for the Gulf Coast Became a Defining Moment for New Urbanism," *Oxford American* (Spring 2004): 108–17; Patrick K. Moore, "'Redneck Riviera' or 'Emerald Coast': Using Public History to Identify and Interpret Community Growth Choices in Florida's Panhandle," *Gulf South Historical Review* (Spring 2003): 60–91; Tim Hollis, *Florida's Miracle Strip: From Redneck Riviera to Emerald Coast* (Jackson: University Press of Mississippi, 2004); Kathryn Ziewitz and Jane Waiz, *Green Empire: The St. Joe Company and the Remaking of Florida's Panhandle* (Gainesville: University Press of Florida, 2005); Wayne Greenhaw, "Summertime," in *Tombigbee and Other Stories* (Montgomery, Ala.: Sycamore Press, 1991); Peter Applebome, *Dixie Rising: How the South Is Shaping American Values, Politics, and*

Culture (New York: Harvest Books, 1996); and David Brooks's biting commentary, *BOBOS in Paradise: The New Upper Class and How They Got There* (New York: Simon and Schuster, 2000), which, without direct reference to them, captured the essence of the Gulf Coast's Bourgeois Bubbas and Bubbettes.

Anyone who wants to see how and why redneckery has survived despite all that has worked against it should check out two documentaries that tell the tale and tell it well—*Mullet Men: Second Place Is the First Loser*, by Charlie Hubbard and Harris Mendheim (Possum Den Productions, 2007), and *The Last American Roadhouse: The Documentary of the FloraBama*, by Alan West Brockman and Joe Gilchrist (The Last American Roadhouse, LLC, 2006). The most recent documentary of events that last weekend in April is Joe York, *Deadliest Throw: Inside the Flora-Bama Interstate Mullet Toss*, a University of Mississippi Documentary Project, 2011, which covers the twenty-sixth annual toss. If you look closely you might find me in the crowd. Supplement these with Ken Wells, *Travels with Barley: A Journey through Beer Culture in America* (New York: Free Press, 2004), whose first chapter, "Anatomy of a Beer Spill," is about the Flora-Bama. More on the Mullet Toss is in Michael Swindle, *Mulletheads* (Birmingham, Ala.: Crane Hill Publishers, 1998).

It seemed that whenever I told anyone that I was writing about the Redneck Riviera they had a story to tell, and if I had sat down and interviewed everyone I never would have finished this book. Those I did interview, and who offered a world of insight into the evolution of the coast, were Jim Appleman, Norma Calhoun, "Sunny" and Ron David, Jennifer Foster, Joe Gilchrist, Karen Triplett Grant, Susan and Peter Horn, Margaret Long, Rusty Shepard, and Lee Sullivan. Tapes and transcripts of the interviews are in my possession. Also in my possession is a copy of *Girls Gone Wild: The Seized Video*, which my buddy Brad bought for me at an adult toy and DVD store on I-35 in Texas, just south of the Red River. Such is the mark of a true friend. He even went to the trouble to watch it to make sure the content was relevant to my research (what a guy!). Though Brad apologized that the disk did not have more about the raid in which the videos were seized, it did reveal (no pun intended) just what Joe Francis was up to and why Lee Sullivan cracked down. I also want to express my appreciation once again to the folks who were interviewed for earlier articles—Cobb Sheriff, Robert Davis, Marietta Lovell, and Bill Wright. The information they gave me helped shaped my thoughts about the development of Seaside. I also appreciate the information on the problems faced by the recreation fishing industry sent to me by Captain Mike Graef of the *Huntress* out of Destin. He and First Mate Craig "Groovy" Davis are my link to a way of life that is threatened in so many ways. My understanding of what BP was doing out in the Gulf and the impact of the spill on the environment was enhanced by information from Captain Roland Blais, passed on to me by his wife, Kathleen.

Since the 1980s, I have corresponded with many people who have vacationed or lived on the coast. These exchanges have helped me better understand the complexity of the Redneck Riviera and why it evolved as it did. I have gone through my files to identify these folks and list them here. Although I fear that I might not thank them all and that someone will be left out, I do want to acknowledge the help of Bob Ansley, Leah Atkins, Judge Pamela W. Baschab, Patsy Body, Lonnie Burnett, Teresa Cancelliere, Ted Childress, Duffie Chisolm, Kathy Davis, Buddy Estes, Lance Galloway, Hunter Harman, Stacye Hathorn, Cheryl Hoffman, Richard Jackson, John Kohler, Walter Lydick, David Mathews, Robert Pender, Robert Rhinehart, Marlene Rikard, Steven Schmidt, Bob Stephens, JL Strickland, Jay and Jody Walker, and Bill Wright. Rebecca B. Saunders of the Bay County Public Library, Scotty Kirkland and Chris Burroughs of the University of South Alabama Archives, William Hatfield of the *Destin Log*, and Frances Coleman of the *Mobile Press-Register* were especially helpful in obtaining pictures of the coast. And a special thanks to Gary Mormino, who sent me all sorts of Florida stuff, and to Joe the TurtleWatch guy, who let me help him mark the nest.

What follows is a chapter-by-chapter guide to the material used in this study. The full citations along with other things I consulted are found in the "Essay on Sources" above.

INTRODUCTION

A copy of the letter from Corporal Jewel A. Rivers to Mrs. Jewel A. Rivers, September 29, 1944, is in my possession. The original is held by his son, Colonel Alfred Rivers (USAF, retired). The reference to the Alabama coast being like "the southern coast of France" is in *Alabama: A Guide to the Deep South* (1941) reprinted as *The WPA Guide to 1930s Alabama*, p. 8. Howell Raines's *New York Times* article appeared on June 21, 1978. Patrick K. Moore's essay "'Redneck Riviera' or 'Emerald Coast': Interpreting Florida's Panhandle through Public History," was published in the *Journal of the Gulf South Historical Association* (Spring 2003). According to Howell Raines he did not coin the term Redneck Riviera, but rather he "picked it up from the general atmosphere." That atmosphere might have included the song "Redneck Riviera," which was recorded around that time by Gulf Shores musician Madison "Shine" Powell, owner of Sam and Shine's lounge, though Raines does not recall ever hearing it. However, Raines is generally credited with being the first writer to use "Redneck Riviera" in print and popularizing the term. See Howell Raines to Harvey Jackson,

January 28, 2011, in possession of the author, and Frances Coleman, "Racial Harmony Belies 'Redneck' Image," in a special section, "Black/White Mobile," in *Mobile Press-Register*, May 13–27, 1990.

CHAPTER 1

Early Gulf Shores is faithfully recovered in Bonkemeyer, *Once Upon an Island,* which contains excerpts from "Sand Castle," which was published in *Southern Living,* July 1984. The coast to the east is chronicled in Long and Shipler, *The Best Place to Be.* Mrs. Long, a resident of the region since the 1940s, based her work on interviews with local folks and on extensive research in local newspapers. She was the source of many of the stories contained here. See also Walter Overton, "Tour Guide to South Baldwin County" (Magnolia Springs, Ala.: Goldenrod Studio, 1938).

The account of the Young Men's Business League of Pensacola lobbying to have Alabama annex the Florida Panhandle was in "Floridians Want to Join Alabama," *Atlanta Constitution,* January 20, 1901. Gary Mormino's *Land of Sunshine, State of Dreams* contains frequent references to the development of the western Florida coast, including the "Coney Island" statement from the 1887 *Pensacolian.* The young men who rode bicycles from Alabama to Pensacola were friends of my mother, and she provided me with a copy of their story. For other accounts of how little the Panhandle and the Pensacola area were developed before World War II see John T. Faris, *Seeing the Sunny South* (1921), and the Florida State Road Department, *Highways of Florida* (1937). The WPA-sponsored *Florida: A Guide to the Southernmost State* (1939) offered a more complete picture of the region but made it clear how undeveloped it was.

Although his purpose was to provide a popular pictorial account of the growth of the "amusement" industry along the Florida Panhandle, a purpose he accomplished quite well, Tim Hollis's *Florida's Miracle Strip: From Redneck Riviera to Emerald Coast* also contains considerable information on the region before the advent of Goofy Golf, including accounts of the difficulties encountered by early developers and the controversies that arose. Patrick Moore's essay "'Redneck Riviera' or 'Emerald Coast'" repeats some of these stories and adds others. In his study Hollis also notes the impact that Alabamians had on the early development of the beaches west of Panama City. Two locally produced studies, *The Way We Were: Recollections of South Walton Pioneers* (Santa Rosa Beach, Fla.: South Walton Three Arts Alliance, 1997); and *Of Days Gone By: Reflections of South Walton County, Florida* (Santa Rosa Beach, Fla.: South Walton Three Arts Alliance, 1999), accomplish for that area what the work of local historians did for south Baldwin County and contain accounts of Butler's store and the Washaway. In the spring of 2000, the Red Bar in Grayton Beach, which now occupies the old Butler store, published a four-page newspaper promoting the establishment. It included a number of reminiscent-style articles, among them "Grayton Beach Stakes Its Claim as One of Area's Oldest Towns," which included an interview with Van R. Butler, scion of the town's pioneer family. For a look at the beach across the bay from Pensacola see *Remember When: A Pictorial Journey of Gulf Breeze*. Information on the Seagrove Company comes from the "Covenant for property located at Seagrove Beach, Florida, between C. H. McGee and Minnie E. Jackson," which is in my possession. See also *Sixteenth Census of the United States for 1940* for information on the racial composition of the region.

CHAPTER 2

Howell Raines's observations on "the redneck way of fishing" are in *Fly Fishing through the Midlife Crisis* (New York: William Morrow and Company, 1993), 28–42. For the best account of early development along the Panama City strip see the early chapters of *Miracle Strip*, which covers the Thomas, Sharpless, and Churchwell developments (6–9) and the arrival of Broderick Lahan (25–26). For Pensacola see *Florida: A Guide*, 239–41.

Before, during, and after World War II Mobile newspapers wrote often in praise of the Alabama coast. There was the *Mobile Register* in the morning, the *Mobile Press* in the afternoon, and the two combined as the *Mobile Press-Register* on weekends. Like so many afternoon editions, the *Press* eventually (1997) was discontinued, and the morning and weekend editions continued as the *Mobile Press-Register*. In particular see the *Mobile Register*, April 20, June 25, a special section on June 30, July 3, and July 16, 1940; and the *Mobile Press-Register*, June 22, June 29, August 10, and August 19, 1941. June 1, 1941, of the *Press-Register* contained another special section on the glories of the coast. The controversy over the fees at Gulf State Park were discussed in a *Mobile Register* editorial, August 16, 1940, which was followed the next spring (April 13, 1941) with an article on the improvements that had been made.

The demands placed on the coast by World War II were the subject of a January 30, 1942, editorial, "The Gulf Loses Its Complacency," in the *Mobile Register*. From that point forward the Mobile papers reported activities all along the Alabama and Panhandle beaches. Efforts by Pensacola authorities and the military to keep soldiers and sailors out of trouble received special attention (see February 24 and 28, 1942). Although there were wartime precautions and on-shore regulations were tightened, people from inland still came to the Gulf, and the newspaper reported their activities. The story of the German spy in Gulf Shores was told in Bonkemeyer, *Once Upon an Island*, 2. The account of the Hooligan Navy is from Cronenberg, *Forth to the Mighty Conflict*, 24–25, while the Panama City beaches' response to the expansion of the shipyard there is in Hollis, *Miracle Strip*, 22–23.

Two weeks after D-day the *Mobile Register* optimistically editorialized on the "Postwar Need for Resort Facilities" (June 21, 1944), and soon the newspaper was filled with accounts of people going to the coast on improved roads (see July 8, 1944). The following summer it was almost as if there had been no war at all (articles and swimsuit ads on June 10 and July 1 are good examples). The summer of 1946 brought more of the same, and the Mobile papers, which had become the papers of record for coastal activities, reported on things that were happening from Panama City to Gulf Shores and points in between (August 1 and 18, 1946) with particular attention to the economic benefit. Sprinkled throughout the paper were advertisements urging Alabamians to "Choose Florida This Summer" (July 7, 1946). Not a week went by without some mention of the delights awaiting anyone who went to the beach. The history of Camp Helen is on the Florida State Park website. Stories of the camp were told to me by "Mr. Ralph," a former boat captain who took textile workers out to fish. Governor Folsom's visits to the coast were featured in the *Mobile Press-Register*, July 28, 1946, and the *Mobile Register*, June 18 and July 3, 4, and 5, 1947.

In 2008 and 2009 the *Destin Log* began the Destin History Project as part of its Progress Edition. Located on the newspaper's website it contains valuable information on Destin and Okaloosa County history, including gambling. Fraser Sherman, "Gambling in Little Las Vegas," *Destin Log*, December 2, 2008, along with the *Tampa Tribune's* 1949 account, remains the best explanation of gambling in the Fort Walton area. The impact of the opening of U.S. 98 and the first "attractions" along that corridor are detailed in Hollis, *Miracle Strip*. Each of the other local histories of the region tells of the rapid expansion of "amusements," eating establishments, and lodging. During the summer of 1947, the Mobile papers begin to chide Alabama for not offering tourists things that tourists can find in Florida. See especially "State Park Seen as Potential Number One Resort Spot on Gulf of Mexico," *Mobile Register*, July 9, 1947, and "Vacationists Jam Facilities from Gulfport Miss., to Panama City, Fla.," *Mobile Press-Register*, July 20, 1947. See also "Property Values Rise in Florida," *Mobile Register*, August 29, 1947, "Bay County Road to Get Publicity," *Mobile Register*, October 26, 1947, and "Gulf Resorts," *Mobile Press-Register*, August 18, 1946, which contains J. E. Churchwell's comments on the difference between prewar and postwar visitors. The Grayton Beach Red Bar, Spring 2000, publication contains memories of that community.

The *Mobile Register* reported the 1947 hurricane and its aftermath, but by December the coast was recovering and people were going down for outings, and in the summer of 1948 the newspaper reported an ever-increasing flow of tourists. Another storm in the fall of 1949 was described in the September 20 *Register*, but once again things quickly returned to normal. The increase in beer licenses was noted in the *Register* (March 11, 1948) and the dangers of marijuana were highlighted in the *Press-Register* (September 12, 1948). However, in its April 3, 1949, issue the *Press-Register* ran a lengthy pictorial article, "Famed Vacation Spots Ready for Season." This was followed on May 15, 1949, by "Gulf Coast Resorts of West Florida Ready for Busiest Vacation Season," which touched on every major resort community from the Alabama line to Panama City. A few days later (July 5, 1949) the *Mobile Register* detailed Governor Folsom's return visit in "Gulf Park Area [had been] Dedicated 'Pleasure Island' of State."

CHAPTER 3

At this point in the book, my memory begins to play a significant role in the story I am telling, for it was in the time period covered in this chapter that I began to make the first of many trips to Gulf Shores, Pensacola, Destin, Panama City, and especially Seagrove Beach. Some of my recollections of those visits were published in "Florida Room: From 'Redneck Riviera' to 'Emerald Coast.'"

The *Mobile Press-Register*, April 3, May 15, 1949, describes the optimism all along the coast as the summer season began. Information on gambling in Fort Walton can be found in Fraser Sherman, "Gambling in 'Little Las Vegas,'" *Destin Log*, December 2, 2008, and the 2008 *Destin Log* Progress Edition timeline of local history. More on the topic appears in the *Mobile Register*, September 15, December 15, 1950, and in Hollis, *Miracle Strip*, 46. Hollis (vii, ix, 14–17, 23) also describes the development (and lack of it) in Panama City Beach and on Okaloosa Island/Fort Walton Beach.

"Time Stands Still in Seagrove Beach," *Seaside Times* (Winter 1992) contains Elton B. Stephens's and C. H. McGee Jr.'s recollections of the early days of the community. Gena Christopher of Jacksonville, Alabama, told me of sleeping in what had been the Stephens's maid quarters when it had been converted into a guest room. The Seagrove Covenant, which outlined all of the community restrictions, is in my possession, as is the letter from Carl P. Heartburg to Minnie Jackson, December 20, 1956, asking her to write the Florida State Road Department and ask them to reroute the road.

Hollis, *Miracle Strip*, remains the best source for the early development of the Panama City beaches, and copies of promotional literature and pictures of the resorts were especially helpful. In the summer of 2009, Karen Triplett Grant took me around the beaches to show me where things had once been and what had survived. Alabama's view of what was happening in Florida and the competition it promised was the subject of "Florida Looks to Plain Folks as Tourist Trade Salvation," *Mobile Register*, June 4, 1950.

The Hangouts at Long Beach Resort and in Gulf Shores stand out in the memories of those of us who were teenagers in the 1950s and 1960s. Hollis, *Miracle Strip*, 64, captures the innocence of the place and the era, while Greenhaw, "Summertime," recalls a rougher edge to the Long Beach establishment. Margaret Long of Orange Beach wrote me (December 15, 2009) about the Gulf Shores Hangout and reunions they hold today. *Once Upon an Island*, 3, contains reminiscences of the place, of which there were many. *Florida: A Guide*, 494, describes Destin in 1939, and my "Florida Room" describes what it had become by the 1950s. In the June 19, 1953, *Alabama* magazine ran a feature article titled "Come Along to Gulf Shores, Alabama's Beach Playground." The next year, May 28, 1954, the magazine published "Gulf Shores Gains as State Resort 'Paradise,'" which detailed the region's growth and its plans for the future. Long and Shipler, *The Best Place to Be*, contains a warmly detailed account of Orange Beach at the same time. For the rest of the coast see Hollis, *Miracle Strip*, especially 94–103, which highlights the arrival of Goofy Golf, and 198–202, where Alvin's Island enters the picture. See also *Mobile Register*, "Vacation Expense to Drop a Little for This Summer," June 12, 1950.

CHAPTER 4

Lawrence P. Lessing, "State of Florida," *Fortune* (February 1948), 65, describes the state at the end of the 1940s, though the best analysis at that time remains Mormino, *Land of Sunshine, State of Dreams*. The bourbon quote is from "Sand Castle" in *Once Upon an Island*, 1. n2, and the observation on serving customers is quoted in Hollis, *Miracle Strip*, 136. The account of Lamar Triplett's relocation to Florida was told to me by his daughter, Karen Triplett Grant. Population figures are from the *Seventeenth Census of the United States*, 1950.

African American beaches along the Redneck Riviera are a neglected topic, and had it not been for the help of Mrs. Ora Wills of Pensacola I might never have discovered them. Her poem, "Florida, Early Fifties," (*Emerald Coast Review* 4) is a delightful description of how she and her family and friends enjoyed the coast. A short history of Johnson Beach is on the Gulf Shores National Seashore, National Park Service website. For Wingate Beach see Lisa Rhue, "Former Black Beach to Become Home to Harbour Lakes," *Pensacola News Journal*, March 2, 1997; and Al Henderson, "Welcome to the Waterfront," at the online site of the *Pensacola Guide for African American Visitors* (2008). The lack of racial restriction in Gulf State Park was covered in Frances Coleman, "Racial Harmony Belies 'Redneck' Image," *Mobile Press-Register*, May 13–17, 1990. See also "Finding Diversity on the Beach," *Anniston Star*, April 29, 2010.

Hollis, *Miracle Strip*, continues the best account of Panhandle growth. The story of the Perdido Pass bridge is covered in Long and Shipler, *The Best Place to Be*, 79,

120–21, and in a letter from Mrs. Long in my possession. See also the *Mobile Register*, July 3, 8, and 16, 1949.

My knowledge of the Flora-Bama comes from frequent visits and from interviews with co-owner Joe Gilchrist. For an excellent account of the place and its history see Ken Wells, *Travels with Barley: A Journey through Beer Culture in America* (New York: Wall Street Journal Book, 2004) which opens with "Anatomy of a Beer Spill, Perdido Key, Fla.," which is about as good an account of the Flora-Bama as you can get. *From Cottages to Condos*, 23–24, has a good short history of the place.

Spring Break has generated more than its share of memories, stories, and newspaper accounts. Mormino, *Land of Sunshine, State of Dreams*, contains a good history of Spring Break and the resulting tensions. Hollis, *Miracle Strip*, 27–28, tells of the efforts by locals to provide wholesome entertainment for the students, while 30–32 relates promotional activities to draw national, and even international, attention to the area. The *Mobile Press-Register*, February 17, 1960, makes it clear that wholesome entertainment was not what the students had in mind. Researching the records of the Panama City Beach City Council and listening to tales told by former city officials convinces me that there was no effective beer ban. Apparently the newspaper was reporting more the hope of action than the actuality.

The construction of motels was a major milestone in coastal development. See the *Destin Log*, Progress Edition 2008; *Once Upon an Island*, 102–3; and Hollis, *Miracle Strip*, 48. Hollis, 13, discusses the consolidation of the beach communities west of Panama City, and that book should be consulted for its description of the whole range of beach amusements and their evolution over time. The impact of U.S. 98 on the development of the region is an ongoing theme, and a particular subject in the *Destin Log*, Progress Edition 2008. *Once Upon an Island*, 102, covers the incorporation of Gulf Shores, while the way Eglin Air Force Base shaped Fort Walton Beach is covered well in Moore, "'Redneck Riviera' or 'Emerald Coast.'"

The Green Knight as a symbol, a landmark, and a business is highlighted in Hollis, *Miracle Strip*, 188–91, and in the *Destin Log*, Progress Edition 2008, which also contains stories associated with the evolution of the Fishing Rodeo. Most helpful of all were the stories told by Norma Calhoun of Destin, who managed the bar at the Knight. Accounts of the hurricanes of the 1960s are in all the local newspapers and in Long and Shipler, *The Best Place to Be*, 122–23. The story of guarding the Flora-Bama during Hurricane Betsy was told to me by Margaret Long of Orange Beach.

CHAPTER 5

My frequent reference to the lack of sophistication among coastal visitors was inspired by comedian Jeff Foxworthy's definition of "redneck" as someone who displays a "glorious lack of sophistication." Not a bad way to look at it. H. L. Mencken,

"The Sahara of the Bozart," first appeared in the New York *Evening Mail*, November 13, 1917. Its impact is analyzed in Fred C. Hobson Jr., *Serpent in Eden: H. L. Mencken and the South* (Baton Rouge: Louisiana State University Press, 1974). Noah's Ark, which is still there, is described in Hollis, *Miracle Strip*, 82. Comments on shrinking swimsuits and hippies came from correspondence with Kathleen Deyo Blais and Teresa Cancelliere.

The impact of the 1960s and especially the 1970s is highlighted in a variety of sources. For the Green Knight the stories told by Norma Calhoun—some of them reprinted in the *Destin Log* Progress Edition 2008, others told to me—capture the flavor of the bar at its best. I also appreciate Kath Davis of Miller's Ferry, Alabama, telling me how she and her friends would drive to Destin after work on Friday to party at the Knight. As for Orange Beach and Gulf Shores, articles by Howell Raines, *New York Times* (June 21, 1978), William Oscar Johnson, *Sports Illustrated* (April 23, 1979), and Robert Jones, *Sports Illustrated* (September 19, 1979), describe the Redneck Riviera at the height of redneckery. Kenny Stabler and Barry Stainback, *Snake*, adds detail and flavor to the many Stabler stories, while Emory Thomas, *Travels to Hallowed Ground*, p. 23, announced the arrival of "raffish Rotarians" and the rest. There are a number of accounts of the Flora-Bama, some on its website, but Ken Wells, *Travels with Barley*, still stands out as the best—so far. The Kenny Stabler "here for the beer" quote came from Paul Finebaum, "Crimson Tide Should Stand by Stabler," *Mobile Press-Register*, June 14, 2008.

Mike Fincher died in 2002. His obituary is in the *Pensacola News Journal*, December 12, 2002, and on his memorial website. Rusty McHugh died a little over two years later. He also has a memorial website. Their music is still alive in CDs that can be bought at or through the Flora-Bama and in video performances preserved on YouTube. Interviews with co-owner Joe Gilchrist added even more Flora-Bama stories to those in print.

In addition to accounts of Hurricane Eloise in Hollis, *Miracle Strip*, 27, 54–55, 57–58, 64, and 138, there was a booklet on the storm—*Eloise*—published the following year. A copy is in the possession of the author. See also the post-Eloise real estate supplement in the *Destin Log*, 1976.

CHAPTER 6

A good article on Gulf Shores before Hurricane Frederic hit is in *Alabama Today*, June 1975. As one might expect the *Mobile Press, Mobile Register,* and *Mobile Press-Register* gave extensive coverage to the storm, as did local histories: *Once Upon an Island*, 3, 108–11; Long and Shipler, *The Best Place to Be*, 79, 108–9, 120, 151; and *From Cottages to Condos*, though as the title suggests, it was more concerned with what came after Frederic than what was there when it hit and pays particular attention to the increase in "snowbird" activity. One of the best accounts of the devastation brought by the storm is "Hurricane," *National Geographic*, September 1980. A good summary of how the Alabama Gulf Coast recovered is in "Hurricane Frederic after 20 years," *Mobile Register*, September 12, 1999. Hollis, *Miracle Strip*, deals with the building of Pinnacle Port (53–54) and Sandestin (18). The *Destin Log*, Progress Edition 2008, highlights the development of Destin and Sandestin and the lack of restrictions placed on growth. The *Log* also traces the ups and downs of the local, state, and national economy; the growing controversy over the development of Holiday Isle; and the rapid commercialization of the coast.

The growth of the "snowbird season" is also chronicled in the local histories and summed up nicely in "Gulf Shores Is No Longer Dormant in Winter," *Mobile Register*, December 27, 1984. The issue of incorporation is also covered in these histories, but see especially *From Cottages to Condos*, 2–11; Long and Shipler, *The Best Place to Be*, 257–61; and *Once Upon an Island*, 62. Fraser Sherman, "25 Years Ago Today in the *Log*: Fight over Incorporation," *Destin Log*, October 23, 2009, and the *Log*'s Progress Edition 2008, covers the community's incorporation and expansion, on which Hollis, *Miracle Strip* (18, 57, and 274–77) also comments. The tension between Destin development and Fort Walton Beach's "no growth" attitude is highlighted in Moore, "'Redneck Riviera' or 'Emerald Coast.'"

CHAPTER 7

The saga of the Trashy White Band and "She Ran Off" was played out in the press all along the coast, but particularly in the *Pensacola Journal*, which on February 9, 1982, published a lengthy account. For later efforts to get the song banned see "Local Band Won't Stop Playing Song," *Destin Log*, June 7, 1989, and "And the Band Can Play On: Judge Won't Halt Controversial Song," *Destin Log*, July 12, 1989. Norma Calhoun, wife of Phil Calhoun, lead singer of the Trashy White Band, gave me copies of articles she had clipped and told me the story. The story of Seaside has been told in a variety of ways. In the summer of 1998, I was given access to the Seaside archives, which include an extensive collection of newspaper clippings, and based on that research I published "Seaside, Florida: Robert Davis and the Quest for Community," *Atlanta History* (Fall 1998). That summer I was also able to interview Robert Davis and a number of other people associated with Seaside, most particularly Bill Wright, an early investor who had his differences with Davis. Those interviews were used in the article and in a subsequent publication, "Developing the Panhandle: Seagrove Beach, Seaside, WaterColor and the Florida Tourist Tradition," which appeared in Starnes, *Southern Journeys*. These form the foundation for the analysis contained here. The account of how the height limit was set for Walton County was confirmed, more or less, by Peter Horn of Seagrove Beach.

Along with Wells, *Travels with Barley*, one of the best accounts of the Flora-Bama is the DVD *The Last American Roadhouse*, which contains Jimmy Louis's version of how the Mullet Toss got started. Another DVD, *Mullet Men*, tells the tale of one man's attempt to win the elusive prize. *From Cottages to Condos*, 68, adds more to the legend of the mullet. Add to this Michael Swindle, *Mulletheads*, and you can find out all you want to know about the Toss, short of being there. It has also been speculated that the mullet was chosen for throwing because, when looked at from a certain angle, it resembles a particular part of the male anatomy.

The music of the Trashy White Band is available on CD and if you get to Destin you can hear them still. Now they are at Calhoun's Pub and Grub, which is run by Norma.

CHAPTER 8

Once again Mormino, *Land of Sunshine, State of Dreams*, 44–45, captures the way "Florida has always straddled the line between respectability and scandal." The *Destin Log*'s historic timeline, published in the summer of 2009, points out the ups and downs of the economy and how local citizens both profited and lost when they did or did not catch the trends just right. Moore, "'Redneck Riviera' or 'Emerald Coast,'" contains information on the condo growth in the region, and Tommy Stevenson, "Green Knight Weathers Destin's Mad Growth," *Tuscaloosa News*, August 6, 1989, looks at developments from the landmark's perspective. See also *From Cottages to Condos*, 5–6, and Long and Shipler, *The Best Place to Be*, 152.

Efforts to break free from the Redneck Riviera image are described in Johnson, "The Key to the Case Is Missing," *Sports Illustrated*, April 23, 1979, which tells of the first effort to ban the term Redneck Riviera. It failed, and though later writers would announce that the label had been dropped, they would be wrong. See also Hollis, *Miracle Strip*, 26–27, and Moore, "'Redneck Riviera' to 'Emerald Coast.'" From the 1970s on, newspaper articles, tourist publications, and magazine accounts would note either that the Redneck Riviera image was fading, or that it wasn't. As for the snowbirds, their arrival had long been anticipated and efforts to attract them noted in earlier chapters were finally paying off. TDC publications record the results. Local complaints were captured in the slogan on a bumper sticker produced by local musician Brent Burns, whose song "If It's Snowbird Season, Why Can't We Shoot 'em" reflects that attitude.

The shifting of Spring Break from Fort Lauderdale and Daytona to Panama City Beach has been examined in every study of the region. Mormino, *Land of Sunshine, State of Dreams*, 317–22, is a good account of the evolution of the ritual. See also Hollis, *Miracle Strip*, 27–29; and *From Cottages to Condos*, 11. One story in particular catches the freewheeling atmosphere of the coast during those days. It seems that the owner of a beach services business noticed that he was spending a lot of money replacing "lost" company T-shirts. Aware of what was happening, he called his crew of young men together, handed each of them a box of the coveted tees, and said, "Boys, I'm not paying you in money anymore. I'm paying you in pussy." No one gave back the shirts and asked for cash. This and many of the other stories here were told on the condition that I not reveal the teller, so I won't. However, I have no doubts that the stories are true.

As far as the music is concerned, in addition to Wells, *Travels with Barley*, and Mormino, *Land of Sunshine, State of Dreams*, I suggest you go to YouTube and seek out the singers and their songs. Along with the music you can see an interview with Rusty and Mike as they talk about life in Destin before they came to the Flora-Bama. *The Last American Roadhouse* also contains a lot of the music, along with interviews with Jimmy Louis and others. Joe Gilchrist took me to Boys Town to talk with Jimmy Louis, who had docked his sailboat there and was living in it and in one of the trailers. Along with the many magazine articles on Seaside and the interviews with Robert Davis and others, some of the best sources for information on the town comes from the *Seaside Times*, the community's in-house newspaper, and the *Seaside Community Report*, which was issued quarterly by the Seaside Town Council. All of these are in the Seaside Archives. See also my article on Seaside in *Atlanta History* and *Southern Journeys* and "Best of the Decade," *Time*, January 1, 1990.

The coastal economy in the 1980s can be traced in local newspapers at the time and in the *Destin Log*, Progress Edition 2008, and the timeline. *From Cottages to Condos*, 6–9, covers the topic in Gulf Shores. Mormino, *Land of Sunshine, State of Dreams*, 67–68, explains "affluenza" and how Florida became "a state of conspicuous consumption." See also Moore, "'Redneck Riviera' to 'Emerald Coast,'" for information on growth patterns along the coast. Interviews with former Panama City Beach mayor Lee Sullivan and "Spring Break attorney" Jim Appleman clarified local laws.

CHAPTER 9

Mormino, *Land of Sunshine, State of Dreams*, 65–67, captures the frenzy of development in Florida in the 1980s and how in the early 1990s "Florida's luck ran out." Local newspapers reflected the spirit of the times and none more so than the *Destin Log*, which the *Tuscaloosa News* (August 6, 1989) asserted was as "indefatigable and optimistic [a] poster of the local economy as one could want to read." When the *Log* began reprinting local history items in the summer of 2009, much of the commentary focused on what happened to the real estate market in prior decades. Moore, "From 'Redneck Riviera' to 'Emerald Coast,'" also assesses the growth. Tannin was highlighted in *Coastal Living* (August 1998).

The saga of Joe Odom filled the newspapers when it took place, but a condensed version of what occurred was published in the *Destin Log*, Progress Edition 2008. For a good look at the "Odom curve" go to www.mapquest.com, and type in Destin, Florida. When the map comes up follow Scenic 98 east, and between Four Prong Lake and the Okaloosa County–Walton County line you will find it. The story of Henderson Park and the Mid-Bay Bridge is also found there. Similar stories concerning Pleasure Island and Panama City Beach are told in the *Birmingham News* (February 7, 1999) and Hollis, *Miracle Strip*, 26, 33. The story of the Red Bar and Picolo's is told in the Red Bar Special Edition newspaper, Spring 2000, and on the Grayton Beach website. Peter Applebome's comments in *Dixie Rising* are on pages 20–21. As for comparisons between what can be found in Seaside and what David Brooks describes in *BOBOS in Paradise*, I invite the reader to do what I did—go see for yourself. The observation about growth bringing in more people to fish was made by Craig "Groovy" Davis, first mate on the *Huntress*. Fort Walton's no-growth policy is well covered in Moore, "'Redneck Riviera' to 'Emerald Coast.'" For the sad fate of the Green Knight see the *Destin Log*'s online history, which includes Fraser Sherman's "The Knight Shift: A Green Guardian Watched Over Destin's Borders."

Like most storms, Hurricane Opal was well covered in the local press and the *Destin Log* was particularly good on the impact of the storm on Holiday Isle and Okaloosa Island. See also Hollis, *Miracle Strip*, 47, 58; and "After Opal, Seaside Diamond Bright," *Seaside Times* (Winter 1995). However, many of the observations here are my own, as I spent a great deal of time on the coast after the storm hit.

Pleasure Island's recovery from Hurricane Frederic and what the Florida Panhandle might learn from it after Hurricane Opal is in "Old South Meets New around Mobile Bay," the *Arizona Republican*, reprinted in the *Anniston Star*, May 21, 1998; "Concrete Paradise," *Birmingham News*, February 7, 1999; "Starr Smith's South," *Montgomery Advertiser*, May 24, 1998; "Coastal Development, Storms Bring More Danger," editorial in the *Mobile Press-Register*, November 30, 1999; and "Fort Morgan, Invasion of the Condos," *Mobile Press-Register*, November 29, 1997. For comments on the snowbirds and the "vexation fee" see *Mobile Press-Register*, April 6, 1997, and January 24, 2000.

CHAPTER 10

The Destin History Project discusses recovery from Opal, while the *Seaside Times* dwells on the community's efforts to restore its beach.

As for *The Truman Show*, it drew comment from across the country. The *Seaside Times* naturally lavished attention on it and had nothing but praise for everyone involved. Other newspapers also featured the project (see "Shooting at Seaside," *Montgomery Advertiser*, June 4, 1998) but it was not long before critics began drawing unfavorable comparisons between the fictional town and the real community. In particular see Paul Goldberger, "Land of Make Believe: Does *The Truman Show* give Seaside, Florida a Bad Rap?" *New Yorker*, June 22, 1998, 41–42; and Jeff Giles, "This Is Your Life," *Newsweek*, June 1, 1998, 62–63. The *Seaside Times* devoted its entire Summer 1998 issue to *The Truman Show* and included in it Davis's reply to his critics entitled "Illusion and Reality."

The evolution of Seaside is covered in my articles "Seaside, Florida: Robert Davis and the Quest for Community"; "Florida Room: From 'Redneck Riviera' to 'Emerald Coast'"; and "Developing the Panhandle: Seagrove Beach, Seaside, WaterColor and the Florida Tourist Tradition," and in the pages of the *Seaside Times*—see especially Robert Davis, "Twenty-first-century Urbanism Evolves," *Seaside Times*, Spring, 1994. See also Caskie Stinnett, "By the Beautiful Seaside," *Travel and Leisure* (March 1988) and Phil Patton "In Seaside, Florida, the Forward Thing Is to Look Backward," *Smithsonian* (January 1991). The building of the interfaith chapel was announced in the Millennium Issue of the *Seaside Times*, Fall 1999. The *Wall Street Journal*, June 7, 1995, contains the critical article. Responses can be found in the *Wall Street Journal/Florida Journal*, August 16, 1995, and in the *Seaside Times*, Summer 1995. See also Millie Ball, "Florida's Seaside: An Architectural Disney World," *New Orleans Times-Picayune*, October 9, 1994, and Robert Davis to Millie Ball, *New Orleans Times-Picayune*, November 20, 1994. Evidence of Davis's in-community critics can be found in the formation of the Seaside Town Council and in the records of its meetings, which are in the Seaside archives. See also the *New York Times*, August 1, 1993.

End of the century activities on Pleasure Island were highlighted in the local newspaper the *Pelican* and on the Gulf Shores website. "Concrete Paradise," *Birmingham News*, February 7, 1999, is an excellent overview of the coast at that time. Coastal pollution problems were explained in the 1998 National Resources Defense Council's annual "Testing the Water" survey. "Concrete Paradise" reported Orange Beach's sewer problems. For a comparison of the high-rises of Pleasure Island and the buildings meeting the height restrictions of south Walton County, see my article "Unparalleled Growth: A Tale of Two Beaches and How They Grew," *Mobile Register*, August 4, 2002. As for the arrival of Latino immigrants, I witnessed it and heard all of the pros and cons. For other perspectives and more information, see issues of any coastal newspaper from the first few years of the twenty-first century and you will find stories aplenty, or go to the Destin History Project.

By far the best coverage of St. Joe Paper Company is Ziewitz and Waiz, *Green Empire*. Accounts of the beginning of WaterColor and later WaterSound are in my articles "Developing the Panhandle" and "Florida Room," and in "Beach Home Alabama," *Birmingham News*, March 12, 2000; "Birmingham and the Beach," *Birmingham News*, April 9, 2000; and "Coastal Delight," *Anniston Star*, June 5, 2004.

The story of Ed Ball rejecting a deal with Disney was told in Mormino, *Land of Sunshine, State of Dreams*, 101.

The story of the Flemings and "The Shark" was told to me by John Fleming, a member of the family, and clarified in his letter to me, July 14, 2010, which is in my possession.

CHAPTER 11

William Oscar Johnson, "The Key to the Case Is Missing," *Sports Illustrated*, April 23, 1979, tells of the first effort to ban the term Redneck Riviera. It failed, and though later writers would announce that the label had been dropped, it hadn't. See "Starr Smith's South," *Montgomery Advertiser*, May 24, 1998; "Sweet Home Alabama," *Golf and Travel*, December 2000; and the *Destin Log*'s Destin History Project. Mormino, *Land of Sunshine, State of Dreams*, 320, points out Panama City Beach's "white necks" campaign and Hollis, *Miracle Strip*, 26–27, highlights other efforts to find the proper label or slogan.

"Beach, Baby, Beach" in American Airlines' *American Way*, March 1, 1996, tells of the families dealing with Grayton's older houses. Doug Pinkston recalled "The Original Grayton Store" in the Red Bar's Spring 2000 publication. Robert Davis, in a January 15, 2000, interview in the *Walton Sun*, goes over efforts to preserve Grayton, his take on how Seaside was evolving, and his plans for the future. The *New York Times* article on Grayton was published June 6, 2008.

According to a local builder who worked on many Seaside projects, Davis also moved to San Francisco so his wife "could escape the boonies of the Redneck Riviera," his son "could get a proper bar mitzvah," and the founder could "find palatable food." The short life of FOOS can be followed in its newsletter, and comments by Seagrove resident Susan Horn shed light on the surrounding events. As for the parade, I have watched it evolve and am watching it continue to do so.

Promotional material and price lists have been available from WaterColor and WaterSound from the start of both projects. For comments on these and other developments along Highway 30–A, in Panama City Beach, and in Destin, see "Coastal Delight," *Anniston Star*, June 5, 2004; Hollis, *Miracle Strip*, 33, 58, 59; and the Destin History Project. For Gulf Shores and Orange Beach see "Starr Smith's South," *Montgomery Advertiser*, May 24, 1998. *Golf and Travel*, December 2000, and *Golf*, February 2001, assess the impact of golf on coastal development.

Thomas Spencer, "Less Redneck, More Riviera," *Birmingham News*, March 18, 2001, chronicles change in the Gulf Shores area, but it could have been written for most of the resort communities along the coast. For the survival of the Flora-Bama see David L. Langford, "Redneck Riviera: Pass the Gator Tail and Beer and Get Ready for the Mullet Toss," May 18, 2001, Associated Press online. Information on

La Borgata came from its website and "Panama City Beach's La Borgata on Standby," *Panama City News Herald*, November 27, 2008. See also Associated Press writer David L. Langford's "Beach with Attitude," *Birmingham News*, July 1, 2001, for more on the Flora-Bama and other local downscale and upscale establishments along Pleasure Island. For a pretty comprehensive listing of hangouts, bars, and clubs from Gulf Shores to Panama City Beach, see *Birmingham News*, April 9, 2000.

The story of Jesus First Ministries was told in the *Mobile Press-Register*, July 9, 2000. The sad demise of the amusements along the Panama City Beach strip is found in Hollis, *Miracle Strip*, 59–66, 143, 177. That book was published about the time that the Miracle Strip Amusement Park closed, an event announced in an Associated Press article, April 14, 2004, that was reprinted in a number of coastal and inland newspapers.

For efforts to find just the right name for the Florida piece of the Redneck Riviera, see the *Northwest Florida Daily News*, July 2008; the *Beach Breeze*, June 4, 2009; and the *Walton Sun*, May 30, 2009. The other side of this effort was expressed to me by Bill Wright, who has lived down there for years.

CHAPTER 12

"Spring Break," *Time*, April 1, 2009, makes the comparison between 1959 and fifty years later and fills in many of the years in between. The Wisconsin-Stout survey and the AMA's warning was the subject of an Associated Press article, "Sobering Survey: Spring Break Drinking Isn't Just Harmless Fun," which appeared in a number of southern newspapers in the spring of 1995. In the years that followed there were more surveys and more articles warning students of the dangers of Spring Break. See also Hollis, *Miracle Strip*, 28–29, and "Spring Break Trouble," *Mobile Press-Register*, April 6, 1997. Mormino, *Land of Sunshine, State of Dreams*, 319–20, tells of the displacement of Spring Break students from Daytona. Efforts by campus religious groups to tame the crowds are in "Spring Break: Beaches, Bikinis, Bars, Bibles?" *Anniston Star*, March 22, 1997.

Copies of the bikini posters are in my possession. The *Birmingham News*, March 28, 2000, reported on Spring Break activities, and Hollis, *Miracle Strip*, 28, neatly sums up that and other promotional controversies. However, the best assessment of Spring Break along the Redneck Riviera is in "Spring Break 2000," *Rolling Stone*, February 17, 2000. Also good on the ritual are David Kohn, "Spring Break Exposed: A 24 Hour Party—Is It Too Much," April 17, 2002, posted on www.cbsnews.com, and Michael Barbaro, "Hot Spots Aggressively Vie for Student Dollars," *Washington Post*, March 9, 2003. Interviews with former Panama City Beach mayor Lee Sullivan and "Spring Break Lawyer" Jim Appleman clarified and expanded on what the students did and how local authorities tried to deal with them.

Appleman and Sullivan were also essential to telling the *Girls Gone Wild* story, which played out in newspapers around the country, particularly in a subsequent *New York Times* article ("Girls Wild and Gone Wrong," December 16, 2007) that covered the controversy in detail. See also *Time*, April 1, 2009, and for Joe Francis's side of the story see "Meet Joe Francis," posted on his website, www.meetjoefrancis .com. Snoop Dogg's involvement in the matter was highlighted in "Parents Beware: Chain Stores Going Crazy Selling *Girls Gone Wild*," National Policy Analysis, October 2003, and "Snoop Sued By Underage Girls Who Appear in *Girls Gone Wild* Video," posted on the MTV website, August 12, 2003. Both cite an earlier Associated Press story that appeared June 25, 2003. For more on Joe Francis see "Joe Francis: 'Baby Give Me a Kiss,'" *Los Angeles Times*, August 6, 2006.

CHAPTER 13

Interviews with Lee Sullivan and Jim Appleman continue to be important in this chapter.

See also "Panama City Pans *Girls Gone Wild*," *North Texas Daily*, March 23, 2004; "Cheap Spring Break Motels to Pricy Condos," Associated Press, May 13, 2002; "Spring Break," *USA Today*, June 6, 2004. The problems west of Gulf Shores are the subject of "Fort Morgan Invasion of Condos," *Mobile Press-Register*, November 29, 1997. Similar problems unresolved are covered by Rick Bragg, "Destin Journal: New Economy Eclipses a Sliver of Old Florida," *New York Times*, August 14, 2000. Margaret Long of Orange Beach was the source of information on the early development of Ono Island. My own views on the resiliency of redneckery at the end of the twentieth century are in "The 'Redneck Riviera': Don't Mourn Its Passing Just Yet, Y'all," *Anniston Star*, March 28, 1999.

Like other hurricanes, Hurricane Ivan was well covered in local newspapers. For a good general account see *From Cottages to Condos*, 9, 24, 79–82. Interviews with Joe Gilchrist, co-owner of the Flora-Bama, reflect the extent of the damage there, as does the DVD *The Last American Roadhouse: The Documentary of the Flora-Bama*; Ryan Dezember, "Mullets Get Some Air at the Flora-Bama," *Mobile Press-Register*, April 27, 2008; and Ryan Dezember, "Hundreds Watch as Flora-Bama Gets Smashed," *Mobile Press-Register*, April 17, 2005. The economic activity before Ivan was reported in "Sleeping Beauty Awakens," which appeared in the local booster publication *Hwy 30-A*, Spring 2004. The real estate market after the storms is chronicled in a host of articles beginning with one of the best, Ryan Dezember, "The Condo Game," *Mobile Press-Register*, July 4, 2004. Written just before Ivan, it not only describes the frenzy of buying and selling that was going on but also establishes the pattern of "flipping" that will follow. See also "Beach Prices Rise after Hurricane Ivan," Associated Press,

January 28, 2005; "Back to the Beach," *Anniston Star*, August 1, 2005, "Condo Fights about Money," *Mobile Press-Register*, August 2, 2005; "Condo Owners Split—Repair or Sell," *Mobile Press-Register*, February 18, 2005. "How the Boom Is Changing Our Lives," *Time*, June 13, 2005, puts the rise in real estate prices into a national context.

How local governments allowed developers to get around zoning regulations is covered in "Upward Growth in Orange Beach Benefits Public," *Mobile Press-Register*, April 24, 2005, while Mayor Steve Russo's problems are the subject of "FBI Says Russo in Lucrative Land 'Flip,'" *Mobile Press-Register*, February 19, 2006. Margaret Long of Orange Beach helped me understand the various aspects of the case. The same growth- and development-friendly atmosphere was found in the Destin area and highlighted in the *Destin Log*, Progress Edition 2008, and the Destin History Project.

When the crash came the impact seemed immediate. I saw the For Sale signs, saw the foreclosure notices, and read in the local press that fewer tourists were coming and that those who were visiting were spending less. I talked with store owners, real estate agents, recreational fishermen, and contractors; all reported business was down. Many were just hanging on. Many didn't make it. In May 2009, the *Defuniak Springs Herald Breeze*, published in the county seat of once-booming Walton County, included two sections, twenty pages announcing "Notice of Tax Sale." A good analysis of the crash along Gulf Shores can be found in Ryan Dezember, "Should Alabama Gulf Coast Condo Investors Have Known Better?" *Mobile Press-Register*, February 8, 2009, and in Kathy Jumper, "Market Struggling in Mobile, Baldwin," *Mobile Press-Register*, March 12, 2009. For the fate of some of the most active flippers see "Whatever Happened to the Dolphin Club?" *Anniston Star*, June 22, 2009, and the comparison between Nature Walk and WaterColor during the recession is in "Riding on the Wrong Side of the Road," *Anniston Star*, June 30, 2008.

CHAPTER 14

Peter Bos's career is covered in the Legendary company history (www.legendaryinc .com), which contains "The Legendary Story." For comments on the growth of Destin see Bragg, "Destin Journal," and the *Destin Log* ,Progress Edition 2008. The shark attacks were reported in the *Destin Log* and *Panama City Herald* at the time, as well as in the national news. As for cleaning the fish, see "Gut Reaction: Destin Unveils 'Three-Pronged' Plan to Salvage Fish Cleaning from DEP Regulations," *Destin Log*, September 24–26, 2008.

The beach mouse controversy was long in growing. The *Mobile Press-Register* listed stopping of condo building on the coast in an effort to protect the beach mouse as one of the top stories of 1984. However, just after the turn of the century the controversy grew. See Friends of the Earth news release, June 20, 2002; "Officials Must Save Species' Habitats," Associated Press, June 20, 2002; "Fort Morgan High-Rise Turned Down," *Mobile Press-Register*, September 6, 2002; "Mouse Stops Condos," *Mobile Press-Register*, June 1, 2007; and, for the final resolution of the case, "Lawsuit on Fort Morgan Beach Mouse Tossed Out," *Mobile Press-Register*, February 10, 2009.

The public ramp controversy played out in the *Mobile Press-Register*, December 2, 18, and 19, 2007. The need for a launch was explained to me by Margaret Long, who lives on Cotton Bayou. She also told the story of how the feral cats got to the proposed site. I joined the discussion with "Beach Mouse Hunt," *Mobile Press-Register*, March 18, 2007, which drew a variety of responses including an op-ed piece by Barbara Allen, "Beach Mice Help Dune System," *Mobile Press-Register*, March 25, 2007, which took me to task on a number of points. Later, when I published "The Boat Ramp, the Mouse, and the Cat," *Mobile Press-Register*, March 8, 2008, the opinion of other locals were expressed in a letter to the editor from Rich Nenstiel, *Mobile Press-Register*, January 4, 2008, and a letter to me from Gene Myers, an Orange Beach boat dealer, January 28, 2008. The letters also responded to an article on the controversy I wrote for the *Anniston Star* ("Reaping What You Sow," January 16, 2008), which was reprinted in the *Mobile Press-Register*. See also "Of Mice and Boats," February 8, 2008, and "Trouble on Ono," March 23, 2008, both in the *Mobile Press-Register*. I appreciate the support given me by George Crozier, retired director of the Dauphin Island Sea Lab. According to Margaret Long, at this writing the ramp is still unbuilt.

The conflict over who has priority on the beach—turtles or people—was traced in an article in the *Walton Sun*, May 30, 2009. I got my first "REMOVE IT OR LOSE IT" tag on August 3, 2007. The *Destin Log*, Progress Edition 2008, and November 22–25, 2008, both cover the controversy. The *Walton Sun*, May 30, 2009, and *Beach Breeze*, July 9, 2009, both address the debate over "Leave No Trace" and who should enforce it. Then there is my column on the matter, "A Tale of Storing 'Stuff,'" *Anniston Star*, October 24, 2008.

For the turtle light debate see ""TDC Passes Turtle Recommendation," *Panama City News Herald*, July 9, 2008; "Dim the Lights, Save a Turtle on Alabama Beaches, *Mobile Press-Register*, November 19, 2008; and my column "Of Darwin and Turtles and Mother Nature," *Anniston Star*, August 1, 2007. Observations on turtles are found in *Once Upon an Island*, 36–37, 41–42, and *From Cottages to Condos*, 55–56. For other commentary on the controversy see my columns "Another Endangered Species," March 14, 2007, and "Sea Turtles, Flamingos and Lights" June 25, 2008, in the *Anniston Star*. I also appreciate the observations of Bill Wright and Walter Lydick.

CHAPTER 15

Fodor's *Gulf South* is quoted in David L. Langford, "The Beach with Attitude," *Birmingham News*, July 1, 2001. I personally made the trip to Calhoun's Pub and Grub and saw it all. The plight of recreational fishermen is described in the *Destin Log* Destin History Project for September 24–26 and November 22–25, 2008, and was explained to me by Captain Mike Graef of the *Huntress* out of Destin. The *Destin Log*, Progress Edition 2008, has numerous entries dealing with fishing. Eventually the recreational fishermen organized and marched on Washington. See "'I Fish, I Vote': Anglers, Captains Find Optimism as They March on Capitol," *Destin Log*, February 23, 2010. For a later commentary that includes more information on the nature of fishing regulations and fish cycles in the Gulf, see Ben Raines, "Scientists Puzzle over Fish Increase after Oil Spill Fishing Ban," *Mobile Press-Register*, November 21, 2010.

Erosion problems on the coast are nothing new. The problems at Gulf Shores were described in "Erosion Claiming Gulf Shores' Beaches," *Anniston Star*, September 23, 1998. Although there are and will continue to be many articles and comments in the *Destin Log* on the question of restoration, nourishment, and "who owns the beach," the best comprehensive account of the controversy is Andrew Rice, "A Stake in the Sand," *New York Times*, March 19, 2010. Arguments against restoration by Okaloosa Island residents, especially against how it would be funded, are in the *North West Florida Daily News*, April 5, 2009. See also "Whose Beach Is It Anyway?" *Anniston Star*, December 2, 2009.

The controversy over Alabama's lack of convention facilities had been going on for some time and in 1999, *Mobile Press-Register* editor B. J. Richey alerted me to a plan by Alabama governor Don Siegelman to turn the park over to private developers "for expansion into a ritzy resort." The *Mobile Press-Register* reported the issue firing up again in "Auburn Manages Gulf State Hotel," June 12, 2004. Efforts were made to stop the plan and when it went to court Garry Mitchell of the Associated Press published "Gulf State Park Hotel Dispute Costs Tourist Money," February 8, 2009. Charley Grimsley, former state conservation commissioner, published "Gulf State Park Litigation," *Mobile Press-Register*, April 5, 2009, which laid out his opposition to the governor's scheme. Supporters of the plan tried to get it approved by the legislature—"Gulf State Park Hotel Supporters Take Case to Legislature," *Mobile Press-Register*, April 20, 2009. Then when the Supreme Court ruled against the plan—"Gulf Park Court Case," *Mobile Press-Register*, April 27, 2009—a compromise plan was put forth—"Alabama Officials Seek Compromise for Park Hotel," *Mobile Press-Register*, April 2009. Compromise has failed, so far.

The tax problems of Peek's Motel were reported in the *Panama City News Herald*, May 31, 2009, and explained more fully to me by Karen Triplett Grant.

As things got worse local boosters tried to put the best face on it. The real estate section of the *Destin Log*, Progress Edition 2008, continued to find silver linings to most clouds, and "Peter Bos' surprising forecast," reported in the *North West Florida Daily News*, June 27, 2008, brought praise. Also see two articles in the *Destin Log*, Pat Rice, "Are We Close to the End of Our Real Estate Woes?" June 27, 2009, and Jack Simpson, "History Will Repeat Real Estate Resilience in Destin," July 2, 2009, which together give a brief history of the ups and downs of the real estate market. However, reports like Ryan Dezember, "Bama Bayou Goes Bust: Grand Plans for Orange Beach Gateway Fizzle," *Mobile Press-Register*, April 12, 2009, may have been more reflective of the situation and the mood.

Efforts to pump money into the economy with a successful but less rowdy Spring Break were highlighted in "Spring Break Fever," *Mobile Press-Register*, March 14, 2009, and the *Walton Sun*, April 4, 2009. On November 26, 2009, Jerryeyler's Weblog announced "Panama City Beach—PCB Biz Group: Paris Hilton, Kardashians Here in Spring," and a short time later word got out that Panama City Beach was not going to have MTV back ("Spring Break: No More 'Deals with the Devil,'" *Panama City News Herald*, December 2, 2009). As far away as Duquesne University in Pittsburgh, students were told MTV was out ("Panama City Beach Ousts MTV Spring Breakers," *Duquesne Duke*, February 25, 2010). However, shortly after that article appeared, the Emerald Coast website announced "MTV will come back," and it did.

Some felt Spring Break was evolving into a more restrained celebration but there was still rowdiness, students still ran amok, the beer still flowed, and there was tragedy (MSNBC report, "ND Recruit Dies in Spring Break Accident," April 3, 2010).

CHAPTER 16

The best general discussion of Florida beaches and beach culture is found in Mormino, *Land of Sunshine, State of Dreams*, chapter 9, "The Beach," 300–354, and especially the subsection "The Technological Beach," 339–354, which gives an excellent background of nourishing. A good account of the issue up to when the case headed for the U.S. Supreme Court is Fraser Sherman, "Life's a Beach—If You Can Get to It," *Destin Log*, Progress Edition 2008.

From the time the first nourishment case went to court the controversy was followed by the *Destin Log*, and the reporting there is excellent. In particular see issues from October 2 and 28; November 9, 10, and 12; and December 1 and 2, 2009. Equally important was the online commentary that revealed how the issue divided the community and how free and easy access to the beach was important to almost every facet of the tourist economy. However, for the clearest explanation of the history of the controversy, the issues involved, and the final resolution see *Stop* the Beach Renourishment, Inc. v. Florida Department of Environmental Protection et al., No. 8–1151, argued before the United States Supreme Court, December 2, 2009, decided June 17, 2010. See also Jess Bravin, "Beach Erosion Weighed in Property-Rights Case," the Wall Street Journal, December 2, 2009, and "Whose Beach Is It Anyway," Anniston Star, December 2, 2009. A copy of the oral arguments in the case was sent to me by George Crozier, former director of the Dauphin Island Sea Lab, who attended.

Seaside's efforts to limit access to its beach and its community is covered in the Seaside Times, Spring 2007 and Holiday Edition 2007. Reaction and dismay from Seagrove Beach next door was expressed to me by family and friends.

The story of the Deepwater Horizon disaster unfolded while I was preparing to go to the coast to write the chapter on the nourishment case and finish the book. The oil spill changed my plans. Through that summer I watched the crisis unfold and tried to write about—it wasn't easy. The best coastal reporting came from the Mobile Press and Press-Register, which was able to monitor how the oil drifted onto the Redneck Riviera beaches and keep up with efforts by BP and the federal government to contain the spill and minimize the damage—both to the environment and to the company's reputation (and bottom line). See especially David Ferrara, "Baldwin Lodging Suffered Greatest Impact of Oil Spill, Tourism President Says," Mobile Press-Register, November 6, 2010. At this writing it is difficult, if not impossible, to find a single source that explains what happened, but a few months after the well blew National Geographic published a special issue, "The Spill," October 2010. Although its focus is more on the Louisiana coast than on beaches to the east, it provides a good look not only at what caused the blowout but also the danger that offshore drilling poses for the Gulf. Rolling Stone, June 24, 2010, looked at the political fallout following the explosion in Tim Dickinson, "The Spill, the Scandal, and the President."

The Destin Log, the Panama City News Herald, and the Pensacola News-Journal covered the progress of the spill and the impact it had on their beaches and their economy. The New York Times, June 14, 2010, describes the problems BP and others were having containing the oil.

Coastal Living, September 2010, contained a feature article, "Seaside Classic" (72–79), which highlighted the porches in that Panhandle community and made no mention of the spill. The only comment contained in the issue is a short article on Oceana, an antipollution group, which suggests readers sign a petition to stop offshore drilling and check out oceana.org.

Comments from folks along the coast came from Captain Roland Blais, Kathleen Blais, Susan Horn, Peter Horn, Didon Comer, Benny Bennett, the Bentons, Captain Mike Graef, Joe Franklin, and all the folks from Puckett.

CHAPTER 17

In the summer of 2010 coastal newspapers were full of reports, rumors, speculation, and, in some cases, hard facts about the causes and consequences of the Deepwater Horizon disaster. The oil spill was in the national news as well.

What dropped from the news was the online debate over who owned the beach. Even before the U.S. Supreme Court handed down its June 17 decision the spill was pushing other issues off the front page. After the court ruled against the foes of nourishment the debate trailed off to the occasional comment. However in the *Destin Log*, Roland Guidry, "The U.S. Supreme Court Ruling in Layman Terms: The Beach Is Still Private," June 24, 2010; Brady Cobb, "Beachfront Owners Must Be Vigilant after High Court Case," August 23, 2010; and Kerry McNulty, "City Must Take Back the 'Public' Point," October 4, 2010, make it clear that in the minds of some the issue is not settled.

As for the oil, in May the *Destin Log* began publishing "Twitter talk" concerning Destin and the spill for, as an article on May 10, 2010, announced, "From a Tar-Ball Brigade to Lighted Barriers, City Rolls out Action Plan at Emergency Meeting (with Training Schedule)." The next day al.com published an AP report headlined, "Tar Balls Reported along Beaches in Gulf Shores." Destin's defiance of the Florida Department of Environmental Protection's request was in the *Walton Sun* on May 10, 2010, while Kevin Costner's "oil cleanup idea" was highlighted in the *Christian Science Monitor*, May 20, 2010. The *New York Times* reported on the national implications of the spill, BP's search for a solution, and efforts by the Obama administration to deal with the crisis (May 12 and May 27). Representative Joseph Cao's suggestion to BP executives was reported widely. See *New York Daily News*, June 15, 2010. Meanwhile local efforts to protect the beaches and the marshes appeared in the *Mobile Press-Register*, May 12, 2010, while concern for what might happen if a hurricane hit appeared in the *Walton Sun*, May 27, 2020. "Storage Tank for Deepwater Horizon Washes Ashore on PCB" was published in the *Walton Sun*, June 12, 2010. President Obama's June 14 visit to Gulf Shores was covered by the *Mobile Press-Register*. This was followed by an Oval Office speech reported in the *Press-Register* along with many other newspapers. Had the president stopped in Mobile on the way down he would have seen a protest in Bienville Square that was reported in the *Press-Register*, June 13, 2010. See also "Obama Declares Gulf Coast 'Open for Business,'" *Anniston Star*, August 15, 2010.

Other stories and comments on the situation came from Captain Roland Blais, Kathleen Blais, Marlene Rikard, and Stacye Hathorn. Some background on oil and tar balls on the beach can be found in my column "The Days of Gooey Stuff on Our Beaches," *Anniston Star*, May 20, 2010. The death of Captain Kruse was reported in the *Mobile Press-Register*, June 24, 2010, with a follow-up article on June 26.

Jimmy Buffet's sister wrote a letter to future Gulf Coast guests that was circulated on the Internet. Her brother's concert was reported in the *Mobile Press-Register* and shown on CMT. Clips of it can be found on YouTube along with some from his drop-in concert at LuLu's at Homeport. Carl Hiaasen's column, "Now You Don't Trust BP, but It's Too Late," was in the *Miami Herald*, June 12, 2010.

"Best Florida Beaches Guide" is in *Florida Travel and Life*, online, summer 2010. Katie Tammen, "'That Smell' Is in the Air as Lynyrd Skynyrd Comes to the Emerald Coast," *Destin Log*, July 19, 2010, was followed by an online commentary by "Swanklin" who opposed bringing Skynyrd in and by "Destinite" who told "Swanklin" to "get a life." You can follow the course of BPs efforts to cap the well and efforts by coastal interests to clean the beaches and marshes while they figured out how to recover the lost revenue in the *Mobile Press-Register, Destin Log, Panama City News Herald*, and other coastal newspapers. The reference to Lynyrd Skynyrd and "Free Bird" is from John Shelton Reed and Dale Volberg Reed, *1001 Things Everyone Should Know about the South* (New York: Doubleday, 1996), 170.

As a postscript to what the recession did to the once-booming upscale real estate economy, about the time this book was going to press the St. Joe Company, which had invested so heavily in "yuppie vacation housing near the Panhandle beaches," found that when the real estate bubble burst the "yuppies went away" and the company was left with houses and developed lots that it could not sell. Add to this the impact of the BP oil spill and St. Joe officials were seriously considering putting the company up for sale to save it. See "St. Joe for Sale. A Case of Too Many Eggs in One (Panhandle) Basket," *St. Petersburg Times*, February 10, 2011.

Index

Chambers of commerce *(continued)*
Walton, 46; Panama City / Panama
City Beach, 39, 74. *See also* Spring
Break; Tourist associations / tourist
development councils; Tourists
Choctawhatchee Bay, 15, 16, 108, 130
Churchwell, J. E., 20, 24, 29, 36, 54
Civilian Conservation Corps (CCC), 12, 27
Coastal Vision 3000, 193–94
Condominiums: height limits on, 126–27,
130–31; impact of incorporation on,
109, 111; and overbuilding, 149–50;
post-Frederic, 98–99, 103–5; replacing
motels, 213–14, 243, 249; speculating on
and "flipping" of, 221–26; mentioned, 95,
97, 113, 142, 147, 182, 243, 249. *See also*
Motels; Real estate

Davis, Robert: and evolution of Seaside,
138–42, 155–57, 166–70; founds Seaside,
115–19; impact of, on coast, 122–27, 147,
152–54, 175, 182; mentioned, 49, 130, 149,
180. *See also* New Urbanism; Seaside
Deepwater Horizon. *See* British Petroleum /
Deepwater Horizon
Destin, Dewey, 215, 229, 248
Destin, Fla.: dealing with growth of, 149–50,
230, 244; and early tourism, 59–60,
79–80; founding of, 15–16; and Hurricane
Eloise, 94–97, 103; and Hurricane
Opal, 155–56, 162; incorporation of,
109–11; and Odom's Curve, 147–49;
post-Eloise growth of, 105–7, 130–31; and
renourishments, 263–69; mentioned,
18, 22, 35, 44, 48, 50, 65, 113, 126, 170.
See also Beach; Bos, Peter; Chambers
of commerce; Condominiums; Fishing;
Green Knight; Holiday Isle; Real estate;
Spring Break
Destin Log, 115, 130, 116, 149, 228
Dune County, proposed, 108

Eglin Air Force Base, 25, 43, 79, 111, 112, 156
El Centro (Fla.), 21

Emerald Coast, 131, 193. *See also* Beach;
Chambers of commerce
Escambia County (Fla.), 19, 43, 69; Santa
Rosa Island, 13, 15, 45. *See also* Pensacola,
Fla.; Pensacola Beach

Fincher, Mike, 92, 136
Fishing: and British Petroleum/Deepwater
Horizon, 281–82, 287–89, 292; deep sea,
244–46, 270; at Destin, 15, 35, 44, 59,
79, 80, 97, 205, 230–31, 244, 247, 271; at
Orange Beach, 11–13, 34, 35, 59, 246–47,
271
Fleming family, 19, 177–78
Flora-Bama: and Frank Brown International
Songwriting Festival, 92, 122, 129;
and Hurricane Frederic, 103–4; and
Hurricane Ivan, 218–20, 260; made
famous, 89–93; Mullet Toss, 119–22, 146;
origins of, 71–73; mentioned, 81, 87, 114,
186, 200, 205, 243. *See also* Gilchrist, Joe;
Louis, Jimmy; McClellan, Pat
Foley, Ala., 11, 13, 33, 57, 93
Folsom, James E. "Big Jim," 12, 33, 37, 44–45.
See also Pleasure Island
Fort Morgan (Ala.), 27, 30, 158, 185, 214
Fort Walton Beach, Fla., 18, 22, 24, 29, 96,
111–12, 146, 155–56; acquires beach, 47;
Billy Bowlegs Festival in, 61; gambling
in, 24, 35, 41, 43, 46–47, 65–66; and "no
growth" movement, 112, 155; origins of,
15; relations of, with Eglin Air Force Base,
79, 111–12. *See also* Okaloosa County;
Okaloosa Island
Francis, Joe, 206–11

Gilchrist, Joe, 71–72, 91–93, 119, 122, 136–37,
155, 218–20, 260; and Interstate Mullet
Toss, 92, 120–22. *See also* Flora-Bama
Girls Gone Wild, 206–12
Golf, 108, 138, 177–78
Goofy Golf, 62
Grayton Beach (Fla.): founding of, 16–19;
upscale development of, 94, 151–52; way

Miracle Strip Amusement Park, 1–3, 22, 77–79, 190–91. *See also* Beach: amusements

Mobile, 11, 25, 37

Mobile Press-Register, 25, 32, 34, 69, 232

Mobile Register, 26, 27, 31, 38, 55

Mormino, Gary, 136

Motels, 54–55, 61, 79, 131; Holiday Inn, Gulf Shores, 76, 101; Holiday Inn, Panama City Beach, 76; older, torn down, 213; Peek's, 252–54. *See also* Condominiums; Real estate

Music, 136–38; Rusty and Mike (McHugh and Fincher), 92, 136, 231. *See also* Boys Town; Buffett, Jimmy; Trashy White Band

Nature Walk, 227

Navarre (Fla.), 14, 15

New Urbanism, 147, 166, 168, 175, 182, 216, 268

"No growth" movement, 4, 112, 155

Nude beach / queer beach, 113

Obama administration, and BP spill, 271, 273, 276, 285

Odom's curve, 148–49

Okaloosa County (Fla.), 18, 24, 46, 59, 69, 108, 131, 221

Okaloosa Island (Fla.), 15, 47, 66, 111, 155–56, 162, 265–67, 280; Gulfarium on, 60, 79, 156. *See also* Beach; Fort Walton Beach, Fla.

Ono Island (Ala.), 90, 136, 146, 216. *See also* Beach mice

Orange Beach, Ala.: early history of, 10–13, 15–16, 25; and Hurricane Frederic, 98–103; incorporation of, 110, 155; post-Frederic development of, 108–10, 130, 151, 158, 214–15, 222–26; postwar development of, 31, 34–35, 48, 59; mentioned, 19, 72, 160, 171, 220. *See also* Beach; Condominiums; Fishing; Gulf

Shores, Ala.; Hurricanes; Motels; Real estate; Spring Break

Panama City, Fla.: early history of, 16, 19, 22; postwar, 32, 38, 44–45, 47, 50, 53; and World War II, 28–29; mentioned, 61, 65, 69, 112, 257

Panama City Beach, Fla.: carnival atmosphere of, 76–78, 84–85; clubs in, 170–71; creation and incorporation of, 76–77; early development of, 20–23, 36–39; *Girls Gone Wild* in, 206–12; and Hurricane Eloise, 95–97, 103, 130; Peek's Motel on, 252–54; popularity of, 142–47, 150; mentioned, 54, 60, 74, 105, 111, 180, 217, 222, 242. *See also* Beach; Chambers of commerce; Condominiums; Hangout; Miracle Strip Amusement Park; Spring Break

Panhandle of Florida: Alabama / lower South influence on, 34, 52, 65, 68; development of, 215; mentioned, 34, 82, 107, 162, 220, 254, 275

Peek's Motel, 252–54. *See also* Motels; Real estate

Pensacola, Fla.: attempt of, to join Alabama, 13; connection of, to beach, 13–14, 19; and Fort Barrancas, 25, 30; and Johnson Beach, 68–70; Naval Air Station, 25; postwar tourism in, 34–35, 38; and Wingate Beach, 68–70; and World War II, 28–29, 112; mentioned, 22, 31, 47, 65, 69, 71. *See also* Hurricanes

Pensacola Beach (Fla.), 13–14, 37, 43, 59–61, 66, 79. *See also* African Americans; Santa Rosa Island

Perdido Bay / Perdido Pass / Perdido Key, 11, 25, 37, 42, 68, 71, 103, 277, 281, 286

Phillips Inlet / Lake Powell (Fla.), 16, 19, 53, 177–78

Pinnacle Port, 105–6

Pleasure Island, 12, 100, 151, 155, 172, 205, 215, 217, 220, 260, 281; named, 45

Politics, inland versus coast, 18, 80–81, 108–10, 219, 254–55. *See also* Baldwin County; Escambia County; Okaloosa County; Walton County

Puckett, Miss., 238–39, 292–94

Race, 23, 68–70, 114–15. *See also* McGee, C. H.

Raines, Howell, 4, 24, 90, 179

Real estate, 66, 94–95, 103–7, 130–31, 146–47, 158–61, 180–81, 214–16, 221–28, 244; flipping, 109, 222–26, 228; and recession, 225–28, 255–57. *See also* Bos, Peter; Condominiums; Davis, Robert; McGee, C. H.; Motels

Red Bar and Picolo's, 151–52, 181

Redneck Riviera: affluence increases in, 146–47, 153–54, 215; characteristics of, 10, 18–19, 36, 59, 63, 66, 209, 243, 254; named, 4, 90, 119; and Hurricanes Frederic and Eloise, 94–101; music in, 136–37, 295–96; oil spill off coast of, 269–70, 281; tourist development of, 129–30, 132–33; mentioned, 71, 87, 99, 113, 115, 158–59, 179, 184–86, 190, 225, 227, 247, 249, 269–70, 278. *See also* African Americans; Flora-Bama; Green Knight; Trashy White Band

Religion: and Jesus First, 188–90; and Noah's Ark, 84; in Seaside, 167–68; and Spring Break, 199, 202

Roadhouses/bars, 83, 85, 87; Gulf Shores / Orange Beach, 89; during World War II, 30, 32, 35. *See also* Flora-Bama; Green Knight; Stabler, Kenny

Rosemary Beach (Fla.), 175

Russo, Steve, 222–23

Sand Castle cottage, 11, 28, 99, 102

Sandestin (Fla.), 105–6, 130, 146, 229, 257

Santa Rosa County (Fla.), 69

Santa Rosa Island, 13, 15, 45

Scenic Highway 30-A, 53, 113, 116–17, 149, 152; development along, 173–77, 221–22,

226, 295; and Minnie E. Jackson, 52–53, 94–95. *See also* Grayton Beach; Seagrove Beach; Seaside

Seagrove Beach (Fla.): and Elton B. Stephens, 48–49, 52; founded, 49–51; and Friends of Old Seagrove (FOOS), 183; growth of, 169–70; and Hurricane Eloise, 94–96; and Jackson family, 3, 52–53, 94–95; parade, 122, 183–84, 293; relationship of, with Seaside, 267–68; mentioned, 16, 18–19, 22, 35, 59–61, 113–15, 122, 126, 151, 167. *See also* McGee, C. H.

Seaside (Fla.): founded, 116–19; growth of, 122–27, 138–42, 152–54, 164–70, 267–69; as holiday town, 166, 168; and Hurricane Opal, 156–57; influence of, 146–47, 176–77, 216; and Tannin Village, 142, 147; *The Truman Show* in, 164–67; mentioned, 49–50, 130, 231, 257. *See also* Davis, Robert; New Urbanism

Sharpless, W. T., 19, 20

Snoop Dogg, 209–10

Southern influence on region: increasing affluence, 104–5, 152–54, 158–59, 166, 168–69, 175–77, 256; origin of residents, 13–14; preferred amusements, 55, 83, 190; proximity to South, 2; Puckett, Miss., 238–39, 292–94; Spring Break, 199–200, 203. *See also* Alabama influence in Florida

Spring Break, 73–76, 80, 83, 133–35, 195; and *Girls Gone Wild*, 206–12; in Panama City Beach, 195–214. *See also* Tourist associations / tourist development councils

Stabler, Kenny, 89–91, 93, 109, 216

Stephens, Elton B., 48–49, 52

St. Joe, 173–77, 194, 227, 257; WaterSound, 175, 257. *See also* WaterColor

Sullivan, Lee, 150, 203–10, 212

Sunnyside (Fla.), 21

Tannin Village (Ala.), 142, 147

Teenagers, 35, 55, 63, 67

CPSIA information can be obtained at www.ICGtesting.com
Printed in the USA
LVOW041552130113

315519LV00014B/843/P